SEVEN TO SEVENTEEN

PLAYS FOR SCHOOL AND CAMP

SEVEN TO SEVENTEEN

Plays for School and Camp

*Twenty-one new plays for boys and girls,
printed for the first time*

COLLECTED AND EDITED BY
ALEXANDER DEAN

SAMUEL FRENCH

NEW YORK   LOS ANGELES

SAMUEL FRENCH, LTD.   LONDON

1940

Copyright, 1931, by Samuel French

MANUFACTURED IN THE UNITED STATES OF AMERICA
BY THE VAIL-BALLOU PRESS, INC., BINGHAMTON, N. Y.

To

WILLIAM ALEXANDER GROVER
NANCY DEAN GROVER
ELIZABETH DEAN FRANCIS
MARY DEAN LEROY
THOMAS GROVER
PAUL DUDLEY DEAN JR.
ELIZABETH CROWNINSHIELD DEAN

the "Seven to Seventeen" members of my family, this collection is affectionately dedicated by their uncle.

INTRODUCTION

The uses of the one act play are rapidly changing. There was a time when three or four short plays constituted a program which took the place of a three act play in the season's repertory of a producing group. Audiences, however, constantly voted against such a policy and the program of short plays is rapidly disappearing as a major production of the Little Theatres.

The one act, however, is not failing in its use and popularity but is still very much in demand. Its uses have changed. It now exists for a new purpose,—that of the special occasion. It is now produced either by itself, or with another one act, or in conjunction with a short lecture, or musical program or special stunts for the purpose of furnishing entertainment at informal club meetings, school convocations, and general get-togethers. Also a great use for it has developed in courses of play production and class room study.

Further the one act play is now being used by every sort of organization as the means by which they may commemorate special occasions such as Armistice Day, Christmas, Washington's birthday, Shakespeare's birthday, Fourth of July, and the many other special days in the calendar.

The growth of the Play Tournament in every part of the country has also increased the demand for the short play.

Thus the one act play, far from decreasing in use or popularity, has found new and greater uses. As a result of this, specialized collections of one act plays are beginning to appear in order to satisfy the demands of specific uses. In time even more of such collections will be edited because general collections contain too many plays not suited to the occasions for which a director needs them. The collection of special plays is valuable to him because it not only furnishes a play for the immediate occasion but gives him plays for similar occasions to follow. From one volume the plays for several seasons may be procured.

For this volume of specialized plays I have chosen those that will appeal to actors and to audiences that range in years from seven to seventeen. These people in their schools,—especially boarding schools—and clubs and camps are continually looking for plays to put on "Saturday night,"—the time to have good entertainment by themselves and for themselves. In every social dramatic club, many members can offer various "specialties" for half the program, but there is nothing so satisfactory for the climax as a one act play.

The specialization of the one act play naturally is having a very definite influence on the fundamental requirements of the play. A collection of women's club plays, in their subjects and writing, would be very different from one for school assemblies to celebrate the holidays and festivals of the year. A volume of plays for study and dramatic presentation classes would necessarily be different in their kind from one collected for the purpose of group entertainment.

Certain very definite requirements have been demanded of the plays in this volume. Not only do the plays have subjects which are understandable to those ages, and characters which are within their experience to act and to appreciate, but they are primarily for the entertainment of actor and audience. The plays further are actable. Many dramas do not act as well as they read. Many plays do not read as well as they act. Although it is desirable to have a play read and act well, whenever it was necessary to choose between one or another of the two, the actable play was selected. That means the story and plot in each one is of primary importance. This is even true of the plays based on historical incidents, although most historical plays pay more attention to the history than they do to the play. The dramatic situation and suspense value prevail in these plays when actually presented on a stage.

Another factor is the demand for a great variety chosen in the series of plays to be given during a season. No matter how much an audience may like a certain kind of play, variety is almost certain to have a greater appeal than a steady diet of one particular type. A farce, a fantasy, a melodrama, a burlesque, a story play, a comedy, presented in turn in the weekly programs, will give the repertory the added charm of contrast. Not only is the widely contrasting type of play included in this volume, but plays for the contrasting ages of seven, fourteen and seventeen. There are plays for the midgets and juniors, for the seniors, for the faculty or councillors,—not only for each group separately, but many for them mixed. There are plays for all boys, for all girls, plays where the boys can play the girls' parts, where the girls can play the boys' parts. There are several plays where John in the cast can become Mary, and Henry can become Ethel, as well as where Ellen can become Sam, and the story is just as plausible. Then there are plays which must have both girls and boys. If the camp has only girls, it can cooperate with a nearby boys camp. If the club is mixed, all the better. Older or younger, larger and smaller girls or boys, every kind and combination can find not just one or two plays, but twenty which are suitable to its needs.

Some plays require a large number of people, other plays a few. But in no case is the burden of putting over the play carried by one person. The parts in the play are nearly always of equal importance, length and interest. This, of course, does not include the mob which is in several. Not only does this uphold the morale of a club, but it aids the director in facing one of his greatest if not the greatest problem,—of how to get on a play with a small number of rehearsals.

No play herein demands an elaborate stage setting. I have long contended that the good play of today is one that can be presented as in the old days, on a wooden platform with an architectural or neutral background,—that the good play can carry itself. Several plays can have beautiful and elaborate settings if a group has a stage craft class that enjoys the designing and constructing of detailed sets. None of the plays depend upon a setting for its value so none of them demands it. Many of the plays can be played out of doors by a school club in the late spring, or in the summer by a camp. But these also can be played any time, any place. Finally at the end of the volume are a few longer plays, four scenes, two acts, a full pageant,—because usually once during a season, a school, club or camp activity wishes to give a gala performance.

So it is that the one act play has progressed from general to specific use, and in filling the demands of the dramatic groups in schools and camps for their "Saturday Night" play, have arrived with these qualities. The actors and audience of the dramatic club want a good time, a surprise, and a play that will act. And just as each group, varying in tastes, desires, and natural make-up are assembled under one roof, so these plays varying in kind, requirements and periods, have been collected for them in one volume.

ALEXANDER DEAN.

New Haven
January 1931

CONTENTS

ROYALTY

All the plays in this volume are printed through the courtesy of and by special arrangement with the authors. Included in this collection are both royalty and non-royalty plays. The royalty plays, except for "The Next-Best Man," a two-act play, may be presented by amateurs upon payment of the following fees:

1. When no admission is charged, five dollars for each performance, payable three days before the date when the play is to be given.

2. When admission is charged, ten dollars for each performance, payable three days before the date when the play is to be given.

"The Next-Best Man" may be presented by amateurs upon payment of fifteen dollars for all performances whether or not admission is charged.

Professional rates, including those for radio broadcasting will be quoted upon application.

Whenever the play is produced the following must appear on all the programs:

1. Title of play.

2. Author.

3. The following statement: "This play is contained in the volume of plays "Seven To Seventeen," published by Samuel French.

When there is no printed program this statement should be read before each performance.

RING LEADER

BY

JOHN WILLIAM ROGERS

A ROYALTY PLAY

THE CAST

DICKEY
STUMP
DUSTY
STANFORD
MR. NOEL
DR. OSLO

THE SCENE

*The house master's bedroom, Laurel House, at the Viking
School for boys, sometime after midnight.*

*The room is neat but austere in its simplicity. In the center of
the left wall, a door opens into the hall. In the center of the
rear wall is a window. In the right wall up stage is a door
leading into a shallow closet. The door is open and discloses
a bath-robe hung on its hook. Nearer the footlights stands a
white iron single bed, its head against the right wall.*

*A small desk stands in the corner up left between the hall door
and the window. There is a chair beside it and two other
larger chairs are in the room, one below the bed, the other in
the center of stage left. Beside the desk is a plain wrought-
iron, standing lamp. The shade to the lamp is probably green.*

THE CHARACTERS AND COSTUMES

*The four boys are all in pajamas. In order to give their figures
individuality, pajamas as different in pattern as possible
should be worn.*

DICKEY, *13 years, the smallest in white.*

STUMP, *16 years, in some elaborate figured pattern.*

DUSTY, *16 years, in vivid stripes.*

2

STANFORD, *17 years, the biggest, in blue or green.*

DR. OSLO, *60 years old, is white-haired, dignified and academic looking. He wears his trousers over his pajamas and wears a dark dressing gown and slippers as though he had already been in bed and gotten up.*

MR. NOEL, *house master of Laurel House, is 23 and wears any sort of street clothes. He must be an attractive young man with a very sympathetic voice. He is very nervous except when making an effort to be calm.*

---•---

At the rise of the curtain the room is unlit but the bright moon-light beyond the window lends a faint glow to everything so that the audience is able to make out the scene dimly. The hall door Left opens slowly and four figures in pajamas advance into the room very cautiously. They are all eagerly trying to make out what is on the bed and they are of uncertain courage. Each form seems to want the others in front of it. Suddenly DICKEY *giggles nervously.* STANFORD *gives him a resounding thump on his back.*

DICKEY [*breaking out indignantly, in a half whisper*]. Hey, who you hitting!

[*The effect of his voice is electric upon the individual members of the mass. With one accord they make for the hall, all squeezing through the door together. The door is closed quickly but softly behind them.*

There is a moment of silence in which nothing happens in the room; then the door is again opened, a little more confidently. The figures hesitate in the doorway.]

DICKEY [*in the door, speaking with intense conviction but lowered tones*]. Aw, he climbed out of the window, I tell you.

STAN. Well, what are you *scared* of then?

DICKEY [*indignantly*]. I'm not scared.

STAN. Then go on in.

[*The group enters,* DICKEY *in front. With sudden decision, he leaves the rest, walks forward across the patch of light that is the window and cautiously feels the surface of the bed.*

Finding no one there, his courage suddenly rises and he smites it triumphantly.]

DICKEY [*louder in confident tones*]. See, he isn't here. I told you I saw him climb out the window. I've watched him do it three nights. [DUSTY *closes door.*]

STAN [*judiciously*]. So he waits till the lights are out and he thinks we are asleep, does he? [*Crosses to Center.*]

DICKEY. Yeah, Stan, that's what he does.

STAN. Getting away with murder!

DUSTY. The old giraffe. [*He goes to window up Center.*]

STAN [*impressively*]. It's got to be stopped.

DUSTY. Where does he go, Dickey?

DICKEY [*crossing to the window and pointing through it*]. He just sort of kept in the shadows there as much as he could and made for the school gate. He had his hat on.

STAN. Going down town, I bet. [*Going to window.*]

DUSTY. Probably got a jane.

STUMP. Yeah, got a jane. [*Going to window.*]

STAN. How long does he stay?

DICKEY. I don't know. I always get sleepy.

[DUSTY *turns on the standing lamp to the consternation of the rest.* DICKEY *drops quickly to the floor.* STUMP *dives for the closet and* STANFORD *starts to make for the hall door, but stops himself.*]

DICKEY. Hey.

STUMP. Hey.

STAN [*collecting his authority*]. Put out that light, Dusty. What do you think you're doing?

DUSTY [*persuasively*]. Aw, ain't anything to be scared of. If old Christmas should come back, we could tell him we were sick or something and only trying to find him. What could he say to us, climbing in the window *himself?*

STUMP [*recovering and coming out of the closet*]. Yeah, climbing in himself. [*Reassured,* DICKEY *and* STUMP *relax and cross to the window.*]

DUSTY. He'd have to do some explaining to us.

STAN [*to* DICKEY *and* STUMP]. Hey, you dumbbells. [*He rushes*

forward and pushes them away from in front of the window.]
Keep away from that window.

DICKEY [*aggrieved*]. Say, Stan, what's the matter with you?
[*He crosses to closet and investigates it.*]

STAN. Don't you know the head's room looks right out at this
window. [*Crossing down to bed.*]

DUSTY [*obligingly*]. I'll pull the shade down.

STAN. No, you don't. . . . Dusty, you better put that light out.

DUSTY [*crossing to desk*]. Aw, I will in a minute. Le's see what
old Christmas's got in his desk.

STUMP [*crossing to desk*]. See if you can find any grades,
Dusty.

[*On the desk* DUSTY *spies a pair of horn-rimmed glasses
and puts them on the end of his nose, giving a heartless burlesque of* NOEL *in the class room.*]

DUSTY [*coming out to the center and pointing to* STANFORD *on
bed*]. Stanford, give the names and dates of the first eighty
emperors of Rome. [*Pause.*] Come to my class unprepared
again, have you? [STUMP *and* DICKEY *laugh and* DUSTY *turns
on them severely.*] A little more quiet in the back of the
room, there. [*He relaxes his attention, then looks back suddenly in the manner of a teacher trying to catch a pupil at
mischief.*] What's that? . . . None of your lip there. [*His
eye falls on the old bath-robe hung on the closet door. He
rushes over and slips it on to change himself into* NOEL *the
house master. Draping himself elaborately, he begins a second imitation.*] Now look here, fellows, any more noise out
there tonight, fellows, and there'll be trouble. Understand,
fellows. . . . What's that, Stanford? I don't want to hear
anything more out of you either. [DUSTY *marches elaborately
over to the desk and sits down, continuing his motions of looking back suddenly to discover mischief.*]

STUMP. What are we going to do, Stan? [*He crosses down to
bed.*]

STAN. Do?

STUMP. About old Christmas climbing out of the window like
this. [*Leans against foot of bed.*]

STAN [*evasively*]. I haven't decided.

DICKEY [*pained*]. We ought to do *something*. [*Sitting in chair Left.*]

STAN. We'll do *something*.

STUMP. I'll tell you. Let's lock the window so he can't get back in.

DICKEY [*delighted*]. Yeah.

DUSTY [*sitting at desk, but facing the other boys*]. Aw, he'd only go round to the front door. Le's do something *really*.

STUMP. I'll bet the head sure would be mad if he knew. Look how he kicked out old Tompkins last year.

DUSTY [*loftily*]. He'd kick Christmas right out of school, too.

DICKEY. House masters haven't got any more right to be off the grounds after lights than we have. . . . What if the house should catch fire?

DUSTY [*starting up brightly*]. Want to *have* a fire?

STUMP. Yes, let's.

STAN. Say, are you guys crazy!

STUMP. Well, I'll bet the head sure would be on old Christmas' tail if he knew.

DUSTY [*rising and becoming* DR. OSLO *in manner*]. Br—br— You can pack your trunk just as soon as you like, Mr. Noel. [*Clears his throat.*] You're not the type of young man I want associated with my school. Brr-brrr— You're fired, Mr. Noel.

DICKEY. Serve him right after the dirty way he's treated Stan all year.

DUSTY [*keeping the pose of the head*]. Brr-brr— What's that, Mr. Noel? Who'll teach the history classes? I'll take them myself. Used to be quite a teacher of history myself in my day. Ha—ha, won a prize in history myself when I was a boy. Pack your trunk, Mr. Noel, you're fired.

STAN. Yeah, get Noel kicked out and the head *will* take the history classes. Then what chance would I have to pass in history?

DICKEY. Oh, come on, Stan, it's such a peachy chance to get old Christmas fired. [*Screwing up his face.*] Pleee-ase!

STUMP. Yeah, Stan.

STAN. I've got to pass that history to graduate. Noel gripes a lot but he may let me through.

STUMP. Aw, you can get that little grind, Fluffy Roberts, to tutor you.

DICKEY. Sure you can.

DUSTY. Be awfully noble and go to the head. Tell him you hate to say anything but you've noticed Mr. Noel climbing out of his window at nights and as one of the older boys you thought you ought to tell him about it. Not safe to have the house unprotected.

STUMP. Gee, you can get in awfully strong with the head.

DICKEY. Maybe he'd pass you in history just for being noble.

STAN [*with decision*]. I'm not a tattle-tale.

   [*Everyone sees the logic of that position too clearly to argue. They all think hard.*]

DUSTY [*leaping up brightly*]. I'll tell you. We could just let the head find it out accidently. *Accidently*, see. One of us could be sick or something and go and wake the head. He'd be mad at being waked this time of night and say, "why don't you tell your house master?" We'd say, "We tried to, sir, but couldn't find him in his room." Then let nature take its course.

STUMP. That's a great idea.

DICKEY. Yeah, Stan. . . . You do it, Dusty. You're a good actor.

DUSTY. No . . . The doctor said the next time I came to him he was going to give me castor oil every night for a week.

DICKEY [*thinking seriously*]. Who would be best?

STAN [*slowly*]. He'd lose his job.

DUSTY. You mean *Christmas?*

STAN [*nodding*]. Yeah.

DUSTY [*with outraged patience*]. Well, isn't that what we're trying to make him do?

DICKEY. Don't get soft-hearted, Stan, look how dirty he's treated you all year.

DICKEY. The head's keeping you on bounds right now because of what he reported about you.

STUMP. He went to the head about *you*, didn't he?

DICKEY. You had just as much right to keep a couple of gold fish in the water cooler as he did to climb out of the window.

STUMP. How did you know he was going to want a drink?

DUSTY. And didn't he just tell you, you probably wouldn't graduate if there was any more trouble?

STAN. Yeah.

DUSTY. Well, gosh, Stan, it's nearly eight weeks until school's out. You know you can't keep out of trouble eight weeks.

STAN. There's something to that . . . [*Warming his wrath.*] And I guess you're about right. Ever since last fall he's been picking on me and I'm getting pretty darned tired of it. Every time anything happens around this dump, I'm the first person to get blamed. Tried to blame me for that stink bomb last night.

STUMP [*bursting out laughing*]. Ha—ha! That was funny.

DUSTY. The way you put one over on him *last night*. Gosh, you looked innocent, I almost thought you were.

STAN. He doesn't like me. Ever since he came, he's had it in for me.

DUSTY. Yeah, remember when school hadn't been open two weeks an' he caught you shaving the back of Fluffy Roberts' neck. . . . Right away he said, "I've heard all about you, Stanford Calloway, as soon as I came here. You and I are going to have trouble."

STAN. And we've had it.

STUMP. Yeah—right off, he started picking on you. I noticed it.

DUSTY. He wasn't as innocent though, as we thought he was going to be—and he sure does play a good game of tennis.

STAN [*magnanimously*]. Oh, it's all right for a guy to be strict. I *like* a guy that's strict. Ain't any fun doing things if you can just walk over them like we could over old Turkey Neck last year. But Christmas is so strict, he's *mean*.

STUMP. Yeah, he's mean. Look at last week. Put the house lights out fifteen minutes early for a whole week, just because a couple of boys got into a water fight in the shower and wouldn't own up.

DICKEY. And look, Stan, how he flunked you in that history test last week.

STAN. Well, he's been sort of decent about that. I told him I forgot it was coming and forgot to bone up for it and he's going to let me take it over.

DICKEY. Well, he wasn't decent about that football game last fall.

DUSTY. You haven't forgotten how he made you miss the biggest football game of the year. Remember, Stump? Buck Whitely kicked three goals from the field.

STUMP. You bet I remember.

DICKEY. And all because the street car you were coming back to school on went off the track and you were two hours late getting back to school.

STUMP [*indignantly*]. Said you could have gotten off and taken another car.

DICKEY. It wasn't your fault the car went off the track.

STAN. But I could have taken another car if I'd wanted to.

DUSTY [*reminiscently*]. Gee, that football game was a peach of a game. Remember Scar McGhee broke his left leg and had to be carried off on a stretcher? Gosh.

STUMP. My cousin saw that game and he said our team played better than the Freshman team at Harvard this year.

DICKEY [*wonderingly*]. He did!

STUMP. Yes, sir, that's what he said.

STAN [*who has been growing bitter under the bitter memories of the football game*]. Well, if you're going to do something, stop gassing and le's do it.

DUSTY. Good. I'll tell you. You be sick, Stan, and Stump and I will take you over to the head's house.

DICKEY. What about *me?*

DUSTY. You?

DICKEY. Yeah.

DUSTY. You're too little. You'll have to go to bed.

DICKEY. Aw, gee, Dusty— [*Bursting out rebelliously.*] Wasn't I the one that found Old Christmas sneaking out?

STAN. Now, Dick, be a good sport. We'll tell you about everything that happens.

DICKEY [*clouding*]. Aw, naw. I told you about Christmas, didn't I? Let Stump go to bed.

STUMP [*with elaborate patience*]. Don't you see, Dickey, we've got to make it look natural. I'm bigger than you are and naturally—

DICKEY. I don't see what difference that makes—

DUSTY. Well, naturally the biggest boy would be the one—

DICKEY [*suddenly*]. Wait— I got a way. I could hear Stan groaning and go in to see what was the matter, then wake you up, Dusty. Don't you see? [*He looks eagerly from* DUSTY *to* STANFORD *and sees he has made his point.*] Yeah! [*With an air of superiority he turns to* STUMP.] Stump, *you* can go back to bed.

STUMP. Aw, gee.

STAN. Now listen, Stump, you're not going to gum up everything. Dickey found it out. You go to bed.

STUMP [*accepting his fate*]. Well, gee.

DUSTY [*forgetting* STUMP'S *woes and turning lightly to the others*]. Now let's get it all straight . . . [*Slowly in the manner of one rehearsing a plot.*] Dickey wakes up and hears you groaning in your room, Stan. He goes to see what it is and finds you awfully sick. He wakes me and you say to call Mr. Noel. We come in here and find the room empty and the bed not slept in. You're groaning so, Stan, we get scared. Why, there's only one thing to do, I say. Go and tell Dr. Oslo. You come along with us and we tell the head what's happened. [*Excited.*] Oh, boy, le's go! . . . Get on the other side of Stan, Dickey. Now look sick, Stan, le's practice. [DUSTY *and* DICKEY *support* STANFORD *who agonizes on the bed. The three take a step or two together when* STANFORD *stops short and speaks inquiringly.*]

STAN. Say—what's the matter with me?

DUSTY. Belly-ache.

STAN. No—no. They always give you such foul medicine. I'm going to have something where you don't have to take a chance of dirty medicine.

DICKEY. Mastoid! My brother had mastoids! He had to have an operation.

STAN [*with decision*]. Well, I'm not going to have any operations.

[*Everybody concentrates on what disease to chose.*]

STUMP [*doubtfully*]. My grandma is always having side-atica.

STAN. Side-atica, what's that?

STUMP. Well, it's got something to do with your side. She's always having a pain here. [*He puts his hand on his hip.*]

STAN. What does she have to take for it?

STUMP. I think they just massage her with one of those electric machines.

STAN [*considering*]. Well—that's not so bad—

STUMP [*overly conscientious*]. I don't *think* she takes any medicine. But I couldn't swear it, Stan—

DUSTY [*impatient*]. Oh, come on. Side-atica's fine. Anyway you can be cured before they start giving you medicine. [*He opens the door.*] We better get our bath-robes— Wait, lemme get rid of this. [*He takes off* NOEL'S *bath-robe and gives it a spirited kick to the center of the room.*]

STAN [*suddenly alarmed*]. Wait! [*He listens and the sharpness of his tone arrests the others who look at him.*] Put that light out, Stump! . . . Quick! [STUMP *turns off the light.*]

DUSTY. What is it?

DICKEY. What is it?

STAN. Somebody's coming. . . . That was the front door. . . . They're coming *this way.*

STUMP [*frightened*]. Wh-what are we going to do?

DICKEY. It's Christmas!

STAN [*irritable with nervous tension*]. Wait! Be quiet! [*They all listen.*] Gee, it's the head!

DUSTY. The head!

STAN. It's the head's step! . . . Hide! Hide!

[DICKEY *promptly drops to the floor and tries to roll under the bed.* DUSTY *makes a dive for the shallow closet.*]

STUMP [*turning round and round in bewilderment*]. Where, Stan, where?

STAN. Oh, jump out of the window. [STUMP *starts toward the window.* STANFORD *grabs him and throws him back in the direction of* DUSTY *and the closet.*] No, you fool!

DUSTY [*promptly shoving him back from the closet*]. You can't come in here.

[STANFORD *throws himself upon the bed, face down, like a man asleep, while* STUMP, *like the proverbial ostrich, merely stands rigidly facing the wall between the door and the desk. The boys have barely had time to get in place when* DR. OLSO *knocks. There is no response to his knocking and after knocking a second time he calls.*]

DR. OSLO. Mr. Noel, it's Dr. Oslo. [*He waits and then opens door.*] I saw your light and wondered if anything— [*He waits for an answer.*] Noel! [*Now he begins to play the flash light about the room, then he flashes it on the bed and mistakes the figure of* STANFORD *for the sleeping* NOEL. *Keeping the light for a moment on* STANFORD *he murmurs to himself.*] Sound sleeper, Noel— [*He sweeps the flash around the room for a final inspection. Then he closes the door.*]

DICKEY [*after a moment, looking out from under the bed*]. Is he gone?

STAN [*fighting down at* DICKEY *with an arm*]. Be quiet.

[STUMP *stands rigidly by the wall,* DUSTY *comes slowly out of the closet back to the center of the room.*]

DUSTY [*sighing as deeply as possible*]. Gosh!

STAN [*warning*]. Look out! Look out!

DUSTY [*more at ease*]. Oh, he's gone. [*Pointing at* STANFORD *and doubling up with amusement.*] He thought *you* were old Christmas, *asleep.*

DICKEY [*rolling out from under the bed and standing up*]. He must be blind without his specs.

STUMP. Didn't know Stan from old Christmas.

DUSTY. If that isn't the house cat's night-gown.

STAN [*rising up on the bed and coming to a sitting position, his feet on the floor*]. We better get out of here!

DUSTY [*sinking down on the floor and drawing his knees up under his chin*]. Wait, wait, let me get my heart started to beating again.

[DICKEY *sits down beside* DUSTY *on the floor.*]

STAN [*between disgust and amusement*]. Stump, the crazy loon, standing there and the head flashing the light all over him.

DUSTY. The head was crazier than Stump—never saw a thing and looking right at him.

STUMP [*enjoying it with the rest*]. I sure was scared.

DUSTY. Here we are trying to get Old Christmas Tree fired and Stan takes his place in bed for him, so he doesn't even get caught being out.

STAN. Well, it never would have happened, if the head hadn't seen that light. I told you not to turn it on.

[*The silhouette of* MR. NOEL's *head and shoulders rises in the frame of the window outside. It is there long enough for the audience to see it clearly, but the boys are so filled with mirth they do not notice it. During the next few speeches it appears and disappears with the motions of some one trying to make out what is going on in the room and yet not be discovered.*]

DUSTY. I know, Stan, but think of the head taking you for Old Christmas Tree asleep. That's funnier than getting him *fired*.

STAN. Old Christmas Tree—Old Sour Apple Tree.

DUSTY. Well, Old Sour Apples won't ever know how much he has to thank us for.

STAN [*rising from the bed*]. Well, let's get back to bed, it's getting late.

STUMP. I'm sure going to hate to get up in the morning.

DUSTY. Wish I hadn't been sick twice already this month.

[NOEL *climbs up in the window.* DICKEY *sees him and utters a cry of horror.*[

DICKEY. Aa—ww—kk. [*He scrambles to his feet.*]

STAN. What's— [*Standing by the bed, startled.* NOEL *enters the room. He stumbles over* DUSTY *who lets out a startled yell.*

NOEL *manages to keep on his feet and in an instant he has the light on surveying the room.*]

NOEL [*as he looks around*]. What's going on here? [DICKEY *moves slowly toward the door as though trying to slip away,* NOEL *grabs him by his pajamas and drags him back.*] Wait a minute— Wait a minute! Come back here. [*He holds on to* DICK *for a few instants before releasing him. All the boys are extremely startled, and uncertain just what to do.* NOEL *crosses to door Left and speaks deliberately.*] It looks like a meeting of the Society for the Destruction of the School. I'm glad I happened around. [*Abruptly dropping his satire.*] What does this mean, Stanford?

[STANFORD *looks at him as though the answer would not come into his mouth.*]

DUSTY [*standing up*]. Stanford wasn't feeling well, Mr. Noel.

NOEL [*to* DUSTY]. Is your name Stanford?

DUSTY [*subsiding*]. No sir.

STAN [*in exactly* DUSTY'S *tone*]. I wasn't feeling well, Mr. Noel.

[NOEL *waits for him to go on.*]

NOEL. Well. [*More painful silence.*]

DUSTY. He came to tell you, sir, and when he couldn't find you in here, he thought it was funny—I mean strange—yes sir, *strange.* He was afraid something might have happened to you, so he—so he called us to decide what we'd better do about—about—

NOEL. You were all in here just worrying over my health.

DUSTY and STUMP [*together*]. Yes, sir.

DICKEY. Yes, sir.

NOEL [*flaring up*]. None of your impudence.

DUSTY [*with pained innocence*]. Why, Mr. Noel!

NOEL [*looking around*]. Same old crowd— Same old tricks. . . . I see you're in bad company again, Stump. I warned you, didn't I?

STUMP. Yes, sir.

NOEL [*after a slight pause*]. You better get back to bed. [*They all start to move with alacrity toward the door.*] Wait a minute! [*They stop in their tracks.*] You report here tomorrow morning after breakfast. I'll arrange something to keep you so busy you won't have time to bother about my health. [*Suddenly turning to* STANFORD.] Oh, you're sick, aren't you, Stanford?

STAN. I don't feel so well, sir.

NOEL. No, I guess not. . . . [*A tone of sincere regret.*] It's too bad about you, Stanford. I told you last week if I had any more trouble out of you, it was likely to cost you your diploma.

STAN [*breaking out in desperation*]. Well, Mr. Noel, when you slip out of your window after lights—

NOEL [*sharply*]. What's that?

STAN [*holding his ground*]. House master's haven't got any more right than we have to climb—

NOEL [*with a warning gesture*]. None of your lip there, young fellow. [STANFORD *remains silent, but his sense of rebellion at what he thinks is injustice is stronger in his mind than anything else. The other boys feel the strength of* STANFORD'S *contention and look questioningly at* NOEL. NOEL *himself is conscious of the weakness of his position and for a moment he is uncertain.*]

NOEL. So . . . now you've taken to ordering house masters about. . . . Well, we'll just get that settled right now. [*Indicating* STUMP, DUSTY *and* DICK.] You three get on to bed there. [*They hesitate.*] Yes, to bed. And see that you *get to bed*, you understand? [*They move toward the door.* DUSTY *and* DICKEY *look back compassionately at* STANFORD.] And don't you forget you're expected here right after breakfast.

[NOEL *closes the door after them and turns to* STANFORD *who is standing just ready for an open rebellion regardless of the consequences. But* NOEL'S *manner suddenly changes, he becomes the diplomatic teacher trying to extract valuable extra curriculum information from a pupil.* STANFORD'S *mood of open defiance is gradually disconcerted by the change in* NOEL.]

NOEL [*almost affably*]. Now let me get this straight. You're undertaking to tell me just what house masters may and may not do.

STAN [*sullenly*]. Not exactly that.

NOEL [*elaborately polite*]. Perhaps I misunderstood you.

STAN [*doggedly*]. I only said house masters weren't supposed to go off the grounds after lights any more than we are.

[STANFORD *stares at his feet.* NOEL *looks at him hard, studying him. He seems vitally interested in how much* STANFORD *knows.*]

NOEL [*slowly, while crossing to Left Center*]. You say I climbed out of the window. [*Quickly.*] How do you *know* I climbed out of the window?

STAN [*hesitating*]. I saw you.

NOEL [*quickly*]. You couldn't have seen me. Your room's on the far side.

STAN [*still standing by the bed*]. I mean somebody else saw you. . . . I'd rather not say who.

NOEL. Saw me to-night?

STAN. They've seen you for three nights.

[NOEL *has lost his superior school-teacher's assurance. He is trying to to mask his intense concern with* STANFORD'S *answers under an air of coolness, but he is like a man playing a big fish on a line he knows is too weak.*]

NOEL. Did they see me come back?

STAN. No, sir, they didn't see you come back.

NOEL [*pausing, then suddenly*]. Stanford, what was that I heard just as I came in about getting me *fired?*

STAN. Well—er— [STANFORD *looks at him, startled.*] That was just a kind of a joke, sir. We were wondering what the head might do, if he found out. [STANFORD *looks at him for help but gets none.*] You've been so strict with us, you know. [*Thinking pause.*]

NOEL. You were going to make it your business to have the head find it out? [STANFORD *hesitates.*] Were you?

STAN [*with decision*]. Yes, sir. [STANFORD *looks at him expecting any sort of an outburst from physical violence to bitter reproaches.* NOEL *hesitates a moment and completely surprises him by his calmness.*]

NOEL [*pleasantly*]. Sit down, Stanford. [*He indicates the chair Right and sits down chair Left.* STANFORD *sits chair Right and stares at him a little bewildered.*] You're right, Stanford. I have gone out three nights . . . *just* three nights as it happens. . . . And you're right I went without—making *formal arrangements* to go. [*A slight pause.*]

STAN [*unable to think of anything else*]. Yes, sir.

NOEL [*rising abruptly and speaking with a sudden inner rebellion*]. Do you know, Stanford, that some things aren't any of your business ?

STAN [*uncomfortably*]. Yes, sir. I— Yes, sir.

[NOEL *walks to the window and looks out aimlessly.*]

NOEL [*now almost amused*]. Well, you seem to have made it pretty successfully your business.

STAN. I—

NOEL [*coming back to his chair, his manner taking on a definite amiability*]. The fact is you *have*—so I've got to take you into my confidence.

STAN. Confidence ?

NOEL. I believe I can trust you, can't I ?

STAN [*astonished*]. Why, I think so, sir.

NOEL. Well, I'm going to tell you something. [*He sits impressively.*] Do you know what insomnia is ?

STAN. Why—er—isn't that when you can't sleep ?

NOEL. That's it— You can't sleep !

STAN [*wonderingly*]. Have you got insomnia ?

NOEL [*for an instant he hesitates. Then he speaks with definiteness*]. No. No, I haven't got it, but there's a fellow in this town that has. Stanford, it's simply terrible. That man hasn't slept for weeks and weeks. He's nearly crazy.

STAN [*sympathetically*]. I should think he would be.

NOEL. He was sick, you see, and the flu left him that way.

STAN [*impressed*]. I didn't know flu would do that.

NOEL. Sometimes it does— Not often. . . . Well, this chap is a friend of mine. That is, I knew his brother at college. This

chap and his wife have been nice to me since I came here. You
know, had me to dinner and that sort of thing. His wife is a
wonderful cook. You can appreciate what a good home-cooked
meal is once in a while.

STAN. I sure can.

NOEL. Well he—the chap—got sick and had to give up his job.
Of course the money stopped coming in and there were bills
—doctor's bills, grocery bills, medicine bills, you know how
it is.

STAN. Yes.

NOEL. Well, somebody had to keep things going and so his wife
went out and got a job. She's got a good job and he's getting
better. Everything would be fine, only he's got insomnia and
can't sleep.

[NOEL, *seeing he has* STANFORD *under his spell, pauses
dramatically. He rises, takes off his coat and hangs it in the
closet. He instinctively reaches to the hook on the door for his
bath-robe and is puzzled not to find it.* STANFORD *realizes what
he wants and picks up the bath-robe from the floor, and takes
it to* NOEL *standing by the closet.*]

STAN [*rather guiltily*]. Is this what you're looking for?

NOEL. Why, yes. [*He takes the robe and looks hard at* STANFORD
*as though he had a swift vision of how it got there. He puts
on the robe and continues his story standing up Right.* STAN-
FORD *crosses to chair Left and sits.*] You see he— [*Very
nervously.*] A chap with insomnia can't get to sleep and he's
so nervous he just can't stay awake alone. He's got to have
somebody awake with him. It would be easy if his wife didn't
have to work in the day. But she can't work all day and sit
up all night. You can see that.

STAN. No, sir, I should think she couldn't.

NOEL [*emphatically*]. That's just it. He wouldn't let her sleep
and the other night she got to a point where she was just about
wild. She saw she was going to lose her job if she didn't get
some sleep and so she sent for me. Naturally, when I got her
message I hurried down as fast as I could to see what was
the matter. . . . As soon as I got there, I realized there was

just one thing, that woman had to have some sleep. I said to her, "You go in and lie down. I'll sit up with him a while." [*Pausing impressively.*] After a while, for the first time in weeks he began to feel a little drowsy.

STAN [*completely interested*]. Really, Mr. Noel!

NOEL. Naturally his wife was grateful and asked me to come again. Last night when I went back, he actually dozed a little. And to-night—I left him snoring.

STAN. I'll bet his wife *is* grateful to you.

NOEL. Anybody would have done as much.

STAN. Just the same it was decent of you to give up your sleep —and take a chance.

NOEL. Oh, myself. That didn't matter. I could have explained all right about myself. I was thinking of him—the chap. It's for his sake I felt it better not to, don't you see? I want to keep everything quiet for his sake.

STAN. Yes, sir.

NOEL. You know, having insomnia and all that, a man doesn't want it noised about. He doesn't want everybody knowing it. *You* can see how he would feel.

STAN. I understand exactly.

NOEL [*pausing for effect*]. And I can count on you, Stanford, to use your influence about this.—To keep everything quiet?

STAN. You sure can, sir. I'll see that the others don't say a word. They're the only ones that know.

NOEL [*offering his hand*]. Thanks, I hoped I could count on you. . . . It's pretty late now, you'd better—

STAN [*rising*]. Yes sir. [*He starts toward the door and when he gets there turns around shyly.*] Can I say, sir, I appreciate your confiding in me like this.

NOEL [*sharply*]. Confiding—

STAN. Your telling me about things confidentially— [*He looks at* NOEL *expecting him to say something, but the latter is looking hard in the other direction. Slowly* STANFORD *starts out of the room.*] Good night, sir.

NOEL [*suddenly*]. Wait a minute, Stanford. [STANFORD *turns around.* NOEL'S *manner changes from easy glibness to some-*

thing more sincere and direct.] You've never lied to me, have you?

STAN [*puzzled*]. Lied to you, sir?

NOEL. To get out of a scrape.

STAN [*thoughtfully*]. Well, no sir—when you've put me squarely up against it. Not when you've gotten me in a corner I haven't.

NOEL. Well, Stanford, I've just been lying to you.

STAN [*not sure what he means*]. Lying to me, sir? I don't believe I understand.

NOEL. You caught me in a corner to-night and I just lied to you to get out of it because I can't tell you the truth. But it isn't worth it—my *job* isn't worth it.

STAN [*embarrassed*]. I—

NOEL. Rules are rules and you caught me breaking them. I saw a chance to avoid the issue by working on your sympathy. I told you that cock and bull story.

STAN [*slowly*]. You mean all that—all that about the insomnia was a—

NOEL. A lie. You had me in the corner and for a moment I saw a way I could get out. . . . It's a way I don't care to take.

STAN [*trying to get everything straight*]. Well, gee.

NOEL. So you've got something on me after all.

[STANFORD *looks at him uncertainly a moment, then slowly breaks into a grin.*]

STAN. Well— That sort of puts us in the same boat, doesn't it? . . . I guess you've got enough on me.

NOEL. I haven't got anything on you, Stanford. You and I have squared our accounts as we went along. I made you pay.

STAN [*smiling, thoughtfully*]. Well, couldn't you give me a little credit in advance now? I'm likely to get into trouble again almost any time, Mr. Noel. . . . We could exchange. . . . I could forget your climbing out of the window if you'd—

NOEL. You mean you'll protect me if I'll protect you.

STAN [*eagerly*]. Yes, sir. That's it.

NOEL [*as if deliberating*]. What about the others?

STAN. Dusty and Dick and— [NOEL *nods.*]

STAN. Oh, I can fix them up.

NOEL. Is that your proposition to me?

STAN. Prop—? . . . Yes, sir.

NOEL [*deliberately, with decision*]. Well, I don't accept it.
   [*They look hard at each other.*]

STAN [*misunderstanding and resenting what he believes to be
   NOEL's meaning*]. You mean you expect to go on punishing
   me whenever you feel like it, while you get away with everything.

NOEL [*slowly*]. I mean tomorrow morning you and I will go to
   the head together.

STAN [*surprised*]. Go to the head!

NOEL. You're going to tell him you came into my room to-night
   and found me gone— While you were here I climbed back
   into the window. You're going to tell him the truth.

STAN [*slowly*]. But the head's more particular about that sort
   of thing than anything—why last year he fired—I mean discharged—

NOEL [*drily*]. Fired is a good expressive word.

STAN. Well, if he found out—

NOEL. *Whatever* happens, I've got an account against me to be
   squared. I'd hold *you* to it if it were against you.

STAN [*thinking*]. But isn't there some other way—without risk-
   ing going to the head I mean— . . . I'm not thinking of myself Mr. Noel. . . . I've been in this school four years, I
   know how Dr. Oslo feels about things like this.

NOEL [*with some curiosity*]. A little while ago, you weren't so
   concerned about my job.

STAN. I know, sir. . . . But this makes it look different.

NOEL. What does?

STAN [*trying to answer the question for himself*]. I don't know
   how to tell you—but it does. . . . Your being frank like this.
   . . . You seem *human*, all of a sudden!

NOEL [*slowly*]. Does it surprise you to find a—teacher human,
   Stanford?

STAN. I didn't mean to be impertinent, sir.

NOEL [*coming down to bed*]. You aren't.

STAN. I suppose I meant that all at once you seemed just like us.

NOEL. Thank you, Stanford. . . . [*Sits on bed.*] I expect we're *all* more like you than you realize—that's just our weak point. We don't want to let you see, if we can help it, just how much like you we are, how human we are. We're afraid you won't respect us as teachers. That's the only reason why it's hard to tell you why I had to go out. But I couldn't let you go away like that just now. It came to me that it was a lot more important that I keep my own self-respect as a man than that I go on preserving in your eyes my dignity as a teacher. . . . You see, Stanford, there was a girl—not just an ordinary kind of a girl but a very special one. I knew that the moment I set eyes on her. I've never met any one like her before and I'm quite sure I'll never meet another if I live to be a hundred. . . . I only just met her last Sunday night and she doesn't live here, she's just visiting. She's going away tomorrow. . . . I don't suppose you'll understand, Stanford, but I simply *had* to see that girl again before she left.

STAN [*slowly and very seriously*]. I kind of understand, sir. . . . I sort of felt that way myself, once.

NOEL. There were some things we *had* to say to each other. . . . I couldn't let her leave without saying good-bye.

STAN. No, sir.

NOEL. There was only one way. I took my chance. With my eyes open— [*With feeling.*] And it was worth it. Now I'll take my medicine . . . I guess she'll understand.

STAN. But, Mr. Noel—

NOEL. I'm thinking of myself, Stan, that's why, under the circumstances, you'd better go with me to Dr. Oslo. . . . [*There is a knock upon the door.* NOEL *stands up.*] Come in.

[*The door opens and* DR. OSLO *enters. He blinks as if he were astonished at what he sees.*]

OSLO. Brr— [*He clears his throat.*] I saw your light again—is anything the trouble ? [*Seeing* STANFORD.] Something the matter with you, Stanford ?

STAN [*standing up*]. No, sir.

NOEL [*coming down Center*]. Stanford and I were having a talk.

OSLO [*frowning*]. Extraordinary time of night for talks, Noel.

NOEL. It's been a rather unusual talk, Dr. Oslo.

STAN. I wasn't asleep and Mr. Noel was awake.

OSLO. I can't say I approve.

NOEL. As a matter of fact, we were coming over to your office in the morning to tell you the whole thing. It's late but as long as you are here—

STAN [*with a rather frantic gesture*]. Mr. Noel— Dr. Oslo, Mr. Noel wanted me to come to you and [*He looks at* NOEL.] before I talked with him, I had thought about it. But Mr. Noel has made me see I'd rather not talk about it to you or any one else, sir.

NOEL [*honestly considering*]. I'm not sure.

OSLO [*irritated*]. Well, Brr-rr [*He clears his throat.*] I'm sure it can't be important enough to stand arguing about this time of night.

STAN [*quickly*]. It isn't, sir. It really isn't.

OSLO [*a bit shortly*]. Well, you get to bed then.

STAN. Yes, sir. [*He darts out of the room as if afraid of being stopped.*]

[OSLO *looks hard at* NOEL *and then at the bed which is slightly rumpled but not turned down.*]

OSLO [*trying to reconcile things in his own mind*]. I came in here a little while ago.

NOEL [*genuinely astonished*]. You did, sir!

OSLO [*re-assured by* NOEL'S *surprise*]. You're a sound sleeper, Noel.

NOEL [*still more baffled*]. Was I—asleep?

OSLO. Turned my flashlight all over you like this. [*He plays it on the bed.*] Called you.

[NOEL *stares at* DR. OSLO *incredulously.*]

NOEL [*ready to hear anything*]. Did I—answer?

OSLO [*with a gesture of dismissing the subject*]. No, you went on snoring. Brr-rr [*He clears his throat.*] I can't say I approve of these late talks. [*He yawns.*]

NOEL. Don't myself, Dr. Oslo. It isn't likely to happen again.

OSLO [*moving to the door*]. Well, I think we'd both better get to bed and try to *stay* there for the rest of the night.

NOEL [*smiling*]. A good idea. Sorry my light made you uneasy.

OSLO [*yawning sleepily*]. Good night, Noel. [*He goes out.*]

[NOEL *stands staring after him a moment. Takes a deep breath and breaks his revery. Takes off his bath-robe and throws it across the foot of the bed. Then like a detective he goes over and examines the top of his mussed bed and the rumpled pillow. He unties his tie and unbottons his shirt while he is making the examination. There is a faint tapping outside his door. He looks up sharply and listens. Reassuring himself that it was nothing, he takes off his shirt, all but one sleeve, when the tapping comes more decided.*]

NOEL. Come. [STANFORD *enters.*] Oh, it's you.

STAN [*inviting himself in.*] Yes, sir.

NOEL. Well?

STAN. I just wanted to tell you, Mr. Noel, you can count on me to keep the others quiet. [*A little importantly.*] We'll keep everything confidential between us—just you and me.

NOEL [*looking hard at him*]. Stanford!

STAN [*slightly uneasy under the gaze*]. Yes, sir?

NOEL [*deliberately*]. Doctor Oslo said he was in here while— Do you know anything about it?

STAN. Why, yes, sir. I didn't hear him coming until it was too late to hide. I just lay down on your bed as if I was asleep and he thought I was you. [*A look of extreme comprehension lights up* NOEL's *face.*]

NOEL. Say, son, I thought you and I had just squared our accounts.

STAN [*conscientiously*]. Oh, we have, sir!

NOEL. Well, if I listen to you any more to-night— Before you're through, you'll have me believing you have just saved my life. [*Pause for effect. He speaks brusquely, but there is a half smile on his face.*] Stanford, you get to bed!

[*A quick curtain as* STANFORD *after one swift look at* NOEL *makes for the door; and the latter, relaxing his pose of authority, finishes taking off his shirt.*]

CURTAIN

STAR DUST

BY

ALICE GERSTENBERG

A ROYALTY PLAY

THE CAST

SLICK
GINGER
WUZZY
SCHMITTY
A MAID
A SECOND MAID

THE SCENE

The side veranda of a summer hotel about four o'clock on a fine afternoon.

A door up Center leads into the hotel. To the right of the door is a lattice window. Before the window a porch swing or davenport; there are two chairs at Left but there is no feeling of livableness about the furnishings. A railing, running from down right across stage to Left, gives the effect of the height of a porch. A post at the corner down Right is entwined with rose vines, and the vines creep in and out of the railing. At Left stairs seem to descend off stage. Bushes mask the reality of a flat floor if a platform is not obtainable.

THE CHARACTERS AND COSTUMES

SLICK and GINGER, exceedingly pretty and feminine, are dressed as briefly as possible in tennis clothes.

WUZZY is dressed in the latest style, over-dressed, but prettily over-dressed. Her gown handicaps her movement and hat, gloves and parasol accentuate the ultra in artificial femininity.

SCHMITTY, chic and attractive, wears aviation trousers, coat, cap, with goggles pushed back over her head.

———•———

At the rise of the curtain, SLICK *and* GINGER *are climbing over the railing at Right, balancing their rackets and tennis balls with some difficulty as they try to escape the thorns of the roses.*

SLICK. Look out, Ginger, these roses have thorns!

GINGER. I should say they have, let's climb back again and come up the stairs.

SLICK. If I start a thing, I see it through!

GINGER. I'm with you to the finish, Slick!

SLICK [*sucking her arm to ease a thorn prick*]. Oh, well, the roses are worth it.

GINGER [*standing outside the rail, she sniffs a rose*]. Oh, so fragrant! You know I always stop to sniff flowers. It's the least I can do to thank them for growing!

SLICK. You'd improve your tennis if you'd stop admiring the scenery. [*She lands on the porch.*]

GINGER. But we've got to admire the scenery. That's another way of thanking the mountains for being beautiful.

SLICK. I'll remember to let you get through thanking before I begin to serve.

GINGER. But that's the only way to get all the ginger out of life, to be open-eyed about it every minute. [*She climbs over rail to porch.*]

SLICK [*laughs*]. Well, open your eyes a little more when my balls comes over. [*Looks up at the hotel.*] Or all the hotel guests will be dashing down to you with spectacles!

[*They sit on Right of front railing; they are still breathing rather heavily as if somewhat fatigued from a strenuous game; they pull out their vanity cases and combs to freshen up faces and hair, which is conveniently short.*]

GINGER. You certainly play a slick game, Slick! Where'd you get that grand back-hand slam?

SLICK. Three brothers brought me up on it.

GINGER. You can even skip stones on water like a boy.

SLICK. Learnt it young.

GINGER. Wish I had brothers, only female inhibs at our house.

SLICK. Where do you get your ginger from, then?

GINGER. Just self-defense, got to have it against two older sisters. Soon as I'm through school and can get a job I'm going to strike out for myself. Want a cig? [*Offers a package of cigarettes.*]

SLICK. No, thanks, I'm off of 'em—in training.

GINGER. I'd better be too. [*Puts the package away from her.*] Want to win the next set.

SLICK. I can't play you till tomorrow. Kenyon Drake's motoring me up to the Casino at five for tea.

GINGER [*consulting her wrist watch*]. You've just a half hour to dress.

SLICK. Dress? I'm going like this.

GINGER. Going like that to the Casino with Drake!

SLICK. Why not? What's wrong about it?

GINGER. Don't you know Kenyon Drake's gone conservative?

SLICK. What y' mean?

GINGER. Didn't you see him go gaga last night at the dance over Fuzzy Wuzzy in her long ruffled skirt and coy nipped-in waist line? Was she gatish! Just like a round-barrel pink bonbon baby covering up the telephone!

SLICK [*with a sudden change of expression*]. Yes, I saw him dance with her.

GINGER. My sisters wagged about it all night. I got up and slammed the door between our rooms because I wanted to sleep, but I heard enough. They said Wuzzy's made up her mind to catch Kenyon. When I said that Kenyon's been going around with you, Slick, they just laughed and said you were only a sub-deb and didn't count. That Kenyon treats us like the children we are.

SLICK. I'm seventeen!

GINGER. They try to be so superior. Makes me rage! I've got more sense than they have, anyway.

SLICK. Kenyon says that to me.

GINGER. But does he mean it? Maybe he's been stringing you, Slick. You'll have to go fluffy ruffles yourself if you want to play against Wuzzy. She can't match you at tennis but in ball gowns—

SLICK [*toying with her tennis racket*]. I won't dress up for him! Besides, I haven't any silly long things and don't intend to get any.

GINGER. Some of us have to stay strong-minded to save the freedom the old girls fought for. I won't let my hair grow long and I won't sweep away the dust for the maids with trains!

SLICK. I told Kenyon I wouldn't. He laughed, said I was a model of clean health and didn't need clothes!

GINGER. You're a magazine cover, Slick. They all say so, but they've seen you play ball on the beach and they treat you like a pal. My sister Cynthia says there's more mystery about Wuzzy all covered up in coats on the beach and in Godey book revivals at dances. Cynthia and Hortense sit in front of the mirror trying to look alluring too in the new styles and they say I have to learn to be feminine, to wear them. But I don't want a coming out party and am going to fight it.

SLICK. Dad says I don't have to have any.

GINGER [*playing with a tennis ball*]. Mother says I have to. You don't really have to, living in New York, but in a suburb, it's different—a lot of old-fashioned family life, everybody talking and living to suit the neighbors. I'd ask you to visit us, but it wouldn't be any fun. I'll get a job in New York and be independent. No girl is really free until she earns her own money. Then you and I can see each other there. I'm glad to have met you this summer, Slick; glad you chose this place.

SLICK. So am I. Dad likes having his golf roll off from the veranda.

GINGER [*looks out front*]. It *is* a stunning course! So green and smooth!

SLICK. My brothers will like you, Ginger. Fred and Sam are coming up next week-end.

GINGER. I suppose they prefer girls all dressed up like china bric-a-brac too.

SLICK. No they don't; they say their wives will have to have a sense of humor.

GINGER. They must be super wonderful men. But Kenyon's different. He'll let a girl win him by cheating.

SLICK. Cheating? *Carol*

GINGER. Wuzzy's awfully tricky. ~~Cynthia~~ and Hortense help each other too, making the men believe they're very popular. Hortense is going to marry Mr. Henderson if she can't find anybody better this summer.

SLICK. The man that came up here in his special train?

GINGER. Yes, his circulation is poor but he has a fine railway system!

SLICK. Oh, I couldn't marry a man I didn't love.

GINGER. I couldn't. I wouldn't.

SLICK. But it would be terrible to be in love and not be loved in return!

GINGER. I'm glad you don't really care then if Kenyon's asked Fuzzy Wuzzy to marry him.

SLICK [*stops toying with her tennis racket*]. Asked Fuzzy Wuzzy—what do you mean—you said—to marry him?

GINGER. Yes, Hortense heard him. Wuzzy and Kenyon were sitting out the dance over there last night. Hortense and Mr. Henderson were sitting inside at the window. They couldn't help hearing.

SLICK [*stands up*]. Kenyon asked Wuzzy to marry him?

GINGER. Don't you believe it?

SLICK. And did Wuzzy—what did Wuzzy say?

GINGER [*beginning to realize a situation*]. Kenyon's not much good anyway, Slick. It can't really matter. He's not worth you —you see— [*She stands up and puts her arm about* SLICK.]

SLICK. Then Wuzzy—

GINGER. They settled it; proves how dumb he is; I've been telling you right along you ought to drop him—

SLICK [*has been trying to control herself but at last unable to, slips to the swing and buries her face in her arms while her body shakes with suppressed sobs*]. I can't—I can't—I can't—

GINGER [*watches her a moment*]. I didn't know it meant so much to you, Slick! I was afraid you were beginning to care and wanted to stop you because I've been hearing from Cynthia how Wuzzy has been angling for Kenyon. She's had her net out for him. Now he's swallowed hook and line and has been hauled into shore to be caged in her own little basket.

SLICK [*in intense grief*]. I haven't a chance in the world against Wuzzy.

GINGER. I don't think you have, Slick, with a man like Kenyon. You never could be Wuzzy's type if that's the type he wants and I don't see why you should care a whoop about him. He's not good enough for you and that's the truth! Come now, forget it! Dry your eyes and look at the sky! [*She crosses to Left and looks up.*] There's Schmitty up there taking her lesson; she's doing all kinds of stunting this morning; she's got fine nerve—gee, I want to learn how to fly too!

SLICK [*paying no attention to* SCHMITTY *but sits up in swing*]. Why didn't I know this! Why did he ask me to tea this afternoon? What does it all mean?

GINGER. Mean? I guess it doesn't mean anything except he's going to tell you about Wuzzy, or else, it's just as Cynthia says, he doesn't consider us grown up yet.

SLICK [*trying to be brave through grief*]. But I *am* grown up— excuse me for crying—it's soft of me—I've never really cried before—much—but I can't help it! [*Buries her face again.*]

GINGER [*crosses to Right and puts her hand on* SLICK's *head*]. Oh, I'm sorry I told you, Slick, but you'd have to know it anyway. And if he told you, he'd see you like this and you wouldn't want him to see.

SLICK [*trying to have courage in the moment that comes early to all lives when the first sorrow seems to strike too deeply for endurance*]. No, I've got to hide it— [*She sits up.*] hide it —but I don't know how I can go on—living—

GINGER. You'll forget—in time—

SLICK. No, I'll never forget. What's the use of trying to go on living? What's there to live for?

GINGER. Your father—your brothers—

SLICK. I never can be happy again. I can't endure it—I'll jump into the ocean and end it—I want to go where it's dark and where I won't be anything any more—I can't go on—thinking —thinking—

GINGER [*looking off Left, she shakes her*]. Some one's coming! Take my vanity—you need rouge—it's Wuzzy—

SLICK. I can't meet her.

GINGER. She'll see you run. Pretend you're combing your hair— I'll talk to her— [*Crossing Left.*] Hello, Wuzzy, where you going, all dolled up?

[SLICK *hurries to the back of the porch at Right and combs her hair.*]

WUZZY [*enters up the stairs at Left*]. Hello, Ginger. Hello, Slick.

SLICK. 'lo.

WUZZY [*looking about on the Left near the chairs as if she were hunting something she had lost*]. Have a good game?

GINGER. Always do.

WUZZY [*not interested*]. Who won?

GINGER. Slick; she usually does—she's going to be a world famous champion some day.

WUZZY [*without enthusiasm*]. That'll be nice.

GINGER. Looking for something?

WUZZY. No— Oh, no— [*Crosses Right to the swing, sits down and thereafter surreptitiously moves the pillows as if seeking something.*]

GINGER [*Left Center*]. Out for some air? Maybe you can't take in much of it in that get up.

WUZZY. I like the view; people don't use this veranda very much, do they?

GINGER. It's out of the way, but it's a short cut for us to the courts. We come down the back stairs and go through the ballroom. You were out here last night, though, weren't you?

WUZZY. Yes, always on Wednesday and Saturday nights between dances.

GINGER. Have a good time last night? How could you dance in that round, long skirt?

WUZZY. I sit out here a lot.

GINGER. You're all shirred up this afternoon too.

WUZZY. I'm going to the Casino for tea with Kenyon Drake at five.

GINGER. Oh, you are!

WUZZY. He's coming for me here.

GINGER. Going alone?

WUZZY. He said he had asked you, Slick. It's half past four so hurry up and get dressed. [SLICK *sits on rail, Right.*]

GINGER. Slick prefers another game with me.

WUZZY. Then I can have him all alone. That'll be nice.

GINGER. Sure, that's just what Slick's been planning. You see Slick knew Kenyon was going to propose to you and didn't want to spoil your fun.

WUZZY. Why, you clever little girls!

GINGER. Yes, we are. You ought to give Slick a handsome present for helping your cause with Kenyon.

WUZZY. Oh, have you, Slick?

SLICK. I hope you'll be very happy.

WUZZY. Kenyon's promised me the most gorgeous new engagement ring. I was engaged once to a man down south, who belonged to such a good family they wouldn't buy new jewelry so I was supposed to accept an old ring all out of style. I was furious and just said I couldn't put— Oh! Oh! [*Looking off Left, her hand flies to her heart.*]

GINGER. What's the matter? Waist too tight?

WUZZY. That aeroplane out there! It just took a terrific swoop!

SLICK. Oh, that's only Schmitty having her lesson!

GINGER. She's trying to be another Lindy. If she doesn't end up by being an Admiral Byrd crashing a South Pole!

WUZZY [*relieved*]. Oh! So I said I wouldn't live with second-hand things and that was that. Kenyon's got enough to give me a smart new house. He thinks you're an awfully nice child, Slick; said in about five years after you'd been out a while and knew how to act sophisticated you'd be able to choose any man you wanted.

GINGER. Stop calling us children. If letting your hair grow is making you feel older you'd better have another bob.

WUZZY [*with her hands to her hair*]. Bob my curls? After I've gone to all the trouble of growing them in?

GINGER. Are they really all your own? [*Feels them.*] Honestly growing on your head?

SLICK. Wuzzy, are you madly in love with Kenyon?

WUZZY. Can I puzzle you? Men love to be puzzled. That's a question I shall never answer, not even to him!

SLICK. If you did love him, you couldn't help saying it, could you?

WUZZY [*laughs*]. Oh, Slick, you're always so *sincere!*

GINGER. Kenyon likes Slick because she is sincere.

[*The whirr of an aeroplane begins faintly off stage Right and continues getting nearer and louder.*]

WUZZY. There you're wrong. Kenyon says Slick is too sincere, it makes her too direct.

GINGER. Kenyon's an old-fashioned man who hasn't enough brains to understand Slick.

WUZZY. Oh, yes, of course, Kenyon's old-fashioned. That's what makes him such a dear! He's so very *blind!*

SLICK. Blind?

GINGER. Dumb! You mean—dumb!

WUZZY [*smiling*]. We won't quarrel about the terms, he's so— [*Her expression changes to terror as she looks off Right and a terrific noise is heard off stage Right.*] Oh! It's coming down!

GINGER [*looking Right with an expression of fear*]. Something's wrong!

SLICK [*with duplicate action*]. Trying to land!

WUZZY. Oh, I can't look!

GINGER [*cries in fear*]. Schmitty! [*Dashes across the stage and leaping over the railing at Right, clears it with ease and disappears.*]

SLICK. Schmitty! [*Follows GINGER, leaping the rail with equal ease and disappears Right.*]

[*Excited voices are heard off stage Right and shouts and noises in confusion.*]

WUZZY [*cries*]. Schmitty! [*And forgetting her dress leaps to follow the girls, but her skirt catches in the rose thorns, her*

*hat falls off, taking with it a bunch of artificial curls; she re-
mains a ridiculous mass of material on top of the railing in a
swimming attitude, caught by thorns on every side and ex-
crutiatingly funny in her struggles to extricate herself. She
raises her voice in screams of shock and pain.*] Help!—Ouch!
—Hel——ep! Ouch! Help! Help! [*Voices and commotion
continue off stage but no one comes to rescue her.*] Ouch!
Ouch! Hel——ep!—Hel—eppp!!! I'm caught! Darn those
thorns! Help! [*Commotion continues off stage but no one
comes to rescue her.*] Please somebody come and get me off!
Ginger! Slick! Slick! I can't move! They're pricking me!
Ouch! Ouch!

[A MAID *enters from the hotel door and runs toward Left to
the stairs, but hearing* WUZZY *turns Right to help her.*]

WUZZY. Help! Help!

MAID. Oh, oh, are you hurt?

WUZZY. What do you think I'm yelling for? Look out, look
out! They're cutting me! Ouch, ouch, ouch, ouch, ouch!

MAID. I can't help it, Miss. They stick! Your dress is caught all
over!

WUZZY. I jumped this railing last year! Oh! what fool skirts!
[*She gets down from rail.*]

MAID. It's all torn, Miss, and such a pretty dress, it is.

WUZZY. My waist's just killing me. Some kind of a bone is in
my side! Can you get a kink out of me there?

MAID. Yes, Miss, be that helpin' you, Miss?

WUZZY. You came along just in time. I would have fainted!

MAID. I was dustin' the ballroom, Miss, when I heard the
noise.

WUZZY. Oh, yes, what happened?

MAID [*looks off Right*]. They came down all right but they
wouldn't have come down on the golf course if somethin'
wasn't wrong.

WUZZY. I seem to be the only one that crashed.

MAID. Yes, Miss Wuzzy.

WUZZY. What time is it? I've got to change my dress, I'm to be
called for here at five.

MAID. Oh, can I sew it up for you, Miss?

WUZZY. Oh, do you think you could?

MAID. I could take tucks in it. It's got so many tucks it wouldn't show.

WUZZY. Oh, please, do. Let's hurry. [*Hurries with* MAID *into the hotel and disappears.*]

[*Voices of* GINGER *and* SLICK *are heard off Right.*]

GINGER [*off stage*]. Please don't follow. She's all right but let her alone till she gets her breath. No, she's not hurt. No, she's not faint. She's just got to get back her wind! Please keep the crowd back!

SLICK [*climbing over rail Right and leaning over to help* SCHMITTY]. Sit down here and rest a while, Schmitty, away from the crowd.

SCHMITTY [*enters by climbing over the rail Right with a laugh which is just a little shaky*]. I'm all right, really I am, just got to breathe.

GINGER [*who has been helping* SCHMITTY *from below, now enters directly after her*]. 'Course you couldn't breathe with a crowd around like that.

SCHMITTY. I did swallow some grass and dust, I think. Whee! What didn't we do to that golf course! [*She sits on swing, Right.*]

GINGER. The hotel won't care about that when they know you're both safe. The pilot went white under his tan.

SCHMITTY [*on the swing*]. It wasn't his fault at all. I've been at the controls for an hour. Once we got into an air pocket but I managed that. We were having a fine skim when all of a sudden the motor didn't sound right. We didn't take any chances at its failing but just staged a glider contest with ourselves as a spectacle for you.

GINGER [*sits at Right of down stage rail*]. Oh, I want to fly. Will you take me up?

SCHMITTY. As soon as I get my pilot's license. Not till I feel absolutely sure. I feel sure for myself now, but the responsibility of other people—that's different.

SLICK [*sits on chair Left Center*]. You do have to know where you are going.

SCHMITTY. You do have to know *how* you're going. There's no fooling with the law in flying.

GINGER. Risky sport but—

SCHMITTY. Not risky, scientific. The laws are in the sky just as we have scientific laws on earth. It's up to us to learn how to use them. When mistakes happen, it is the mistake of our own judgment or the imperfection of the machine.

SLICK. Take *me* up soon, I don't care if I crash.

SCHMITTY. But I do. I don't want to be a smart-alecky dunce trying to show off how little I know. When we're flying at night nearer the stars something very wonderful comes over me—

GINGER. Maybe it's star dust.

SCHMITTY. It sort of filters through me and makes me feel as if I were a part of the sky, or as if we were swimming through a sea of energy. I don't seem to have a body; at least, I don't seem to feel my body as much as my mind and I feel sort of indestructible; can you understand that?

SLICK. But I don't want to keep on thinking forever. I'd rather stay close to earth then and die.

SCHMITTY. Why, Slick, that doesn't sound like you.

GINGER. Slick's got a headache.

SCHMITTY. Best way to cure it is to get your thoughts off the earth.

GINGER. I wish she could. Something's gone wrong and she's mad. She wanted something awfully hard and she's lost it.

SCHMITTY. Yes?

[*There is a pause.* SLICK *blinks with tears and swallows with difficulty.* SCHMITTY *looks at* GINGER. GINGER *looks at* SCHMITTY *but does not explain.*]

SCHMITTY. Listen, Slick, I don't know what's worrying you but whatever it is, the minute you lose self-control, you crash! You know in flying when the wind is stronger against us than we want, we use our brains and our controls and guide our-

selves out of it. Maybe some day when we learn how to guide
our lives scientifically we'll really be masters. Maybe you've
been going headlong into a storm and have been miraculously
turned aside from it.

GINGER. I'll say she has! She's really in luck!

SCHMITTY. Sometimes our knocks are good luck in disguise!
I'll ask one of the pilots to take you up to-night for a shower
of star dust. You'll feel quite supreme then!

SLICK. Oh, will you, Schmitty?

SCHMITTY. You know when we were ready to take off Kenyon
Drake came along. His foursome had just reached the 18th
hole. I asked Kenyon in fun if he'd go up with me, and what
do you think he said?

[*As* SLICK *and* GINGER *look at* SCHMITTY *expectantly, waiting for her to continue the* SECOND MAID *comes out of the hotel
door and approaches them.*]

THE SECOND MAID. Oh, Miss Schmidt, we are so glad you are
safe!

SCHMITTY [*laughs*]. Yes, I had a good lesson to-day!

THE SECOND MAID. Do one of you young ladies know to whom
this curl belongs? [*Shows a curl she holds in her hand.*] I
found it there in the swing this morning when I was cleaning.

SCHMITTY. Not to me.

GINGER. Not to me.

SLICK [*takes the curl and looks at it*]. I know. [THE SECOND
MAID *enters hotel, center door.*]

WUZZY [*enters from the hotel door in a hurry and crosses to
Left*]. Oh, Slick, Kenyon's in his car out there. Are you coming? Hello, Schmitty, glad you didn't hurt yourself!

SCHMITTY. Good gracious, Wuzzy! Where are you going—for
a *buggy-ride?*

SLICK [*she crosses Left and holds out the curl*]. Here. Take this
with you. *I'm* not going!

[WUZZY *snatches the curl angrily, tosses her head and goes
out Left.*]

SCHMITTY [*laughs*]. *She'd* never fly, except into rages!

SLICK. Schmitty, what did Kenyon say?

SCHMITTY. Oh, Kenyon said he'd never fly with a *woman*.

GINGER. But of course, *he* couldn't! It takes new men to understand new women!

SLICK [*steps forward, with a sudden brilliant smile and with an inspirational light in her eyes; grasps her tennis racket in renewed power for achievement*]. All right, Ginger, let's play *again!*

CURTAIN

WHAT'S A FIXER FOR?

BY
H. C. POTTER

A ROYALTY PLAY

THE CAST

THE SCENE

A corner of the Midway of the Mighty Marvin Carnival Company on a State Fair Grounds at noon on a sunny day in September.

Down Right, part of the "Office" Wagon or tent is seen. A short flight of steps lead to the ground from the open door. Signs: "Keep Out—This Means You" and "Notary Public" are tacked over the door. "Marvin Shows No. 8" is painted on the side of the wagon. Across the back of the stage is stretched a six-foot wall of brown canvas, supported at intervals by poles. At Left is seen the beginning of a line of "Rag Fronts" or side-show banners displaying the charms of "Jolly Irene —947 lbs.!" Blue sky is seen over the canvas wall. One or two crates labeled "Marvin Shows" up Center and a battered camp-stool near the wagon complete the picture.

Note:—Before the actual play begins there can be a parade of the side-show band, clowns, performers and freaks, lasting several minutes. Also this play offers an opportunity of forming a whole program around the carnival. It can be done by having the parade first and then the different specialty acts introduced by the barker. At the close as many of these stunts as are desired, the play can begin without a lowering of the curtain.

THE CHARACTERS AND COSTUMES

ADGIE *wears a gypsy costume; bandana, beads, puttees, long-sleeved, magenta dress. She has a lion act with the Mighty Marvin Carnival Company. She has about thirty-five carnival-worn years to her credit. She is brandishing a whip.*

BARLOW *is about twenty-five. He is a hard-boiled, mean-looking man dressed cheaply and with a certain amount of flash.*

JAKE, *a rough-neck, is dressed in a battered hat, shabby suit, and battered shoes.*

DUGAN *is a man of about thirty-five or forty. His dress is calculated to impress; diamond stick pin and ring, rakish hat, colored shirt, "fancy" suit. He belongs to all the fraternal organizations he can get into—and he has emblems and pins for those he can't! These are an essential part of his Trade. As the "fixer" for the outfit he radiates confidence and a sense of importance. His job is to gloss over all the faults, appease irritated townsfolk or carnival workers, "sell" the carnival idea to suspicious mayors, police chiefs, and Boards of Health. His middle name is "trouble"—he lives on it. His tongue runs like a well-oiled machine—he can persuade almost any one to do almost anything.*

JANE *is a hardened old trouper with a grouch on the world. She wears a torn shirtwaist, old skirt, black apron with change pockets, broken-down shoes, etc.*

THE COOK-HOUSE BOY *is fat and wears a white round visorless cap—a dirty white shirt and apron.*

At the rise of the curtain the usual sounds of the carnival Tom-tom, Triangle, Hot Dog Vender, Shooting Gallery, donkey engines, start and continue as a faint undercurrent throughout the play.

Then from Left ADGIE *followed by* BARLOW *and* JAKE *enter quarreling.*

ADGIE. I'll see the fixer first—

BARLOW. Fixer?—

ADGIE. You ain't gonna get them—you ain't gonna get them!

BARLOW. Quit raisin' such a row.

ADGIE. Them lions is mine, I tell you!

BARLOW. We been through all that! [*He advances toward her. She threatens him with her whip.*]

ADGIE. Get back!!

   [BARLOW *motions to* JAKE. JAKE *stealthily crosses around behind her.*]

BARLOW. Them lions is ours and you know it!

ADGIE. Yours? Get out of here before I hit one of you! [JAKE *springs, she turns and raises whip just a moment too late, and* JAKE *holds her arms from behind.*] Help! Help! Dugan! Dugan!

BARLOW. Gimme that whip!

   [JAKE *throws whip and continues to hold* ADGIE.]

ADGIE. Get your dirty paws off me! Dugan! Dugan! [*She struggles with* JAKE *and moves down Right.*]

   [DUGAN *enters onto steps of wagon unseen by* BARLOW.]

BARLOW. Now, maybe you'll listen to reason!

ADGIE. Charlie—

JAKE. Shut up!

DUGAN. What's this?—a free outdoor exhibition?

ADGIE. Dugan! He's trying to steal my lions!

DUGAN. Wait a minute. [JAKE *lets go of* ADGIE *and crosses to Left.*] Wanta raise a crowd? [*He crosses and looks off stage Left then turns and crosses to Center.*] Now this is just a friendly argument, that's all— What's the trouble?

ADGIE [*Right*]. Charlie, he's trying to take my lions away!

BARLOW [*Left*]. They ain't hers, any more, they're mine! She made a legal sale—!

ADGIE. I did not!

DUGAN. Take it easy, Adgie, take it easy. [*Crosses to* BARLOW.] Legal sale, you say? Do you—represent the law, young feller?

BARLOW. No—I—don't!

DUGAN. Fair Association?

BARLOW. No!

DUGAN. You—a—local man?

BARLOW. No!

DUGAN. In the show business?

BARLOW. Yeah.

DUGAN. Dugan's my name. [*Puts out hand, which* BARLOW *shakes.*] Who you with?

ADGIE. Charlie! you ain't . . .

DUGAN [*Left Center. To* ADGIE]. Just a moment! [*To* BARLOW.] Who you with?

BARLOW. B. C. Barlow's United Shows—my name's Frank Barlow.

DUGAN. B. C. Barlow, eh? Know him well. Great showman and a square dealer—you're his son, eh?

BARLOW. Yeah.

DUGAN. Well, what's the trouble?

BARLOW. Ain't no trouble, Mr. Dugan—this lady sold us her lions—and, ah—now she won't us take 'em away.

ADGIE. Honest, Charlie, he's lyin'.

BARLOW. Lyin', huh? Here, Mr. Dugan, take a look at this. [*Takes paper from pocket and hands it to* DUGAN.]

DUGAN. What's this?

BARLOW. It's a photographic copy of a bill of sale she signed six weeks ago in Lima, Ohio. . . .

ADGIE. Charlie, I never!

DUGAN [*Crossing Center*]. Now listen, Adgie, no sense in raising a row. You just keep quiet and I'll see if I can't settle this to the satisfaction of all parties concerned. . . . Now let's see. [*He reads.*] "I—Adgie Modeno— So and so, and so and so, and so and so— Hey—this your signature?

ADGIE [*Right*]. Yes—but I never signed that!

DUGAN [*Center*]. Did you sign anything?

BARLOW [*Left Center*]. You'll notice the signature is witnessed by a notary public.

[JAKE *looks over* DUGAN's *shoulder.*]

DUGAN [*Center*]. Yeah, I noticed that. [*Notices* JAKE.] Who are you, Nosey?—The Notary Public?

JAKE [*Center*]. Nosey! [*He starts to hit* DUGAN.]

BARLOW. Jake!

JAKE. Aw, leave me take a sock at that guy!

[JAKE *crosses up Left.*]

BARLOW. Pipe down! [*Then to* DUGAN *with a threat in his voice.*] He just came along to see that everything goes all right.

DUGAN [*crossing up Left*]. Oh, I see.—How dedo—Dugan's my name— Smoke?—Here have a cigar. [*Hands him one.*]

[JAKE *looks at* BARLOW *as if to say "all right?"* BARLOW *nods.* JAKE *takes the cigar.*]

DUGAN. Mind if I keep this—seeing that it's only a photographic copy—

BARLOW. Go as far as you like.

JAKE. Seein' it's only a photographic copy.

ADGIE. Charlie— You ain't gonna let him take my Leo and my Myra?

DUGAN. What can *I* do about it? This man's got a genuine bill of sale—signed by you—

ADGIE. Yes, but I thought it was a bond—

DUGAN. I can't help what you thought it was— Mr. Barlow, I'm tryin' to get this straightened out for you—

ADGIE. For him—ain't you gonna help me?

DUGAN [*to* BARLOW]. You see what I'm up against? [*Then to* ADGIE.] Now Adgie, I want you to go over to your show and tell your talker to close down for the day. Tell him to move over to the Athletic Show.

ADGIE. You mean I ain't got a chance?

DUGAN. Well, it looks bad.

ADGIE. Layin' down on me, eh? Then do it yourself. If I'm through here, I don't take no more orders from you!

DUGAN. You heard me.

ADGIE [*crosses Right—then turns*]. And if you think—

DUGAN. Beat it. [*She exits Right.*] Say, would your friend like to look over the show?

JAKE. Naw.

DUGAN. We got a Ten-In-One, Palace of Illusions, nice little girl show— [*To* BARLOW.] Maybe he'd like to go down and have a bite at the cook-house?

BARLOW. He stays right here.

JAKE. Yeah, I stay right here.

DUGAN. Suit yourself—I thought I'd like to talk confidentially—

JAKE. The old man says "Stick to Frank," he says. And that's what I'm gonna do. Maybe you'd like to try and throw me out?

BARLOW. Willya pipe down! Now look here, Dugan. I brought this guy along as a witness. No use tryin' to get rid of him, see? Any talking you do, do it in front of him.

DUGAN. Well, I just thought he'd like to look around, that's all. What I wanted to ask you was—confidentially, of course, was this—as one showman to another—don't you think you're giving the girl a rough break?

BARLOW. We need the act—she signed the papers—

DUGAN. Sure, I understand—but don't you think you're taking the bread outta her mouth? That's all she's got in the world —that act. She didn't know she signed a bill of sale. Don't you think that maybe—

BARLOW. Just because I'm young, don't think I'm a sap! We got the goods on her and I'm here to collect—quit stallin' around and hand over them lions.

DUGAN. What's she gonna do—starve?

BARLOW. What do I care?

[*There is a short pause.*]

DUGAN. Well—sure you won't—

BARLOW. Come on!

DUGAN. All right—I was just trying to show you her side, that's all—

BARLOW. Now listen, Dugan, if you put this through for me, I'll make it worth your while.

DUGAN. Yeah?

BARLOW. Of course, we got everything on our side as it is, but if she don't gimme the lions now, we'll have to go to law about it and we need the act—right away.

DUGAN. Where are you playin'?

BARLOW. Crawfordsville.

JAKE. About fifty miles from here.

DUGAN. I'll see that you both get back to-night.

BARLOW. Jake, tell that guy to drive his truck in.

DUGAN [*an idea strikes him*]. Say, would you mind askin' him to drive in the lower gate?—The midway is pretty well crowded now—if he comes in the front way, it'll only cause a disturbance—you know—

BARLOW [*off his guard*]. Yeah, sure.

DUGAN. You understand—we don't want any more rows— I'll send a couple of hunkies down to help you crate 'em up —all right?

BARLOW. That's O.K. Well, Mr. Dugan, guess that settles it. We'll get right after them lions—I wanna thank you for all your help— [*He and* JAKE *start off Left.*]

DUGAN. That's all right— What's a fixer for if it ain't to fix things?

BARLOW. See you later. [*They exit Left.*]

DUGAN [*as they go off he watches them*]. Always glad to help a fellow showman. [*Then when they are out of sight, he turns to wagon and calls.*] Jane!—Hey Jane!

JANE [*from inside the office wagon*]. Yeah?

DUGAN. Come out here—and step on it!

[JANE *enters and stands in the doorway.*]

JANE. Spill it.

DUGAN. I want you to go down to the cook-house and round up four punks—

JANE [*standing on top step*]. What do you think I am—Western Union? Do you realize that twelve years ago I'da been one of the big shots on the Barnum Show only—

DUGAN AND JANE [*together*]. —my partner left me and got *married!*

DUGAN. Yeah—sure—I know. Now listen. Adgie's in a jam— if I don't get her out she's through for the season—maybe for good. [JANE *starts to speak*.] Wait a minute—I ain't through yet. [ADGIE *enters from Right to hear the last of this*.] Get four big guys and tell 'em to go over to Adgie's show.

ADGIE. Say, if you think I'm gonna let you crate up my lions— [*She sits on camp-stool near steps*.]

DUGAN. Wait a minute—gimme a chance! Now Jane, tell those guys not to let anybody near them lions and if anybody asks them who give them the orders—they don't know—see?

JANE. All right.

DUGAN. And tell Mitch over at the prop wagon that there'll be a guy along in about ten minutes to ask for help to get his truck outta the mud and he's to help him, see?

ADGIE. Is this outfit a carnival or the Society of the Helping Hand?

JANE. How do you know there'll be a guy down there?

DUGAN. Never mind, I know.

JANE. The boys'll kick. The mud is terrible out there.

DUGAN. Don't you suppose I know that too!

JANE. Say, what is this?

DUGAN. Leave the thinking to me. Now you beat it right down to the cook-house.

JANE [*crossing to exit Left*]. To think I'd come to this when ten years ago I was with the Mighty Haag Outfit and was singing "There'll be a Hot Time in the Old Town To-night" on the back of an elephant!

DUGAN. And I suppose the elephant got married.—Beat it! [*She exits Left*. DUGAN *starts pacing up and down paying no attention to* ADGIE *who is still sitting dejectedly on the office wagon steps*.]

ADGIE. What did I ever do to you, Charlie Dugan? You're lettin' them take my act without a peep outta you. [DUGAN *still paces up and down without answering*.] Six seasons with the

Marvin Shows and what does it get me? [*Still no answer.*]
And I thought you was my friend! [*Still no answer.*] A fine
fixer you are! [*This hits.*]

DUGAN. Aw, shut up. [*He continues to pace.*]

ADGIE. You're a quitter. Why, you don't care what happens to
the performers so long as the dough rolls into the office
wagon.

DUGAN. Aw, don't bother me.

ADGIE. Charlie, what am I gonna do?

DUGAN. I don't know yet. [*Stopping his pacing.*] Well, let's
get at this from the beginning! What did you sign it for?

ADGIE. They told me it was a bond—I had to have money to
jump the show with.

DUGAN. Get in a jam?

ADGIE. No. Charlie, it was the crummiest outfit under canvas!!
I just couldn't stand it any longer.

DUGAN. I know—that guy Barlow is the biggest grafter in the
business.

ADGIE. I gave 'em my notice—Leo was sick—infected foot.
My Leo that I raised from a kitten!—[*Then lashing out.*]
But why wouldn't he be? The ring stock was mangy. Fever
and distemper running through the menagerie like wildfire.
Rotten canvas—leaky and windy cars—every lot like the
last one: up to the hubs in mud because Barlow wouldn't
pay enough for a dry one.

DUGAN. Cut the sob story and get to the business—that's what
I'm interested in.

ADGIE [*rises*]. Barlow comes to me, "What's this about quittin'
the Show?" he says. I told him this and that. "Adgie," he
says, "haven't I always treated you fair and square? Haven't
I—"

DUGAN [*Left Center*]. Come on, come on. Your wasting my
time. What did he offer you?

ADGIE [*Right Center*]. That all comes later.

DUGAN. Well, let's have it now.

ADGIE. But he didn't offer me anything until we talked for about
a half hour.

DUGAN. Well, skip the half hour!

ADGIE. How can you help me outta this jam unless you know the story?

DUGAN. All I want to know is what did he offer you and what did you sign? [BARLOW *and* JAKE *enter from up Right behind wagon.*] Barlow is liable to be back any moment an— [*He sees them.*] Well, ready to start loading?

BARLOW [*Center*]. Say, that's a swell way you sent us—the truck's up to the hubs in mud just outside the gate.

DUGAN [*Left Center*]. Say now that's terrible—tell you what I'll do. Go on down to the prop wagon—it's next to the cookhouse—ask for Mitch—tell him I said you could have half a dozen hunkies. They'll get you out all right.

BARLOW. All right—much obliged. [*He goes up Right.*]

DUGAN. Say, Barlow, have you got a letter from your old man authorizing you to do business for his outfit? Just a matter of form, you know.

BARLOW [*crossing to Center*]. Sure— [*Produces a letter.*]

JAKE [*in a cock-sure tone*]. We got everything!

DUGAN [*crosses to Center. Takes letter—glances at it—puts it in his pocket*]. All right. Well, if you go down to the prop wagon, Mitch'll fix you up. [*The two start off up Right.*] Come back here when you get ready and we'll sign the receipts and—

BARLOW. Receipts?

DUGAN. Sure—for the boss— He's great on business details. System, you know. [*He laughs.*] Terrible, ain't it!

BARLOW. The out-door racket's gettin' more like a business every year—not like the old days, eh?

[BARLOW *and* JAKE *exit behind wagon, up Right.*]

DUGAN. No, sir, you're right, brother— [*They are out of hearing.*] What would he know of the old days—the rotten little tank-town grafter. [*Turning to* ADGIE.] Well?

ADGIE. Well, Barlow offers me $200 to make the jump. "Only," he says, "I gotta have a bond."

DUGAN. O.K. so far.

ADGIE. So he hands me a paper.

DUGAN. Which was not a bond but a bill of sale— Ha-ha! The old bill of sale racket! You performers'll sign anything to get out of a jam! You'd think you'd learn some day—but you never do. [JANE *enters down Left.*] Well—did you have a nice trip?

JANE. Aw—I come back as quick as I could.

DUGAN. Go get some paper.

JANE. Go roll your hoop!

DUGAN. I want you to do some typing for me.

JANE. Say, am I cashier for this outfit or your private secretary? Answer me that. When I was with Bowers Society Dog and Pony— [*She exits into the office wagon.*]

DUGAN. All right, all right. [*To* ADGIE.] Now, Adgie, go on down to the Athletic Show and tell your talker you may need him.

ADGIE. What for?

DUGAN. Now, don't stop to ask me questions. We gotta work fast.

ADGIE. Dugan, you think there's a chance?

DUGAN. Listen, will ya? When Barlow comes back to sign the papers—

ADGIE. I won't sign no papers!

DUGAN. That's right— Not at first. But when I tell you to, go ahead and sign.

ADGIE. Sign away my act? I thought you was goin' to do somethin'.

DUGAN. Now Adgie, you trust me, don't you?

ADGIE. Look at what happened the last time anybody got good to me.

DUGAN. Will you please do as I say—didn't I tell you to tell your talker to stand by for the outside bally?

ADGIE. Yeah—and didn't you tell Barlow to come back and sign receipts?

DUGAN. Adgie, you know I'm *your* friend.

ADGIE. How do I know—I'll tell you this, Dugan. If you double cross me on this racket—

DUGAN. Don't be a fool—

ADGIE. Take a look down that midway—plenty of kids on the grounds to-day, eh?

DUGAN. What's kids got to do with it?

ADGIE. I'll tell you! If you double cross me, this outfit'll be in the biggest jam you ever saw—I'll go down to the cages and turn them cats loose—right down that midway! [*She whirls around and exits Right.* DUGAN *turns to office wagon.*]

DUGAN. Jane!—Step on it. [JANE *enters from wagon.*] Now don't waste any time telling me about when you was an acrobat with Cook's Colossal Flea Circus. Listen: draw up a *receipt* from the B. C. Barlow Shows to Adgie Modeno for three lions—and make a carbon of that. Got it?

JANE. Yeah.

DUGAN [*slowly*]. Now listen—draw up *a bill of sale* from B. C. Barlow to Adgie for two lions.

JANE. A bill of sale?

DUGAN. A bill of sale! Make two carbons of that.

JANE. What! with all the work I got—

DUGAN. When I holler, you bring me *four papers*. [*Glances over his shoulder—then lowers his voice.*] The two on top are the receipts—*but* the two on the bottom are the carbon copies of the bill of sale!

JANE. Is Adgie buyin' more lions?

DUGAN. No, she's buyin' her own lions back again.

JANE. Oh—the old bill of sale racket! I get ya.

DUGAN. Get busy! [*She exits into wagon.* BARLOW *and* JAKE *enter up Right behind wagon.*] Back already, eh? Well, we're just getting the papers typed—be ready in a minute, I'll go get Adgie. [*He crosses down Right and turns.*] Say, she may be a little hard to handle. I've been talkin' to her but—you know—women like her—tough customers. Now I tell ya, if I get her ready to sign, don't hold the deal up none. We'll rush it through, eh? Quick and Quiet. [*He exits Right.*]

BARLOW [*Center*]. Papers drawn and everything rosy. Pretty easy, pretty easy.

JAKE [*Left*]. I wisht you'd leave me take a sock at that guy!

BARLOW. I'm runnin' this racket.

JAKE. I'd like to hand him a four-foot pole chain—in the back of the neck! [*He hits himself in the back of the neck.*] Baby!

BARLOW. He's O.K. if he's handled right—an' the old man says "Dugan's the slickest fixer in the business."

JAKE. Slick? Well, maybe he's all right as a fixer for a lousy carnival, but he wouldn't be no good with a high-class circus.

BARLOW [*Left Center*]. Well I don't know—he's got personality—

[DUGAN *and* ADGIE *enter down Right.*]

ADGIE [*Right*]. Now, remember what I said—

DUGAN [*Center*]. Now, just a minute, Adgie, while I get them papers. [*To* BARLOW.] Don't forget—quick and quiet—Jane!

[JANE *enters from wagon with the papers.*]

JANE. Wait a minute, wait a minute. [DUGAN *takes the papers.* JANE *stands in the doorway.*] Let's see—O.K. Here's one for you to read, Adgie. [*He gives her top paper—a receipt.*] and here's one for you, [*He gives* BARLOW *the 2nd paper—the other receipt.* BARLOW *reaches for the other papers but* DUGAN *withdraws them.*] These two are just carbons. [BARLOW *and* JAKE *read theirs. A* COOK-HOUSE BOY *enters from up Right behind wagon and calls* DUGAN.]

BOY. Charlie. [DUGAN *crosses up Right.*] The grease joint gotta bad mess of hamburger from the butcher in this town.

DUGAN. What's his name?

BOY. Strauss—they want you to go down and make it good.

DUGAN. Tell him to take the meat back and I'll see Strauss personally.

BOY. O.K.

DUGAN. O.K. [*The boy exits up Right.* DUGAN *crosses to* BARLOW *Left*]. The boy says your truck's O.K. now. The driver says you better hurry or you won't be back to-night, in time to make the jump.

BARLOW. All right, we'll get right after these papers.

ADGIE. Just you wait a minute. You're not goin' to get away with this!

BARLOW. Now, Madame, there's no sense in delaying this any further. It's all legal. You're only making trouble for yourself.

DUGAN [*speaking at the same time*]. Aw, Adgie, I've told you there isn't a chance. Now why not be sensible?

ADGIE. No, sir! I get a lawyer before I go a step further.

BARLOW. We been through all that.

ADGIE. No, we haven't. Not by a long shot.

JAKE. Aw—go lay down!

DUGAN. Now keep quiet everybody. Calm down. Take it easy. Now Adgie—you signed a bill of sale, didn't you?

ADGIE. Yeah, but I thought it was a bond and anyway—

DUGAN. But you signed it!

ADGIE. Yes—yes—yes— You oughta know that by this time!

DUGAN [*topping her*]. All right! That's all there is to it, I'm sorry these men won't be broad-minded about it—but business is business.

BARLOW [*taking out his pen impatiently*]. Yeah—business is business!

JANE [*with a wink at* DUGAN]. Charlie Dugan, you know that ain't right— Don't you sign, Adgie!

DUGAN. Jane, you keep quiet—this ain't your deal— [*Crosses to* ADGIE.] All right, Adgie—you sign here. [*Shows her where to sign.*]

ADGIE. It's O.K.?

DUGAN. Yeah. It's O.K. [*She signs.* DUGAN *crosses quickly to* BARLOW.] Barlow, sign yours, quick, before she changes her mind! [BARLOW *signs the receipt.*] Yes, sir. That's O.K. [*He presents the other two papers.*] Now these two carbons.

JAKE. Hey! Better read them!

[DUGAN *snatches papers and crosses to* ADGIE.]

BARLOW. Shut up! Wanta queer everything?

DUGAN [*to* ADGIE]. Go ahead, Adgie.

ADGIE. All right, Charlie.

DUGAN [*crosses back to* BARLOW]. Make it snappy—she's liable
to blow up any minute!

BARLOW. Gimme the papers.

JAKE. The old man said—

BARLOW. You keep outta this, Jake. It's all O.K.

DUGAN. Come on—make it snappy!

BARLOW. I'm ready. [*He signs the third paper.*]

DUGAN. O.K.—now put your John Hancock on this one. [BAR-
LOW *signs the last paper.*] There we are— [*He crosses to*
ADGIE *with all three papers.*] Here you are, Adgie—sign these
three, now. [*He crosses back to* BARLOW *with the first paper
—which* ADGIE *has been holding all this time.*] Here's her
receipt. [BARLOW *signs.*] All right, sir! [*He crosses to* ADGIE
and gets the other three papers.] Now, Jane! Witness them
all—put the seal on them. Bring out a copy for Mr. Barlow—
[*He "dog-ears" one paper.*] Bring out this one. Put the rest
in the safe.

[JANE *takes them and exits into wagon.* DUGAN *relaxes.*]

BARLOW. Well, I guess we'll start loadin'. Jake—go on down
and tell that truck driver to start cratin' 'em up.

DUGAN. Just a minute, Barlow— [*With a lazy smile.*] There
really ain't no use in sending Jake down there.

BARLOW. What's the idea?

DUGAN. You ain't gonna get them lions.

BARLOW. Come on—cut the comedy—go ahead, Jake!

DUGAN. Wait!—Hey, Jane! [JANE'S *voice is heard grumbling,
then she enters from wagon with the dog-eared paper.* DUGAN
takes it.] Here, lemme see. Yeah, that's the one—wait a minute, Jane. Get in on this. [*He crosses to* BARLOW.] Here you
are, young feller.—And also— [*He counts four bills into*
BARLOW'S *hand and gives him the paper.*] Fifty—one hundred—one fifty—two hundred. [*He shoves a cigar under*
JAKE'S *nose.*] Have a cigar!

[JAKE *takes it.*]

BARLOW. Two hundred bucks!—What's the racket?

DUGAN. That's the dough Adgie owed your old man. It means

she's through with your mangy circus, and it means— Get Off The Lot!

BARLOW. That won't go down. I don't want the dough, I want the lions!

DUGAN. You'll take the dough and like it!

ADGIE. Jane, he's done it. Oh, Charlie!

DUGAN. You keep out of this.

BARLOW. Look here, Dugan! We got the original bill of sale signed by that broad back in the B. C. Barlow safe!

DUGAN [*crossing Right*]. Yeah?—Take a look at that.

BARLOW [*looks wildly at the paper*]. What the—

DUGAN. If you read close you'll find you've sold them cats back to the lady—

BARLOW. Yeah, but—

DUGAN [*topping him*]. You got the cash for 'em—

JAKE. You think you—

DUGAN [*Right. Topping him*]. Now blow!—Next time your old man's gotta dirty deal like this one, tell him to come himself.

[ADGIE *goes wild—flings herself at* DUGAN.]

ADGIE. Charlie Dugan!—Charlie—

DUGAN [*Right*].—Jane, take her off me!

[JANE *does so.* BARLOW *Left Center draws a gun.*]

BARLOW. I'll be hanged if I'll stand for this!

JAKE. Frank, don't pull no rod!

BARLOW. Double cross me, will ya? [ADGIE *and* JANE *make a break for help toward down Right.*] Wait! [*They stop.*] One move outta you two and you won't move again! Now, Dugan—let's have the keys to that strong box!

DUGAN [*crossing slowly toward* BARLOW]. What are you going to do—squirt water at me? [*Pointing to the gun.*]

BARLOW [*Left Center*]. Come on with them keys.

JAKE. Put up the rod and—leave me ask him! [*Rolls up his sleeves.*]

DUGAN [*crossing slowly toward* BARLOW]. Suppose I call the boys? One "Hey Rube" outta me and you'd be in a jam.

BARLOW. You'd never draw breath for another.

DUGAN. Yeah, but where 'ud you be ? These people like me. One yell from me an' the cook-house couldn't use you two for hamburger. [*Very near to* BARLOW.] Come on you—put up that cannon— [*There is a tense pause.*]

[*As he says "cannon" he throws his leg forward behind* BARLOW, *pushes him back with one hand as he grabs the gun with the other.* BARLOW *falls backwards to the ground. All this happens like a flash.*]

DUGAN [*to* JAKE]. Here!—you know better than that! [*Hands him the gun.*]

BARLOW [*on the ground Left Center*]. Wait a minute—this paper ain't a legal bill of sale!

DUGAN [*Center. Lazily points to the sign on the office wagon "Notary Public"*]. Yeah? Pipe the sign! Notary Public!

BARLOW [*getting up from ground*]. We'll go to law about this!

DUGAN. Try it—just try it!—Come on, Barlow, the show's over. Kindly pass out with as little crowding as possible.

BARLOW. I'll send my lawyer down to-morrow.

DUGAN. Don't waste the carfare.

BARLOW. You lousy crook.

DUGAN. Crook! That comes well from you! [*To* JAKE.] Hey, Nosey! put this kid in the truck, wheel him back to Barlow, and tell him his boy ain't growed up yet. Now get off the Fair Grounds, and don't come back. [BARLOW *and* JAKE *exit up Right.*] And when you get back, tell your old man you did business with Dugan!

[*The dialogue from this point up to the re-entrance of* BARLOW *should be run together in a confused jumble. An occasional line coming out of the rejoicing. As much ad libitum may be inserted as desired.*]

ADGIE *and* JANE *together.* { ADGIE. Charlie, I can't tell you—I— Oh! Charlie—
JANE. Now when I had my trained pig act!

DUGAN. Come on now— Get back to your show. You've wasted enough time to-day.—Get outta here, Jane.

JANE. Charlie, you put it over!

ADGIE. Charlie—I'll pay back the two hundred—

DUGAN. You're sure right you will— Jane, that comes out of her envelope this week, get me?

JANE. O.K. with me, Charlie.

[JANE *nods and exits into wagon.* COOK-HOUSE BOY *enters from Left.*]

ADGIE. I don't know what to say.

BOY. Hey, Dugan!

DUGAN. After this don't say it with ink. [ADGIE *exits Right.*]

BOY [*Left*]. Hey, Dugan!

DUGAN [*crossing Left*]. Ya—

BOY [*Left*]. Dugan, they want you down to the Athletic Show —a couple of the local boys are startin' a fight—looks like trouble— [*He exits Left.*]

DUGAN. Be right there—

[*Enter* BARLOW *and* JAKE *from up Right.*]

BARLOW. Look here, that truck's still in the mud.

DUGAN. Say, that's terrible!

BARLOW [*Center*]. Your hunkies won't help us—we gotta get outta here!

DUGAN. Who's stoppin' you?

BARLOW. But we're stuck in the mud!

DUGAN [*turning*]. Go buy a shovel! [*To* JAKE.] Have a cigar! [JAKE *takes it*—DUGAN *turns and exits Left.*] Now just a minute, folks, it's just a friendly argument—

JAKE [*Center*]. I knew I shoulda socked that guy! [*Throwing the cigar down.*]

CURTAIN

TH' 'NITIATED

BY

E. P. CONKLE

A ROYALTY PLAY

THE CAST

Simp
Rod
Willie
Toodles
Mack
The Initiated

THE SCENE

Sparks' Grove at night.
A log and a stump on the Right; an old-fashioned well and seat on the Left. In the Center are coals from an old bonfire. The hoot of an owl; the bark of a dog. A low moon, perhaps. And shortly, a boy's voice somewhere back of the brush.

———————•———————

Simp. Huckleberries.
[*Silence.*]
Simp. Huckleberries!
[*Silence.* Simp, *carrying a knapsack containing 2 old tin pans and other camping utensils, enters stealthily from the Left. Seeing no one, he crosses more boldly. He looks around; he then sits on the log to wait. Shortly another boy's voice is heard.*]
Rod. Huckleberries.
[Simp *gets up.*]
Simp. Gooseberries.
[Rod *enters from Right.*]
Rod. Howdy, Simp.
Simp. Is that you?
Rod. Ef my pa didn't misname me, et is.
Simp. No more of the fellers is come yit.

64

Rod. They air a-comin'. I heerd 'em chatterin'.

Simp. Et's past time fer th' meetin'.

Rod. Le's . . . set. I'm . . . ta'rd!

Simp. We ort to start a fa'ar, I reckon. Et's in th' by-laws.

Rod. Le's start her a-settin', then.

Simp. You got some matches?

Rod. I got some, but they hain't got no heads on 'em.

Simp. How could a feller start a fa'ar with 'em, then?

Rod. Nobody asted a feller to. I got t' use my matches fer toof-pickers. [*He gets up.*] They is some stored over thur b'hint th' well.

Simp. You go git 'em while I git some chips gathered up.

Rod. What you got ag'in goin' gettin' 'em?

Simp. I . . . I . . . I don't like t' go nigh that plague-gonned thing. I . . . *I'm* ta'rd. [*He sits on log.*]

Rod. So'm . . . I. [*He sits on log.*]

Simp. Then . . . le's set yur till th' other fellers comes.

Rod. Mebby we could start a fiction fire with two sticks an' a speck-a moss.

Simp. Yeh. I s'pose we cud *try* et.

Rod. Ef we wasn't both too ta'rd to.

[*They get two sticks, sit on the ground Center, opposite each other by the old fire, and gather up a few dead leaves and sticks and begin to start a fire by rubbing the two sticks together.* Toodles, Willie *and* Mack *enter Left. Immediately they stop.*]

Toodles. Strowberries!

[Simp *and* rod *turn.*]

Simp. Strowberries?

Rod. Et hain't strowberries! [*He gets up.*]

Willie. I telled him et wasn't strowberries; but he wouldn't hear t' me.

[*The boys come forward.*]

Mack. Et's dew-berries, ain't et?

Rod. Et's huckleberries, what it is!

Simp. I could-a shot you fellers fer comin' up without givin' th' parst-word!

WILLIE. You could-a shot *at* us.

SIMP. Et's in th' by-laws. . . . I could-a shot you!

TOODLES. What could you a-shot us with?

SIMP. My pa's got a double-baarled shot-gun I could-a used.

TOODLES. But yer pa's gun air over home over th' pantry door!
An' *I* am *yur*.

SIMP. I . . . I . . . I never thunk-a *that*.

WILLIE. You wouldn't-a shot us no ways, would you-a, Simp?

SIMP. I reckon I *couldn't* afford t' waste no catridges. But, I got
th' right to. I air th' Big Goslin Goose, ain't I?

MACK. I reckon you got th' right; but hev you got th' *aim?*

SIMP. I could-a hit you when you turned flat-ways t' run.

WILLIE. Yeh . . . but I run th' narrer way, though!

ROD. Don't talk 'bout runnin' no ways. Le's set down. I'm . . .
ta'rd. [*Sits on log.*]

TOODLES. Me, too! [*Sits on log.*]

SIMP. Willie, you got some matches?

WILLIE. Nope.

SIMP. Rod, you got some matches?

ROD. Nope.

SIMP. Mack, you?

MACK. Nope.

SIMP. We'll hev to make it seem—our old fa'ar ain't even gone
out.

WILLIE. What you ta'rd about now, Rod?

ROD. Ain't I been doin' what was passted at th' last meetin'?

MACK. I didn't know nothin' passted.

WILLIE. I didn't know nothin' could git past us fellers.

ROD. Wasn't et passted I was to keep my wether eye on Tippie
Hacker so he wouldn't come up an' spy on us while we set? I
mean . . . *met*.

MACK. He'd shore like t' spy on us; but us fellers is too smart
fer him.

SIMP. Where's he at, Rod?

ROD. He told me he was goin' up th' Holler, an' he set out
a-goin'. I let-on I didn't care a fig, an' let him take th' halter.
When he got to Toller's Bridge, I was plumb tuckered out.

I reckon he's up to his gramma's by now . . . ef he didn't stub his toe an' fall down.

WILLIE. Us fellers shore put one over on him!

ROD. I air shore plumb all tuckered out! My ma says I was borned all down at th' mouth.

SIMP. A-course, we ain't got nothin' 'specially ag'in Tippie, only he ain't bright.

TOODLES. He don't know what is seven an' what is 'leven. I reckon I don't neither; but then . . . I'm diffrunt!

ROD. *You* got plendy-a other sense, like horse-sense.

MACK. Yeh. An' nonsense!

TOODLES. Tippie is so plague-gonned kindhearted an' softy. He ain't got no . . . chivaltery . . . about him. No git-up an' gumption!

WILLIE. I shore got git-up an' gall! I hain't got no gumption; but I got plendy-a spunk an' brass! [*He sits on seat by well.*]

MACK. Y' don't reckon Tippie felled into th' crick, do you?

SIMP. Been kind of a good riddance ef he was to.

MACK. Would-a spoiled all th' town's drinkin' warter.

WILLIE. Et 'pears like th' town ain't drinkin' much warter nowdays.

ROD. You fellers seen th' way I tracked Tippie all over. He didn't catch onto a thing. That shows he ain't . . . bright.

TOODLES. Yeh . . . ef he couldn't ketch onto *you!*

[*The boys laugh. All but* ROD.]

ROD. He ain't got no business in our Goslin-Goose Club!

WILLIE. I never knowed him t' take a bath ner t' change his underwears.

MACK. Half th' time he don't wear none.

SIMP. He couldn't git in ef he was a millionaire. Us fellers has got to be firm. Ef we was to begin lettin' in dumb-bells, come a time when we wouldn't have nothin' but dumb-bells in.

MACK. Reckon we got a-nough in *now*, ain't we, Simp?

[*The boys laugh.* WILLIE *jumps up.*]

WILLIE. Fellers . . . I heerd a . . . a noise!

[*All turn toward* WILLIE.]

ROD. Over . . . thur?

WILLIE. Yeh. [*He crosses to the log.*] By th' well-curb.

SIMP. What did et sound like? [*Getting up quietly.*]

WILLIE. Like a feller sawin' off a soup-bone.

MACK. Mebby et was a . . . ghost! [*Getting up, and backing to Right.*]

TOODLES. A . . . ghost? [*Getting up.*]

WILLIE. Somebody is allus thinkin'-a them critters!

ROD [*getting up and backing off to Right*]. They hain't no sech thing as a . . . ghost! Et's allus a old white horse or a bare tree-limb!

MACK. My ma says she once raised her head out-a th' kivvers an' seen a ghost loomin' up b'fore her by th' cupboard door. An' my pa says she yelled bloody-murder an' socked him in th' nose.

WILLIE. I jist about seed one, onct. Ef et hadn't-a been my pa out in th' wood-shed takin' a bath, et would-a been a . . . ghost!

ROD. I heerd tell of plendy-a ghosts all around places fer-off. They air ginally hanted places.

MACK. Et's ghosts makes hanted places hanted. Otherways they wouldn't be hanted. Ever'body says my gramma was hanted. She seen spirits ever'wheres. She sure looked tough, too. She's where I git my . . . vigger!

SIMP. You fellers is all silly. They hain't no sech things as a . . . ghost. How could they be? [*Sits on log.*]

[*No one can answer that. Then a noise comes from the well. An audible, distinct noise. All turn. From its dark depths rises a . . . ghost. It is a medium-sized ghost. It goes Ooooooooh! and climbs over the curb.* SIMP *jumps up and the boys move more closely together, on the Right, speechless.*]

TOODLES. Looky . . . fellers . . . et's . . . !

WILLIE. We *air* lookyin'!

TOODLES. . . . a . . . a . . . *live!*

ROD. Et's comin' . . . this-a-way!

MACK. You rise up an' meet et, Simp!

SIMP. Why-far should *I?*

MACK. You air th' Big Goslin Goose!

WILLIE. Should we run or should we set an' meet et?

THE GHOST. Jist set . . . ef you air so ta'rd. Ooooooh!
[*The boys shiver.*]

ROD. Looky at et . . . wiggggle!

WILLIE. What should we do? Et's comin' closter!

TOODLES. Et looks like a mean one t' me! I . . . I . . . I'm
going to . . . [*He starts to exit. All start to follow.* THE
GHOST *puts out an arm.*]

THE GHOST. Fellers. Jist keep yer pants on.

WILLIE. I cain't tell whether mine is on or off!

SIMP. Whut . . . whut . . . whut you . . . want?

THE GHOST. 'Nitiation.

MACK. What?

THE GHOST. 'Nitiation.

TOODLES. 'Nitiation?

THE GHOST. I don't chaw my t'baccer twict. I wants a . . .
'nitiation.

SIMP. Who you want et fer?

THE GHOST. Fer me myse'f.
[*The boys gasp.*]

TOODLES. A . . . a ghost t' be . . . 'nitiated.

THE GHOST. Shore. Git yer doo-flummies ready.

MACK. Et'd be . . . unconstertutional!

WILLIE. Us fellers cain't take in no . . . ghost! Cain . . .
we?

SIMP. Et hain't in th' by-laws as sech.

THE GHOST. You wouldn't take in leetle Tippie Hacker, so
you kin take in *me!*

TOODLES. What'll you do to us ef . . . ef we don't?

THE GHOST. I'll make hedge-cheese out of th' mess-a you, I
will! I got m' grinder right over thur t' do et with!

MACK. Air you a . . . a real ghost?

THE GHOST. Ooooooh!
[*The boys quake.*]

THE GHOST. I . . . air!

WILLIE. Kin you . . . flutter?

THE GHOST. Oooooooooh! I kin.

Toodles. You ever eat young fries like us fellers?

The Ghost. Ooooooh! I do. . . .

[*He takes a step toward them. They move toward* simp.]

The Ghost. . . . ef I hain't . . . 'nitiated! (*He advances slowly to Center.*]

Rod. Simp, le's 'nitiate th' ghost. I . . . I . . . I got t' be hittin' fer my home! My ma . . .

The Ghost. Yistiday I swallered a baby like et was a oyster. I'll git *you* an' grate you on th' horse-raddish grater! I'll squash *you* through yer ma's sieve like you was a parsnip! I'll lay *you* down an' harrer you over, an' run you through a corn-sheller, I will! I'm gittin' . . . desprit! When I git's desprit I kin chew shingle-nails an' swaller bailin'-wire!

Rod. Whuuuuuut you goin' t' do t' . . . t' Simp?

The Ghost. I'm goin' to put him inter a hay-baler an' make alfalfy hay out-a him. Then I'm goin' to feed him to a bay mare!

Willie. I . . . I hear my pa a-hollerin' fer me. I s'pose I ort to . . .

The Ghost. Don't nary a feller wiggle a toe. Ef you don't 'nitiate me I air goin' t' smite you inter . . . pergatory! I'll order th' earth t' open up an' swaller you . . . clean whole! You want me to . . . ? [*He puts out his hand.*]

Mack. Simp . . . Simp . . . I move t' allow . . .

Simp. Don't move! Et'll . . .

Willie. I move t' allow us t' interduce ghosts into th' Goslin Gooses at onct b'fore us fellers is all swallered up . . . clean whole! I cain't afford t' be swallered up. I'm too . . . precious!

Mack. I got t' saw wood t'morrer or my pa'll git down his razor-strop ag'in this week!

Toodles. We got t' ram him into th' Club, Simp!

Simp. Is they . . . is . . . ?

The Ghost. Et's . . . blooooooood! Ooooooh!

Simp. . . . is they . . . annybody hain't . . . ag'in et?

Rod. Nobody sayed a . . . a mumblin' word . . . I heerd!

SIMP. Et's passted by a couple-a flickeys. Us fellers'll take you
in ef . . . ef you won't tell Tippie Hacker what is th' 'nitiation. He wants t' git inter our midst, he does!

THE GHOST. What's th' matter with Tippie Hacker?

WILLIE. He air a . . . a dumb-bell!

THE GHOST. Is that so? Ooooooh!

WILLIE. Don't . . . don't do et, ghost! Don't *oooooh* so much!
Le's git down t' busyness so's we kin putter on home.

TOODLES. Prob'ly yer pa needs him to scratch his back b'fore he
goes t' bed, ghost.

THE GHOST. I got no pa; I got no ma. All I got is . . . p'taters.

ROD. P'taters?

THE GHOST. Irish p'taters . . . early Ohio p'taters . . . cob-
blers . . . sweet p'taters . . . marshed p'taters . . . fried,
an' stewed, an' boiled, an' with dumplin's . . . an' with salt-
pork, an' with butter-beans, an' ooooooooh!

[THE GHOST *dances around.*]

MACK. Stop et, ghost! Et makes me all chizzelty!

SIMP. We cain't 'nitiate no one ef we air all chizzely.

THE GHOST. Toodle-de-oodle-de-deee! Git yer old tin dish-pan
from b'hint th' weeds yander, feller.

MACK. What you know 'bout my warsh-pan? You never . . .

THE GHOST. I air a ghost, ain't I?

MACK. I never pinched you . . . yit.

THE GHOST. A ghost knows . . . ever'thing.

TOODLES. You know what I air thinkin' 'bout right now?

THE GHOST. Shore!

TOODLES [*backing off*]. Lands-a-mercy!

THE GHOST. An' I air goin' to get you, too, ef you don't git yer
pan.

[ROD *goes to knapsack by log and gets from it a tin pan.*]

SIMP. Why . . . why does a ghost want t' join us fellerses
Club? We . . .

THE GHOST. I got my own p'ticulars. I'll tell you at th' next
congergation.

WILLIE. You goin' t' be yur th' next time us fellers meets?

THE GHOST. I'll be right yur stronger as horse-raddish!

MACK. I ain't a-comin'.

THE GHOST. Yes, you air! Every one-a you fellers will be right yur or I'll hunt you out an' . . . hant you!

TOODLES. We don't like fer no ghosts hangin' 'round us!

THE GHOST. No ghost won't be hangin' 'round.

SIMP. What you mean, ghost?

THE GHOST. Use your 'magination; you fellers is bright boys, hain't you?

[WILLIE *fills tin pan with dirt.*]

[*They puzzle.*]

WILLIE. I . . . I reckon . . . so. Simp says we is.

THE GHOST. Now . . . let her go Gallagher, fellers. I'm ready t' ride yer old nanny-goat!

SIMP. I reckon we got t' do et . . . t' keep from bein' devastaterd. I ain't got no objections ag'in no . . . ghost. [*Crosses to Center.*]

THE GHOST. Et's a good ideey you ain't. Lessen I would turn you inter a broken-down cow b'fore Jack Robi'son could say *scat.*

SIMP. You ready t' go ahead?

THE GHOST. I shore hain't ready t' go a-foot!

SIMP. Well . . . I'll let her flicker. They is only one pusson 'round here I couldn't tolerate t' 'nitiate none.

THE GHOST. Is that . . . Tippie?

SIMP. Et's . . . him. He cain't keep up with us fellers. He's dumb an' . . .

THE GHOST. Jist . . . 'nitiate.

SIMP. Whut?

THE GHOST. Jist . . . 'nitiate.

SIMP. All right. Come on, here, Rod.

[ROD *comes forward with the pan.*]

SIMP. Git yer other things, fellers.

[*Out of the knapsack* WILLIE *gets an old tin pan. This he beats on at intervals.* MACK *gets a knotted stick.* TOODLES *gets a handful of weeds.*]

SIMP. Now . . . set yur.

THE GHOST. *Set?*

SIMP. Yeh. This air a settin' club. We air all too ta'rd t' stand.

WILLIE. So us fellers all stands a-settin'.

[THE GHOST *sits Center opposite* SIMP. *The boys sit around them in a semi-circle.* MACK *stands up.*]

MACK. Say "I do!"

THE GHOST. "I do" whut?

MACK. Jist do *that!* Say "I do!"

THE GHOST. I . . . do.

SIMP. Say et low an' mumblin' like a ghost.

THE GHOST. I air a ghost. I kin say et however-ways I take a notion, cain't I?

MACK. You got anny doubts?

THE GHOST. Whut about?

MACK. Most annything.

THE GHOST. No.

MACK. Go "ta-ra-ra-ra-boom-de-ay!"

THE GHOST. Ta-ra-ra-ra-boom-de-ay.

MACK. Now . . . cross yer toes an' say "X.Y.Z. I ain't interested in no women an' never will be."

THE GHOST. Leave them lines out. Go on.

MACK. Red Rooster, give th' ghost th' kibosch. [*He sits.*]

[ROD *rises. He approaches* THE GHOST. *He sprinkles dirt on* THE GHOST'S *head from his tin pan.*]

ROD. Dirt . . . is . . . good. But not t' eat. Ooooh.

THE GHOST. Dirt is . . .

MACK. Don't repeat et!

SIMP. Et hain't in th' by-laws as sech.

MACK [*to* SIMP]. Big Goslin, air all all O.K.?

SIMP. Toodle-de-doo. X.Y.Z. Perceed on.

MACK. Willie Rooster, give th' royalty clanks. [*He sits.*]

[WILLIE *arises and strikes three times on the pan. Then he sits.* TOODLES *rises with his weeds.*]

TOODLES. Leetle Gander . . . yur they is.

MACK. Eat a weed, Ghost.

THE GHOST. I p'fer pepper-grass.

TOODLES. They ain't no pepper-grass out now. Et air all etten up. This is sheep-shower. Et hain't nettles.

THE GHOST. Sheep-shower is all right. You hain't got a-nough thur.

TOODLES. I got all I could lay hands onto. Yur. "Eat an' be filled."

THE GHOST. Don't keer ef I do. [*He puts weeds in his mouth and chews, later he spits them out.*]

SIMP. Et air royal grub. Go on with th' ceremony, leetle Gander.

MACK [*rising*]. Yur is th' royal shinnanigans. [*He stirs the coals of the dead fire with a half-burned stick.*] Hocus-pocus . . .

THE GHOST. You goin' t' burn a hole inter me?

SIMP. A ghost cain't feel no pain, cain he?

THE GHOST. I . . . I . . . I reckon . . . not. Go ahead. I kin stand whut you fellers cain set down to. An' a lot more!

MACK. Et hain't hot, ghost. Et's only cold ashes.

WILLIE. You shouldn't-a telled him!

THE GHOST. You kin make 'em hot ef you air a mind to. I hain't . . . afeerd!

TOODLES. Us fellers us'ly p'fers cool ones ourse'fs.

THE GHOST. You fellers hain't got much gumption, hev you?

SIMP. Air you . . . ?

THE GHOST. Go ahead, leetle Pullet.

[MACK *takes the stick and makes a black cross on* THE GHOST'S *forehead.*]

MACK. Eeenie-meenie-meiny-mo . . . one is fer me . . . an' one is fer thee!

ALL. Huckleberry!

[MACK *sits.* SIMP *gets up.*]

SIMP. You swear t' allus go in when it rains?

THE GHOST. Yeh. I allus swears when et rains.

SIMP. You swear t' never tell on us fellers . . . what we done?

THE GHOST. Yeh. You didn't do a great sight.

SIMP. X.Y.Z. You air hereby a member of th' Goslin Gooses. Goest thou likewise an' doest likewise! [*He sits.*]

[*The ceremony is all over. The boys shift their positions with a sigh.*]

THE GHOST. Air I . . . *in?*

MACK. You shore hain't *out!*

THE GHOST. Whut air th' objeck of this Club?

MACK. No objeck a-tall.

WILLIE. 'Ceptin' when our ma's objeck to us stayin' out real late.

THE GHOST. Ef et's all over, then . . . oooooooh!
   [*The boys jump up.*]

WILLIE. Dooooon't, ghost!

MACK. You hain't sech a bad feller, ghost. When you don't do . . . thet!

THE GHOST. I got to git back on home, now. [*He gets up.*]

ROD. You goin' t' git back down into th' well?

THE GHOST. I got a-nother meetin'.

SIMP. Who you goin' t' meet?

THE GHOST. M' Dutch uncle down on Eli Higginses south forty.
   [*He starts to exit Left. He does a little dance by way of diversion.*]

THE GHOST. Tippie . . . Tippie . . . Tippie . . . !

SIMP. Whut you . . . mean? Hey!

THE GHOST. Tippie . . . Tippie . . . Tippie . . . [THE GHOST *flits from their midst to the edge of the clearing Left.*]

THE GHOST. See you *bright* fellers ag'in . . . sometime! Huckleberries! [*He exits Left. The boys stand speechless.*]

TOODLES. Gee! Ain't a ghost . . . funny! [*Crossing up Left and looking after* GHOST.]

WILLIE. Whose ghost you reckon et was?

ROD. Whose?

WILLIE. Shore. Ever' ghost b'longs t' some livin' pusson. I got a ghost sommers. So hev you fellers.

MACK. Hev . . . I?

ROD. I bet my pa's ghost looks like heck! Whose you s'pose he was? I reckon *he* was a *he*.

TOODLES. I ain't got no ideey whose he was.

SIMP. I . . . hev!

ALL. Whose?

SIMP. I got m' ideey.

[*He sits down Center.*]

ROD. Guess I'll set down, too. I'm . . . ta'rd! [*He sits on log.*]

MACK. So'm . . . I! [*He sits on log.*]

WILLIE. So'm . . . I! [*He sits on ground Right.*]

TOODLES. Whew! [*He sits on ground up Left.*]

MACK. What . . . ideey you got . . . Simp?

SIMP. I got a good ideey us fellers is all a bunch-a dumb-bells ourse'fs.

WILLIE. Ef we *air* . . . mebby we could 'low t' let Tippie inter th' Goslin Gooses arter all.

SIMP. "*Mebby we* could 'low t' let Tippie in"—why us fellers . . . already . . . *has!*

[*The boys' mouths open and close without utterance.*]

CURTAIN

THE PALACE OF KNOSSOS

A PLAY OF THESEUS AND THE MINOTAUR

BY

ELIZABETH McFADDEN

A ROYALTY PLAY

THE CAST

Cichas
Agig
Ariadne
Gorgo
Hatasu
Chief Guard
High Priestess
Theseus
Datis
The Thing that Laughs

Other guards, attendants on the priestess, Cretan dancing maidens, Greeks (seven girls and seven men) to be sacrificed in the labyrinth.

THE SCENES

The throne room of the Palace of Knossos, corridors and rooms down through the labyrinth, and the temple. Midnight. About 1450 B. C.

(Requires one simple set only. See Production Note at end of play.)

THE CHARACTERS AND COSTUMES

Cichas, *a guard, is a young fellow and newcomer to the palace. It has been a hard day for* cichas. *He is a simple lad, brought up as a fisherman, used to sailing his little boat in the blue waters of the Ægean Sea near his father's hut. The great palace with its crowds of foreigners, its strange ceremonials, its dark and tragic secrets has gotten on his nerves.*

Agig *is a veteran guard in the King's service. He is probably*

78

vice-president of the Amalgamated Order of Palace Guards.

ARIADNE *is a slender girl of perhaps sixteen. A vivid young aristocrat with more than a touch of royal power in her manner. She is beautiful to look at and dressed as though for a coronation,—a splendid figure in her robes and jewels.*

HATASU *is an Egyptian woman of sixty-odd, an intellectual type, very ceremonious as becomes the governess of the princess. Her costume is Egyptian.*

THESEUS *is about twenty-four years old, tall and very muscular. His costume is a tunic of woolen or linen, and over that a voluminous cloak (chalmys) fastened to the right shoulder. His armor consists of a helmet and the sword which* ARIADNE *restores to him.*

THE CRETAN GUARDS *wear a tunic more closely fitting than the Greeks, their characteristic "wasp-waists were accentuated by a wide belt." They wear feathered head-dresses and carry shields and spears.*

THE CRETAN DANCING MAIDENS *wear the very distinctive costume described by Mrs. B. E. Williams in her book "Gournia" as "an elaborate tight-fitting bodice, laced in front into a small waist, with short sleeves, sometimes puffed, and a low open neck. . . . The waist confined by a broad belt . . . bell-shaped skirts, the style of which is varied by pleated ruffles and straight bands, while often the skirt is flounced from top to bottom with ruffles of varying width and colors. Long waving tresses, twists, and coquettish curls, that might be the work of a French coiffeur de dames, were affected by the beauties of the Knossos court."*

THE CRETAN TORCH-BEARERS *are dressed like the Cretan guards without the helmets, spears or shields. The Cretan men according to Hawes' "Crete the forerunner of Greece," "were bronzed, . . . with beardless faces, and dark hair, which they wore coiled in three twists on the head, and falling in three long curls over the shoulders."*

THE GREEK MEN *are dressed like* THESEUS *but without his sword.*

THE GREEK GIRLS *wear the traditional flowing robe with a*

*band coming over the shoulders, crossing in front, and pass-
ing back near the waist. The sleeves were plain, close, short.
The hair worn in a Psyche knot or bobbed.*

———●———

Scene I

*The throne room. A door down Right leads to the labyrinth
and one at the Left to the banquet chamber. Back Center against
the wall stands the throne of King Minos. It is flanked by low
stone benches. Rich hangings at the doorways and behind the
throne dignify the room.*

*Two floor lamps taller than a man stand Right and Left. Most
of the wicks have been put out but one still burns and in its
flickering light the shadows in the room seem to creep forward
and cringe back again.*

At the rise of curtain the two guards, CICHAS *at the left door and*
AGIG, *at the right door, move restlessly.*

CICHAS. Sh! What's that?

AGIG. What?

CICHAS [*gesturing toward the doorway Right*]. That noise. Listen! Don't you hear? Queer roaring. Like the sea.

AGIG. Oh! That. Wind. Rising.

CICHAS. Not—not the— [AGIG *makes a quick gesture of silence.*]
What?

AGIG. In the palace we do not speak of—Him who lives in the
labyrinth. Better not!

CICHAS. The night is full of sounds!

AGIG. Rhea! You'll hear a lot of queer noises if you stay here.

CICHAS. What makes them, Agig?

AGIG. The labyrinth itself, some of them. It's all walls and
openings. The wind goes through it like a harp. You should
hear it in the winter when the gale from the sea blows through
it. Whew!

CICHAS. Oh, the sea in storm—like that!

AGIG. Hum. Sometimes. Or—like women—screaming.

CICHAS. You mean—those weren't real cries? That we heard?

AGIG. Not yet.

CICHAS. You said the Greeks would be driven into the labyrinth tonight. I thought those cries—

AGIG. You'll know it when the Greeks are driven in.

CICHAS. When will it happen?

AGIG. Any time now. When the King gets through with them.

CICHAS. What does the King do to them?

AGIG. Has 'em up before him, at his banquet. To make him laugh. Up there now. Didn't you hear them laughing a while ago?

CICHAS. What do the Greeks do? To make the King laugh?

AGIG. They dance and sing. The girls. The men tell stories.

CICHAS. On the last night of their lives! Knowing what's before them!

AGIG. *Not* knowing what's before them, you mean. [*Crossing to Right Center.*] Take heart, Cichas. It isn't you that's going down into the labyrinth tonight. Rhea! There's one I'm sorry to see go.

CICHAS. One?

AGIG. The chap that wrestled this afternoon. You see the match?

CICHAS. I was on guard.

AGIG. You ought to have seen it!

CICHAS [*crossing to Left Center*]. Old Lytos said the Greek knocked Chedor out.

AGIG. In the first round! Never saw Chedor beaten before. Went down like a stone from the sling and took the count.

CICHAS. Theseus, they called him. The Greek.

AGIG. Aye. Theseus. What a man!

CICHAS. And still they'll kill him?

AGIG [*with a gesture of helplessness*]. Pledged to the sacrifice! The gods would not forgive. It's a pity, though. A good-looking chap. Even our little princess had her eye on him.

[*There comes the sound from the Right of distant ghostlike laughter. Not human laughter, but more like the strange haunting sounds that wild animals make at night.*]

CICHAS. What's that?

AGIG [*listening intently and crossing to Right door*]. From the labyrinth. [*He turns his head and listens to sounds*

Left.] They're moving in there. The banquet's breaking up.

CICHAS. Now, shall we see the Greeks?

AGIG. Aye. The only entrance to the labyrinth is there. [*He points through the doorway off Right.*] Out through those bronze gates. I sit here sometimes and listen to what goes on and—I'm glad they're bronze,—and thick!

[*The wind shrieks through the night.*]

CICHAS [*cowering*]. I wish I were some place else. The air seems thick as mist.

AGIG. Phantoms! On these sacrificial nights the dead crowd close about us. The stars wheel on. [*He turns quickly and stares at the doorway down Left.*] Someone comes! Fast. [*He rushes to Center.*]

CICHAS. S-s-s-s-someone a-a-alive?

AGIG. Yes, yes. Hush!

[*Both stand staring at the doorway Left. The curtain is pushed back. The* PRINCESS ARIADNE *stands in the entrance.*]

ARIADNE [*Left*]. Agig!

AGIG [*Right Center. Making a deep obeisance and giving a salute with the weapon he carries*]. Your Royal Highness.

CICHAS [*Left Center. Making the same salute*]. Princess Ariadne.

ARIADNE. Stop it! Don't stand there bobbing like idiots. Where is he? What have they done with him?

AGIG. May one ask who?

ARIADNE. Who? Theseus! The Greek! The one that wrestled. Not—in *there?* They have not sent him in?

AGIG. Not yet, Your Highness.

ARIADNE [*With immense relief*]. Goddess! Be thanked! There is time. [*She speaks haughtily to* CICHAS.] Stand afar. [CICHAS *takes himself off to the shadows up Right.*] Agig! *She beckons to* AGIG. *He crosses to Left. Her manner grows coaxing.*] Are you my friend?

AGIG. You have none surer, Princess.

ARIADNE [*exerting all her charm*]. Don't I know it? Didn't you carry me when I was a baby? And hold my hand when I was a little girl. We went walking, you and I, out into the great meadows to pick flowers. Think, Agig, spring! And the fields all yellow and white and blue. Crocuses, and the iris. Lilies of Crete. And the soft wind from Egypt. And the blue sea. Agig, you loved me then!

AGIG [*moved*]. Then and now. Princess, your slave!

ARIADNE [*with a cry of delight*]. Ah, I knew you! This you must do, my Agig. This! Tonight. When the Greeks to be sacrificed are driven into the labyrinth, I will speak to Theseus.

AGIG. But how?

ARIADNE. Here. Alone. Send out the other guards. Keep him back.

AGIG [*drawing back in terror*]. Princess! I worship Rhea! I serve King Minos.

ARIADNE. Why, so do I!

AGIG. I cannot let the Greek escape. Pledged to the sacrifice. He must go in.

ARIADNE. And so he shall. When I have had speech with him.

AGIG. And when he's in, that is the end. No one comes back.

ARIADNE [*terror showing in her face and poise*]. Agig, tell me. Has no one ever gone through those gates—and come back?

AGIG. Never a living soul. The dead return. On nights like this.

ARIADNE. But *why* can they not come back?

AGIG. It is a trap.

ARIADNE. How "a trap"? [AGIG *hesitates.*] Agig, I will know.

AGIG. Daedalus built it when you were a child.

ARIADNE. Oh, that I know; and that it is a maze of many windings and men get lost but I should think that would be amusing. Like a game. But there is something there that makes men shudder. And I have heard sounds—!

AGIG. Better not to know, my princess.

ARIADNE. But I will know. Always when I ask my father or Prince Sitis they put me off. I am a child no longer. Tell me, Agig, what do you know? What happens there?

AGIG. I know nothing, but this is what they say. Beyond the gates, at first there are splendid rooms, richly decorated; then as you pass, the walls grow narrow and there are many doors, opening into winding corridors that lead to stairs descending deep and ever deeper—all one twisting maze.

ARIADNE. Yes. And—

AGIG. And there is inky darkness and a roaring wind that lifts you with its very clamor and sweeps you on and down. A whirlpool suction that draws you. Ever on and down.

ARIADNE. Mother of the gods! Protect him! And—at last?

AGIG. The way grows rougher. Jutting rocks catch at you; broken stairs, where you trip and find no walls to save you, send you headlong; rooms no bigger than a coffin. All in endless coiled confusion.

ARIADNE. Agig! Why don't they turn back?

AGIG. Still the wind drives them on, sucks them down, screams in their ears. So they flee on. Deep underground. In cold and hunger. Bewildered. They call and the wind echoes with wilder cries. Till at last—they go mad—and die.

ARIADNE. But if a man had something that could guide him back?

AGIG. There is no such thing. But even if there were—

ARIADNE. Yes? What then?

AGIG. They still must turn and face—the Thing That Follows!

ARIADNE. The One that Laughs? [AGIG nods.] And then?

AGIG. I may not tell.

[From a distance on the Right comes the unearthly laughter. The two cower. Gradually ARIADNE regains her courage.]

ARIADNE. Listen to me, Agig. Theseus shall go in.

AGIG. You promise that?

ARIADNE. I promise. But first I will speak with him.

AGIG. Well, I will do your bidding.

ARIADNE [with queenly poise shot through with joy]. I shall remember you, Agig. All the days of my life. For this one hour. [She turns toward the throne.] He shall see me like a queen. Call in my maids. [She gestures toward the doorway Left. AGIG goes to the doorway and speaks to someone outside. ARIADNE goes to the throne and seats herself. She gestures to CICHAS and toward the lamps. ARIADNE'S dancing maidens en-

ter, led by GORGO, *her chief lady-in-waiting.*] More light.
[CICHAS *goes out Left, returns immediately with a lighted
torch and touches the lamps with it. The room becomes bril-
liantly illuminated.* ARIADNE *speaks to her girls.*] Music and
dance. [*The girls dance to the music that one or two make with
their instruments.* ARIADNE, *tense but composed, sits waiting
watching the doorway Left.* AGIG, *there, raises his hand in
salute.* ARIADNE *makes a gesture of silence. The dancers stop.*]
The Greeks?

GORGO [*near the door Left, listening*]. No, Princess. That's
Madame Hatasu, looking for you!

ARIADNE. Oh, Gorgo! Always on my heels! Can't she leave me
alone?

[*Enter* MADAME HATASU *from Left.*]

MME. HATASU. Your Royal Highness! Oh! How you have
frightened me! I've been looking for you everywhere!

ARIADNE. But why?

MME. HATASU. Do you know what time it is? What will your
royal father say?

ARIADNE. He doesn't mind.

MME. HATASU. What are you doing here? Gorgo, I'm surprised
at you! What are you doing, Princess?

ARIADNE. Can't you see? I'm sitting on the throne.

MME. HATASU [*awed a trifle in spite of herself*]. You're a
strange—princess! At the dead of night! On your father's
throne!

ARIADNE. Why not? Some day I shall be a queen like the one
you're named for. Queen Hatasu of Egypt.

MME. HATASU. But why are you here now?

ARIADNE. I come here to feel my power. To plan for the days to
come. You disturb me, Madame Hatasu. I want to think.

MME. HATASU. And—and—of what do you think, Princess?

ARIADNE [*with feline intensity*]. Sometimes of those I shall have
thrown into the labyrinth! [MME. HATASU *cowers.*] Sometimes of the great power I shall hold as queen and of the
mercy and—generosity I shall show to those I wish to reward.

AGIG [*Left Center*]. Madame Hatasu, it is an omen! Perhaps the Goddess Rhea herself has brought her here to sit on her father's throne.

GORGO. Yes. A vision for her eyes alone, Madame.

AGIG. Leave her now and you will soon see her back. Safe in the queen's megaron.

ARIADNE. Yes! Go, be quick, lest you spoil the vision!

GORGO. Or anger the Princess!

MME. HATASU. Osiris, guard me! Isis, protect us! I will go sacrifice. Come, Gorgo! I am afraid!

GORGO. You? Of what?

MME. HATASU. Everything is so, so bewildering in this strange palace.

[ARIADNE *indicates to* GORGO *to go with* MME. HATASU. *The two women go out down Left.* ARIADNE *gestures to the others to dance and they begin again. As the dance comes to a close,* AGIG *at the doorway down Left raises his hand to indicate that someone is coming. The dancing girls step aside and stand back by the throne.*]

AGIG. The Greeks!

[*Enter through the doorway Left a procession of people as follows:* TWO TORCH-BEARERS *carrying their lights,* TWO GUARDS *bearing the Cretan insignia of the double-axe, a* HIGH PRIESTESS *of the Earth Goddess and* FOUR WOMEN ATTEND-ANTS *all in their ceremonial robes and high head-dresses, more* GUARDS. *Next come the* GREEKS, *seven men and seven girls, marching two by two, a man and a girl. Their eyes are bound, their arms are tied with ropes. More* GUARDS *bring up the rear. The* GREEKS *are pale but bear themselves with quiet and gallant poise.* THESEUS, *the last of the Greek men, is very tall, a splendid fighting figure. As the last of the* GUARDS *enter, the* HIGH PRIESTESS *near the gates down Right makes a gesture to the* CHIEF GUARD.]

CHIEF GUARD. Halt! [*The marching stops. A* GREEK GIRL *laughs hysterically.*] Silence, there! Ground arms. Dress. Attention.

[*The* HIGH PRIESTESS *and her* ATTENDANTS *face toward the gates in an attitude of adoration, their right hands on their foreheads.*]

HIGH PRIESTESS. Goddess of Earth, we bring thee sacrifice. Approach. Look down. Accept. [*She turns to one of the* ATTENDANTS *who hands her a rhyton in the shape of a bull's head. She carries it to the gate and pours out the offering of wine, speaking as she does so.*] In the name of Crete. In the name of Minos. In the name of the Unseen One that Follows. [*The ghostly laughter from the Right comes clear and close almost as though it were in the very room. The* GUARDS *and* PRISONERS *cringe in fear. A woman's clear voice comes from a distance saying: "Lo, I am here." The* HIGH PRIESTESS *turns to the* CHIEF GUARD.] She comes. The Goddess comes. Open the gates. Drive in the Greeks.

[*The* GREEKS *huddle closer. A woman's sob is heard. Then a clear voice (one of the* GREEK GIRLS), *begins a dirge. A man's voice joins in. As they go out, the singing masks their fear, though once or twice it falters. The* GUARDS *prod the victims forward with their weapons; there comes an occasional cry from a girl. The* GREEK MEN *present an invincible front of courage.*]

[AGIG *and the* CHIEF GUARD *have thrown open the gates of the labyrinth, retreating and urging the* GREEKS *before them.*]

[*The* HIGH PRIESTESS *and her* ATTENDANTS *break into a ritual dance, retreating across the back of the stage to the Left.*]

HIGH PRIESTESS [*veiling her face*]. Away. It is done. To the temple of the Snake Goddess. Come. [*She goes out Left and the others veiling their faces, follow her, the one holding the rhyton exorcising as she goes.*]

[ARIADNE *comes down to* AGIG *as the last of the* GREEKS *approach the gates Right and lays her hand on his arm. He nods and turns to the* CHIEF GUARD, *indicating* THESEUS.]

AGIG. Halt. I'm holding this man out.

CHIEF GUARD. You cannot do that.

AGIG. Only for a few moments. Orders. I'll be responsible. [*He draws* THESEUS *out of the ranks of the Greeks toward the Left.*] Stand aside, Theseus. Loose him.

[CICHAS *unties his arms and unveils his eyes.*]

THESEUS. No, no. I want to go with my people.

AGIG. You'll wait. [*The last of the Greeks are driven through door Right. The gates are closed with a crash of metal. The dirge dies away in the distance. The* GUARDS *exit Left.*] Patience. By going last you will meet the Thing that Follows before your people.

CHIEF GUARD [*handing a soft clay tablet to* AGIG]. Sign. One lot Greeks. [AGIG *signs. The* CHIEF GUARD *takes the chance to say in an undertone.*] Say, Agig, Chedor's been at me all afternoon to get him speech with this chap. He wants him to show him the blow that put him to sleep this morning. He's out there now in the court. [*He gestures out Left with his head.*] Can't you let him speak to him for a minute?

AGIG. Later, yes. Tell Chedor to wait out there.

CHIEF GUARD. Good. He'll be there. [*He exits Left.*]

ARIADNE [*to her maidens*]. Go. Back to the megaron. [*The* GIRLS *go out Left. One, evidently second to* GORGO, *pauses and looks back, hesitating about leaving the* PRINCESS *alone.* ARIADNE *gestures her off.*] Go. Go, let none await me.

[*The last* GIRL *goes out.* ARIADNE *goes to* THESEUS *Left. They stare silently, each a magnet to the other, drawn yet questioning, doubtfully.*]

[AGIG *has been standing down Right listening to something in the labyrinth. Now he goes Left to* CICHAS *who is trembling as far from the labyrinth gates as possible.* AGIG *motions* CICHAS *out, he exits Left eagerly.*]

AGIG. The time is brief, Your Highness.

ARIADNE [*comes to him Left and lays a ring from her finger in his hand.* AGIG *draws back and does not want to take it.*] Yes, yes, you must. It will support you when you need it most.

AGIG. I am not doing this for pay, Your Highness.

ARIADNE. I know. Dear Agig. My friend. [*She makes a gesture to him that he will think of later as a solemn salutation of farewell. He bows to her and goes out Left. She turns back to*

THESEUS. *At last they are alone. The distant dirge rings in their ears.*]

THESEUS [*Right Center. Holding out an imploring hand to her*]. Princess! I must go with my people.

[ARIADNE *stands looking at him, her love in her eyes. In that moment she has caught a sort of radiance. Her imperious manner has dropped from her. She is just a young girl in her first fresh beauty.*]

ARIADNE [*Left Center. In a voice of low music*]. Theseus! You shall go before long. But first I must speak with you. [*She pauses hardly knowing how to begin.*] Today, I saw you wrestle! Saw you overthrow our Cretan champion.

THESEUS. That was—just a bit of fortune, Your Highness.

ARIADNE. And as I watched you, suddenly it came to me, who you are. You are Theseus, son of King Aegeus, are you not?

THESEUS. Yes, Your Highness.

ARIADNE [*with girlish enthusiasm*]. All my life I have heard tales of you and of your deeds! Oh! you are he who slew Corynetes, and Sinis the Pine-bender, and the wicked Sciron, and Procrustes the Horrible who cut off his guests to fit his bed! From the time I was a little girl I have dreamed of you and of your bravery!

THESEUS. You do me too much honor, Princess.

ARIADNE. Not Princess. Ariadne. Say it.

THESEUS. Ariadne.

[*They have been growing closer to each other with every word, moving in a growing enchantment which they do not realize.*]

ARIADNE. I know every great deed that you have done, O Theseus! How you took the bullocks from the Athenian cart and flung them higher than the temple. How you caught the flame-spitting Bull of Marathon and sacrificed it to your God Apollo.

THESEUS. It pleases me that you should remember my poor deeds.

ARIADNE. Why did the Greeks send *you* to this awful sacrifice?

THESEUS. They did not send me. I came of my own will.

ARIADNE. But *why?*

THESEUS. If you must know—that I might kill the Minotaur and free my countrymen.

ARIADNE [*in exultation*]. Oh! I knew it! That is like you! But, weaponless?

THESEUS. Your Royal Father bade them take away my sword. Still I have these. [*He shows her his clenched fists.*]

ARIADNE [*throwing aside her heavy outer robe and drawing forth a sword she has been holding underneath.*] You shall not go unarmed. [*She holds out the sword to him. He stares at it amazed, overjoyed, then takes it.*]

THESEUS. *My* sword! My very sword! Princess! How shall I thank you? [*He slips it through his sword belt. It is concealed by his cloak.*]

ARIADNE. I have something else for you. [*She hands him a ball in a little container. He takes it wonderingly.*]

THESEUS. A ball. Of silken cord. For what? [*He draws the cord out through a small hole in the box. They are close together. She lays her hand on his arm and speaks in a nervous whisper.*]

ARIADNE. It is a clue box. Nos made it for me. Listen close, my Theseus. When you leave me they will take you into the labyrinth. I cannot save you from it though I would.

THESEUS. Ariadne! Your wish consoles me.

ARIADNE. There are two dangers there. One is the Thing that Laughs.

THESEUS. Him I will slay.

[ARIADNE *shakes her head doubtingly.*]

ARIADNE. Against—even you may not prevail. Superhuman. The creature of the Earth Goddess. Demoniac. A ghoul.

THESEUS. Still I shall fight.

ARIADNE. And—if you should be victor?

THESEUS. Then find our way back. Beat through your guards. Fight our way to freedom. We are seven men. Greeks! Picked soldiers.

ARIADNE. You do not know the labyrinth. It is a winding maze. The cord's for that. When you go in tie one end to a bracket in the wall. Whatever way you take, pay out the thread so that it goes with you. Then when you have fought—if you still live—

THESEUS. A man can die but once, my Ariadne, and once a man must die. To the brave the gods are kind.

ARIADNE. Ah, Theseus! If you can worst the Evil Spirit there, you shall not die. Hold tight the thread. It will lead you safely to the upper air. Can you break through those gates?
[*He goes to them, examines the hinges and locks.*]

THESEUS. Aye! The point of my sword can turn those locks around.

ARIADNE. If you come out of those gates by dawn our guards will never stop you! They will think you demons of the underworld. Then—to the North Road—and the sea.

THESEUS. And our Grecian ship!
[*The ghostly laughter comes again from the Right.*]

ARIADNE. Ah! If you did not have to go!

THESEUS. Ariadne. You have given me life and make it not worth the living. Am I never to see you again? To feel your loveliness? To look in your sweet eyes?

ARIADNE [*yielding herself to his arms*]. Theseus! My love!

THESEUS. My strength dissolves before you. Little Princess.
[CICHAS *comes hurrying on from the Left, still carrying the lighted torch.*]

CICHAS. If Your Highness will forgive me, Agig says it is time for the gentleman to go.

ARIADNE. Go, then, Theseus. [CICHAS *motions* THESEUS *off toward the Left.*] Why that way?

CICHAS. Princess, Chedor does much desire to speak with His Worship; then Agig will send him in.
[*The two men start out. When they are almost at the doorway Left,* ARIADNE *speaks with sudden breathless resolution.*]

ARIADNE. Cichas! Give me that torch. [*Wonderingly* CICHAS *hands the torch to her. She turns to* THESEUS.] We shall meet again. Trust me. [*They stand a moment looking into each other's eyes. Their hands touch. He puts her fingers to his lips.*

ARIADNE'S *voice trembles with emotion.*] May all your gods and mine go with you! May Rhea sleep when you slay her Thing that Laughs!

THESEUS. May the world be as kind to you as you have been to me! [*He turns and follows* CICHAS *out Left.*]

[ARIADNE *stands tense, watching them go. Then she swiftly takes off the heavy trailing robe of state, flinging it back over the throne. In her short simple dress she looks younger than before. Evidently much frightened but nerving herself and holding the torch she goes to the gates of the labyrinth, struggles with the heavy lock, gets it open, throws her weight against the bronze doors which yield slowly. She goes through. They close behind her. In the moment that they have stood open a refrain from the dirge comes through.*]

[*After a pause,* AGIG *and* CICHAS *enter with* THESEUS, *his eyes bound, between them.* AGIG *is intent on* THESEUS, CICHAS *on his own fears. They do not look around the room, but go straight to the gates.*]

AGIG. If I had my way, after the fight you put up today, you should go free.

THESEUS. My friend, even for that I thank you.

[AGIG *opens the gates, pushes* THESEUS *through, the gates close with a crash. The laughter comes.*]

AGIG. And now you know how a brave man goes to his death.

[*He turns toward the throne expecting to see the* PRINCESS *there. He stares at her robe, goes up to it, brushes it aside wonderingly as though he had thought she might be hiding behind it.*] Why, where's Her Highness?

CICHAS [*staring round, roused from his own danger*]. She was here! A minute ago.

AGIG [*slightly alarmed*]. Just now? As we came through with him?

CICHAS [*confused, trying to think when he had seen her*]. Why, yes! She must have been. She didn't pass us out there. [*He points off Left.*] She spoke to me. And then, she was there on the throne as we took him through.

AGIG. Sure?

CICHAS. Why, yes. Yes!

AGIG [*accepting this*]. She slipped out as we took him in. She cannot bear to think of that young man's fate.

[*The wind has been whistling through the palace at intervals but the dirge has faded into silence. Now there comes the sound of a shrieking wind; or was it a human cry?*]

CICHAS. Listen! was that—the wind?

AGIG. Wind? Or woman? Now you'll hear sounds that will burn in your mind. The last time—

CICHAS. Don't! I can't bear it! Must we stay here now?

AGIG. No. We can go if we like.

CICHAS. I'm going! Better the open sky than this haunted air that wraps itself around your throat.

AGIG. I'm with you. Put out those lights.

[CICHAS *extinguishes the wicks in the tall lamps. The room lies in total darkness except for a faint oblong of light that marks the doorway down Left. They hurry out through that exit.*]

[*Pause, during which the darkness deepens. The scene is changed by removing the throne, the hangings, the robe of the* PRINCESS, *and the two tall lamps. A single great vase placed to mark the new room.*]

[*During the pause the wind wails softly at first then louder, till it goes shrieking through the night. The laughter comes. In the darkness these sounds seem to increase as though we too had passed through the bronze gates and were now in the labyrinth.*]

SCENE II

A moving light flickers through the doorway down Left and focuses finally into the torch held high in the hand of ARIADNE. *She comes in, a slender little frightened figure. As her torch lights the scene she finds herself in this bare room with walls that suggest stone, and the exit at the Right. Midway through the room she stops and stands listening. She is shaking with terror but trying desperately to nerve herself to show a gallant front to* THESEUS. *She hears someone coming. Her face shows fright, then as she recognizes the step, relief and joy. She draws back against the wall and waits.*

Enter THESEUS, *Left, sword drawn. He is carefully paying out the thread from his left hand. He comes rather slowly and cautiously in from the dark, for he has no torch, looking around him, beating the wall softly with his sword, feeling his way, working toward the light. As he gets to it, he sees* ARIADNE.

THESEUS. You! Here! My Ariadne!

ARIADNE. I did not want to live if you must die. [*As he comes up to her his arms go round her; he holds her close, protectingly.*]

THESEUS. Apollo, thanks! Now I know that the gods mean you shall be mine. [*Faint ghostly laughter comes from a distance.*] Aha! Are you there, O Minotaur? I'll fight you here and now.

ARIADNE. No, no. Not here. You cannot swing your sword. We must go on till you have a broader space.

THESEUS. Come swiftly then.

ARIADNE. Give me the ball.

[*He hands it to her. She goes out first, holding the torch so that it lights their way. He follows with drawn sword. The light flickers off to complete darkness. Laughter. The chant of the wind.*]

Scene III

A narrower room created by drawing the curtains just above the entrances and characterized by a typical piece of Cretan decoration: a rough stone seat.

Again the blackness is broken by the flicker of the torchlight out Left. ARIADNE *appears in the doorway followed by* THESEUS, *who is watching something behind him, at least something he dreads may appear.*

THESEUS. Stop, rest a moment.

ARIADNE. Yes. [*They pause, draw close to each other, and stand*

listening. He puts a comforting arm around her.] Listen!
    [*From far off to the Right in the labyrinth comes the dirge
of the Greeks. The wind seems to lift and play with this music,
at times drowning it completely with the wailing and roaring
of its own sound, at times sucking it off into silence, at times
bringing it nearer.*]
THESEUS. They live still. Shall we try to reach them?
ARIADNE. Yes, yes. Come on.
THESEUS. Something is following us.
    [*They listen.*]
ARIADNE. It's coming! The Thing! Quick, Theseus, come!
    [*They go out right. The light again fades to blackness. The
wind brings a grotesque version of the dirge, a roaring whistling variation of the music.*]

SCENE IV

A mere passageway hemmed in by leaning walls.
The flickering torch approaches from the Left. ARIADNE *and*
THESEUS *enter. He is now carrying the torch in his left hand
and watching behind him with ready sword for the Minotaur.*
ARIADNE. Quick, Theseus. Oh, be careful. There are holes in
the pavement here.
THESEUS. If it comes to a fight, you run on ahead. Get as far
away as you can.
ARIADNE. He's getting nearer!
    [*They hurry straight on through the doorway out Right.*
    [*Blackness. A moment's pause. Then in the entrance Left
stands* THE THING THAT LAUGHS. *Two gleaming greenish eyes
about ten feet from the floor and wide apart, a slavering
mouth that gleams, a dim shadow of a great hulk that yet is
nothing but a shadow. Slowly with a rhythm it crosses the
stage, chuckling its ghostly laughter. The dirge is blown in,
jazzed by the wind.* THE THING *passes out Right.*]

SCENE V

*Again the scene is changed. A larger more irregular room, en-
tered by a flight of stone steps leading from the entrance Left.*

ARIADNE *and* THESEUS *hurry down the steps. They spend no time here in talk. The terror that pursues them is growing closer. The song of the Greeks comes from quite near by. They run out.*

Darkness and the wind shrieking.

A pause. The green eyes appear at the doorway, Left, cross the stage, and go out Right.

SCENE VI

A queer grotesquely shaped little room with overhanging stone-work, part of which has fallen down and forms a rude seat. The approaching light, ARIADNE *and* THESEUS *enter Left on a dead run. He is supporting her.* ARIADNE *sinks on the stone seat, exhausted.*

ARIADNE. Theseus, I am spent! Go on! Save yourself. The others.

THESEUS. Leave you? Not for Olympus!

ARIADNE. We may have thrown It off the trail. Listen! Can you hear anything?

[*They listen. Utter silence.*]

THESEUS. Clever of you to think of doubling on our tracks back there.

ARIADNE. At least we've a moment's rest.

[*From right outside the door comes the whip of* THE THING'S *laughter.* ARIADNE *leaps to her feet and flees terror-stricken out Right,* THESEUS *following her closely, holding high the torch.*

[*Almost before its light is gone the eyes appear and the dim shadow gallops across the stage and out after them. The wind shrieks and thunders through the labyrinth.*]

SCENE VII

The "Beehive temple" of the Earth Goddess. A shadowy spacious room, the height and extent of which is lost in darkness. ARIADNE *enters first, running,* THESEUS *behind her, looking back as though ready to turn and fight at any moment.*

ARIADNE. Theseus! The temple!

THESEUS. Yes. Here I can fight. Keep back. Take the torch.

ARIADNE. Give it to me. [*He thrusts it into her hand and pushes her behind him.*]

THESEUS. Throw the light against him. Keep me in the shadow. Quick. Keep behind me.

ARIADNE. Yes, yes. [*She starts to swing the torch so the rays will shine on the doorway Left. Her strength gives way, the torch swings downward and drops from her hand. They are left in inky blackness.* ARIADNE *gives a stifled scream.*]

THESEUS. Apollo! Guard us! [*The green eyes of* THE THING THAT LAUGHS *appear in the doorway Left. They sweep the room looking for their prey. There is utter silence.*] Ariadne!

ARIADNE. Yes?

THESEUS. Keep against the wall. Go out if you can find the door.

ARIADNE. Goddess! Defend us!

[*Still the strange silence like a lull in a tempest. The wind is stilled. There is no dirge. Suddenly the eyes and the slavering jaws rise in the air and lunge at* THESEUS. *There is the sound of a plunging body. A blow. The confusion of conflict, blows. Pause. Renewed battle between the man and* THE THING. *Gradually the noises lessen. Stop. There comes a groan. Was it human? Silence.*

[*After another pause a girl's whisper breaks the stillness.*]

ARIADNE. Theseus?

THESEUS. My love. Are you hurt?

ARIADNE. No. Are you?

THESEUS. A wound or two. Not deep.

ARIADNE. Is It—dead?

THESEUS. I think so. I felt my sword go deep.

ARIADNE. Goddess of Earth! Forgive!

THESEUS. I wish we had a light.

ARIADNE. Wait! I've got the torch. Maybe I can kindle it again. [*She works over it for a moment.*] There's a spark of fire in it!

[*The spark begins to glow in the darkness. The light shines in her face, revealing it for a moment. She blows it gently, it flames higher, at last burning brightly. She throws the light here and there looking for the* MINOTAUR. *It has vanished.*]

THESEUS. He's gone.

ARIADNE. Back to the underworld. Now I know that you are the greatest hero in the world.

THESEUS. I could not see him; that was what scared me.

ARIADNE. You! Scared!

THESEUS. Of course! Don't be silly. Every man's afraid. That's what steels his arm. And clears his eye. And straightens his aim.

ARIADNE. Oh! I believe I like you scared. And fighting on!

THESEUS. And I like you better every way you are! [*He turns the torch on her.*] Frightened and daring. Imperious and humble. My love! My little princess love!

[*The dirge begins again in an adjoining chamber.*]

ARIADNE. Listen! They think that you have been killed.

THESEUS. [*goes to the doorway down right and calls through*]. What, friends! Datis! Geleon! Argadus! Come out. You're safe.

[DATIS *appears at the entrance down Right, sees* THESEUS, *and turns back to shout to the others.*]

DATIS. Ho, there! Argadus! Theseus is safe. He has vanquished the Minotaur. Come here! [*He comes running in to the temple and grasps* THESEUS, *embracing him in his delight. All the others, men and girls, come running in, surround* THESEUS, *laughing, crying, at the sudden reprieve from death. They all talk at once, crowding up to* THESEUS.]

THE GREEKS. Praise to Apollo! Theseus! Great Theseus! Safe, safe! Is he dead? "Vanished!" Now, by Zeus!

[*After a moment* THESEUS *shakes himself free from them and goes to* ARIADNE *who has been standing to one side watching them.*]

THESEUS. Do not thank me for your lives, my friends. Thank the Princess Ariadne, daughter to the King of Crete. Thank her and welcome her for she is now our princess.

[*The Greeks stare amazed.*]

DATIS. What do you mean? Was a Cretan merciful?

A GREEK GIRL. But how came she here?

GELEON. Princess, we give you thanks. How did you come to save us?

ARIADNE. That you shall hear. In time. But now, before day dawns, let us escape. My father will never forgive the deed done here. Never forgive you, Theseus. No, nor me.

THESEUS. Do not fear. We shall get to the ship before they find us. Where is the clue?

ARIADNE. Here. I have the box. Come. Follow.

[THESEUS *takes her hand and turning holds out his hand to the next girl who takes it and offers her hand to the man near her.*]

DATIS. Shall we go without giving thanks to Apollo for our safety?

MANY VOICES. No, no! A dance to Apollo. Thanks to thee, Apollo. Apollo! Apollo be praised.

[*The girls begin to sing, the men join in. They swirl into a dance that expresses their almost hysterical joy. As they dance, from some cranny high in the walls or ceiling of the temple, a brilliant ray of sunlight streams down on them.*

[*The Greeks accept the light as a miracle, a personal answer from the Sun-God himself. They break off the dance, prostrate themselves and cry out:*]

Apollo comes! He answers! The Sun-God comes!

[*A girl's clear soprano begins a hymn of praise to Apollo, voice after voice takes it up. The chorus mounts exultant, ringing triumphant to a climax of solemn emotion. All the agony, all the relief, the joy of life and love is poured out as the music rings on and on.*

[THESEUS *turns to* ARIADNE *and takes her in his arms.*]

CURTAIN

PRODUCTION NOTE

The Palace of Knossos may be given with extreme simplicity of scene, purely for the sake of its story, or it may be treated as a study in stage settings with elaborate scenery. Most producers will doubtless combine these aims and they need no suggestions from the author.

While the play as written seems to call for different scenes, the entire action may be given against a single background in a neutral tint suggesting a stone or plastered wall. Whether scenery or curtains are used, it should be so arranged as to make doorways down right and left. The movement of the actors against this background after Scene I is constantly from left to right. Each scene is divided from the others by moments of darkness during which the simple properties are changed. A great vase is removed and a stone bench or a tall lamp put in its place. The appearance of the room may be further altered by holding the back curtain at a different slant during one scene and changing the slant or letting it fall straight for the next entrance. Or after the second scene, a curtain could be drawn just above the entrances. In the first scene the gates to the labyrinth may be shown, or imagined as beyond the doorway out right.

The moment of complete darkness between the scenes should be just long enough to permit the actors to pass behind the scenery and get to the left entrance each time. If this is done quickly enough to give the impression of continuity, it conveys the idea of their swift passage down through the stone corridors and subterranean shafts of the labyrinth underlying the palace of Knossos. During the moment while the stage is black the sense of something happening is maintained by the passage across the stage of the Thing that Laughs, or by the singing of the dirge by the Greeks, or by the wailing of the wind through the labyrinth.

After the first scene, the lighting is solely effected by the torch which Theseus carries. This torch must be put out as soon as he leaves the stage, otherwise it will be seen through the scenery as he goes from right to left.

THE REUNION

OR

BEARDING THE LION

A BURLESQUE MELODRAMA

BY

JEROME DAVIS ROSS

A NON-ROYALTY PLAY

THE CAST

DANIEL GULLITT, *a master crook (with mustachios and all)*
COKEY JOE, *his accomplice (a pathetically anæmic drug-fiend)*
JOSIAH FINCH, *a Professor (very upright and exemplary)*
THELMA FINCH, *his daughter (an innocent and mouselike heroine)*
NELL FINCH, *his wife (now decayed, but once beautiful)*
OLD TOM, *a tramp (with a long gray beard)*
AH WU, *a sinister Chinese servant.*

THE SCENE

A dilapidated tenement in the New York slums.

It is a typical setting of the Seventies. The back is made up either of flats or a drop curtain that wavers with the movements of the play. The sides are two or three "wings." The walls were once papered with a dirty brown which has not only gotten much dirtier but has peeled off, showing the brick and plaster and laths underneath (a grand scenic effect of the old school). Down Right there is a table and two chairs. Up stage Center there is a tenement iron bed or couch and down stage Left is another chair. All furniture is dilapidated. A few broken pictures hang on the walls. Altogether the scene impresses one with its terrific squalidness and decay. If possible, the set should be framed by an elaborate "Grand tormentor,"—Painted red velvet curtains tied back in folds to painted marble columns.

THE COSTUMES

The costumes are of the 1850–1860 period. The men wear colored frock coats and tall hats, and the women are dressed in hoop skirts, bonnets and shawls. COKEY JOE is in his shirt sleeves. OLD TOM wears a long dark overcoat and slouch hat, pulled down over his face. AH WU *wears an elaborate Chinese costume.*

———•———

Before the rise of curtain, the stage manager, in overalls, should appear before the curtain and light with a taper the imaginary candles behind the large light projectors. The foots should come up very gradually on each light lit.

At the rise of the curtain, DANIEL GULLITT *is, as the melodramas state, "discovered" alone on the stage, reading a letter and sitting chair Left.*

GULLITT [*reading aloud*]. "And I also wish to let you know that I have altered somewhat the previous arrangement of mailing you the $25,000 for the Bonanza Bar Mining Stock. As I am now in New York on an extended sight-seeing tour with my daughter Thelma, I shall bring the money to your address on the afternoon of the date above mentioned. Yours respectfully, Josiah Finch." Poor credulous fool! He little knows the Satanic rôle I have already played in his life and which I shall continue to play with the aid of Heaven and my own accursed cleverness! [*He laughs wickedly.*]

    [*Enter* COKEY JOE *wing Left.*]

COKEY. Ah, meditatin'? Still waters run deep is best applied to the person o' Dan Gullitt. Youse been thinkin', fer I see a look o' triumph on yer face.

GULLITT. I must always be thinking and planning, Cokey Joe. How else could we two make a living unless I daily conceived new schemes for the pocketing of ill-gotten gains? Robbing the poor, blackmailing the rich, swindling the gullible,—what matters it to me how far, or in what places, my tentacles of greed reach out and suck their weak victims, leaving only poverty and suffering in their wake?

COKEY. Too true. Fer thirty years we's plied our nefarious game,—the curse o' honest men, the problem o' Scotland Yard an' Ludlow Street. You, the master mind an' me the faithful agint. We's reaped a mighty harvest!

GULLITT. And ever will, so long as we sow the seeds! See here, Cokey. I've a letter from Josiah Finch.

COKEY. What? Not old perfessor from Dubuque what's goin' to buy yer phoney stocks an' whose wife yer—

GULLITT. Hush! She may hear us! [*He indicates wing Right 1 and crosses to Center.*] Yes, it's him. He comes here to-day with the cash. 'Tis twenty years since last he saw me so I'm sure he'll not remember my visage. Besides, this newly cultivated mustache— [*He curls it.*]

COKEY. Aye, but if he ever does discover you to be the snake that crept into his happy home them long years ago; if he should chance ter meet with Nell—

GULLITT. We must get rid of her by all means.

COKEY. Supposin' he should rekernize her an' see to what she has fallen? Then the blasted trick would be up! We'd best send her out while the perfessor finishes his little transaction with yer.

GULLITT. A good idea. In her absence I'll unload the stock on Finch. Then with the cash in hand we'll fly to some quiet place until the thing blows over.

COKEY [*aside*]. A very devil in his cleverness, this Dani'l Gullitt! [*He goes to wing Right 1.*] Come in here, Nell! [*Crosses to Left.*]

    [*Nell enters wing Right 1.*]

NELL. What do you two want of me? You woke me from a needed sleep. These aching eyes of mine have scarce been closed this fortnight past!

GULLITT. You've got no cause for beauty naps, you hussy! I want you to go to Mulberry and West Streets wearing your yellow bonnet.

NELL [*aside*]. Oh, dear heaven! Once more I must obey the evil bidding of this man. [*Aloud.*] Again you want me to become accomplice in your drug ring?

GULLITT [*with a leer*]. Just so, my dear. You're to play the usual ruse of waiting for a horse-car. When Morphine Mose sees your beautiful headpiece he'll know you to be my agent. Don't let the Bulls see him hand you the "snow."

NELL. Oh Daniel Gullitt, may heaven forgive you, I cannot! For love of you I deserted husband, home and nursing babe.

For love of you I braved the years of sham and poverty. And now I have become ugly, weighed down by low environment, you step on me like dirt! You scoundrel, how I hate you!

GULLITT. Why Nellie, you've no cause to talk that way! If it hadn't been for me you'd still be with a fool husband in that wretched rural spot.

NELL. Alas, too late, I wish I were! [*She sobs hysterically.*]

GULLITT. Hush woman! Cease your bawling. Depart at once and fetch that dope!

NELL [*aside*]. Oh, if I could only spurn his ill commands! But day by day, year by year, he has attained such a power over me that I dare not disobey. [*Aloud.*] Yes, Daniel, I'm going. [*She puts on a horrible hat and exits wing Left 1.*]

COKEY [*crossing to Center*]. Ha, ha! You've got her trained, the ugly zany. To think she once loved you!

GULLITT. Ah, that was twenty years ago. Each year I sank lower and lower, steeped in deep iniquity. And as I fell I dragged her with me until now she loathes my very shadow. But as long as I've use for her she stays. [*Sits chair Left.*]

COKEY. I hope she'll bring that morphine back. I'm gettin' kinda— [*He suddenly twists about.*]

GULLITT. It's all right, Cokey Joe.

COKEY [*pointing out to audience*]. Look, look! My fevered brain must be on fire! Hideous sights confront me. See— can't you see? What awful prodigy is that there?

GULLITT [*aside*]. 'Tis but another symptom of his sad condition. [*Aloud.*] There's naught in sight, Cokey.

COKEY. There it is, I say! Oh Dani'l, can't you see? A horrible serpent all blue and green seems to crawl and twine himself about me! Higher and higher he creeps; his coils are drawn yet tighter!! Help, help!! He is around my neck! I strangle!!

GULLITT. I'll get you something soothing.

COKEY [*falls on his knees on floor*]. No, no, Dan. Fer the love o' heaven, do not leave me! Do ye not see me in the clutches of the fell monster? His eyes, his fiery eyes gaze through me and sear my aching heart! His dribbling mouth foams with glee to see his tortured victim! Oh, oh, oh!!!

[GUILLITT *claps his hands twice and* AH WU, *the China-man, enters wing Right 2.*]

GULLITT. Fang quin ah sin Cokey Joe.

[AH WU *takes large cocaine needle from his brocaded robe, hands it to* COKEY *and retires to backstage.*]

GULLITT. There you are, Cokey.

[COKEY *turns and injects the drug, possibly rolling up his sleeve to make the action as vivid and realistic as possible. He reels to the bed with a sigh of relief.*]

COKEY. If only I could break myself o' that pernicious habit!

GULLITT. You ought to stick to something light, like opium.

COKEY. Aye, once upon a time that would do but it ain't strong enough now. You'll come to morphine by and by, Dan. It's allus the same with everyone. First an occasional puff on the "joy pipe" jest fer novelty, then more and more. Then cocaine and morphine 'til every speck o' flesh is poisoned an' every drop o' blood bubbles in torment and cries "more, more!" [*He comes to footlights Center.*] Oh, decent clean-livin' men, before yer stray remember the picture of a soul writhin' in starvation fer food unspeakable,—one who's branded before all, *a dope fiend!!* [*He returns to bed and sits.*]

[*A knock off stage at wing Left 1.*]

GULLITT. Ah, that must be Josiah Finch! Pull yourself together, Cokey, and remember don't laugh in the fool's face. [*He crosses to wing Left 1 and admits* FINCH.] Professor Finch, I presume. I recognized that dignity and "jenny say quoi" which shows at once in the faces of all great scholars. [*Aside.*] I've never yet seen so weak a looking mug!

FINCH. How do ye do, Mr. Gullitt. Very pleased to meet you. [*Aside.*] I don't like the man. His face seems to recall some criminal. [*Aloud.*] I trust you received my hastily penned letter.

GULLITT. Ah, yes, and I was indeed gratified to learn I should be privileged to carry on the deal with you in person. Such private matters are hardly to be trusted to the mails. They are best contracted in the sanctum sanctorum of one's own domicile.

FINCH. I was rather surprised to be driven to this address. I don't know your great city at all. Just on my first visit, with Thelma, my unmarried daughter of twenty. Somehow this locale didn't seem quite—

GULLITT. Yes, yes, Professor. You'll have to excuse the looks of it. We're about to move to more spacious quarters. [*Aside.*] And more distant ones! [*Aloud.*] May I present er—er— Mr. Cocaine Joseph.

FINCH [*aside*]. Cocaine? Odd name indeed. [*Aloud.*] Pleased to meet you sir.

COKEY. And you danged well ought ter be!

GULLITT. Well, may I suggest we start our business, Mr. Finch?

FINCH. 'Tis what I'm here for, sir.

    [GULLITT *again claps his hands,—this time thrice.* AH WU *glides forward from his stand backstage.*]

GULLITT. Lung sing wham tong stocks.

    [AH WU *takes the stock from his robe and exits mysteriously wing Right 2.*]

FINCH [*delighted*]. A Chinese servant. 'Tis indeed exotic.

GULLITT. I brought him back with me from the East. A queer people, the Chinese. Their calculating minds, their cool, yet bloodthirsty pursuits have always fascinated me. During my stay in the Celestial Kingdom I collected many authentic torture instruments of the early Middle Period of the Late Twang Empire. A most delicious hobby, I assure you.

FINCH. How exceedingly fortunate for me, sir. I am just now writing a work on Playful Pastimes of Old China. I should greatly like to see your collection after we have concluded our business.

GULLITT. With pleasure. [*He crosses to chair right of table Right and sits.* FINCH *sits chair left of table.*] And now to begin. I have here five thousand shares of Bonanza Bar. At five dollars per that makes twenty-five thousand.

FINCH. Forty years of slaving, sir. I hope the venture is as successful as you promise.

GULLITT. Of course, of course. They'll have a dozen shafts down within a month, all of them teeming with that magic elixir of the human race,—gold! I wouldn't sell this to you unless it were good.

COKEY [aside]. Not much, you wily swindler!

GULLITT. Well, Mr. Finch, here's the stock. If you like we'll draw up transfer receipts with Joe, here, as witness. Then I'll have the needed cash and you'll have the surest fortune ever made. How I regret that pressing circumstances force me to sacrifice this to you. 'Tis good you came to-day. I've held off countless offers.

FINCH. Well, I haven't got the cash. I'll write a cheque for you.

GULLITT [aside]. A cheque! That's not so good. Still, if we can cash it before he discovers— [Aloud.] You'd better date it as of today or even yesterday.

FINCH. We must be formal about this, Mr. Gullitt. To write yesterday's date today would scarce bespeak a knowledge of our great American Financial customs and procedure.

GULLITT. Quite so, of course. I only wished to test your powers as a business man. By all means date it of today.

FINCH. On the other hand this concerns my own and my dear daughter's entire welfare. I'll postdate the check a few days.

GULLITT. Zounds, man, you don't think me crooked?

FINCH. Pray mention no such knavish thought, sir. I merely wish to stress my businesslike nature. Besides, to be frank, I have telegraphed some investigators in California and await their judgment as to how rich the mines are.

GULLITT [aside]. Curses! He suspects! He will soon learn there are no such things as Bonanza Bar Mines, that they are such stuff as schemes are made on! We must force him to date the cheque today. [Aloud.] Sir, I must insist upon your inscribing this very day upon your check. I leave town immediately for a place which has no banks.

COKEY [aside]. And no sheriffs, let's hope!

FINCH. In that case, we'd best call the transaction off. [*Aside.*]
His strange manner makes me mighty suspicious.

GULLITT [*arises*]. Finch, I order you to make that out as I
demand!

FINCH [*arises*]. Sir, for forty years I've scrimped and saved
the sum in question. Regardless of the consequences which
may proceed—for I now see you to be a villain who fears
no man or code—my paternal love, my desire for comfort
in senility, my hatred of base coercion,—all force me to
retort in kind; *never!!*

GULLITT. Cokey, then let's seize him! [COKEY *seizes* FINCH
from behind.] A few hours, bound and gagged in that room,
and he'll come through with our demands!

[GULLITT *and* COKEY *struggle with* FINCH, *bind him and
drag him toward wing Right 2.*]

FINCH. Cokey, eh? Oh, now I see it all! Dope fiends, swindlers,
parasites!! Though hacked to bits, though consumed with
dread, starvation, thirst or suffering, I'll still cry *never,
never!!* [*They exit wing Right 2.*]

]*The stage is empty for a moment, then there is a knock
off Left.* GULLITT *and* COKEY *reappear from wing Right 2.*]

GULLITT [*Center*]. You forgot to lock the door,—fool! I'll
watch our pugnacious friend whilst you answer this inopportune knocking.

[GULLITT *exits wing Right 2.* COKEY *crosses to wing Left
1 and admits* THELMA *and* OLD TOM.]

THELMA. Pardon me, but is my father in there?

COKEY. Er— No he ain't, who is he?

THELMA. Professor Josiah Ebeneezer Finch of Dubuque. I am
his only daughter, Thelma.

COKEY. Well, I said he ain't here.

THELMA. Papa mentioned this address at the hotel this morning. He's so absent-minded, the poor darling, that I thought
I'd best follow him to see that he got in no trouble.

COKEY. How many times has I gotta say he ain't here?

THELMA. No matter, my good man. I shall wait until he arrives. [*Crosses to Center.*]

COKEY [*Left Center aside*]. How can I allow her to remain and yet conceal his whereabouts? [*Aloud—indicating* OLD TOM.] Who is this ragged fellow?

OLD TOM [*Down Left*]. Old Tom, sir, jest Old Tom.

THELMA [*Center*]. Poor soul! I picked him up in some deserted alley where woeful pangs of hunger had driven him to sniffing about the garbage cans. He showed me how to find this address.

COKEY. At any rate you'll both have ter git out!

THELMA. Oh, don't sir! 'Tis storming so, and we can keep warm within until Papa gets here. [*The wind blows outside.*]

OLD TOM. Old Tom can't do no harm, sir.

COKEY [*aside*]. Perhaps the sights o' his little angel lass in agony will force the old man to do as we say! Ha, ha! I'll let her stay. [*Wind blows.*]

THELMA. Heavens, what a storm! I wish Papa would get here and take me home.

COKEY. Now, no noise from either of yer.

[*As he exits wing Right 2, a groan from* FINCH *is heard.* THELMA *rushes over and bangs on wing.*]

THELMA. Open! I have heard my dear father cry for help!

GULLITT [*coming out of wing Right 2*]. Nonsense. 'Tis but the wind howling in the garret.

FINCH [*off stage*]. Help! Oh, oh, save me!

THELMA. Release my father on the instant, you vermin!!

GULLITT. My dear lady, you are wholly mistaken or else quite mad. I am a peace-loving and respectable citizen. Never would I hold another fellow human against his will. Such cowardly things revolt me.

THELMA. I just now heard my father call for succor, I say! I am a pure maiden, and yet your actions compel me to voice unladylike expressions: Sir, you have fibbed!!!

GULLITT. How now, you spritely Amazon! [*Aside.*] Demme, but the girl's good looking! What dainty peeps from yon petticoat! What a well-turned— [*He clutches her wrist and says aloud.*] We shall perhaps become acquainted, my dear? [*He pushes her back to Center.*]

THELMA. Unhand me, wretch! [*She rushes to wing Left 1 crying for help.* COKEY JOE *is near wing;—he seizes her throws her on to bed.* OLD TOM *starts to rush upon* GULLITT. *The latter hits him over the head with a pistol and he falls unconscious on floor up Left by head of bed. Both* THELMA *and* OLD TOM *are bound.*]

GULLITT [*as he hits* OLD TOM]. There, you vagabond! Take that! . . . Well, my lass, and you,—poor fool, I fear your little act of bravery will cost your father many sighs. You'll learn that Dan Gullitt is not the man to be trifled with. Once aroused by feeble, vain attempts to foil me, I become akin to vulture of the sky or lion of the jungle! Cokey Joe, bring Finch in here! Have Ah Wu wheel on the Manchu Rack!

COKEY. Oh, Dani'l ye wouldn't do *that* before the gal's own eyes?

GULLITT. Be silent, man. No more delay, I say! The sight of her poor father on the dread instrument of the Yellow Devil will drive the lass well-nigh insane. Their suffering,—his physical, hers spiritual, will bring submission quickly!

COKEY. The awful memory of that last victim lingers yet. My blood curdles at the thought!

[*He exits wing Right 2 and brings* FINCH *on, still bound and very much shaken.*]

THELMA [*rising*]. Oh, Papa! Have they been annoying you, the beasts!

[GULLITT *pushes her back.*]

FINCH. Alas, the sight which greets me! Could not you two have plied your ghoulish work on me alone? No, like true cowards, you needs must seize little Thelma, my solace in declining years. Plague me to your heart's content! What care I? I who until this day ne'er realized the lowness of humanity; I who, strained in every aged fiber, cares not to live! Kill me then, but let my angel daughter be! Her right to long-saved earnings will not by me be signed away!!!

GULLITT. You'll sing a different tune shortly, my friend. [*Leering.*] I am, as you may have observed, particularly ingratiating to students of the ancient civilization of the

East. You have expressed a desire to view my curiosities, therefore I am pleased to show you a most unusual Chinese torture instrument,—the Manchu Rack.

[*He claps his hands and* AU WU *wheels out from wing Right 2 to up Right the Rack, a large rectangular framework, with Chinese letters and dragons painted on it.*]

THELMA. Oh, you beast! You brute!!

GULLITT [*crossing to up Right by the Rack*]. A most ingenious contraption, Professor. Shall I relate its history? Invented in the Second Manchu Dynasty for obtaining confessions of criminal guilt. I have found it indeed invaluable. The victim is placed within here. [*He indicates.*] Each careful twist of this wheel—so, and his bones are stretched more tautly. Each touch, so—and his hellish agony increases! Well, Professor, what think you?

FINCH. Daniel Gullitt, God in His Heaven looks down and surveys all!!

COKEY. I'd advice yer, Perfessy, I would! It's too terrible—

GULLITT. Think of being separated limb from limb! Think of the bloody dismemberment while yet alive! Think of your daughter here, whose eyes needs must be riveted on your mutilated torso, whose fevered brain will nevermore be normal after the gruesome sight!!!

FINCH. You have heard me! To falter now would be to lose all self-respect and happiness!

GULLITT [*Right*]. Put him on the rack, Cokey!

[FINCH *is placed on the Rack by* COKEY *and* AH WU. GULLITT *claps his hands once and* AH WU *from behind turns the wheel very slowly.* FINCH *writhes.*]

THELMA. Oh, that I should live to see this day! [*She sobs.*]

COKEY [*Right Center*]. Give in, Perfessy, ye'll never last!

[GULLITT *claps again and* AH WU *continues.* FINCH *emits an agonized cry.*]

FINCH. Oh—my—poor—weary—weary—body—!

GULLITT. This Spartan stance will bode no good, sir. You'll spare yourself by acquiescing. No answer?

[*Another clap of his hands.* FINCH *writhes terribly; this is terrible to behold.*]

FINCH. Dear Heaven—give—me—strength—!

GULLITT. Poor old fellow, my heart feels for you! [*But he smacks his lips and claps again.*]

THELMA. Oh, Dear God, have mercy!!!

FINCH. For—you—my—little—Thelma—! [*He collapses.* THELMA *sobs hysterically.*]

COKEY. Hold on, Dan! He's unconscious now. 'Twill be useless to keep this up. [*Aside, sadly.*] Yours is a mind of iron, but a heart of stone! Dani'l Gullitt, at times I pity ye!

GULLITT. Ah Wu. [*Claps his hands once.* AH WU *wheels the Rack to backstage with* FINCH *still tied to it.*] We'll revive him later with a shot of dope and then start our work anew. The girl and bum are safe enough alone.

COKEY. I see the tramp ain't yet awake. That was a perfect knockout fer ye.

[*They exit wing Right 2,* THELMA *emits low, squealing sobs.* OLD TOM *is just beginning to come to.*]

THELMA. Oh, divine Providence, is there no way of bringing aid? Has all the world been turned upside down? Never before, in wildest fancy, did I conceive of such a plight! [*More sobbing.*]

OLD TOM [*stirring at last*]. Er—er—Where am I?

THELMA. Poor Tom! I'd quite forgotten you.

OLD TOM. Everybody fergits Old Tom.

THELMA [*rolling on to her side and turning to him*]. How I grieve to think that my innocence has led you into this hardship.

OLD TOM. No hardship, Missy. 'Tis a pleasure to aid a dear, sweet lady.

THELMA. How kind of you to say so, Tom. [*Aside.*] I must comfort this poor soul, for I was taught, "Blessed are the Poor." [*Aloud.*] Do you find it awfully dreary living in alleys?

OLD TOM. Aye, 'tis a willful, woeful world, Missy, and us

poor wretches here on Mott Street is fergotten by the other half.

THELMA. It *is* a rather bourgeois neighborhood.

OLD TOM. Aye, Missy, it is that! Ye had no call to be down here alone and unaccompanied.

THELMA. I didn't know it would be like this. I've never been in New York before.

OLD TOM [*sitting up and edging over to* THELMA]. 'Tis a great, great city, New York. The rushin' of the people in the streets and the crushing of the carriages and gruntin' of the pigs in the gutters. . . . Do ye like it too, Miss?

THELMA. Indeed Tom, until this very day, I've loved everything about it. But all my happiness, I fear, will be transformed to grief and sadness.

OLD TOM. Ye must not judge too hasty, Miss. All folk that live in this city be not so evil as them what lives here.

THELMA. Oh, I daresay not, Tom.

OLD TOM. There be all kinds o' people and all kinds o' places to make this World; Down here there be the honest poor and the crooked poor. Up on Fifth Avenue, it be the same way,—the honest rich and the crooked rich. 'Tis a strange city. . . . Have ye seen much of it?

THELMA. I've been everywhere,—even Brooklyn. Last night Papa took me to the Policeman's Ball. How wonderful it was! All flags and bunting and confetti.

OLD TOM. Yes, Miss, I've heard tell that them Police Balls was grand affairs. Be it true that they have beer and sandwiches there?

THELMA. Quite true, indeed. [*Leans on her elbow.*] And oh, Tom, I met the most adorable young policeman! Would he were only here to aid us now!

OLD TOM [*very close to her by now*]. Now speak on, Missy. Confide yer secrets in Old Tom.

THELMA. In all my twenty years I've never known another like him. The gentlemen of Dubuque are all so light-hearted, but he's the staid and serious type all maidens long for!

OLD TOM. 'Tis kinda romantic as ye might say.

THELMA. He looked so handsome in his uniform,—like a hero suddenly materializing out of a young girl's idle fancy. Only to think he was my dream man;—and as the lights grew low, the band softened into a tender *gavotte*. Round and round we whirled and he told me that he loved me. I felt as if I were in Paradise!

OLD TOM. Then ye love him too, Missy?

THELMA. With all my heart! I'd cross mountain and desert and prairie to find him again! But that will never come to pass, and I shall perish, my love unconfessed.

OLD TOM [*aside*]. Oh, if only I could—but, no, I cannot!

THELMA. My situation here is doubly sad for not alone am I tortured, but I must also realize that my dear one can never fly to rescue me. Unbeknown to him, I slowly return to dust!

OLD TOM. What were his name, Miss?

THELMA. Sergeant Dick Trevelynne, I think he said.

OLD TOM [*aside*]. Alas for me that I cannot speak!

[NELL *enters wing Left 1 carrying a small white package.*]

THELMA [*aside*]. Can this be one of God's dear creatures,— so wan and pale that she seems marked for early grave?

NELL [*down Left*]. Pray what are you two doing here in captive bonds?

THELMA [*sits up on the bed*]. We were seeking someone when some base villains tied us thus.

NELL [*aside*]. Spies, I'll wager; it serves them right. And yet my womanly intuition tells me that sweet and simple face cannot belong to one of such a class. I must learn more. [*Aloud.*] For whom were you seeking?

THELMA. For my Papa.

NELL. Oh, for your father. And have you a mother, little girl?

THELMA. Alas, she died when I was but a babe. I never knew her, but all my life I shall pray for her saintly soul. My dear Papa's lips have often described her to me.

NELL [*aside*]. How this cuts at my very heart! [*Aloud.*] I had a baby once, my pet.—She must be just your age now.

THELMA. How sweet! And what happened to her?

NELL. She grew up like you, I suppose,—lovely and beautiful. I pray there may be nothing of wretched me in her!

THELMA. Why, what may be the matter with you, Ma'am?

NELL. Do I look like a mother that was once? I who am degraded and who serve a criminal's bidding? The sight of you stirs up what little decency is left in my miserable body. Somewhere my little daughter must be alive. That thought has given me hope for ten hollow, frigid years! No longer will I remain so low, no longer will I smuggle vile narcotics! [*She hurls her little white package to the ground.*]

THELMA. What are you doing, dear?

NELL. I am making myself worthy of my deserted baby!!!! [*She sobs.*]

THELMA. Come, dry your tears. [*Aside.*] If only she had a decent home with a sunny porch and roses in the garden, and someone to take care of her. I'm sure that then she'd be raised to what she was before. [*Aloud.*] I'm going to ask Papa to let me adopt you!

NELL. How shall I ever thank you, Pet? All I need to make me a saved soul will be a cozy home with a sunny porch and roses in the garden.

THELMA. Why, how did you know? You've described our very house out West!

NELL. Can it be? 'Twas a home like that which I deserted for fell places such as this! It cannot be true! What is your name, dear? [*She goes to bed.*]

THELMA. Thelma Ann Finch, the unmarried, twenty-year-old daughter of Josiah Finch. And you are—?

NELL. Now, only old Nellie, but once Penelope Finch!!! Oh, I knew you were my baby, you sweet one!

THELMA. Mother! [NELL *weeps and embraces* THELMA.] Promise you'll never leave us again! Oh, how glad Papa will be and Rufus too!

NELL. How is Rufus? He was but a puppy when I left.

THELMA. He is old and blind now. Poor dog, his days are numbered!

NELL. And Josiah, your angel father?

THELMA [*remembering for a change*]. Oh, alas! He lies suspended on that fearful instrument, tortured well-nigh to death by fiends! To think that we should all be reunited only to have this sad mishap!

NELL. Josiah's not in the hands of Gullitt and Cokey Joe? There's not a moment to be lost, for they are two derelicts who have reached the stage where human life is valueless! We must act quickly! [*She unties the bonds which hold* THELMA *and* OLD TOM.]

OLD TOM [*jumping up*]. By Heavens, I'll get them now!

NELL. No, no, stay back! They both have guns and Ah Wu, the Chink, is a very demon with his knife. Lie down, pretending to be still bound. Then later you can take them on an off-guard moment.

[OLD TOM *resumes his former position on the floor, wrapping the untied ropes about himself.* THELMA *rushes over to* FINCH, *who has been unconscious all this while.*]

THELMA [*on her knees*]. Papa, darling! Speak to me!

NELL [*on her knees*]. Josiah, my angel! Sent back to me by a beneficent Providence.

FINCH [*waking*]. Er—er—what do I see before me? It is my little Thelma, whose pure and innocent countenance ever comforts me. Yet who is this lady who stands by her side? She appears older;—still her manner bespeaks culture and kindliness. By Heavens, it is Penelope, my long lost spouse!!! A little faded, perhaps, but still with former loveliness of spirit which no years can dampen!

NELL. My beloved! What a happy ending to these ages of hardship!

[*They embrace his knees. Suddenly* GULLITT *bursts in, followed by* COKEY.]

GULLITT. What means this, Nell? You've untied the girl!

NELL. Josiah, Josiah, with my own hands I shall free you! [*She attempts to cut him down from the Rack.*]

[GULLITT *throws the two women to Left stage.*]

GULLITT [*flourishing pistol*]. Keep back, both you women! [*He backs down Right.*]

FINCH. By Jupiter, I recognize you now, Daniel Gullitt! You are he who shattered my connubial bliss so many years ago! He who in guise of traveling man ran off with my dearest hope! I shall have justice at last!

GULLITT [*aside*]. It is too late for half measures. Now he must never escape my clutches! [*Aloud.*] And now I shall have my way without further ado. Cokey! Turn the Rack wheel quickly. We'll wrench his very bones apart!

[COKEY *turns the wheel.* FINCH *writhes and groans.* OLD TOM *remains on the floor waiting to spring.*]

GULLITT. Will you never agree to give me that check? Once more, Cokey!

COKEY. Lord knows, I hates to do this, Dan! [*He turns wheel again.*]

FINCH. When—will—this—anguish—cease?

GULLITT. As soon as you assent to my demands, sir!

NELL [*rushing to Center*]. Oh, Daniel Gullitt, you savage, you cannibal! Release my love immediately or I shall reveal the dire fate of that banker you kidnapped in Omaha!

GULLITT. Er—er—very well, you may cease, Cokey. If we are thus to be prevented from breaking your staunch will by imposing gross physicalities then perhaps you'll fall for something else!

FINCH. Elucidate your nefarious plan, sir. I do not follow.

GULLITT [*down Right. Again flourishing pistol.* NELL *rushes to down Left*]. I give you three seconds to come to terms, Josiah Finch! Otherwise I shoot your daughter.

[OLD TOM *jumps up.*]

OLD TOM. Hold!!!

GULLITT. And who are you to stop me, pray?

OLD TOM [*coming down Left, suddenly tearing off his beard, whipping out a revolver and revealing himself as a handsome young man*]. Sergeant Dick Trevelynne, sir, of New York's finest!! For years I've been on your tracks, Dan Gullitt and Cokey Joe! And now at last you're caught after searches that led through cities and forests, through oceans and wild ravines. I have trailed you round the globe and now I find you right at home! This is luck indeed. [*He releases* FINCH, *who rushes to* NELL *down stage Left.*]

GULLITT. Why—why—how did you get here?

OLD TOM [*or better,* TREVELYNNE]. Mr. Finch asked me how to get to this address at the Police Ball last evening. My suspicions concerning his safety were aroused so I followed him here! You'll serve a pleasant term, you two!

COKEY JOE [*coming down Right*]. Lemme go, Officer, I didn't mean anything, honest!

GULLITT. Hush, you idiot! A thousand curses on you, Trevelynne!

TREVELYNNE. Little good that will do you now.

THELMA [*rushing Center*]. Oh, my hero!

TREVELYNNE. My adorable one! [*They may hold hands, but the embrace will not come until the end.*]

NELL [*down Left*]. And you say you'll take me back, Josiah? Oh, I'm so glad!!

FINCH [*down Left*]. How I've missed you all these years! But that will be forgotten now and we will all three live together in Dubuque.

THELMA [*Center*]. All *four*, Papa and Mama.

FINCH. I don't quite comprehend, my dear.

TREVELYNNE [*Center*]. Permit me to have the honor of your daughter's hand in marriage! I love her and think she loves me, sir.

FINCH. With all my heart. Don't you agree, Penelope?

NELL. Why, anything you say, Josiah.

THELMA. Then we shall all four live together in our little house with the rose garden, far, far away from this sordidness and vice. And maybe some day, in the sweet dawn of the dim future, we'll have—

TREVELYNNE. —little ones to share our joy!

THELMA. Oh, Richard!

COKEY [*sniffling*]. Look, Dan, ain't it touching!

[*Coming to the footlights, they form a straight line in this order from Right to Left*—JOE, GULLITT, THELMA, RICHARD, NELL, FINCH.]

FINCH [*to the audience*]. Just as these two have been caught, so may all base men gain their just desserts, for the wages of Dishonesty are confinement and segregation from all decent souls. Justice and Righteousness will ever triumph, and over all Love will prevail! Bless you, my children.

[THELMA *and* TREVELYNNE *embrace*.]

CURTAIN

THE MOON FOR A PRINCE

BY

GRACE RUTHENBERG

NOTE

This fantasy may be presented by,—
- (1) marionettes
- (2) actors performing like marionettes with the readers off stage
- (3) actors playing the parts in a fantasy.

A NON-ROYALTY PLAY

THE CAST

THE SCENE

The roof of the royal palace.

Across the Back runs the castle wall, cut in square scallops after the habit of castles. At Left a trap door. The MOON *is rising, visible through the branches of a tree.*

At the rise of the curtain the PRINCE *opens the trap door, looks out, and seeing no one about, goes to the parapet which he climbs and sits so that he can see the* MOON.

———•———

PRINCE.

> O moon through the restless trees,
> I'd like for my birthday, please,
>> Just to play for a while
>> With your golden smile
> And to sit on your golden knees.

> I've begged it in Timbuctoo,
> In Spanish and Latin, too,
>> But the court grows unpleasant
>> When begged as a present
> A birthday with nothing but you.

> O moon like a golden flask,
> What's the good of a kingdom, I ask,

122

> If His Highness Your Father
> Won't go to the bother
> Of doing so simple a task?

MAGICIAN [*sticking his head through the trap door*]. What's this? What's this? The royal prince wanting something that nobody gets for him? [*Fawning.*] This will never do.

PRINCE. Oh, Magician, it's you, is it?

MAGICIAN [*thrusting down a long neck in chatty fashion into the* PRINCE's *face*]. And what might the trouble be, pretty Prince?

PRINCE. Why, it's just this. Tomorrow's my birthday and nobody's asked me what I want.

MAGICIAN. Have you not counted the enormous number of packages already lying under the table in the royal nursery?

PRINCE. What I want is not there.

MAGICIAN. O Prince, I trust you have not been punching them. Punching packages, you recall, is forbidden by the royal rules of manners.

PRINCE. What I want is the moon.

MAGICIAN. The moon? [*With satisfaction.*] Ah! Why not ask your royal father for it?

PRINCE. Oh, I didn't mean that. It just fitted into my song. If I were to ask him he might promise, and that would be dreadful, because if the king ever goes back on a promise it is written that his throne shall be hacked into bits and he will be forced to lead the life of a ragpicker.

MAGICIAN. Never mind, pretty prince. Just leave the moon to me and I'll see what a magician can do about it. Go down now and sit on the royal bottom step till I call you.

PRINCE. O good and noble Magician! [*He exits down the trap.*]

MAGICIAN [*wickedly*]. The King will come shortly to take the evening air on the castle wall, and then watch me trick him into losing his kingdom. [*He dances.*]

> The royal Magician
> Is now in position

To comfort his itchity fingers,
  For an ancient decree
  Most important to me
In my wickedest memory lingers.

The King, can I whet him
  To vow this, I'll get him
For once where I want him to be.
  If he will but promise
  The moon, by St. Thomas,
His kingdom is coming to me.

[*He withdraws as the* KING *enters through the trap door, holding up his royal mantle.*]

MAGICIAN [*coming up behind the* KING]. Your Highness?

KING. Eh, what? Oh, it's you, Magician?

MAGICIAN [*sighing*]. Yes, and a sad one.

KING. Why, what's the matter?

MAGICIAN. It's the Prince, the poor little princeling. Nobody can get him what he wants for his birthday.

KING. Why can't they?

MAGICIAN. The kingdom isn't wide enough.

KING. What do you mean by saying my kingdom isn't wide enough? It's so wide a thousand black horses can trot themselves lame one by one without reaching its outermost boundary.

MAGICIAN. Well, then, not deep enough.

KING. Not deep enough? It's so deep it reaches to the innermost part of the earth where the rocks boil up like soap on a Monday.

MAGICIAN. Well then, not high enough.

KING. Not high enough? It's so high the largest eye of the oldest magician never saw its upper edge.

MAGICIAN. If that were true, he could have it.

KING. True? Of course it's true. There is nothing the Prince can ask for his birthday that his father can't give him.

MAGICIAN. Don't be rash. Suppose he were to ask for a white horse with gold fringe on the bridle?

KING. There are seven such in the royal stables.

MAGICIAN. Or a miraculous pudding in which the maraschino cherries were inexhaustible?

KING. He likes raisins better.

MAGICIAN. O royal sir, do you not realize what becomes of a king who goes back on his august word?

KING. Certainly. His throne is broken into bits and the King himself is forced to take up the life of a ragpicker.

MAGICIAN. By my faith, Your Royal Highness, this is fine of you.

KING. I vow that whatever he asks he shall have it.

MAGICIAN. You vow that?

KING. Certainly I vow it.

MAGICIAN. On the golden border of your sacred beard?

KING. On the golden border of my sacred beard. What does he want?

MAGICIAN. I'm sure I have no idea. It might be well to ask him. [*Stretching out his neck to the trap door, he calls "Prince!"*] I will go below for fear he might not like asking while I am here.

KING. Thoughtful Magician! Send him up.

MAGICIAN [*dancing behind the* KING'S *back*].

> Thoughtful Magician!
> He has no suspicion
> Of what his Magician's about.
> As sure as fire crackles
> I'll have him in shackles
> And put his retainers to rout.

[*The* MAGICIAN *disappears. The* PRINCE *comes through the trap door.*]

KING. Now, sirrah, what's this you're asking for your birthday, going around letting people think I can't give it to you?

PRINCE. Oh, but you couldn't, sir. Why, if you promised that, you'd have to break your word and you know what would happen.

KING. What is it?

PRINCE. I wouldn't even tell you, sir.

KING [*nervously*]. Out with it.

PRINCE. For fear you might be tempted to promise it, sir.

KING. Come, come.

PRINCE. By royal decree if the King were to break a promise, his throne, you remember, would be broken into bits and he would be forced to take up the life of a ragpicker.

KING [*fearfully*]. Ah!

PRINCE. I would not tempt you to vow it, sir.

KING. I have already vowed. What is it?

PRINCE. You haven't vowed, sir? Not without knowing?

KING. Yes.

PRINCE [*weeping*]. Alackaday! I asked for the moon.

KING. The moon?

PRINCE. Yes.

KING.

O lovely and elegant moon,
This vow was most inopportune,
    To beg I have forced me.
    My throne has unhorsed me.
They'll smash it to smithereens soon.

Call the Magician. Tell him to get the Moon down.

PRINCE. Yes, yes. The good Magician. [*He hurries off.*]

KING. Hurry!

MAGICIAN [*entering and bowing*]. What will you, O King? Have you found out what the Prince wants for a birthday present?

KING. Yes, the moon. You'll have to get it down.

MAGICIAN. I? Get the moon down? You amuse me. My magic is confined to earth as your Most Excellent Highness knows well enough.

KING. I can't help it, man. Get it down. Use a fishing pole. Use a broom handle. Climb the parapet and jump for it. Only get it down.

MAGICIAN [*bowing and standing still*]. Yes, Your Highness.

KING. Well?

MAGICIAN [*bowing and standing still*]. It cannot be done.

KING. Do it! Do you realize that if I go back on my word my throne will be broken into bits and I shall have to turn into a ragpicker?

MAGICIAN. Regrettable, I am sure. I shall do my best of course. [*He turns to the* MOON.]

> Abraca bree brooo
> Balaga doodle bologny
> Inglenook golobru tinklanium
> Zigelobruski clamchowder.

[*The* MOON *stays where it is.*] I'm very sorry, Your Majesty, but it doesn't seem to be coming down, does it? [*He stretches his neck up to look.*]

KING [*rushing forward to beat him*]. You tricked me into this!

MAGICIAN. After all, you made your own vow, you know. You said you owned everything above or below your kingdom, and the moon is undoubtedly above it. However, however! [*He starts to bustle off.*] I'll go down and see about getting your bundle ready. Ragpickers always carry bundles, you know. [*He bows skimpily, and goes.*]

PRINCE [*reappearing*]. Oh, Father Your Majesty, did he get the Moon down?

KING. No, my son.

> It's absolutely no use, you see:
>   I'll simply have to beg;
> So take my scepter away from me,
>   And the tassel from off my leg.

PRINCE.

> O Father, by your kingly crown,
>   I'll ask for the moon no more.
> I can't have you going about the town
>   Begging from door to door.

KING.

> I'll go with a dog about the town
> And beg for scraps of bread.
> For there are worse lives, I'll be bound,
> Than a beggar's, when all is said.

PRINCE.

> O Father, by your kingly crown,
> I'd rather an empty stocking
> Than see you with a beggar's bone
> Like a beggar come a-knocking.

KING.

> Oh, woe is me, the word is said
> Nor can the King gainsay it.
> Our promise is on our royal head,
> And we cannot betray it.

> So bring me here my beggar's staff
> And bring my beggar's wallet,
> And let the village children laugh
> At my tattered what-d'ye-call-it.

[Embracing him.]

> A blessing on you, O my son,
> Though a beggar's blessing be slender—

PRINCE. Oh, Father, think, what have I done!
KING [*bravely*]. I may rise to be scissors mender.

> Be not cast down, my noble boy,
> Nor have a thought for the morrow.
> I think I shall really quite enjoy
> To beg instead of to borrow.

And only the road to follow all day long!
PRINCE. But, Father, tomorrow is my birthday! You will have none of the cake.

KING. Kiss me farewell, my son. Here comes the Magician. [*He kisses him and the* PRINCE *leaves.*]

MAGICIAN. The throne is all ready for the chopping, Your Highness. Sorry.

KING. What did the Queen say?

MAGICIAN. I warned her that by the sacred order the throne would be broken to bits, and told her not to be sitting on it at the time.

KING. Thoughtful of you!

MAGICIAN. I do my best. [*He stretches his neck toward the* MOON.]

> Abraca bree brooo
> Abraca dum di dinger—

Your beggar's staff is ready in the hall.

> Similacrum bilibu
> Tiddlediwinks by ginger.

[*He withdraws his neck.*] It's no use, you see. I'll precede you. [*He goes as the* MOON, *climbing down the parapet, dangles its thin brown legs over the coping.*]

MOON. Well?

KING [*almost losing his balance on the roof*]. You—you— What are you doing?

MOON. I guess tomorrow's the Prince's birthday, isn't it? And when can a moon do what he likes if it isn't on the Prince's birthday?

KING. But I thought—I thought—

MOON [*swinging his legs which until now have been doubled out of sight behind his round yellow face*].

> Once a year or twice a year
>   Or once a century,
> The moon comes down to see the world
> And stretch his legs that have been curled
>   Behind his face, you see.

KING. Hm!
MOON.

> Twice a year or thrice a year
>   Or maybe only once,
> He dangles down a neat brown leg
> For fear the King might have to beg
>   Or Magician prove a dunce.

[*The* MOON *sits on the wall as the* PRINCE *returns.*]
PRINCE. Let me embrace you once more, my Royal Father. [*He
sees the* MOON.] What—?
KING [*clasping the* PRINCE].

> Our kingdom is saved
> For the moon has behaved
> In this most considerate fashion.
> The Magician shall be
> Cut up into three
> By ourself, without any compassion.

[*The* KING *and* PRINCE *stand one on each side while the*
MOON *climbs down to the center of the parapet and begins
to dance.*]
MOON.

> Hereafter make no promise bold
>   Nor leave your realm to chance,
> For wise men often own, I'm told,
>   A duplex countenance.
> They have been known to wreck a throne
>   Where kings have made a blunder.
> With wicked wile and fearful style
>   To knock his props from under.
> And now, good night! The land needs light.
>   Amid rejoicings fervent

I shall return to glow and burn,
  Your Highness' humble servant.

[*He begins the ascent of the parapet as the curtain comes down.*]

CURTAIN

THE FORKS OF THE DILEMMA

A COMEDY ABOUT QUEEN ELIZABETH
AND THE BOY SHAKESPEARE

BY

PRISCILLA FLOWERS

A NON-ROYALTY PLAY

THE CAST

The Chief Steward *of the Castle.*
Anne Hathaway, *his niece, a serving maid.*
Master Hatton, *bodyguard to the Queen.*
The Boy.
The Lord Chamberlain *of the Castle.*
Lord Leicester, *Dudley of Kenilworth.*
Elizabeth, *Queen of England.*

THE SCENE

Place: *A Tower Room in Kenilworth Castle.*
*An evening in July. An intimate withdrawing room leading
to the Minstrels' Gallery overlooking The Great Hall in
the castle. Up Left is a long casement window of leaded
panes, flanked by heavy draw curtains that hang to the
floor. A large carved chest forms a window seat under the
window. Bright moonlight streams through this window, several of the casements are open. Up Right is a secret panel in
the wall. On the back wall there is a wide Gothic archway
through which one sees the railing of the Minstrels' Gallery
with pennants, banners, etc., hanging as if from the rail into
The Great Hall below. Down Right there is a door with a
Gothic arched top. Completely covering this door is a green
and tan tapestry. There is little furniture, a large impressive
gold table in the Right Center, with a large gold chair behind
it directly facing audience, two candelabra or sconces on the
wall on either side of the archway to Gallery, a large candelabra upon the table. Strewn upon a cloth on the table are
many forks. They should, according to the history of forks,
have but two prongs or tines. For our purposes, however, one
rather large fork, such as one finds in a modern steak carving
set with a dark handle, will serve.*

134

THE CHARACTERS AND COSTUMES

All the costumes are of the Elizabethan style. They vary in color and gorgeousness. The men are all in doublet and hose, the women are in full long skirts.

THE CHIEF STEWARD *is a timid little fat man about fifty. His position is high, but his manner does not come up to his position in grandeur. He wears a great chain and pendant around his neck. His costume is fairly elaborate. He is red of face. He is fussy and mincing in taking his position and work over-seriously. His voice is high-pitched.*

ANNE *is a gay young girl of eighteen. She wears a robin's-egg blue satin gown with a cap of pearls after the mode of the period. Her position is that of a lady-in-waiting.*

MASTER HATTON *is fat and pompous. He is very elaborately dressed and waves from time to time a lace handkerchief.*

THE BOY *is about eleven years old. His very simple costume is soiled and torn. His stockings are torn and his legs are scratched and bloody. He is pale and tired; his hair mussed.*

THE LORD CHAMBERLAIN *is tall and spare. He is slow in movement and rather stupid in manner. His voice is low.*

LORD LEICESTER *is tall and well built. He is romantic in manner and handsome in looks. A beautiful speaking voice adds to his glamorous attire.*

ELIZABETH *in spite of her age is gay, expectant, eager. She is full of contrasting moods. A lively sense of humor changes to romantic feeling and tempestuous torrents. Her dress is very full, made of cream satin. Her red hair is piled high upon her head and bedecked with pearls. She wears ropes of pearls around her neck and her fingers are covered with rings.*

At rise of curtain, ANNE HATHAWAY *is on the down-stage side of table flourishing a two-pronged fork in her hand. She is in a hilarious mood, laughing incessantly as a Pavanne is being practised off stage on the Gallery to be ready for the time when the* QUEEN *should enter the Banquet Hall later. With*

her, bending over examining the forks, is her uncle, the CHIEF
STEWARD. *He is quite impatient with his giggling niece.*

CHIEF STEWARD. Zounds, Anne, hast forgotten the Ququququeen
is within?

ANNE [*putting her hand over her mouth*]. I prithee, Uncle,
show me how 'tis used.

[ANNE *plunges the fork vehemently into a lump or hunk
of bread lying beside the forks. She lifts up the speared lump
of bread and begins to munch from the side of the lump, holding it off at each bite an arm's length. She laughs.*]

ANNE. Fancy this is a joint of mutton, Uncle.

STEWARD [*taking it from her with force*]. Shhhh . . . not
so . . . thththtus 'tis used, the joint so. [*He takes bread in
left hand, fork in right.*] This be used for picking thththus.
[*He pantomimes the picking off of meat with wide gesture.*]

ANNE [*delightedly*]. "By the blood of the scorpion" 'twill never
do in England.

STEWARD. So say I . . . a silly French contrivance lately come
from the De Medici wench, a gift to his lordship . . . 'tis a
fad . . . 'twill never last. . . . God gave us these. [*He twid-
dles his fingers.*]

ANNE [*striking a pose, holding the fork aloft*]. I would give the
world and all to stand on yonder Gallery tonight watching
that banquet of two hundred perplexed Knights and Ladies
thus confronted.

STEWARD. Thththus counfounded. Shhhh. I go . . . enough of
this.

ANNE. Ohhhhhhhhhhh. [*She laughs.*]

STEWARD. WILT cease this?

ANNE. Can't a cat laugh at a Ququququeen?

STEWARD. Look to't . . . someone approaches.

[*He exits Center through the archway.* ANNE *is still laughing when, from the covered doorway down Right,* MASTER
HATTON *enters. He puffs with hurrying.*]

MASTER HATTON. Good Mistress Hathaway, shhhhhhhhh, 'tis
no time for levity. There be happenings.

ANNE [*sobering*]. What sayst?

HATTON. There be a prowler about.

ANNE. 'Tis not possible. Mine uncle and milord Chamberlain have set a strong guard for Her Majesty's protection. Dost lose thy head?

MASTER HATTON. By the soul of my mother, there be a prowler. The Queen's Guard hath warned me. Mark me, Mistress Hathaway, and he be found within these walls, we'll all lose our heads.

ANNE. I'll forswear thee . . . thou art droll.

HATTON [*seeing forks*]. Ahahhhhhhh . . . weapons of a sort.

ANNE. Look you now.

HATTON [*puffing toward Gallery*]. Look you now . . . keep a sharp lookout . . . away . . . there's much afoot . . . dearie me, there be. I return anon. [*He waddles puffing through archway Center.*]

ANNE [*alone*]. A prowler . . . zounds, the man raves.

[ANNE *turns, gathers up the forks in the cloth on the table as we see a hand grasping the window sill and a head is seen as someone, climbing upon the vines of the tower, pulls himself through the window.* ANNE *hears a sound. She looks at window. Sees head. Gives a little scream. She backs Center toward the Gallery, finally turns and shouts over the rail . . .*]

ANNE. Uncle . . . Uncle . . . Milord Chamberlain . . . Master Hatton . . . haste . . . help . . . Uncle.

[*She runs with all speed back to the table, picks up a fork and holding it as one would a dagger, advances upon the figure crawling through the casement. Meantime,* THE BOY *pulls himself wearily into the room.* ANNE *advances upon him, her jaw set viciously.*]

ANNE. How now, prowler, whence come you?

[THE BOY *sinks on the chest, puts his head on his arm and cries.*]

ANNE. Wilt answer? Haste before I strike.

BOY. By yonder vines, astride a moonbeam, Mistress Hathaway.

ANNE [*excitedly*]. Thou speakst my name . . . thou knowst me? How now . . . ? For why came you?

BOY. The Guards, the hounds.

ANNE [*seeing the blood*]. Art hurt . . . why . . . O God in Heaven, what's to do with you?

BOY. I care not. Rest. Let me rest.

ANNE. That I cannot. Who art thou? Thou knowst me?

BOY. An' it please you, in Stratford . . . An' it please you, let me bide here, 'tis a quiet room.

ANNE. Haste, 'tis not—'tis the crossroads of England. Come, I'll aid thee.

BOY. Ohhhh, my legs—how he flogged me— Have they come yet?

ANNE. The guard? I called for aid. . . . Oh, lad, what's to do?

BOY. Hide me, Mistress . . . 'tis not the guard . . . I fear to miss the players.

ANNE. How now . . . what mean you?

BOY. The Coventry Men, Mistress . . . let me hide in yon Gallery—'tis the players now grave, now gay . . . laughing with one eye while the other weeps . . .

ANNE. Thou'd risk thy head to see the players . . . a low tribe, I tell thee. Thou'lt weep with both thine eyes.

BOY. 'Tis the players, Mistress . . . I'll make no sound . . . so quiet.

ANNE [*vehemently*]. Thou poor fool, 'tis the Guard, I tell thee . . . haste . . . into the chest with you.

[ANNE *puts him into the huge chest under the window and sits upon it, waving the fork about, still apparently laughing at it as the* LORD CHAMBERLAIN *and* CHIEF STEWARD *rush breathlessly from the Gallery Center into the room.*]

STEWARD. Anne . . . what's amiss? . . . we heard thee call.

ANNE [*calmly in great contrast to her former agitation*]. Amiss? The larks be singing in thy head, Uncle . . .

CHAMBERLAIN. 'Twas the screeching of yon minstrels . . . prithee stop that music . . . a plague on 't . . . they've practised enough.

STEWARD. Yes, milord. [*He nervously sidles out Center to Minstrels' Gallery and in a moment the music stops.*]

CHAMBERLAIN. And now, Mistress Anne.

ANNE. Hast seen these droll forks, milord, for the more dainty picking apart of food—look, sir, dost mark the number—wouldst take them to the banquet board?

CHAMBERLAIN [*looking about*]. 'Tis not forks for the picking of food, 'tis a prowler we seek.

ANNE. Not so, by my troth, how could such be?

CHAMBERLAIN. He won't be for long, the Queen's Guard hath wind of it.

ANNE. Mayhap in the woods—the forks, milord?

CHAMBERLAIN. Where is the varlet—villain—rrrrrat? An he be within this castle, 'twill be more than a flogging.

[ANNE *flutters over to the chest again and seats herself upon it smiling. The* CHIEF STEWARD *returns Center from the Gallery.*]

ANNE. Most like he tarries to look at the Queen. God knows why. I should not walk an ell to look on such a one.

STEWARD. Shhhhh, child, she's everywhere.

ANNE. Would she were everywhere but here.

STEWARD. Bridle thy tongue.

CHAMBERLAIN. Look about, you bleating mutton, crawl into yon panel.

STEWARD. Yes, milord. [*He enters panel up Right.*]

ANNE. Much ado about nothing, milord. [*She spreads her skirt and leans back.*]

[*The* CHAMBERLAIN *stalks about bumping his staff upon the floor. He lifts curtain over door down Right.*]

CHAMBERLAIN. I'll hang him by the thumbs an I catch him. I'll have him flogged till his last breath an I do.

ANNE. 'Tis cruel.

STEWARD [*emerging from panel*]. Nothing there, milord.

CHAMBERLAIN. Mark you this—if I find him not and others do, I'll claim friendship for him, were he the devil himself.

ANNE. How now, sir.

CHAMBERLAIN. Anyone. I should not admit— [*He pounds with his staff.*] I would not grant so great stupidity in the lack of searching. I would invent excuses—I would claim a reason why he was within the castle. I'd say he was my guest.

STEWARD. A thief, mayhap?

ANNE. You would?

CHAMBERLAIN. Aye.

STEWARD. A murderer—an he had killed the Queen? A friend of milord?

CHAMBERLAIN [*realizing that this would be a bad plan*]. Zounds. On with the search.

[*They move to the door Right.* ANNE *rises quickly, eager for them to go. She steals a look down at the chest. Moves toward table.*]

ANNE. Would it please you . . . be the forks ready for the banquet? There is no need to return to this room, gentlemen [*She curtsies smilingly.*] and I take them hither.

[LEICESTER *from the Gallery Center calls:* "*Milord Chamberlain.*" ANNE *flits back to the chest and stands nearby. The* LORD CHAMBERLAIN *and the* CHIEF STEWARD *stop near door Right and listen.*]

CHAMBERLAIN. Soft—someone comes. My Lord of Leicester knows naught of this prowler—'tis he. . . . Smile, you mutton—stop shaking.

STEWARD. YYYYYYYeeees, milord.

[ANNE *makes a deep curtsy. The two men bow as* DUDLEY, LORD LEICESTER, *enters Center. His brows are knit. His nostrils dilate.*]

CHAMBERLAIN. Milord.

[*The* CHIEF STEWARD *always observes the face of the* LORD CHAMBERLAIN *before he says anything, thus his speeches are always timed a bit after the* CHAMBERLAIN'S.]

STEWARD. Milord.

LEICESTER. Gentlemen, I seek those forks—a plague upon them. [*He goes to table.*]

CHAMBERLAIN. Here they be in readiness for the banquet, all in readiness.

STEWARD. All.

LEICESTER [*seeing* ANNE]. Your ear in private, gentlemen.

CHAMBERLAIN. Mistress Hathaway, by your leave.

ANNE [*a bit terrified, not expecting to leave the chest*]. Yes, milords. [*She slinks out Center, looking back.*]

[LEICESTER *gathers up the forks quickly and thrusts them at the* LORD CHAMBERLAIN.]

LEICESTER. Take them—hide them. [*He looks furtively about.*]

CHAMBERLAIN. Yes, milord.

LEICESTER. Anywhere. The Queen of England must not see them. Make haste.

CHAMBERLAIN. Not use them at the banquet? Not these new contrivances?

CHIEF STEWARD. The Queen doth adore newfangled things, milord.

LEICESTER. Elizabeth of England would make clowns of every knight and lady at the board . . . she doth worship clowns.

LEICESTER. She shall not endanger this banquet by any such embarrassment. She, safely gnawing on her joint whilst the rest of us picked! She, bursting with laughter, her cheeks puffed like a jester's bladder with the juice and tender meat, whilst the rest of us with dry pecks doth try to satisfy our hunger. She shan't use them, no, not if I hang for it. Haste, someone comes.

LORD CHAMBERLAIN. *Not* Her Majesty. This be the one room in all the castle she hath not found.

LEICESTER. She will. Hide them.

[LORD CHAMBERLAIN *passes the bundle to the* CHIEF STEWARD.]

LORD CHAMBERLAIN. Here.

CHIEF STEWARD [*shaking*]. YYYYYes. . . . Whwhwhwh-what's to do?

LEICESTER. Under thy coat . . . haste . . . 'tis silk . . . 'tis she.

[STEWARD *hides forks under his coat and* LEICESTER *quickly seats himself in the large chair, taps with his finger.*]

LEICESTER [*pretending not to hear her approach. To the* LORD CHAMBERLAIN]. There's what as to fish? And meat?

LORD CHAMBERLAIN. Flounders, Carp, Salmon, Sole, Rabbits, Larks, Gulls, Capons, [ELIZABETH *the Queen enters from the Gallery Center. The three men pretend not to hear her.*] Green Geese, Swans, Woodcocks, Pigeons and Peacocks.

LEICESTER [*with severity*]. By the soul of my mother, where's something to eat? Where's the beef?

[ELIZABETH *laughs. The men turn and bow, pretending to see her for the first time.*]

LEICESTER [*rising*]. Your gracious Highness, it doth not please me that you find me in the midst of food.

ELIZABETH [*advances and extends hand to* LEICESTER *who kneels and kisses it*]. Rare food, gentlemen—but have it Beef! 'Tis not food I crave!

LEICESTER. What, Great Queen—ask these gentlemen.

ELIZABETH [*her eyes twinkling*]. 'Tis men. [*All exchange glances*—ELIZABETH *sees them and flares a bit.*] 'Tis the Coventry Men, you fools! Actors, a low common tribe, but one I favor. From the towers to the cellars, I find no one who hath seen them. Have they come?

CHAMBERLAIN. Not yet, Your Highness.

ELIZABETH. When, think you? What manner of play, think you? Do they bring a clown, a droll, a tumbling fellow? Your arm, Leicester. Let's to the clerk of the kitchen—I would know— No, I'll go alone! Where tarries my bodyguard, Master Hatton?

[*She sweeps out door Right.* LEICESTER *motions to bundle of forks under* STEWARD'S *coat.* CHAMBERLAIN *points toward panel cupboard.* LEICESTER *nods "yes," smiles, winks and follows* ELIZABETH . . . MASTER HATTON *enters Center weary and breathless and starts to door Right, following the* QUEEN.]

HATTON. Being bodyguard to Her Majesty is like following the hounds.

CHAMBERLAIN. You need long legs.

HATTON [*crossing to door Right*]. I need a horse.

STEWARD. Quick! These implements!

CHAMBERLAIN. My Lord of Leicester signified there—make haste! She'll return!

[STEWARD *places them in the cupboard up Right.* MASTER HATTON, *however, has hesitated in the door long enough to see this.* ANNE *rushes in through archway. The men are confused, thinking she has noticed them.* HATTON *exits Right.*]

STEWARD [*looking under table*]. Anne—come help us! An assassin—within the castle!

CHAMBERLAIN [*looking out of window*]. Most like in the Queen's apartments—waiting to—

STEWARD. To . . . to . . .

ANNE. Do not worry 'bout him. He is harmless. He's no assassin.

STEWARD. Now the larks be singing in your head.

ANNE. He will not kill the Queen. He is safe.

STEWARD. How you talk, wench!

ANNE. Go you two and search, but you'll not find him.

CHAMBERLAIN. How?

ANNE. Because I know where he hides.

STEWARD. You!

ANNE. Aye! I hid him.

CHAMBERLAIN. Where, wench?

ANNE. I won't tell thee.

CHAMBERLAIN [*rushes and pinions her arms behind her*]. What? You won't!

ANNE [*her face wry from the pain*]. I won't!

STEWARD. Child, you will let us go to the block—all of us!

CHAMBERLAIN. Harboring a desperate [*Twisting her arm.*] yokel!

ANNE. He's a poor little lad. I'll not tell!

CHAMBERLAIN. You will, hussy! I'll flay you!

STEWARD. Strike not, milord! Let me—oh, my child—pity me!

ANNE. I'll not tell. They'll not find him!

CHAMBERLAIN. I'll give thee over to my Lord of Leicester—then you'll tell.

ANNE. And you with me—implicated! What manner of guard then doth the manager of the castle give Her Majesty?

CHAMBERLAIN [after a pause]. Oh, I'll bargain. I'll barter! Deny there be anything amiss and when the banquet waxes merry, I'll give the boy safe conduct. Where! Speak!!

STEWARD [listening at door Right]. Here comes that woman! Oh, child, quick! Speak!

ANNE. You will lay no hand on him—no flogging?

CHAMBERLAIN. Thou art sure they won't find him? Safe conduct I promise. Go, wench—the Queen and Leicester pass this way.

STEWARD [dancing with fright]. Where to go!

CHAMBERLAIN [whispering]. They will not tarry here—they go to the Great Hall—to the Gallery. Wench, away with you. Return later after they pass through! We'll step behind yon curtains. [Pointing to window.] Lest we be seen dallying and excite suspicion.

[ANNE rushes into the gallery. STEWARD and CHAMBERLAIN get behind curtains flanking the window. Enter ELIZABETH and LEICESTER from Right.]

ELIZABETH [laughing]. Didst mark the clown with one leg red —the other green, droll fellow? Will we laugh, think you, Dudley? Will it be merry?

LEICESTER. Fit for a queen to make merry withal—your every wish, my Queen.

[ELIZABETH stops short and looks toward window.]

ELIZABETH. The moon hath come out, Dudley. See how it lies like silver. [She crosses to the window.] Come, Dudley, look, it lies on yonder bank—a sort of magic!

LEICESTER. I cannot look overlong—it affects me strangely.

ELIZABETH [sitting on chest]. Come, Dudley, sit by me.

LEICESTER. There be a more fitting place than this.

ELIZABETH. No, no, just here. 'Tis a worshipful room—'tis private. There [She pulls him gently down beside her.] Oh, [Sighing—looks out at the moon.] Dudley!

LEICESTER. Would you were plain Elizabeth Tudor!

ELIZABETH [*tenderly*]. Would I were a plain woman—to hold her husband's bridle as he mounts.

LEICESTER [*kissing her hand*]. My heart bends lower than my knee.

ELIZABETH [*looking right and left*]. Even this room feels full of—something. A kind of presence. [*The curtains twitch.*]

LEICESTER [*getting into the swing*]. 'Tis love, good Elizabeth!

ELIZABETH [*suspiciously*]. You're sure? 'Tis a private withdrawing room? [*Rises.*] I would have the head of anyone eavesdropping, [*Curtains tremble.*] damned if I wouldn't! Dudley, I would sit upon thee, twine my arms about thee like yon vines.

LEICESTER. Come! [*He takes her in his arms.*] Kiss me!

ELIZABETH [*doing so*]. Again, Dudley! [*Curtain twitches.*]

[MASTER HATTON *enters Right door. He coughs, lifts his eyebrows.* QUEEN *and* LEICESTER *break and turn on him.*]

ELIZABETH [*enraged*]. O, Master Hatton, thou hangst about me more closely than my stays! [*He takes out his sword.*] Is my body in danger! Has a Queen no right under the moon as another hath!

HATTON. A prowler, Your Majesty—he is within the castle!

LEICESTER. What! A stranger? What sayst! Where is my Lord Chamberlain—my Chief Steward!

[*Sounds of a mob come faintly through archway.*]

HATTON. The yeomen seek him—they come this way with the Queen's guard. Gracious Highness, speak to the yeomen— just at the balcony. As compiler of the Royal Memoirs, I advise it. They would have the prowler—they clamor for his blood. They would search.

ELIZABETH. The Queen is occupied— They may gaze on me for one moment—then I shall return and get at this matter of the prowler. He is not within this room? 'Tis private—is it not, Leicester?

LEICESTER. I'll stake my head on't.

[*She sails out into the Gallery Center, followed by* LEICESTER *and* HATTON. *Immediately, the* BOY *climbs out of the chest and staggers over into the panel cabinet, closing it behind him. A moment later, ANNE enters Center through archway. She runs to the curtains and pulls out CHAMBERLAIN and STEWARD—stand fixing their ruffs, their hair, etc. The STEWARD is nearly weeping—the CHAMBERLAIN is wild-eyed but more controlled.*]

ANNE. She's on the gallery. Hurry—

CHAMBERLAIN [*pulling at STEWARD*]. Away! Heard you her words?

ANNE. There's not time. Stand up, Uncle.

STEWARD. I'm all of a tremble! Save us, child, save us! How think you it would be to feel one's head rolling? She hath vowed—

CHAMBERLAIN. Shh! you bleating mutton!

ANNE [*to CHAMBERLAIN*]. Yes, and you'll be bleeding muttons, if I don't save you. Help me save the lad, a fair exchange. Make haste! Stand still. Is't a bargain? Save the lad! I've saved you!

STEWARD. How, child, art sure we are safe?

ANNE. Use your wits.

STEWARD. My knees.

CHAMBERLAIN. She said your wits!! Oh, here she comes!

    [CHAMBERLAIN *and* STEWARD *back up against the wall one Right, one Left and stand very stiff and straight.* ANNE *starts to open chest, then decides there is not time and rushes to other side of room.* QUEEN ELIZABETH *and* HATTON *re-enter Center.*]

ANNE. Milord!

LEICESTER. Out, wench!

ANNE. But a moment, milord! I crave a word—

ELIZABETH. Out Wench! Cans't hear—out!

    [ANNE *backs out Center.* ELIZABETH *observes* STEWARD *and* CHAMBERLAIN.]

ELIZABETH. How, now, Leicester, thy belated managers? [*She looks them over.*]

CHAMBERLAIN [*bowing*]. Your Highness.

STEWARD [*bowing*]. Your Highness.

LEICESTER. Gentlemen, what means this? A prowler within my castle?

[*Gentlemen look at each other—gasp.*]

LEICESTER. Perhaps they do be breathless from haste in getting here. The stairs, milords?

CHAMBERLAIN. The stairs, milord.

STEWARD. Stairs.

ELIZABETH. 'Tis no need of the whys and wherefores of the lateness of these gentlemen.

HATTON. They were here in this room but a moment gone, milord.

ELIZABETH [*looking around.*] Here!

HATTON. Aye—placing a packet in the secret panel.

ELIZABEH [*begins poking about walls.*] A secret panel—a packet? Woulds't see this packet, Dudley?

LEICESTER. 'Tis not important.

ELIZABETH. And two men secrete it? Fie, Leicester, open yon secret cupboard!

[CHAMBERLAIN *and* STEWARD *are paralyzed with fright.* ANNE, *who has been loitering in gallery, summons up courage to enter again—the mob is still heard outside.*]

ELIZABETH [*as* ANNE *goes to* LEICESTER]. Be this wench thy "Master Hatton," Leicester?

LEICESTER. Out, wench!

ANNE. An you flog me, Sir, now I must tell you—they seek the poor lad!

LEICESTER. What lad, wench? Where? For why?

ANNE. The prowler, milord. 'Tis but a lad come from Stratford.

LEICESTER. Wherefore intrude? Doth he not know Her Majesty makes a progress?

ANNE [*trying to soften them*]. Most likely he came to see the Great Queen. A lad, milord.

ELIZABETH. To the hounds with him! Thy hand, Leicester. The packet!

ANNE [*indicating noise of mob*]. Good, milord, spare him from them. They be like hungry wolves for a lamb's blood!

ELIZABETH. They do protect their Queen. What say you, my
Lord of Leicester, hast no management at Killingworth that
we are burst in upon by a servent wench who pleads for some
boy brat? All alike, the devils! Brats—all of 'em! I would
see that packet!

ANNE [*noise increases*]. They come! Oh, spare the lad!

LEICESTER. Spare him? I have no lad—there is no lad.

ANNE. Ah, yes! In the chest.

ELIZABETH. The chest! Ah!

[ELIZABETH *rushes over and opens chest.*]

ELIZABETH. Empty! [ANNE *is amazed and falls back.*] Enough
of this! All of you are mad—there is no prowler. Master Hatton, quiet yon mob of yeomen—command them return to
their homes—begone! [MASTER HATTON *rushes out Center.
Everyone stands petrified—fearing the* QUEEN'S *wrath.*] And
now! I want the packet—the packet. Where is the packet?

CHAMBERLAIN. It—it—

ELIZABETH. You secreted it in a panel. Come now! Where is it!
What's in't?

STEWARD [*indicating panel*]. Th-th-th-there, Your Highness.

ELIZABETH [*almost jumping at panel*]. Aha! Now Leicester!
[*She opens panel. The* BOY *has fainted.* CHAMBERLAIN *and*
STEWARD *lift him up to top of chest.* ELIZABETH *gives a little
scream, and gives* BOY *a close look.*]

LEICESTER. What means this! To the dungeon with him—what
doth he here?

ELIZABETH [*rummaging in cupboard*]. To the hounds with
him, Dudley. The packet . . . ah, the packet.

LEICESTER. Throw him in the dungeon until Her Majesty departs.

ELIZABETH [*emerging with forks*]. Throw him to the hounds!
Hast forgotten, my lord of Leicester, he was a witness? Think
you the Queen of England will let live a witness who would
bruit about how the queen in private—well, think you I would
let live one who— [*She opens packet of forks at table and
forgets the* BOY *entirely.*] What be these— hair ornaments?
[*Begins sticking them into her hair.*]

ANNE [*to* BOY]. There, there, tell my Lord of Leicester for why you came, lad—speak, lad! It was to see the Great Queen, wasn't it, lad? To see the great queen?

BOY [*reviving for a moment*]. Not the Queen—no—not the Queen.

ELIZABETH [*busy with the forks*]. To you, my Lord of Leicester, do I give command—to the tower with yon lad!

ANNE. No, no, Your gracious Majesty—not that! Not the tower!

ELIZABETH. To the dungeon with him—and with the wench too! A prowler in the castle—threatening my life!

CHAMBERLAIN [*able to speak—at last*]. He is no prowler. We know the lad.

ELIZABETH. You know him?

CHAMBERLAIN. We do, Your Majesty. We know him.

STEWARD. We do.

ELIZABETH. What might his name be?

CHAMBERLAIN [*with difficulty*]. Johnnie, your Highness.

STEWARD. Little Johnnie.

CHAMBERLAIN. My Lord of Leicester, think you I would permit a prowler?

STEWARD. Or I? O, dear no.

ELIZABETH. He was in that panel. How came he there?

[CHAMBERLAIN *and* STEWARD *search for an answer.* ANNE *comes to the rescue.*]

ANNE [*center*]. Let the boy tell for why. He sleeps—I'll wake him.

ELIZABETH. Asleep? Think you he was asleep?

CHAMBERLAIN. He's asleep.

STEWARD. Quite.

ELIZABETH [*to* ANNE]. Asleep for long, think you?

ANNE. So sound a sleep must have fallen through the space of one whole hour, Your Highness.

ELIZABETH [*sighing—immensely relieved*]. Leicester, he slept in yon cupboard—he heard nothing.

LEICESTER [*kissing her hand*]. Your Highness.

ANNE. He is free?

ELIZABETH [*with a wide gesture*]. Free of me. Flog him—throw him to the yeomen—anything you like.

ANNE. No, no, I beseech you!

ELIZABETH. The Queen has finished with the boy brat. [*She starts to exit right, then remembers forks and takes one from her hair.*] Wait! Leicester, I would know about these.

LEICESTER [*Right Center*]. A queer contrivance.

ELIZABETH [*Right*]. Dost know for what they are used?

LEICESTER. I know not. Mayhap for the hair as you have them.

ELIZABETH. If anyone can tell the exact use, he may demand anything of me and it shall be granted.

[BOY *rubs his eyes and sits up.*]

CHAMBERLAIN [*down Left*]. I know, Your Highness.

STEWARD [*up Left*]. And I!

BOY [*up Left*]. And I!

ELIZABETH [*laughing*]. Good! Demand of me.

CHAMBERLAIN. May you never cut off our heads, Your Highness.

STEWARD. Amen.

ELIZABETH [*coquettishly*]. May you never *lose* your heads, gentlemen, because of your queen. And you? [*To* BOY.] What is your wish?

BOY. The play was all! I did climb up the vines through yon window. It was wrong but the plays—they do so draw me.

ELIZABETH. With my Lord Chamberlain and my Chief Steward! You all three climbed in together—all friends. [*Laughs.*] Leicester, Leicester! [CHAMBERLAIN *and* STEWARD *hang their heads.*] 'Tis well I promised you your heads, gentlemen. 'Tis well the cupboard held but one. Now tell me—what are these implements?

[CHAMBERLAIN *and* STEWARD *start to reply*—BOY *breaks in.*]

BOY [*rising*]. Forks, Your Majesty! For the picking apart of food, Your Majesty—thus. [*He demonstrates.*]

ELIZABETH [*crossing to table*]. Forks—forks! Leicester, good! We'll use them tonight. How I love newfangled devices!

Come, Leicester, away with yon boy. Let's to sup. [*Crossing to door Center. Looks at* BOY *again.*] What was he doing in the cupboard, think you?

LEICESTER. My Lord Chamberlain will discover. Take the lad below stairs quickly. A banquet comes apace.

ELIZABETH. With forks!

CHAMBERLAIN. Yes, milord.

STEWARD. Yes, milord.

[*They grasp him by the arms and drag him to door Right.*]

BOY [*screaming and trying to get away*]. Help! Help me and it please you!

CHAMBERLAIN. Come lad, come along.

STEWARD. Come along, lad.

CHAMBERLAIN. You know us, lad, come along.

BOY [*kicks and screams*]. That I do! Don't, I pray you! 'Tis he who flogged me! See, I bleed!

ELIZABETH [*Center. Gesturing with fork*]. These be friends, little Johnnie.

BOY. 'Tis not my name, Johnnie—'tis William.

STEWARD. It may be William but he's Johnnie to us.

CHAMBERLAIN. A simple lad who wished to see the inside of a castle—nothing more. I shall take him below stairs by your leave.

BOY. No, no, he will flog me!

LEICESTER. Enough of this!

BOY [*being dragged out*]. Mercy, Your Majesty!

ELIZABETH. Away with his bawling!

BOY. The play, Your Majesty, the play! I did but wish to see the play!

LEICESTER. I'll throw you to·the hounds an you don't go!

BOY. The Coventry men—that's for why I came!

LEICESTER. Ye blithering bratling—take him away!

BOY. Just one play was all, milord! He'll kill me! The play, Your Majesty, the play!

[*They drag him almost to door. Then* ELIZABETH *turns suddenly and raises her hand.*]

ELIZABETH [*up Center*]. Stop! Bring back the brat.

[THE BOY *runs to her and falls on one knee.*]

CHAMBERLAIN. We entreat pardon, Your Majesty. Let us take him. We—

LEICESTER. Silence! Thou [*to* BOY] art a prowler and so shalt thou be punished.

[MASTER HATTON *re-enters from Gallery and watches the scene with great bewilderment.*]

ELIZABETH. He loves plays, Leicester—let the Queen stand between him and thy wrath. Now tell me—what know you of plays?

BOY. Enough and not enough, Your Majesty.

ELIZABETH. How now?

BOY. When my father leads me to the calves and bids me sever soul from body by the slashing of their throats, there comes a faintness on me. 'Tis then, my hands all blood, my arms, my feet, and their so innocent eyes upon you, I do remember plays. The bleeding calf's the funny clown all red and white—I see him tumble, fall at my feet—'tis thus I do my father's bidding. I know not why they do so draw me. Would I loved them less and came not here.

ELIZABETH [*her hand upon his head*]. So well as that? I love plays, lad, merry glorious plays—rise up—thus well do I love them—plays that dull the edge of memory—and one has memories, that stop the foot of Time—and one has years. [*Pause.*] Ahhhh . . . [*snapping to*] Your arm, Leicester.

HATTON. Who will bear the towel and the basin for your Royal hands?

ELIZABETH. The Queen hath a whim.

[*The Lord Chamberlain advances a step toward the table.*]

ELIZABETH. 'Tis her will that the lad bear it.

LEICESTER. Your Majesty.

ELIZABETH. The lad.

[LORD CHAMBERLAIN *and* STEWARD *stand back, right.*]

THE BOY. I? Sitting in the Great Hall? I hearing the play with no fear? Looking till my eyes overflow with the fullness of it?

ELIZABETH. 'Tis the Coventry Men for us, lad. The golden basin for him, wench.

[*The music of the Pavanne begins.* ANNE *puts the basin in the boy's hands, the cloth over his arm.*]

THE BOY. Ohhhhh.

HATTON. Your Majesty, as compiler of the Royal Memoirs what shall I put down as the name of the bearer of the basin at the banquet at Killingworth?

ELIZABETH [*turning impatiently*]. Likewise, Master Hatton, put down that forks were employed at the banquet for the first time by Elizabeth of England . . . your name, lad?

THE BOY. I should be so flogged and my father heard.

ELIZABETH. What's immortality to a flogging? Hatton . . . Oh, name him William.

HATTON. William what?

THE BOY. What matter what—William Ham—William Bacon —a rose by another name would smell as sweet—what's in a name?

ELIZABETH. The boy hath a head, Leicester.

LEICESTER. And he keep it, Your Majesty. [*With a lift of his eyebrows.*]

HATTON. Thy name—for posterity.

THE BOY. 'Tis a good name— My father's the best butcher in Stratford.

HATTON. Thy name?

THE BOY. Shakespeare.

[MASTER HATTON *writes in a book.*]

ELIZABETH. To the banquet board—thou shalt see the play, lad, a jester with cap and bells—a dark villain who is worsted . . . a clown. . . . [*She turns as if to go, then as suddenly turns again to him.*] And thou shalt see another play . . . 200 knights and ladies with forks in a comedy of errors. —to mess.

LEICESTER. A fine mess, indeed. [*He lifts two fingers as if they were forks.*]

[*The* QUEEN *and* LEICESTER *start up Center followed by* THE BOY, *bearing the basin.* MASTER HATTON *bows to* MIS-

TRESS HATHAWAY. *They walk doing a step of the Pavanne as they exit toward the Gallery. The* LORD CHAMBERLAIN *and* CHIEF STEWARD *bow to each other and follow in the procession going out up Center.*

CURTAIN

A WOMAN OF JUDGMENT

BY

LEON M. PEARSON

A NON-ROYALTY PLAY

THE CAST

THE SCENE

The office of MISS EUGENIA POWERS.

On the Right a flat-topped mahogany desk faces the center of the room. A high-backed chair Right faces the desk. In front of it a small stiff chair also faces desk. On the Left a spacious easy-chair with a taborette for papers beside it, partially faces the center of the room. Beyond it on the Left and further down stage by the wall is a smaller armchair. On the walls are pictures of dominating personalities;—Napoleon, William II, Mussolini, and many others.

The door at Right, behind her desk, leads into a private room and the door in the back wall leads into the hallway and other parts of the house. Its opening is hung with portières.

THE CHARACTERS AND COSTUMES

STELLA, *a maid of any age is dressed in uniform.*

MRS. WARING, *a widow, and middle-aged, is dressed in black. She is a gentlewoman.*

ELFREDA WARING, *her daughter, is pretty, quiet, and innocent looking.*

MISS EUGENIA POWERS, *a practicer of a "new psychology," is a large-framed woman, suave, dominating. She wears a tailored suit, trim hat, carries brown kid gloves. When she speaks her voice is low and firm.*

MISS RIDGE, *a detective, is young and attractive in a brusque flippant way. Her clothes are a trifle mannish. Her desire for a dramatic career has been thwarted by an unappreciative New York manager and as a result, she affects a theatrical abrupt manner.*

———●———

At the rise of the curtain STELLA *shows in* MRS. WARING *door Center.* MRS. WARING *has both hands on her hand-bag, and glances timidly about the room.*

STELLA. It won't be long now. If she says she'll be back at four, she'll be back at four. Not two minutes after, either. You can set your clock by her. Have a seat, madam. [*She indicates the easy-chair, Left.* MRS. WARING *crosses to it, but does not sit.*] Now take yesterday morning. I heard the chimes strike in the church tower, and I says to cook, "That's six-forty-five"; and she says, "No, six-thirty." And I says, "No, six-forty-five." And come to find out,—I was right. And cook says, "How'd you know it was six-forty-five?" And I says, "'Cause, I heard the water runnin' in the madam's shower bath, and when I hear that, I know it's six-forty-five." [*Crossing to* MRS. WARING.] You just sit down. She won't be a minute now.

MRS. WARING [*sitting*]. But I don't want to see her.
STELLA. You don't? Who do you want to see?
MRS. WARING. My daughter. I'm Mrs. Waring.
STELLA. Oh! I didn't take notice of your name. I thought you had an appointment. That's what most people comes for. And you looked like one, too,—that is—I don't mean no harm, but you look kind of—well, I don't know *what* to say—anyhow, I'll get Miss Elfreda. *She's* here all right.
     [*She exits, Center.*]
     [ELFREDA *enters, Center. She does not see her mother at first and we get in her eyes an anxious, startled expression, like a fawn. She is pretty now, but prettiest when gay. In any case her expression is of innocence. No criminal, here.*]
MRS. WARING. Elfreda!

[ELFREDA *turns, quickly. They embrace, fervently. The mother's hand on the daughter's face. There are no words. The girl's eyes steady at first, then falling. Then her arms fall. Shame. Her mother repulses the inference, taking her face in hands, bringing it up again.*]

MRS. WARING. Elfreda—? [*Now with the positive downward inflection.*] You didn't do it.

ELFREDA [*directly, simply*]. No.

MRS. WARING [*as if, That's over*]. There! [*She sighs, turning.*] I knew it. That's all I wanted, just to hear you say you didn't. I knew you couldn't have done it. She's coming back and I don't want to—I don't need to see her now.

ELFREDA. I'm going with you.

MRS. WARING. No, no. It would make you look guilty. You mustn't leave now.

ELFREDA. But I'm discharged.

MRS. WARING. But if you didn't do it—?

ELFREDA. She doesn't *believe* me.

MRS. WARING. Have you told her?

ELFREDA. I—I tried to. But it didn't do any good. She said she had proof— [*Recalling the words.*] "incontrovertible proof."

MRS. WARING. Why, what proof could she have?

ELFREDA. She had left the ring in a box in her bureau drawer. The next morning it was in my hand-bag.

MRS. WARING. The maid?

ELFREDA. Stella and Jane were both out.

MRS. WARING. Just for the evening?

ELFREDA. Yes.

MRS. WARING. Perhaps, when they came home—

ELFREDA. But my room was locked. I went to my room at nine, and locked the door, and I didn't unlock it until the next morning, when she came.

MRS. WARING. She came to see—?

ELFREDA. Yes, she had missed it, and she came and knocked on the door, and she said her ring was gone. So I helped her hunt it, and first we looked in her room, and then she said, "Will you look in your room?" "But it couldn't be in *my* room," I said. But she insisted, and came back with me. I wasn't even dressed yet.—And I found it in my purse.

MRS. WARING. *You* found it there?

ELFREDA. Yes.

MRS. WARING. She didn't find it there?

ELFREDA. I opened the bag myself, and there it was.

MRS. WARING. But how did it get there?

ELFREDA [*desperately*]. I don't know!

MRS. WARING. But dear— You didn't do it. And somebody did. We must find out who it was.

ELFREDA. Mother—the worst of it is that nobody else *could* have done it.

MRS. WARING. What do you mean?

ELFREDA. Just that it would have been impossible for anyone to take it but me. I'm the thief.

MRS. WARING. My dear girl! [*Straining for reassurance.*] You *didn't* do it—?

ELFREDA [*simply*]. No.

MRS. WARING [*fortified*]. Well then.

ELFREDA. But nobody in the world would believe me but you, mother dear.

MRS. WARING [*challenging*]. Why not?

ELFREDA. Don't you see—Miss Powers had the ring at eight o'clock, and that was after the maids had gone. She put it away in her bureau drawer, and then went out. I was alone in the house for an hour and a half. When she came back, the ring was gone. The maids were still out . . . I had gone to bed. In the morning she called me, and the ring was found in my purse.

MRS. WARING [*taken aback*]. My goodness!

ELFREDA. All I can do is to say "I didn't take it, I didn't take it." But she doesn't believe me. I want to go home, mother. I *have* to go, anyway.

[*Voices are heard in the hall. The women listen. By an exchange of glances, they say "Is that she?" and "Yes." They glance about the room self-consciously. The girl leads her mother to a chair at extreme left, and stands by her when she sits. The mother looks toward the door. The girl's glance is lowered.*]

[*In the meantime, this is the off-stage conversation, the last line of which, only, need be heard:*]

MISS POWERS. Whose overshoes, Stella!

STELLA. They're Miss Elfreda's mother's.

MISS POWERS. Oh.

STELLA. She's in there, ma'am. They're both in there.

MISS POWERS. Stella, call a cab.

STELLA. Yes, ma'am.

MISS POWERS. And only one place tonight, for dinner.

STELLA. Yes, ma'am.

[MISS POWERS *enters and stands in the doorway, Center, looking directly at the two women. She does not advance, she does not speak. Her glance is neither a friendly welcome nor an unfriendly glare. It is simply the height of self-assurance, of impassivity. Now she advances.*]

MISS POWERS [*not a question*]. This is Mrs. Waring. [MRS. WARING, *rising, is about to speak, but:*] Please don't disturb yourself. [*She urges her to sit again. Now she turns, goes to right, picks up the small chair in front of desk, and lifting it with one hand, brings it to Center; she sits in the chair. Now, waiving preliminaries, she goes to the very heart of their matter.*] I have no desire to give publicity to this unfortunate incident, but you will understand that your daughter must go. [MRS. WARING *straightens up to speak, but* MISS POWERS *raises an arresting hand.*] The ring itself was of no great value, but theft is theft. It was a surprising revelation to me, as you may imagine, and I feel very badly about it. Your daughter had become very efficient and I shall hate to lose her, but the facts being what they are, you can see that it would be impossible for me to keep her. [*She rises and turns up stage.*] I have ordered a cab; in the meantime, if you care to wait in the parlor—

MRS. WARING [*rising*]. She'll go, if you want her to, but not because she's guilty, for she didn't do it! Miss Powers, you

are a student of character. Just look at her and you will see
for yourself—

Miss Powers. I realize that it is very hard for her mother to
believe. Indeed, it was hard enough for me. But the evidence,
in spite of both of us, is incontrovertible.

Mrs. Waring [*who has taken her daughter's hand, now looks
at her, still speaking to* miss powers]. But she couldn't have
done it. [*Now to her daughter.*] Elfreda, tell me the truth,
whatever it is. Did you steal the ring?

Elfreda [*simply, directly*]. No, mother.

Mrs. Waring [*turning*]. You see! What is "evidence" com-
pared to that?

[miss powers *comes forward and stands in front of* elfreda *Left. She says nothing, simply looks her full in the
eyes. The girl meets her glance fairly at first, then wavers.
Her hand moves first; then she shifts her weight; then she
drops her eyes.* miss powers *turns away from her with a
"You see" gesture, and crosses to her desk. Inconspicuously
she picks up a checkered black-and-white pencil; she turns,
and speaks:*]

Miss Powers. Miss Waring.

Elfreda. Yes, Miss Powers?

Miss Powers. Will you come to me, please? [elfreda *crosses
to her Right.* miss powers *holds the pencil in her fingers as
she speaks.*] It is true, is it not, that you were alone in the
house last Thursday evening?

Elfreda. I believe so, yes.

Miss Powers. You know that Stella and Jane went out?

Elfreda. Yes.

Miss Powers. And that I went out shortly after?

Elfreda. Yes.

Miss Powers. When I returned, Stella and Jane had not come
back?

Elfreda. No.

Miss Powers [*bringing the pencil closer to the girl's face*].
Then you must have been alone in the house during the time
I was away?—

ELFREDA. Yes.

MISS POWERS. I had taken off the ring just before I left and had put it in my bureau drawer; when I returned, the ring was found in a purse in *your* bureau drawer. Is this true, or not?

ELFREDA. Yes, it is true.

MISS POWERS. Are you aware of anyone having entered your room during my absence?

ELFREDA. No.

MISS POWERS. *Could* anyone have entered your room?

ELFREDA. No, the door was locked.

MISS POWERS. The door was locked. . . . Who, then, could have taken the ring from my room to yours?

ELFREDA [*faltering*]. No one, except me.

MISS POWERS. If no one else could have stolen the ring, *you* must have stolen the ring. [ELFREDA'S *shameful posture acquiesces.*] Look at me. [ELFREDA *does so.* MISS POWERS *holds the black-and-white pencil steadily before her eyes.*] Did you steal the ring?

[*There is a pause,* MRS. WARING *crosses to Center.* ELFREDA *now looks steadily, with an awed fascination into the eyes of her inquisitor, until she says, not in the whisper of shame, but with a strange fervor:*]

ELFREDA. Yes!

[MISS POWERS, *with a gesture to the anxious mother, turns away, leaving* ELFREDA *staring, transfixed, into space, so that when the girl collapses, it is her mother who sees and supports her and puts the chair Center in place for her to sit.* MISS POWERS *goes to the door, right, leaves the stage for a moment, to return with smelling salts, which she hands to the mother. Now she goes to the door at Center and calls:*]

MISS POWERS. Stella—

[*Then she moves to Right and stands watching the stricken women across the room. When* STELLA *comes to the door,* MISS POWERS *speaks in a low voice:*]

MISS POWERS. The cab come?

STELLA. No, ma'am, not yet. [*Turning, she sees* "MISS ELFREDA" *in misfortune, and says:*] Anything wrong, ma'am?

[MISS POWERS *does not glare reproof; she merely looks at the girl with steady impassivity, which is more wilting than the other, and the girl, backing, goes clumsily out. A door bell rings.* STELLA *exits Center.*]

MISS POWERS. I dare say that's your cab. [ELFREDA *rises. She and* MRS. WARING *cross toward the door.*] Don't pay the man. It will be charged to me. [*They are about to go, when* STELLA *appears in the doorway.*] The cab?

STELLA. A Miss Ridge, ma'am.

MISS POWERS. Isn't the cab there?

STELLA. No, ma'am. It's a Miss Ridge, to see you, ma'am.

MISS POWERS. Miss Ridge?

STELLA. Yes, ma'am.

MISS POWERS. She'll have to wait.

[*But* MISS RIDGE *enters Center at this moment.*]

MISS RIDGE. I'll come in if you don't mind. [*She surveys the group of women, then speaks to* MISS POWERS:] This is Miss Powers?

MISS POWERS. I'm very busy now,—you'll have to wait out there.

MISS RIDGE [*turning to* ELFREDA]. And this is Miss Waring? [ELFREDA *nods.*] Miss Elfreda Waring— And this, her mother.

[MRS. WARING *and* ELFREDA *back off to Left.*]

MISS POWERS. I can't see you now,—you'll . . .

MISS RIDGE [*removing gloves*]. Indeed you can. [*This gayly; then shrewdly, to* MISS POWERS:] Shall we be seated?

MISS POWERS. Who are you?

MISS RIDGE. I beg pardon for not answering before. I am, by profession—

[STELLA, *entering, provides an interruption.*]

STELLA. The cab is here now, m'am.

MISS RIDGE. Cab? For whom?

MISS POWERS. Well, good-by, Mrs. Waring.

MISS RIDGE [*to* STELLA]. Hold on. Send the cab away.

[STELLA *looks to her mistress for authority.*]

MISS POWERS. Good-by, Elfreda.

Miss Ridge [*Left*]. Just a minute, Miss Powers. It will be some time before anyone of us will need a taxi. You'll have to pardon my abruptness. It's an unfortunate mannerism I have, but useful in my line of work, particularly in the pinches. I guess you psychologists would call it a kind of defense mechanism. Is that right? [*Seeing the lingering* STELLA.] Are you still there? I thought I told you—

Miss Powers [*Right, near bursting*]. Will you be good enough to tell me who you are.

Miss Ridge [*She turns from* STELLA'S *expression of dismay and confusion to say to* MISS POWERS *very quietly*]. Miss Powers, I am a detective. I trust now you will believe me when I tell you there will be no use for a taxi-cab.

[*The eyes of the two women have met, and are fixed so for another moment, until* MISS POWERS, *turning to* STELLA, *says:*]

Miss Powers. Tell him to go.

Stella [*grateful for agreement*]. Yes, ma'am!

[*She goes.*]

Miss Ridge. Now. I'll tell you what I'm here for. [*To* MISS POWERS.] You don't mind if we sit down. [MISS POWERS *replies with a gesture and all sit,* MISS POWERS *at Right,* MRS. WARING *in small chair Left,* ELFREDA *in large chair, Left Center,* MISS RIDGE *Center*.] This is not going to be any inquisition, I'll just tell you my story, and see what happens. It's not going to be a funny story and it won't put you to sleep either.

Miss Powers. This sounds very mysterious, Miss Ridge, but I suspect that your mystery is solved already.

Miss Ridge. You don't say!

Miss Powers. I have already examined Miss Waring and she has confessed. So you will perhaps save your own time and the young lady's feelings—

Miss Ridge. Well, well, when did this happen?

Miss Powers. Only a few minutes ago.

Miss Ridge. Really. And do you say this taxi-cab was to take Miss Waring away?

Miss Powers. Yes.

Miss Ridge. Where?

Miss Powers. To her own home, I suppose.

Miss Ridge. Do you mean to say that you would send off, willy-nilly, to go her own sweet way, a person whom you had discovered to be guilty of forgery?

[Miss Powers' *reaction to this is not vocalized, but* Mrs. Waring *exclaims:*]

Mrs. Waring. Forgery? Not forgery!

Miss Ridge. No?

Mrs. Waring. No indeed!

Miss Ridge. This is interesting. What *was* it?

Mrs. Waring. Not anything, really. She's not really guilty of anything. But the *charge* was theft.

Miss Ridge. Theft?—Money?

Mrs. Waring. It was a ring. Miss Powers thinks that she took a ring. It does look awfully incriminating—the way it happened, but I'm perfectly sure—I asked Elfreda and she told me that she didn't.

Miss Ridge. Did Miss Waring have the ring?

Mrs. Waring. Yes, and it seems that no one else— Oh, but I don't want to go over all that again,—it's not *that* you came about.

Miss Powers. Apparently not. I believe you were going to tell us what you did come about.

Miss Ridge. Last night I got a call from a man I used to know when I was on the Herald. He wanted me to come to his office right away. I went over. Nobody there but him. Sitting at his desk with a lot of checks spread out in front of him. Paid checks. Bank statement;—you know. Now three thousand dollars doesn't mean *that* to him. [*Snap of the fingers.*] Got plenty. But doesn't like to be jipped out of anything,—even a nickel. He had three checks there,—a thousand apiece, made out to Cash. He can't remember writ-

ing them,—swears he didn't write them. His own signature.
So there you are. Puzzler, isn't it?

MISS POWERS. Miss Ridge, we are more puzzled than you are.
You have not yet told us why you came *here*.

MISS RIDGE. Oh, I was coming to that. [*Through the following
speech, she impersonates herself and the man, reproducing the
scene in direct discourse.*] I said, "If you didn't write those
checks, who did?" "*That*, my dear young lady, is what *you're*
supposed to tell me." "All right, who else can make your signature like that?" "Dunno, Professional forger, I guess."
"How about a secretary?" "What, do you mean—*my* secretary?" "Precisely." "Well, I'd hate to think—" "Generous
of you,—but think just the same." "M-m." [*Musing.*]
"Don't they sign your name to some of the letters?" "Yes."
"They imitate your signature, don't they?" "Yes, but they're
no good at it.—Hold on!—Last year I had a girl,—*uncanny*
the way she could write my signature." "Ah-ha, a clue," I
said, and there we sat looking out over the roofs of the city
from the top story of—

MISS POWERS. Just spare us the scenery, Miss Ridge, and tell
us the name of your—client.

MISS RIDGE. I was on the point of telling you the name of the
office building. Let's see,—how did I put it?—"looking out
over the roofs of the city from the top story of"—the Widener
Building.

ELFREDA. The Widener Building!

MISS RIDGE. Yes. But why did you ask?

ELFREDA. I used to work in the Widener Building.

MISS RIDGE. For Mr. Frank Mayhill?

ELFREDA. Yes, for Mr. Mayhill.

MISS RIDGE [*rising, speaking quite simply*]. Well, Miss Waring, I came here to ask you if you signed these checks.
[*She displays them.*]

ELFREDA [*simply, without confusion*]. Oh, no.

MISS RIDGE. You're quite sure?

ELFREDA. Yes, I'm *sure*.

MISS RIDGE. That's all I wanted to know,—that you didn't

do it. [*She pockets the checks and turns to* MISS POWERS.]
Please pardon the intrusion. Professional duty, you know.
Have to dig up another clue. It's going to be difficult, I'm
afraid. [*She turns toward the door.*] Well—good-by, everybody.

[*She is on the point of waving farewell, when* MISS POWERS
halts her.]

MISS POWERS [*rising*]. You're not going?

MISS RIDGE. What is there to stay for?

MISS POWERS. Of course, it's your own affair, but—

MISS RIDGE. Do you mean to suggest, Miss Powers, I have been
a bit hasty in my—

MISS POWERS. Of course, I haven't the slightest desire to in-
criminate Miss Waring, but—

MISS RIDGE. I quite understand. [*She turns to* ELFREDA.] Is it
true, Miss Waring, that while you were working for Mr.
Mayhill you learned to imitate his signature?

ELFREDA. Yes, I think I did it very well. He told me so once
himself.

MISS RIDGE. But it never occurred to you, of course, to take
one of his checks and sign his name,—

ELFREDA. Oh, no!

MISS RIDGE. That would be forgery. And the penalty for forgery, as you may know—

ELFREDA. I don't know *what* the penalty is, but I know I would
never think of doing that!

MISS RIDGE. To be sure. [*She scratches her head, turning
front.*] Well, there seems to be nothing more to say. [*To*
MISS POWERS, *naïvely.*] Do you have any suggestions?

MISS POWERS. Miss Ridge, I should like to see you alone for
a few minutes.

MISS RIDGE. Very well.

MISS POWERS [*crossing to the door, Right*]. Perhaps you two
will be good enough to wait in here. [*She opens the door.*
ELFREDA *goes out. As her mother is about to follow,* MISS
POWERS *stops her.*] On second thought—I'd like to have
you stay, if you will. [*She closes the door. The three women*

are left in the room.] Sit down, Mrs. Waring. [MRS. WARING *sits chair Center*, MISS RIDGE, *chair Left Center*. MISS POWERS *speaks in tones of confidence.*] I feel it my duty to tell you of a matter which I could not very well discuss before Miss Waring. You will find what I have to say hard to believe, Miss Ridge, and you, Mrs. Waring, still harder. But it is true, as I can prove to you, if necessary, by demonstration.

MRS. WARING. What *do* you mean?

MISS POWERS. Your daughter, Mrs. Waring, is an unconscious kleptomaniac.

MRS. WARING. Klepto—!

MISS POWERS. Hsh! It is a strange psychic condition, rarely known to the profession, one that *I* have never met before. She is a thief who does not know that she is a thief. This will account, you see, for her protestations of innocence. Her thieving has usually been petty, and I have put up with it, never supposing it would go as far as this. I was anxious to bring from her an admission of this last theft, hoping it would shock her into consciousness of her acts. It is a strange thing, and a very sad one.

MISS RIDGE. That's a new one!—*Unconscious* kleptomaniac.

MRS. WARING. But she never in her life—!

MISS RIDGE. Go on.

MRS. WARING. She never has done anything like that.

MISS RIDGE. That habit usually shows up early, doesn't it? Even in childhood.

MISS POWERS. It develops as the result of a strange and unfortunate inhibition,—when, perhaps, the release impulses have been thwarted, and the patient—

MISS RIDGE. Hold on. "The release impulses have been—" What was that again?

MISS POWERS. I said "thwarted."

MISS RIDGE. Oh, yes. [*Turning to* MRS. WARING.] Have you known any period in your daughter's life when her release impulses have been thwarted?

MRS. WARING. I—I'm afraid I don't know what you mean.

MISS RIDGE [*the irony is gentle*]. Mrs. Waring, you must think. Here is Miss Powers, an eminent psychologist, who is doing everything in her—what shall I say?—who is doing all she can to help you to understand your own daughter. How can you expect her to help unless you are willing to tell her what incident, or what person has thwarted her exhaust— [*correcting herself*] no, no,—her *release* impulses?

MRS. WARING. I *am* willing, but unless you will explain—

MISS RIDGE. Don't look at me. *I* didn't say it. It was—
    [*Gesture to* MISS POWERS.]

MISS POWERS [*not unhit, rising*]. If you don't care for the terminology, Miss Ridge, perhaps you would like to *see* what I mean.

MISS RIDGE [*rising, delighted*]. Splendid! [*Turning.*] Mrs. Waring, this is rare experience. We are about to see a demonstration of the inhibition of release impulses.

MISS POWERS [*firmly; having quite a struggle to inhibit her own release impulses!*] No! A demonstration of the mania itself.

MISS RIDGE. Oh. Do you mean—with Miss Waring as the object?

MISS POWERS. With Miss Waring as the *subject*,—yes.

MISS RIDGE. Oh, yes of course,—subject— Do you mean that you propose to—

MISS POWERS. To let Miss Waring commit a theft, before your very eyes.

MISS RIDGE. What!

MISS POWERS. You must hide so she won't see you. I'll put an alluring object, such as a piece of money or jewelry on the table. You will see her take it and then when she is questioned, you will hear her deny having done it.

MRS. WARING. It's not possible!

MISS POWERS. I shall show you.

MISS RIDGE [*to* MRS. WARING]. I can't believe it, either. But let's try it.

MRS. WARING. I know Elfreda will never do it!

Miss Ridge. Of course not. But then Miss Powers, herself, will be convinced. [*To her.*] Where shall we go?

Miss Powers. You will go into the living room for a few moments. Then when I come to the door and clear my throat, you will come and stand behind the portières.

Miss Ridge. And what is to be the—bait?

Miss Powers. Anything of value, jewelry, or—

Miss Ridge [*showing her hands*]. I've a gold coin here— [*She takes a small purse from a coat pocket.*] twenty dollars.

Miss Powers. Capital.

Miss Ridge [*she can't resist it*]. I'll say it's capital!—Where shall I put it?

Miss Powers. There on the desk.

Miss Ridge [*doing so*]. Now the stage is set. [*Crossing back.*] Come along, Mrs. Waring, we are the villains,—the spies. [*They start to exit Center.*] You'll clear your throat, will you?

Miss Powers. Yes, like this.

[*She does so.*]

Miss Ridge. I think we can hear that.

[*They exit Center. Left alone,* miss powers *surveys her scene. She crosses to the desk and takes from it the pencil, which she conceals on her person. Her course determined upon, she turns to the door, Right, opens it, and summons her subject.*]

Miss Powers. Miss Waring.

[elfreda *appears at the door.* miss powers *has crossed to Center.*]

Elfreda [*looking around*]. Where's mother?

Miss Powers. Close the door, please.

Elfreda [*anxiously*]. Where's mother?

Miss Powers. She's waiting. Come in, Elfreda, and close the door. [*The girl does so.*] Now, come here to me.

[*Not sternly.*]

Elfreda [*crossing*]. What is it? [*In distress.*] What do you want?

Miss Powers. Your head is aching. [elfreda *droops her head,*

and brings her hands to her eyes.] I want to relieve you. Sit
over there.

[*She indicates the easy-chair at Left.*]

ELFREDA. Oh, no, not that! Please! Just let me go. If I can
only get away! [MISS POWERS *looks firmly into her eyes,
and again indicates the chair. The protests are weaker now.*]
Please don't do it again! [*She crosses weakly to the chair.*]
I'd rather have a headache.—What is mother doing?

MISS POWERS. She will be here in a moment. Sit and wait.

[ELFREDA *relaxes and drops into the chair, which seems to
enfold her. Her head is thrown back and her eyes are closed.
There is an audible sigh.* MISS POWERS *passes her hands over
the girl's eyes. Presently she produces the pencil and holds
it in front of* ELFREDA'S *face, in a vertical position. When
she opens her eyes, she seems transfixed by the sight. Though
she protests with her voice, she yields with her eyes.*]

ELFREDA. Oh, no, no, please don't.

MISS POWERS [*starting to move the pencil slowly across the
path of the girl's vision*]. You will come out when I tap.

ELFREDA [*less vigorously*]. Oh, don't, please don't.

[*Her eyes are fixed.*]

MISS POWERS. Do you understand?—When I tap.

ELFREDA [*weakly*]. Yes.

[*The pencil continues to describe an arc before the eyes
of the increasingly helpless girl, who now leans forward
eagerly, with lips parted.*]

MISS POWERS. You are more comfortable now.

ELFREDA. Yes.

MISS POWERS. The pain has gone away.

ELFREDA. Yes.

MISS POWERS [*speaking in the rhythm of the pencil movements*]. To love, and to soothe, and to heal and caress, this is
the consummate blessedness.—Reply.

ELFREDA [*also in rhythm*]. Yes,—yes,—yes,—yes.

MISS POWERS. Now—rise. [ELFREDA *does so with the ready
obedience and implicit faith of a child.*] Sit again. [*She sits;*
MISS POWERS *crosses to the desk.*] In a moment I want you

to come here to this desk, take a book, sit down, and read. Then after you have read for a few moments, look up at me. I shall be reading over there. Then take this coin, do you see? —this gold coin, and slip it into your shoe, like this. [*She demonstrates; now she crosses to her again.*] Remember, Go to the desk. Read. Look up at me. Take the coin. Put it in your shoe. Then read the book again. Do you understand?

ELFREDA. Yes!

MISS POWERS. One moment. [*She goes to the door, Center, opens it, and clears her throat; she turns back.*] Now rise. [ELFREDA *rises.*] Now go.

[*As the girl crosses,* MISS POWERS *turns the easy-chair to face left, sits in it, and takes up a magazine to read.* MISS RIDGE *and* MRS. WARING *appear behind the portières. They see* ELFREDA *sit at the desk and take up a book. She gazes into the book, then looks up to* MISS POWERS. *She looks at the gold coin. She takes it and slips it into her shoe. She returns to the book.*

[MISS POWERS, *out of the corner of her eyes, watches the execution of her commands. Now she taps with the pencil on the wood of her chair, and crosses at once to Center, with the result that the observers do not see the change in* ELFREDA'S *expression as she comes out of the trance.*

[*The girl's hands go to her face, and a shudder passes over her body.* MISS POWERS *now crosses to her.*]

MISS POWERS. I'll call your mother.

ELFREDA. Yes! Where is mother? [*She rises.*] Can we go now? Oh, I wish we could go home.

[MISS POWERS *has crossed to Center;* ELFREDA *follows her.*]

MISS POWERS. I am entirely willing that you should go. It is Miss Ridge who has detained you. [*She turns to door Center.*] Oh, you are here. Come in. [*As they enter,* MISS POWERS *crosses to her desk.*] It is sometimes more convincing to have the evidence of one's own eyes.

ELFREDA [*Right Center to her mother, who remains dumbfounded just inside the door*]. She says we may go now!

MRS. WARING. But Elfreda,—you told me—

ELFREDA. Mother! Don't look that way!

MISS POWERS. One moment. Before you go, Miss Waring, let me ask if you have seen anything of a gold coin that was here on the desk.

ELFREDA [*to her*]. A gold coin?—No.

MISS POWERS [*Right*]. There was a twenty-dollar gold piece here on the desk this afternoon.

ELFREDA [*Right Center*]. You're not accusing me!

MISS POWERS. I am simply stating the fact. Miss Ridge will testify that she saw the coin here; it has disappeared within the last few minutes.

ELFREDA. Miss Powers,—I did not see a gold coin, and I did not take one. If you are accusing me, all I can say is that you are mistaken. Please let me go from here. You are trying to make a thief of me at every turn.

MISS POWERS. You may go, as far as I am concerned. But I suspect that Miss Ridge will have something to say first.

MISS RIDGE [*Left Center. To* ELFREDA]. Tell me, have your wages been paid you in full?

ELFREDA. What do you mean?

MISS RIDGE. Does Miss Powers owe you any wages—any money?

ELFREDA. Why, no.

MISS RIDGE. What were your wages here?

ELFREDA. Twenty dollars a week.

MISS RIDGE. Did she not owe you a week's wages?

MISS POWERS. I paid Miss Waring in full this morning.

MISS RIDGE [*to* MISS POWERS]. Please. [*To* ELFREDA.] There was nothing owing you?

ELFREDA. No.

MISS RIDGE. Then why did you take a twenty-dollar gold piece from the desk just now?

ELFREDA [*gasping*]. Why—I—I didn't!

MISS RIDGE. But I saw you. It was a mean advantage to take and I am sorry. But I was watching from that doorway, and I saw you.

ELFREDA. You *saw* me—?

Miss Ridge. Yes.

Elfreda. But I didn't take it! I haven't seen it!

Miss Ridge [*crossing to Right Center.*] My dear girl, don't deny it. I saw you. Your mother saw you. You took the coin and put it into your slipper.

Elfreda. Into my slipper!—But I don't know what you mean! I haven't seen a gold coin.

Miss Ridge. Take off your right slipper. [*She holds her arm. The girl does so and stares into the shoe.*] What do you see?

Elfreda. But *I* didn't do it!

Miss Ridge. Come now, that's too much. We saw you. We all saw you. And now you deny it. [*She takes the slipper, and regains her coin.*] I was trying to help you, but this is too much. [elfreda *collapses;* miss ridge *turns just in time to catch her.* mrs. waring *comes to her and helps support her to the chair Center.*] Say you did it. Come along, it will ease your mind.

[miss ridge *makes it her business to restore the girl's slipper to her foot.*]

Elfreda [*sobbing*]. I—I guess I must have. I don't remember!

Miss Ridge. That's better. Now then, the other business. Keep your mind clear and tell the truth. You'll find that it pays,—with me.—You have told me that you were expert at reproducing Mr. Mayhill's signature. I should like to see you do it. [*She takes a notebook from her pocket, and seems to be feeling for a pen.*] Here, this will do— [*She crosses to desk and takes up the checkered pencil, and is about to hand it to* elfreda.] Now do the best you can, please.

Elfreda. No, no, not that.

[*She shrinks back in horror.*]

Miss Ridge [*Right Center*]. What's the matter?

Elfreda [*Center*]. Not that! I couldn't do it with that!

Miss Ridge. What's the matter with it? [*She looks at the pencil.*] Does look sort of funny doesn't it? Oh, Miss Powers, may I see the ring you said was stolen.

Miss Powers. I am not wearing it just at present.

Miss Ridge. No, I noticed that. Would you mind getting it?

Miss Powers. If you need to see it.

[*She crosses up Center.*]

Miss Ridge. I should like to. [miss powers *goes out Center.* miss ridge *speaks to* elfreda *with increased earnestness.*] Now, if you want me to help you, tell me the truth. It's your one chance.

Elfreda. I will!

Miss Ridge [*Right Center. Taking her hand*]. Don't you remember putting that coin into your shoe? Answer me as you would your mother.

Elfreda [*Center. Eagerly*]. No, I don't. I didn't do it!

Mrs. Waring [*Left Center. In agony*]. Elfreda!

Miss Ridge [*restraining her*]. No, no, please.—Now these checks. Think. Don't you remember signing Mr. Mayhill's name to these checks?—Look at me, Elfreda.

Elfreda. No. I'm sure I didn't do it.

Miss Ridge [*taking her hand*]. And the ring. You didn't take the ring either, did you?

Elfreda. No!

Miss Ridge. I believe you!

Elfreda. Oh, thank you!

Miss Ridge. Now this pencil— [elfreda *shudders and turns away.*] Don't worry. This is the last of it. [*She breaks it in two in her hands.*] There!

Elfreda [*standing. In relief*]. Oh!

Miss Ridge. Tell me,—why do you have such a horror of it?

Elfreda [*in anguish*]. Oh, I can't tell you. It's . . . it's . . .

Miss Ridge [*passing a broken piece in front of her eyes*]. Was it like this?

Elfreda. Yes! Yes! [*She crosses and throws herself into chair, Left Center.*]

Miss Ridge. Eureka! Eureka!

Mrs. Waring. What is it?

Miss Ridge [*crossing to telephone on desk*]. Don't you remember the old story about Archimedes and the bathtub? [*To the telephone.*] Baring 8343.

Mrs. Waring. I—I don't understand.

Miss Ridge [*in high spirits*]. You know! Specific gravity, and all that sort of thing. [*To the telephone.*] Give me the chief, please. [*To* mrs. waring.] Or was it Newton?—No that was the apple. This was the bathtub. [*To the telephone.*] Hello, Chief?—This is Aunt Susan. Well, I cracked it. . . . No, no, it wasn't the girl after all. [mrs. waring *goes to* elfreda, *Left Center.*] I could see that the minute I looked at her. It was the old lady herself. [*At this point* miss powers *returns at center door and stands in mute astonishment, ill concealed;* miss ridge *goes on.*] Believe it or not.—Well it was this way,—it seems that she had the girl hypped—waved a pencil in front of her eyes, cast a spell over her, and made her do the dirty work.—Sounds like a story book, doesn't it? Wait till the Herald gets hold of this! Don't you see? She hypnotized the girl and made her sign the checks, and then when the breeze began to blow the wrong way, tried to get rid of her by making her do a little theft, accusing her of it, and driving her off— Yes, nick of time. [miss ridge *has not looked up on the entrance of the other woman; she continues.*] What's that?—Oh, she's right here.—No, right here in the room. I'm speaking from her 'phone.—Chief! I'm surprised at you.—Ladies don't fight.—Oh, no,—no wagon, we'll come in a taxi.—No, not a chance. There won't be any trouble. Besides, Chief, she's a woman of judgment.

[*These last lines are spoken slowly and end the conversation; she replaces the telephone, and looks pleasantly at her prey, as*

THE CURTAIN FALLS

TOAST AND TEA

A PLAY ABOUT THE BOSTON TEA PARTY

BY

ALEXANDER DEAN

A NON-ROYALTY PLAY

THE CAST

HENRY HARPER
ARTIE DINWIDDIE
HEZEKIAH HALL
BENJAMIN EDES
HENRY PURKETT
GEORGE HEWES
PETER EDES
FRANCIS ROTCH
CAPTAIN O'CONNER
COLONISTS *and* MOHAWKS

THE SCENE

The stern deck of the ship, "The Dartmouth," lying alongside Griffin's Wharf, Boston. A late afternoon, the sixteenth of December, 1773.

At the rear, rises the highly built stern with the British Flag waving on high. On the right is the side of the boat, beyond which is the open sea. The rail is solid and no water can be seen. On the left is the shipside that borders the wharf. An opening in this, a third of the distance from the footlights to the back, allows a gang-plank to form an exit, but merely a few steps down this carries one off stage. A small chest, familiarly known as "half chest," of tea, rests down stage from the entrance. On the up-stage side is a lantern hung to the rail. In the center of the stage rises the mizzenmast, but this towers out of sight, allowing only a bit of loosely hanging sail to drop near it just before it becomes indiscernible to the audience. At the foot of this is another half chest of tea. All about the deck and piled high are chests. Behind these in the

*very rear is a hatchway which is used and spoken of as an exit,
but is not seen. The chests are mostly arranged on the right-
hand side and back part of the stage. There are two specific
arrangements of these chests and except for these they may be
arranged to suit the stage manager. Firstly a passage must
be kept free around the right hand side of the deck. Secondly
a small formation known as the coop, seen by the audience but
not by the actors. It is between center stage and the right rail.
This coop is down stage near the footlights and is formed by
boxes of tea, resting on top of one another so as to form a
hiding place.*

THE CHARACTERS AND COSTUMES

HENRY HARPER *and* ARTIE DINWIDDIE, *seamen of the ship,
"The Dartmouth" are short, chunky and strong in their
bodies but are stupid and simple in their ideas and emotions.
They are sunburned and have small beards. They wear such
costumes as old salts would wear today. Big boots, flannel
shirts, mackinaws.*

HEZEKIAH HALL, *captain of "The Dartmouth" is a tall, fat,
pompous English sea captain. He wears similar clothes but
they are in better condition and are more suggestive of an old
uniform than of old clothes.*

BENJAMIN EDES, *a colonist, is severe, ponderous and large.*

HENRY PLUNKETT, *a colonist, is tall, thin, and lugubrious.*

GEORGE HEWES, *a colonist, is short, fat and jovial.*

PETER EDES, *14-year-old son of* BENJAMIN EDES, *is strong,
short and sturdy,—fast in movement and mind. He is a typical colonist,—bold, outspoken and brave. Characteristically
of the period he knows what America is passing through and
appreciates vitally and enjoys keenly the significance and importance of life at this time.*

FRANCIS ROTCH, *an Englishman, owner of "The Dartmouth,"
is middle-aged and refined.*

At the rise of the curtain HENRY HARPER *is swabbing the deck at the left, and* ARTIE DINWIDDIE *is sitting on a chest of tea, Center, mending rope.*

HENRY HARPER [*sniffling*]. H'a bloody job this, h'awashin', h'an' h'ascrubbin', h'an' h'aswabbin' this ere deck naow, when the good Lord h'ain't stopped h'adoin' h'it for a hull day—for the hull four h'an' twinty 'ours!

ARTIE DINWIDDIE. Five h'an' twinty, Enery.

HARPER. Four h'an' twinty in the day, h'I says.

DINWIDDIE [*proudly*]. Five h'an' twinty, h'I says, h'an' h'ain't h'I your bo'sun?

HARPER. Yes, but—

DINWIDDIE. H'an' don't your bo'sun know more'n you wot h'is h'only h'a common seaman?

HARPER. Yes—but—

DINWIDDIE. H'an' h'I says there be five h'an' twinty, don't h'I?

HARPER. Five h'an' twinty h'it h'is, sir; h'an' h'it's rained h'every wan of 'em h'in this God-forsaken country.

DINWIDDIE. You want to be a bo'sun some day, don't you, Enery? [*With grand air.*] Then learn to respect the learnin' o' your superiors.

HARPER [*sniffling*]. Rain h'an' Christmas! Christmas, h'an' we h'ain't 'ome yet!

DINWIDDIE. The king h'an' gov'nur h'is all too good to 'em.

HARPER [*blubbering*]. They h'act like we didn't h'own 'em. H'I 'ope the tea rots like h'it do in Charleston or chokes 'em dead. Curse me h'ef h'I don't!

DINWIDDIE [*sneering*]. H'a lot o' good their guard over there do 'em. [*He looks off Left.*]

HARPER [*simpering*]. I'd knock their puny faces further h'in then they is naow—h'I would.

DINWIDDIE [*fiercely*]. No, you wouldn't!

HARPER [*boldly*]. H'an' w'y not?

DINWIDDIE. Cos, I'd do h'it h'afore you.

[*They work a moment in silence. The ship's clock below strikes six o'clock or four bells, ship time.*]

HARPER. H'Artie, did you h'ever see wan o' them h'Injuns?

DINWIDDIE. Douzins.

HARPER. Wot they look like?

DINWIDDIE. H'all red h'an' wild like.

HARPER. H'ain't they h'awful?

DINWIDDIE. Be so to mos', but h'ain't to me.

HARPER. 'Onest, h'ain't you h'afeared?

DINWIDDIE. Nop—not h'Artie Dinwiddie. W'y, ef warn was to step 'is foot h'on this 'ere brig, h'I—h'I—

[*At this moment, footsteps are heard coming up the gang-plank.*]

DINWIDDIE. Oh, Lor', wot's that? [*He hides behind a chest Right.*]

HARPER [*hiding also Right*]. H'Injuns, p'r'aps!

DINWIDDIE. You look, Enery.

HARPER. No. You look, h'Artie.

DINWIDDIE. I dasent.

[CAPTAIN HEZEKIAH HALL *enters up the gang-plank.*]

HALL [*bellowing*]. OO-HOO! OO-HOO!—Helloa there—Helloa!

HARPER [*weakly; from behind the chest*]. Aye, aye, Cap'em.

DINWIDDIE [*relieved*]. Oh-h-h-h.

HALL. You lazy lubber, you—

DINWIDDIE [*humbly*]. Aye, aye, cap'em. [*He comes forth from behind the chest.*]

HALL. Wot you hidin' from?

HARPER [*to* DINWIDDIE, *as he also emerges from his hiding place, and continues his work*]. Oh, h'I say, h'Artie, h'I thought you wasn't h'afeared.

DINWIDDIE. H'I—h'I was—h'I was jesta—jesta testin' 'ow good h'a bo'sun you'd be.

HALL. 'Idin' from your work, is it?—well, I'll learn you. [*He swings off to hit* DINWIDDIE *with his cane but* DINWIDDIE *dodges and jumps to his rope and braids the frayed ends wildly.*] W'y are the lamps, fore an' aft, larboard an' starboard lit, an' this one ain't? Eh? [*He points to the lantern fastened at the head of the gang-plank.* DINWIDDIE *lights this.*]

HALL. Anythink been 'ere?

DINWIDDIE [*humbly*]. No, sir.

HALL. Ain't Rotch brung back the passport, for our sailin', from the gov'nur?

DINWIDDIE. 'Ow could he, sir, when nothink h'ain't been 'ere, sir?

HALL [*yelling*]. Silence!!! [*Troubled in mind, he stalks about the deck.*]

HARPER. Please, sir, wot did the meetin' decide, sir?

HALL [*sharply*]. Wot meetin'?

HARPER. Will they let h'us take the tea back, sir, so's we will be 'ome by Twelfth Night, sir?

HALL. W'y ask me? How do I know? Blamed fools, don't know themselves. They sit up there in the Old South Meetin' House from ten this mornin', aspeechin', an' apreachin'. They adjourned till three, then agin at half atter four—an' they be agabbin' since. Always sech talk. Nothink kin make out wot they say—all parlimentary, an' court-like, an' dry. Dry as toast, I calls it. All about their rights.

HARPER. Their rights, sir? Don't the king own 'em?

HALL [*turning sharply on him*]. Course he do. [*Marching up and down.*] Thought they'd try an' force Rotch to take the tea back to Lunnon. Well, they can't. H'it's heresy agin God Almighty, agin his chosen king, George the third. [*To DINWIDDIE.*] Is their guard there?

DINWIDDIE [*without looking*]. Yes, sir.

HARPER [*looking off to the left*]. No, cap'n, h'it h'ain't. H'it h'ain't.

HALL. It ain't! There! What'd I say? Don't like it. There's trouble; trouble I tell you. I smell it.

HARPER. H'an' h'all day, sir, twos h'an' threes has come down to the wharf h'an' looked to h'us like we had the leprosy.

HALL. They did, ey? Wot did they do?

HARPER. They pointed, h'an' whispered, h'an' whispered—

HALL [*yelling.*] Silence!

HARPER. Aye, sir.

HALL. Get below, you numskulls—below in the hold, crawl

shoreward, an' up to the bow hatch. Then fasten it tight from below.

DINWIDDIE [*humbly*]. But, Cap'n, it will take us till Christmas.

HALL. Do as you're told, an' clear out o' my sight, you idiots. [*He drives them down the hatchway behind the chests, and follows them himself.*]

[*From behind the chests on the extreme Right,* BENJAMIN EDES, *stepping lightly, crosses to the gang-plank, and makes a large beckon. He then crosses to the hatchway and watches it closely.* HENRY PURKETT *and* GEORGE HEWES *appear up the plank Left.*]

EDES [*crossing to them*]. Speak low, and remember if we are apprehended—we are here to persuade the captain to sail back without the permit from Hutchinson.

HEWES [*Left*]. We need not stay long with you. [*Rubbing his hands in expectancy.*] Everything is going superbly.

PURKETT [*Left. As from the grave*]. On the contrary all is wrong.

HEWES. Well, above two score have already signed the paper and have consented to be prepared for action. Concerning you?

EDES. Things here are simple. Mostly arranged as we imagined. The only way to board is by this plank. Here, the hatch, that leads below to all the quarters, and still further below to the hold, wherein lies the tea. The hold stretches forward to the bow, and there another hatch connects more directly the main deck and the chests. But the way is difficult to find and just now Hall has ordered this forward hatch to be fastened from below.

PURKETT. You have done a fair bit of task, brother Edes.

EDES. And so I ought, for 'tis nearly two hours that I've hid and ducked and sneaked among these chests to find what little I know. Tell this all to the men.

PURKETT. You can do so yourself, Edes, for Gill says for you to leave here and go to your shop and remain there with the Mohawks.

HEWES. While I go to the meeting and wait for Rotch to return. Then I, upon the words of Rotch or rather upon some few that Samuel Adams may deem wise to add, will let loose a wild unearthly whoop—that to be the sign for you to allow the braves to sally forth.

EDES. Suppose, by chance, this Rotch should bring back the passport?

PURKETT. He won't. The good never happens.

EDES [*sharply in quick retort*]. Don't be a fool.

HEWES. Tut, tut, children, tut, tut. The fool speaks—let wise men listen. One whoop with the passport; two, without. Like this— [*He starts to show them.*]

EDES. You are the fool. Would you scare up these English pigs and have them find us in their sty.

[*At the gang-plank appears* PETER EDES. *He carries an unlit lantern in one hand, and in the other, waves on high two pieces of paper.*]

PETER [*in a loud whisper*]. Pup, oh, pup!

EDES. Sh-h-h, would you loose all with your piping pate?

PETER [*jumping up and down and crying in a loud whisper*]. But, pup, pup!

EDES [*impatient*]. Yes, yes—

PETER. Mr. Gill sent this to you. [*Holding out one of the two sheets of paper.*] It's the signatures of citizens who have volunteered.

EDES [*signifying to the men that this is just what it is.*] Why did he send this to me?

PETER. Pup, ask me.

HEWES. How should I know?

PURKETT. Something bad, I know.

PETER. I guess it's because he didn't want to be caught with it on him in case the king's men got 'spicious and captured him, and searched the shop, and you, and all the Indians.

PURKETT. So that's what you guess?

PETER. Yes, sir, and you want to know why I guess it?

EDES. Don't guess.

PETER. No, sir. I'll think. I think so, because I heard him say to

Paul Revere, "The unfortunate that gets caught with this tell-tale will get the devil," and then he gave it me for you.

EDES. Eh? What? He did, he did?

[HEWES *and* PURKETT *laugh.* EDES *folds the list of names and tucks it in his belt.*]

PURKETT. And what's this other paper you have?

PETER. He gave it me as a present, for bringing the other. Isn't it dandy? I haven't had a piece of paper as good as this since last Christmas.

PURKETT. I hope you're going to put it to some good use, child, and not squander it in idle play.

PETER. Yes, pup, I'm going to write Betsy Warren that if she doesn't stop her mother from drinking tea and make her become a Daughter of Liberty, I'll take Hannah Mercy for my best sweetheart. [*The men laugh.* PETER *folds the piece of paper carefully and places it in his outer pocket.*]

EDES. Come, we must be off, or we'll be surprised. All's settled finely.

HEWES. Fine as silk. Let's away.

PURKETT. On the contrary, all is wrong.

HEWES. Aren't we prepared for action?

PURKETT. Again you speak of action. Again you mean violence. Well, I shall stay here and see no violence is done.

EDES. It is a small matter. But let it please you. You may notify us the time you think it safe to strike.

PURKETT. You speak as if that had not been in my head, the while.

PETER. Pup—oh, pup. Let me stay with him!

EDES. Silence, child, be seen and not heard.

HEWES. You act, Brother Purkett, as if this ship was yours, and you could lounge at leisure.

EDES. As we now do at great risk.

PURKETT. If I encounter one, I'll engage him in converse.

EDES. Oh, no, you won't. If you remain, you'll hide until the whoops are given and then upon convenience give me, at the shop, a signal from here.

PETER [*jumping up and down*]. Please, pup, please let me!

EDES. No—no—no— We'll leave the lantern, the lad brought, and you after lighting it lower it over the rail there.

PETER. So, pup? [*He lowers the lantern over the left railing between the gang-plank and the audience.*]

EDES. Aye, Purkett, as the lad does so; and we'll see it from the shop.

HEWES [*he has been investigating the chests of tea*]. Imagine Brother Henry hidden in here! [*He signifies the coop.*]

EDES. That's where he must sit.

PETER. Let me try. I can squat there.

PURKETT. You speak as if there were some doubt of my— [PURKETT *backs into the coop, and sits, but his head and shoulders are in the open and his feet stick out into plain sight.*]

PETER. I know the signal.

EDES. Your head, oh, your head!

HEWES. It always spoils everything.

PURKETT [*crossing away from the coop*]. It's not necessary for such concealment.

PETER [*crawling in and smuggly sitting entirely out of sight*]. Pup, see me. I can hide!

EDES [*to* PURKETT]. Excuse me, but it is. [*Off stage*, HALL's *lumbering voice, "You numskulls—you lazy clouts!"*] Hall comes. We must be off!

PETER. Pup, see me; let me stay!

EDES. No. Come!

HEWES. 'Low the lad to stay. He'll do as good a bit as Brother Henry could.

EDES. No.

HALL [*off stage but nearer*]. I'll fix you, I'll fix you!

EDES. I agree, boy, but remember the signals.

PETER. One whoop with the pass; two, without. [HEWES *exits down the gang-plank.*] If it's one, I'll slip away quiet-like. If it's two, then when the coast is clear, I'll dip the lighted lantern over so. [*He repeats the signal with the unlit lantern.*] And you'll see it from the shop.

PURKETT. Don't forget, you youngster, for I'll take good care that they'll not come unless you assure us there's no force here to cause great violence. [*He exits.*]

EDES. Good luck, my boy, don't lose your head and make a fuddle, but achieve a task well worthy of a colonist.

[EDES *turns to go.* HALL *appears at the top of the hatchway, calling back, "You blundering, blustering bumpkins." The list of names slips from* EDES' *belt onto the deck.* EDES *is just stooping to pick it up when* HALL *turns and sees him.*]

HALL. Hello, hello, there!

EDES [*keeps an eye on the paper, but giving his attention to* HALL *so as not to make him suspicious*]. Captain Hall? [*He looks at* PETER *and then at the paper.*]

HALL. The very one. [PETER *almost panic-stricken emerges from the coop and crawls around the right side of the deck behind the chests and then up from the rear.*]

EDES. I'm Benjamin Edes, of Edes and Gill, printers. [*He sees* PETER *and senses that he is intent upon rescuing the lists.*] Our shop, at the head of this wharf. [*He points off at the place between the gang-plank and the audience, to his left.* HALL *steps up to the rail.*] You can see from here. Just lean over a bit.

[HALL *suspicious—leans over gingerly.* PETER *crawls up, takes the paper and retreats back, and returns to his coop by circling around the right of the chests. When he arrives, he holds the list in his hand and listens intently.*]

HALL. Well, s'pose I kin.

EDES. Captain Hall, by sunrise tomorrow, the revenue officers in the ordinary course of events and law, will board this ship and unload the cargo of one hundred and fourteen chests of tea.

HALL. I've heard o' that. Also that the consignees won't resign as you hoped for.

EDES. The consignees will go to the customs house and pay the tax and duty.

HALL. An' the king's scheme will be crowned with success.

EDES. I beg to differ. That will never happen.

HALL. An' w'y not, pray?

EDES. Violence, sir, violence. The colonists will settle affairs to suit themselves, sooner than bow thusly to the tyrant. The guard will fire on you if you attempt to unload the tea by force.

HALL. God is on our side, an' will punish you rebels!

EDES. To avoid violence—I have been asked by a group of citizens to ask you to consider—supposing the Governor refuses Mr. Rotch the passport for returning the cargo to England —to consider setting sail without it.

HALL. If I would, I could not, for you know that the ship cannot pass the castle without a permit from Gov'nur Hutchinson.

EDES. Won't you try another channel?

HALL. Adm'r'l Montague has placed these vessels under his command an' will stop it.

EDES. Come, you don't mean to imply he would fire on you?

HALL. I cannot.

EDES. But think of the violence!

HALL. You speak like one wot knows too much.

EDES. I know the colonists and I should think you would by now.

HALL. I cannot.

EDES. Remember the colonists have given you warning, and a chance to escape. The blood of any struggle be upon your soul!

HALL. I cannot without a passport.

EDES. You won't?

HALL. I won't.

[*A pause. It is all that* EDES *can do to control himself. He turns and crosses to the head of the gang-plank.*]

HALL. An' naow, good evenin' to you, Mister Edes, of Edes an' Gill, printers, the establishment wot kin be seen from here. Good evenin'.

[EDES *turns and looks at* PETER *who helplessly holds out the list; but* EDES *turns and exits down the plank.* HALL *stands looking out.* PETER, *nervous and upset, sees that there is nothing to do but keep the list, so he folds it carefully and start-*

ing to put it in his outer pocket, changes and places it in his inner pocket. HALL *turns and on the look-out for more suspicious persons walks to the Center and towards the coop where* PETER *tries to be more inconspicuous. Enter up the gang-plank, a middle-aged man in colonist costume. He is very much in a hurry and runs into* HALL. *It is* ROTCH.]

HALL [*yelling in his customary bullying manner*]. Hey? Wot, blockhead?—

ROTCH. Beg pardon. Beg pardon.

HALL [*very humbly*]. Mister Rotch! Excuse me most particularly, sir. I ought to hev looked to what I was asaying.

ROTCH. All my fault, Hall.

HALL. Not yours, sir. [*Bowing meekly.*] Your humble servant's.

ROTCH. The die is cast. This morning on a mere chance, but willing for any possibility to avoid a clash, I tried the Customs House again for a clearance, and that being refused, I applied at the colonist's request to the Governor.

HALL. Yes, yes?

ROTCH. Hutchinson has thrown down the gauntlet and flatly refused the passport.

HALL. Bless me, you don't say!

ROTCH. Refused the passport until the vessel has been regularly cleared out for sailing.

HALL. You ain't agoin' to their bloody meetin'?

ROTCH. Right away. I just dropped here first to warn you to be on the lookout for any suspicious actions. Everything been safe?

HALL [*very positive*]. Yes, sir; I was just agoin' to say with me here, everythink is secure, sir.

ROTCH. Well, I'm worried. I know there's trouble.

HALL [*anxious at all costs to agree with his master*]. I was just agoin' to say, sir, I think there's trouble brewin'.

ROTCH. I saw three men in converse go shoreward on this wharf.

HALL. I've seen 'em too—thousands o' 'em. They was here, atryin' to force an' bribe me to sail.

ROTCH. Not bribe?

HALL. Offered me a hundred pounds, sir. I reckon they wanted the Castle to fire on us—an' ruin us, an' they not be liable for it. Naow I have a feelin' they're agoin' to burn the ship.

ROTCH. Nonsense, Hall. They're dead set against the tea, but not the ship.

HALL. I was just agoin' to say, sir, them was my very sentiments. The colonists don't mean bad, do you think so, Mr. Rotch?

ROTCH. Not at all.

HALL. No. I don't think so either.

ROTCH. There are too many men of property active in their meetings—Hancock, Phillips, Howe, and Adams. You don't think one of them are about here spying?

HALL. Lor', sir, impossible. W'y a body couldn't come within five an' twenty feet of this 'ere ship without me scentin' 'em. An' as for their bein' 'ere naow, I'd know it quick.

[*Poor* PETER *is scared.*]

ROTCH. Where's the crew?

HALL. Below, sir. Every mother's son o' 'em.

ROTCH. Just you keep a sharp lookout for spies. Don't be afraid of violence to the ship, but *watch that tea.* [*He exits down the plank.*]

[*The ship's clock strikes five bells.* PETER, *who for the past scenes has been listening attentively, becomes too much interested, and in his eagerness leans too far to one side. The chests lose their balance and tumble with* PETER, *sprawling in their midst.* HALL *rushes forward and faces* PETER, *before he rises.*]

HALL [*bellowing*]. Oo-ho, young feller!

PETER [*mimicking him*]. Oo-ho, old man!

HALL. Blast me, ef I don't cut the heart out o' you same like I would the eye of a pertater. [PETER *casually rises and brushes himself.*] Wot's your object 'ere?

PETER. Just wanted to see the ship Dartmouth, got aboa'd by curiosity in my inspection and heard you come, so hid.

HALL. 'Spect me to believe that?

PETER. I was going ashore just as soon as all was silent, the men not about, as it was before you came.

HALL. You be, be yer?

PETER. Yes, I be.

HALL. Naow, quite providential, first an' las', I see ye. Wot be your name?

PETER [*a moment's hesitation*]. Jack Sprat.

HALL. You young imp, I'll crack yer agin a stanchion, an' heave yer overboard.

PETER. 'Spect me to believe that?

HALL [*after a slight pause, he changes his tone to coaxing*]. Don't want to buy any tea, do yer, young gen'l'm'n? I'll sell yer as little or as much as yer want.

PETER. You must think we colonists aren't in earnest. Your stupid king can't realize we're fighting for our rights.

HALL. I'll sell you this 'ere tea plus the tax cheaper 'en you kin buy it in Lunnon.

PETER. No, you won't.

HALL. W'y not, sir?

PETER. Well, if your just tyrant gave it me free, and all's I had to do was to pay the tax, I wouldn't carry it home.

HALL. It's cheaper than the vile stuff you're smugglin' from the Dutch.

PETER. See here, old man, we colonists are fighting for a principle. We're not looking for a bargain in groceries.

HALL. Well, young chap, ef you ain't willin' ter commit yourself an' you ain't 'ere ter buy tea, it's jest as I thought— you're 'ere for spyin'.

PETER. And for what should I be spying?

HALL. That's just it, w'y? [PETER *laughs.*] Bloomin' funny, ain't it?

PETER. Yes.

HALL. Wot is, you spalpeen?

PETER. It's funny to think that you think that I'm going to tell you what I think.

HALL. Wot makes you act so? Wot makes you hate us English?

PETER. I don't hate you English, none of us do. Why, we people

of the colonies are descendants of Englishmen. We inherit
our ideas and principles from you just as we do our blood and
life.

HALL. You're disloyal.

PETER. Do you call it disloyal to fight for England in the
French and Indian Wars? Didn't we give our best men and
tax ourselves for our mother country then?

HALL. But these 'ere taxes are a tiny think. Won't mount to
more than three hundred pounds a year.

PETER. Petty quarrels it is, sir, but as Samuel Adams says, "No
taxation without representation."

HALL. Come naow, I'll fix it with yer fine. Blow me ef I don't.
[*He shakes some coins in his pocket.*] How much do you
name?

PETER. Oh, so you want to buy my secret?

HALL. Say the price.

PETER. A feller my age can spend an awful lot of money.

HALL. A shilling. Are they after the ship, or the tea?

PETER. You said you would make it worth my while.

HALL. Make it a sov'ren. Are they after the ship, or the tea?

PETER [*scornfully*]. A sov'ren!

HALL. Blow me, a pound. But not a penny more. Is it the ship
or the tea? Come naow. [PETER *jumps up and down in his excitement.*] Two pounds. Tell me, lad. [*No answer.*] The ship
or the tea, or—or—or— [PETER *roars with laughter.*] Good
lor', bye, don't say it's me they're after, not me, Hezekiah
Hall, not me. [*He takes* PETER'S *hand and forces a bag of
coins into it.*] 'Ere, take this, but jest tell me ef it's me
they're after. [PETER *looks at the bag in his hands, then smiles
contemptuously.*]

PETER. Say, old man, let me tell you something straight. Don't
you ever think a real American will sell his country. [*He
throws the bag at* HALL.] We're not made that way.

HALL [*picking up the bag*]. Lor', bye, how you kin talk. You're
a reg'lar American!

PETER. You've suppressed our free commerce, you've entered
and searched our homes at your pleasure, and have forbidden

public meetings and free speech. You treat us like foreigners and slaves.

HALL. Give me a chance to get ashore afore they come.

PETER. Know this, old man—a free people aren't obliged to support a tyrant who destroys liberty.

HALL. Who's learned you all this wot I can't understand?

PETER. My pup taught it me by rote, but in heart and spirit Samuel Adams did, and John Hancock and William Warren did, and all the colonists do.

HALL. Bye, I asks you 'umbly [*he kneels*] ef it's me they're atter?

PETER. And the privilege of fighting a tyrant and preserving democracy, at least in this part of the world, is given to the people.

HALL. Don't speak so learned, bye, so learned an' parlimentary, an' dry—dry as toast I calls it, an' jest as hard to swallow.

[*In the distance two long, drawn-out Indian war-whoops are heard.* HALL *exclaims "Wot's that?" and jumps up.*]

PETER. Not you, old man, they're not after you. There's bigger fish in the sea than you.

[HALL *examines the intense excitement of the boy who fetches his lantern from the chests, takes out a flint and lights it. During this:*]

HALL. And you knowed it all the time?

PETER. I reckon I did. [*He walks to the plank, but* HALL *blocks his exit.*]

HALL. Where baound?

PETER. What do you mean?

HALL. There's bigger fish in the sea than me, is there? Well, I'll learn you that there's as good fish in the sea as has ever come out of it. [*Roaring.*] Put down that light!

PETER. You let me go!

HALL. Mabbe I will, an' mabbe I won't!

PETER [*running to the gang-plank*]. You dasent keep me here.

[HALL *grabs the lantern and places it down stage from the exit.*]

HALL. You ain't purtendin' you thought you was agoin' ter hev me floppin' without payin' for it?

PETER. Well, you won't have to let me go. [*He grabs for his lantern, but* HALL *intercepts him. He stands away with his back to* HALL *trying to gather his poor shattered wits.*]

HALL. Bein' kept 'ere, I guess, rayther makes you slack an' ruffle like a sail when you luff ship.

PETER. You coward, you—

HALL. Naow tell me what's goin' on?

PETER. Never. Look! LOOK! What's that? [*He points directly behind* HALL, *who starts and turns with his back to the lantern.* PETER *makes a dive for it, but* HALL *is quick and keeps on turning and reaches the lantern first. He throws back the lad violently.*]

HALL. Tryin' to get clever, be ye? I'll stop this gallopin' with you an' shut you up in the hold w'ile you tell me wot's up.

PETER [*calling*]. Pup, oh, pup!

HALL. You've no call to shout.

PETER [*jumping up on a chest and using his hands as a megaphone*]. Pup—Mr. Gill—

HALL. Mr. Gill, is it? Edes and Gill, the printer's shop wot kin be seen from here. Seen an' heard?

PETER. Yes. Heard.

HALL. They can't hear you.

PETER. Why can't they hear me?

HALL. There's nothink there.

PETER. They are too.

HALL. So, that's where they is, is it? You tumbled right into the hatchway that time. Wait till Mr. Rotch gits back an' learns there's a conspiricy agin' the king agoin' on right in the leeward to his ship. [PETER *laughs.*] I'm glad as how you see it funny.

PETER. It is. In the first place, they won't be there when Mr. Rotch calls out the king's men and secondly the list of volunteers isn't there either.

HALL. Oh, there's a list, is there? A list of the traitors. [*Bellowing.*] Where's that list?

PETER [*getting up higher in the chests*]. I—don't— Do you really think I'm going to tell you?

HALL [*rushing after him*]. You little varmint.

PETER. Come on, you Britisher, beat us colonists if you can!

HALL. Kim down.

PETER. Strike America! America is free, and a free people can't be conquered.

HALL. That's your Sam Adams an' his dryness. It's rubbish. Kim down!

PETER. For their heart and soul is theirs.

HALL. Kim down or I'll call for help. Bless me w'y didn't I think of it afore. [*Calling.*] 'Enery 'Arper, you blundering— Naow, I'll learn you ter respect your superiors.

PETER. "To respect my superiors!" The way you do, Mr. Rotch. Why, you didn't dare tell him that you allowed all the crew but two to go ashore.

HALL. You scamp, them two will draw up the gang-plank so that your blunderin' trick will blunder—

PETER. You fawning old world slave, you don't respect him no more than I do you, yet you blow and bow and soap your hands and say "Yes, your honor, black *is* white."

HALL. Your spyin' friends will be hit like they'd tripped on a hatch an' battered the mainmast with their heads. [*Calling.*] Dinwiddie—

PETER. And when his back is to you, you'll turn and beat your bo'sun, make him swear the moon is cheese; and he, upon your exit will flay and cuss his seamen who'll next vow that the moon is soap and green at that. And so it goes with your old-world classes and your ranks—each a beater and then in turn being beaten.

HALL [*crossing to the hatchway. Calling*]. Dinwiddie, Bo'sun Dinwiddie. [*Calling down the hatchway.*] 'Arper—Bo'sun Dinwiddie!

VOICES [*off stage*]. Comin', Cap'n, comin'!

HALL. Naow I've got you! [PETER *seeing his chance to escape crawls softly down.* HALL *sees him.* PETER *does not notice* HALL *is watching him.* PETER *makes a dash for the exit, but* HALL *reaches there first.*] You young imp, stand away. [PETER *quickly sees that* HALL *does not get his hands on him. Then he rushes to the hatchway.*]

PETER. Remember the hatchway has a padlock and key. The gang-plank is yours, but the hatchway is mine. Mine, old man, mine! [*We hear the cover slam down and a chain rattling as if it were being padlocked.*]

HALL. You clever raskill, w'y don't you go up forrard naow, an' lock the hatch in the bow?

PETER. Yes. So that after I go, you can unlock this. [*We hear in the distance, the war-whoop, once, twice.* PETER *crosses to the captain.*] Captain Hall, won't you please let me go? It's nothing of you they want.

HALL [*proudly*]. It's agin' the king.

PETER. Think of my disgrace, sir. They trusted me to serve the colonists, and I have failed. Oh, I'll never be able to live down this. [*A great rattling and pounding from the closed hatchway and two men's voices crying,* "Wot's wanted?" *and* "H'open the 'atchway," *etc.*]

PETER. My pup will be so ashamed of me, I can't bear that. I can't.

HALL. Hold your tongues, you blubberheads, and crawl down into the hold, then shoreward and up through the bow hatchway.

DINWIDDIE. It will take us till Christmas, Cap'n.

HARPER. Can't do it.

HALL. Crawl out through the gun ports, an' up 'ere on the stays. Now the king's men are victorious!

PETER. I'm not afraid of their getting here. It will take them too long. But please, please give me my lantern and let me go.

HALL. Calm daown, bye, it's the coolest player wot's takes the kitty.

PETER. I'll come in the morning to thank you, and my mother'll come, and—so will Betsy Warren,—we're going to be married—oh, sir, I'll do anything if you'll only let me go.

HALL. Wot kin you do?

PETER. Anything you want. [HALL *laughs.*] I'll— [PETER *stops and thinks—then adds slowly*]. I'll give you the list of names of those that—

HALL. You will? You will?

[PETER *slowly takes his right hand and starts to put it into his inner pocket, but stops as an idea comes to him. Then he puts his hand in his outer pocket and brings out the blank piece of paper folded, as he says:*]

PETER. Yes—I—will.

HALL. Aa-ha. Let me see it. Let me see it. [*He crosses to* PETER *but* PETER *withdraws, keeping the paper behind him.*]

PETER. No. No. No, you don't, until you let me get between you and the plank.

HALL. Won't you trust me?

PETER [*contempt*]. I—trust—you?

HALL. Well, get ahead, but you stand close w'ile I read it. [*Both are distrustful of the other.* HALL *stands in the center of the stage and* PETER *near him, but on the side of him near the exit.* PETER *hands him the paper and starts to run.*] Hold on there! [*And* HALL *grabs him, holding on to him tight.*] You acts too 'spicious for Hezekiah Hall. [*He opens the paper and sees it blank.*] You raskill, you varmint! I'll fix yer, I'll fix yer! [*And throwing away the paper he shakes the lad considerably and throws him from the exit.*] Jest one think for you. You'll be hanged, hanged by the neck till you rot!

PETER. You can't scare me with your threats.

HALL. An' that ain't the worst on it. You'll be taken to England.

PETER. It's a lie. You're all lies.

HALL. Come naow, don't purtind thet your eddication an' Sam Adams ain't told you that the king is agoin' to take you rebels to England for trial. You know that.

PETER. Suppose I do, what then?

HALL. "What then?" You little turnip, don't you know you've been caught aspyin' agin' the king on a king's ship? That means you is to be shipped to England an' atterwards be tried by Bridishers.

PETER. Taken alone?

HALL. Tried an' hung among strangers. As a example for all the trespassing an' rebelling colonists.

PETER. Not without my pup—surely not without pup?

HALL. An' w'y not?

PETER. Not if I give you the real list?

HALL. You're aquizzing me.

PETER. Pup dropped it. [*Taking it out of his pocket.*] And here it is. [*He unfolds it.*]

HALL. Leave me have it in my hands.

PETER. I'll stand by the plank, if you please. [*Again* HALL *lets* PETER *circle to the other side of him and again he watches him carefully for any escape.*]

HALL. None o' your tricks naow, or I'll— [PETER *hands out the list of names, but just before* HALL *takes it, he withdraws it.*]

HALL. Wot's you afeared o', naow?

PETER. I just can't, I just—

HALL. To England then.

PETER [*handing the paper and again* HALL *is about to lay his hands on it when he withdraws it*]. It makes me feel so awful.

HALL. Wot's botherin' you? You're gettin' off free.

PETER. Give me my lantern then. [HALL *allows him to pick it up.*]

HALL [*stepping nearer* PETER]. Come naow. [PETER *holds it out. The ship's clock strikes six bells.* HALL *steps towards him to take it, when* PETER *suddenly withdraws it, throws down his lantern and tears up the list.*]

PETER. No, no, no, I won't. I won't. It's just like betraying my country to save myself. Oh, I'll let you take me to England alone among the enemy, I'll let you hang me as a spy, do anything you like with me, but I'll never harm a head of my countrymen, I'll never desert my country.

HALL. Well, I'll be blowed. [*And he takes his stand by the gang-plank and sets the lantern by him.*]

PETER [*continuing to tear the paper to the winds.*] And you'll never know who was in the Tea Party, you won't, nor I won't, nor nobody won't. Never, never, never!

HALL. You little fool, wot did you do that for? [*He flies at* PETER *just in time for* PETER *to throw the last handful of torn paper in his face.*]

PETER. Holler, old man, holler. You can't scare me. You can't do anything to me, but holler, and swear and beat me. But I'll never regret what I've done. Never!

HALL. We'll see how long you say that after Dinwiddie comes.

PETER. Give me my lantern. You've no right to take that from me.

HALL. Keep away naow. [PETER *makes a dart for his lantern, and* HALL *grabs it first. Before the captain recovers himself,* PETER *grabs the lit lantern that has hung the while from the rail. But* HALL *is quick enough to block the entrance.*]

HALL. You want a lantern.

PETER. Yes.

HALL. You want one too much to suit this 'ere gen'l'm'n.

PETER. Yes?

HALL. I don't believe you're over your bustin' tricks yet.

PETER. Really? [PETER *is watching his chance to give the signal.*]

HALL. Yes.

PETER. Yes? [PETER *circles around* HALL *and gets near the upstage left rail.*]

HALL. Stand away there. Wot you want a lantern for?

PETER. It's dark, isn't it?

HALL. Course it's dark, but you ain't agoin' off this boat, so what matters it to you ef it's pitch, or not? [PETER *now circles around* HALL *and is near the down-stage left rail, between* HALL *and the audience.*]

PETER. If I'm goin' to die, I'll want to make my last will and testament, don't I? [*He raises the lantern to lower it over the rail.*]

HALL. Last will an' testament! Bah! [*Flying at him.*] 'Ere, 'ere. Keep by the mizzenmast.

PETER [*backing towards the Center, and waving the lantern with a motion similar to its going over the rail*]. Of course, why not?

HALL. Wot hev you got to leave anythink?

PETER. Pigs and pigeons, and marbles. [*He is trying to find a place from where he can see his father's shop. He stands on a chest.*]

HALL. Pigs, is it? 'Ere get off that chest.

PETER. Yes, and my favorite piece of string. [PETER *jumps down.*]

HALL. See 'ere, young scamp, you've fooled with me long enough. Blow me ef you ain't up to some trick—

PETER. You take this long to realize that? You surprise me, sir.

HALL. Put down that lantern.

PETER. Make me!

HALL. "Make me!" I'll make you. [HALL *flies at* PETER, *who tries to dodge him, but* HALL *though heavy is spry. He grabs the lantern.*] Make you! I'll show you I won't hev no dancin' round my deck wavin' no lantern an' agivin' no signals for traitors. [*He crosses during this to the rail and on the last sentence, he, with the lantern in both his hands and a high movement, throws the lantern overboard. The spot is where they had practiced giving the signal.*]

PETER [*screaming and jumping up and down with delight*]. There. There. You've done it. You've done it. [*Many wild war-whoops are given and cheers and yells.*] Listen, old man, listen. They're coming, they're coming.

HALL. Who?

PETER. All of them. Hear them yelling.

HALL [*calling*]. Dinwiddie, Dinwiddie. [*Rushing to the hatchway.*]

PETER. Hear them, hear them running on the wharf? [*He looks over the rail and the sound of the approaching Mohawks increases.*]

HALL. Where's the key to this padlock?

PETER. I threw it into the ocean.

HALL. Hang me myself.

PETER. Going after it?

HALL [*rushing to the right rail*]. Dinwiddie, Dinwiddie.

DINWIDDIE. Aye, aye, sir!

HALL. Where are you, man?

DINWIDDIE. Comin'.

HALL. Hurry up. The world is upon us. Hurry!

[*A great troop of about twenty colonists—some of them dressed fully as Mohawks rush up the gang-plank and scramble to the tea chests. All the while they are whooping, yelling, and uttering unearthly shrieks. Some rush up to* HALL *and grab him, drag him to the mast and tie him to it. They take a half chest of tea, by the gang-plank and allow him to sit on it, while he is remaining prisoner. He objects, uttering,* "Blow me, wot's all this mean? You'll pay for this. The king will see you're punished, etc., etc." [*We see others open each and every chest of tea and pour the contents into the ocean, and whole chests are thrown over too.*]

[PETER, *standing down Left, is jumping up and down with his excitement, and calling* "Pup, oh, pup!" *By this time the troop of braves has finished entering and the three leaders bring up the rear.* EDES *hears* PETER'S *call and rushes up to him. The noise of the Mohawks dies down.*]

EDES. What ailed thee, boy?

HEWES. You well nigh ruined everything.

PURKETT. You should not have taken so long.

PETER. But, pup, I couldn't help it, really I couldn't. I— [*And they continue for a while to listen in a group while the noise increases. Above all, we hear the cry.*]

FIRST INDIAN. The tea's in the hold.

SECOND INDIAN. Let nothing escape us.

THIRD INDIAN. Down in the hatch.

FIRST INDIAN. It's locked.

SECOND INDIAN. Where's the key?

THIRD INDIAN. Break open the padlock.

SEVERAL INDIANS. Break open the padlock. Etc., etc.

[PURKETT *scenting violence leaves* PETER *and the group, and calling,* "Here, here," *rushes up stage to the group beside the hatchway.*]

PURKETT. No violence, absolutely not a bit of it.

THIRD INDIAN. Break it open.

[*Many yell and then we hear the chain rattle, and a cover thrown back and after unlaying the hatch, they go down in the hold. Then those below hoist upon deck the chests, and those above break open the chests, and scatter the tea about and heave it overboard where it is damaged and lost.*]

HALL [*at suitable intervals*]. Lack-a-day. To think I should live for sech a day. Oh, my tea, my tea. Dinwiddie— Blast me, 'Enery 'Arper.

HEWES [*breaking open a chest*]. Well, Peter, you were a brave lad.

PETER. You think I did right now, don't you, pup?

EDES [*severely*]. You were slow, boy, too slow. You well near spoiled all.

HEWES. You did a fine piece of work, boy, fine. Nobody could have done better, and there's few [*with a look at* PURKETT] that I know, that could have done as well. [*He goes to the rear of the ship giving orders.*]

EDES [*to* HEWES]. Never should have been allowed to stay.

PETER. That's all the thanks I get, and no matter how terrible he treated me, I kept thinking how proud my pup would be of me.

EDES. And so he is, Peter, too proud.

PETER. Pup! [*And he throws his arms around his father's waist and hugs him tight.*]

EDES [*patting* PETER'S *head*]. Too proud, Peter, but you wouldn't have me boasting and praising my own lad before our neighbors, would you? [*He breaks open a chest.*]

PURKETT [*rushing down from the crowd about the hatchway*]. Heydey. Heydey. What have they done?

EDES [*pouring the tea overboard*]. Well what?

PURKETT. Violence, Edes. In spite of all my warning! They've broken this badlock. Ruined it. What shall we do now?

PETER. Buy them another.

PURKETT [*relieved as the bright idea strikes him*]. Well said, boy, and so I shall, tomorrow, the first thing. I will make note of this.

[PURKETT *walks away making a knot in his handkerchief.*]

PETER. Pup, mayn't I have just a little tea for myself?

EDES [*breaking open a chest*]. Hush, boy, hush.

PETER. Just a little to keep in a tiny bottle to show off?

EDES. No. No.

PETER. Look, pup, look. [*He points to the left side of the ship where a short stout man in colonist costume is slyly stuffing all the tea he can into his side pockets, and his coattail pockets, in his hat, and in every possible place.*] Who's that?

EDES. Captain O'Connor of Charlestown.

PETER. He's getting enough to fill many a bottle.

EDES. He's busy with idle fingers, is he? [*Rushing to him.*] Hey, you traitor, O'Connor.

HEWES. Tea thief. Thief.

VOICES. Who? Where?

[O'CONNOR *looks about him, sees* EDES *coming for him, and starts to run to the plank.* EDES *catches him and grabs him by the coat collar. But* O'CONNOR *slips out of his coat and runs down the gang-plank.* PETER *and several others kick him as he passes.*]

EDES [*by the exit and holding up the coat*]. The coat tails of a thieving traitor.

VOICES. Hang him, hang 'im!

PURKETT. Here, here. I cannot permit such—

EDES. Why, hang the coat tails to the whipping-post in Charlestown.

VOICES. Hooray! Hooray!

[*They group, yelling and whooping, return to heaving the tea overboard.* EDES, PETER, PURKETT, HEWES *are by the exit, giving orders, directions and working the while.* HARPER, *from the right side of the ship crawls up into sight and steps over the railing onto the deck. He crouches behind the chest of tea and peers out at the hullabaloo. Then returns to the rail and in a loud whisper.*]

HARPER. Pst, pst, Dinwiddie.

DINWIDDIE. Is it safe?

HARPER. Come on. [*He peers out from behind the chest and sees the captain.* DINWIDDIE *appears over the rail.*] Look. Look at the poor, old dog-fish.

DINWIDDIE. Show respect, mon.

HARPER. Look wot the h'Injuns has did to 'im.

DINWIDDIE. Let's be away.

HARPER. Don't the Cap'n want yer?

DINWIDDIE. Sure he do, but he h'ain't agoin' ter git me.

HARPER. Don't be h'afeared o' the h'Injuns.

DINWIDDIE. Them h'ain't h'Injuns.

HARPER. Wot be they then?

DINWIDDIE. Devils. Big red devils. H'I be agoin'.

HARPER. H'I'm gone. [*They crawl back.*]

PETER [*coming forward*]. Pup, oh, pup!

EDES. What is it, child?

PETER. A bit of tea has got into my shoe.

EDES. Throw it out. Don't bother me.

PETER. Let me leave it there. Oh, mayn't I?

EDES. Hush, child, hush. [*He turns to resume his work.*]

PETER. Oh, hurrah! Now I can have it for every one to wonder at—in a little bottle, tied with a piece of red ribbon. [*The ship's clock strikes seven bells.*]

HALL [*wailing*]. All my cargo! There— [*looking off at the Right*] they're aboardin' the other brigs. Alack-a-day!

PETER [*laughing*]. Hello, old man.

HALL. Hello, you raskill.

PETER. Are you learning your lesson, sir? Learning it so that you can teach your tyrant that although this Tea Party is a petty quarrel, it means that Americans are a free people and they will fight for liberty, and democracy, not only for themselves, but for England; not only for England, but for the world; now, and a hundred, and two hundred years hence? They'll fight for it forever and forever and forever.

HALL. Hold your tongue with your parlimentary preachin' and learnin'. It's dry.

PETER. Dry, yes, dry as toast, Captain, but quite important at a Tea Party.

[*The tea is nearly over. The hullabaloo increases.*]

PRODUCTION NOTE

Looking at the stage descriptions, you will perhaps at first feel that it is quite impossible for you to set this scene on your bare stage or platform. But the truth is, it will be very simple. Keep foremost in your mind that today, suggestiveness in scenery is more important and more in vogue than careful detail. The hatchway is purposely out of sight in order that a trap door may be unnecessary. The characters may go out of any opening in the back. The directions call for solid rails but if necessary tennis nets may be used. Fasten one end of this net to the tormentor, or the proscenium, or a post down stage, and run the net around the stage in the shape of a ship's stern until the net comes to the corresponding down-stage post on the other side. A British flag in the rear will add much. Keep this waving by playing an electric fan on it from behind the scene. The stern need not be built high, but boxes of tea, piled up, can be employed to cover this deficiency. A mast is essential and a certain amount of rigging and rope. Equally necessary are the chests. A great many are needed. Ordinary packing boxes may be used, painted or stained a dark gray, with large red labels. Visit a tea and coffee store and ask to see a tea chest. Then you can easily copy them. They should be piled high in the back and lower in front. This enables you to utilize tables on which to pile them; those in front will keep the tables hidden. You cannot have too many chests for not only are they to serve as a covering for deficiencies in the setting and the formation of the coop, but they are used in the Tea Party proper, apparently being lifted up from the hold through the hatchway.

In place of a back drop and wings use blue tarlatan, cambric, cheese cloth, or any convenient blue material. Hang this in a semi-circumference, beginning at one side and going entirely around the scene to the other. Keep this at least five feet from

the ship's railing. A good but unimportant detail would be to
have the blue in the rear lighter than that at the sides. This will
do for the air and water, and will add distance to the perspective.

The dialogue during the Tea Party proper should follow
promptly and rapidly. Under no conditions should it impede
the action of a well-planned destruction. The actual time of
the "Party" was about six-thirty or seven P. M., so the lights
should be low. This means that many deficiencies and crudities
of the set may be blended into a perfect whole. The colonists
are all dressed in the style of 1773. Carrying out details, they
would wear tri-cornered hats, mufflers, mittens, knee-breeches,
and shoes with large buckles. Peter's costume is similar but
suitable for a small boy. Pictures may be found in any book
of American History.

The Mohawks wear full Indian costume with blankets, toma-
hawks and hatchets, and head covering of feathers. Other
participants are not so well disguised,—merely smudging their
faces and wrapping a blanket around their colonist's dress.
Some appearing at the last use no disguise at all.

AT THE FOUNTAIN

BY

RICHARD C. BULL
AND
EDWARD G. STEINMETZ, JR.

A NON-ROYALTY PLAY

THE CAST

MR. FLUMDETTER, *the druggist*
JOE, *the clerk*
NEVADA, *a colored maid*
BILL ⎤
LEN ⎬ *High School boys*
TOM ⎦
BLUTTS, *a high-pressure salesman*
JANE ⎤
SUE ⎦ *two High School girls*
THE MAN FOR MANAYUNK
MR. WASSERMANN, *an excitable father*
LILIAN, *his daughter*
MRS. VAN DER VEER DE LANCY, *a matron*
CLARISSA, *her poodle*
FRANK, *a young man*
KITTY, *his best girl*
MISS BLUM, *a spinster*
FOUR SMALL BOYS

THE SCENE

The soda fountain of a small-town drugstore on a Saturday afternoon of a summer's day.

On the Right a soda fountain runs the depth of the stage. Behind and down stage of it is a door which leads into the prescription department. In front of it are four stools. On the counter are the usual paraphernalia including jars containing peanuts, gumdrops, etc. A door down Left leads onto the street. Above this is the large window which is mostly covered by large cardboard advertisements and a solid railing. A post-

*card rack stands near the street door, Left. A typical drugstore
table and chairs are in the Center of the stage. A telephone
hangs on the Right wall below door.*

THE CHARACTERS AND COSTUMES

FLUMDETTER: *An elderly man with spectacles and a gray coat.*

JOE: *A youth in a soda-clerk's white coat.*

NEVADA: *A colored maid in a shabby lightweight coat.*

BILL, LEN and TOM: *"Boys about town." They wear snappy
bow ties and sweaters.* BILL *wears a skullcap.*

BLUTTS: *A high-pressure salesman. He wears a straw hat, a
natty suit, and flashy socks.*

JANE and SUE: *High School girls. Bobbed hair, attractive
summer dresses.*

THE MAN FOR MANAYUNK: *An old rustic in duster, rubbers
and spectacles. He is bent, carries a cane, and is rather successfully concealed by a long beard. He is rather shy and
always speaks in an apologetic manner.*

WASSERMANN: *An excitable father. He is hatless.*

LILIAN: *His little daughter. She wears pigtails with colorful
bows tied thereto.*

MRS. VAN DER VEER DE LANCY: *A stately matron with a
lorgnette.*

FRANK: *A young man wearing a straw hat, blue coat and white
duck trousers.*

KITTY: *His best girl. She wears a flowery dress and wide-
brimmed straw hat.*

MISS BLUM: *An elderly spinster in a dark dress and high,
ornate hat.*

THE SMALL BOYS: *Gray linen and khaki suits, no hats, and
perhaps two of them without stockings.*

———•———

At the rise of the curtain MR. FLUMDETTER *is puttering around
behind the counter.* JOE *enters from the street door, Left,
whistling merrily.*

Mr. Flumdetter [*looking at his watch*]. You're five minutes late again. What's your excuse this time?

Joe. Well, you see, Mr. Flumdetter, our cat—

Mr. Flumdetter. Never mind. I wouldn't believe you anyway. Just try not to let it happen again.

Joe. Oh, no, sir, I won't.

Mr. Flumdetter. And, Joe, you've got to be careful with the vanilla ice cream this afternoon. It's running low. Put custard in all the sundaes—no one will know the difference. We're running short of chocolate syrup, too.

Joe. That's all right. I'll put lots of coffee and licorice in it to make it go farther.

Mr. Flumdetter. And by the way, don't put so many nuts on the sundaes.

Joe. Why, they're the berries! [*He goes behind the counter, takes a white duck coat from a hook, and puts it on.*]

Mr. Flumdetter. Well, the berries are just as expensive. This is a business,—not a public charity. No free treats.

Joe. Yes, sir.

Mr. Flumdetter. And I'm not paying you to flirt with the customers, either. This isn't a matrimonial agency.

Joe [*behind the counter and peering around*]. We've got too much whipped cream today. It won't keep.

Mr. Flumdetter. Then lick a spoon of it every time a customer comes in, so that they'll want some.

Joe. How about writing on the mirror with it?

Mr. Flumdetter. That would just draw the flies.

Joe. That might remind people to buy flypaper.

Mr. Flumdetter. Use your own judgment—if you have any.
   [nevada *enters from Left, breathlessly, carrying a large paper bundle.*]

Nevada. Mistah Flumdetter, ah gotta have five quarts of chaw-clit ice cream 'stead of vanella, and ah doan wanta make a mistake again 'cause the Missus am havin' the leddies in fo' Satiddy afternoon bridge, and they all eat an awful lot, 'specially Miss Blum; so the Missus says to me: "Nevada, you all go down an' git five quarts of vanell—ah mean chawclit—ice cream fo' the leddies. So ah come. But ah got to thinkin' that vanella was mah favorite ice cream, and when ah got back ah remembered as ah had got vanella 'stead of chawclit, so ah came right back 'fore the Missus cotched me.

MR. FLUMDETTER. Well, give me the package, Nevada.

NEVADA [handing it to him]. Yas suh, here it is.

MR. FLUMDETTER. Don't make a mistake again because the ice cream gets soft when it's out of the can.

NEVADA. No suh. Ah won't make a mistake again.

MR. FLUMDETTER [handing her five quart bricks of ice cream]. Here's your chocolate. Five quarts.

NEVADA. No suh. Ah won't make no mistake again. Thank you, Mistah Flumdetter. [She exits Left.]

MR. FLUMDETTER. I wish people would write out their orders so their dumb maids would get them straight.

JOE. She sure would make Simple Simon look like Solomon!

MR. FLUMDETTER. Oh,—I meant to tell you not to give such large doses of castor oil when people come in to get it, because yesterday— Say, that reminds me, the windows need washing.

JOE. Yes, Mr. Flumdetter. Is that all?

MR. FLUMDETTER. That's all I can think of just now. I'll go make up those back prescriptions. [He goes out Right.]

[BILL, TOM, and LEN enter sheepishly from the Left.]

BILL [aside to the other two at door Left]. Let's sponge sodas off Joe.

LEN. Hi, Joe!

JOE. Howdy, boys.

TOM. How's the old boy feeling?

BILL. Working hard, Joe?

JOE. You bet!

LEN. Where's old Flapdoodle?

JOE [with a jerk of his thumb]. Back there monkeying around.

BILL. Who's he goin' to kill now?

JOE. Dunno.

[A pause. The three seek inspiration which LEN at last finds.]

LEN. How's the vanilla ice cream today, Joe?

JOE. Short of it.

LEN. How's the chocolate?

[JOE *licks a spoon of whipped cream.*]

JOE. All right.

LEN. It would go pretty well with whipped cream.

JOE. Yes. Lots of whipped cream.

BILL. Not going to waste, is it?

JOE. No.

BILL. Oh.

TOM. I couldn't eat a whole dishful, but just a taste would go pretty well. How about you, Len?

LEN. Sounds smooth as a snake's hips to me.

JOE. Three chocolates with whipped cream? That's forty-five cents.

BILL [*doubtfully*]. Well . . . I haven't any money with me right now.

LEN. Joe'll trust us till next time.

MR. FLUMDETTER [*calling warningly*]. Joe! Joe!

JOE. Yes, doctor?

MR. FLUMDETTER. Don't forget to fix that pump or we'll run out of soda water.

JOE. All right.

[BLUTTS *enter from Left, carrying a small suitcase. The* BOYS *cross to door Left.*]

JOE. What can I do for you?

BLUTTS [*Center*]. Is the boss in?

JOE. Yeh.

[*He makes no move to call him.*]

BLUTTS [*impatiently*]. Well, can I see him? [*Crosses to lower end of counter.*]

JOE. Why certainly sir. [*Exits Right.*]

LEN. Pipe them socks. [*He mimics* BLUTTS *behind his back.*]

BILL. Bet he's selling a cure for the blind.

TOM [*pointing to socks*]. Then he's creating trade all right.

[JOE *returns from Right with* MR. FLUMDETTER *who meets* BLUTTS *at the end of fountain Right.*]

Mr. Flumdetter [*to* Blutts, *shortly*]. Yes, sir?

Blutts. The manager, I assume?

Mr. Flumdetter. Yes.

Blutts. My name is Blutts. Good progressive store you've got here!

Mr. Flumdetter [*dryly*]. I hope so.

Blutts. I'm a man of few words, Mr. Flumdetter, and I'll come right to the point of my visit. I represent the firm of Cardinal and Sons, and we have chosen you as one of the lucky few who are to be privileged to introduce our new writing paper to the public market. It's going to be a wow—the most distinguished-looking paper you've ever seen.

Mr. Flumdetter. That's fine, but I'm well stocked with paper right now.

Blutts. Just a moment, Mr. Flumgetter. This paper has the appeal of novelty, beauty and durability. It's a keen seller and it's going to go like hotcakes. A friend of mine sent a box to his aunt that's high up in society, and the next day he came to me and said his aunt wanted three dozen boxes for card party prizes.

Mr. Flumdetter. But I'm stocked up.

Blutts. Just a moment. This paper has the appeal of novelty, beauty, and dur— [*He realizes that he has already said that and covers it up.*] Well, anyway, take a look at it. It comes in three qualities. The first is what we call "Acme." [*He takes a sheet from his suitcase.*] That's this here. You'll notice the broad horizontal stripes. Second is the "de Lux"—that's this diamond pattern. [*Demonstrating it.*] Then here's the "Buckingham"—

Mr. Flumdetter [*interrupting impatiently*]. But I've already said I've got too much paper.

Blutts. Just a moment, Mr. Dumfletter, I want to tell you about this "Buckingham" paper. [*Leaning towards him and speaking confidentially.*] This paper was designed at the suggestion of Princess Mary of England—she's King George's daughter—the one who married the Canadian, or was it Australian?—not so long ago. Well, anyway, we asked her to create a paper that would be the criterion of "chick." Well, one day she was out horseback riding, and got caught in the rain, and that gave her the idea for this paper. These black designments are the horses, and get the thunder and cloud effects in harmonizing and contrasting colors.

MR. FLUMDETTER. That's all very fine, but they wouldn't have any appeal around here, and I'm stocked up anyway.

BLUTTS [*paying no attention to him*]. Now I want to tell you about the five color combinations. The first we call "Dawn" —that's coral and chalk. Next is "Morning"—a cheery paper to write on to sick friends and things like that. That's indigo and cerise. Then we have "Moon"—flame and leaf green— that's for love letters. "Twilight," this here, is our conservative paper in faun and lavender. And last is "Night"—the dressy paper and the best of 'em all.—It's a knockout— black and yellow. Why my cousin wrote a letter to—

MR. FLUMDETTER [*interrupting impatiently*]. You're wasting my time and yours, sir. Good day. [*He turns to* JOE.] Joe, have you fixed that pump ye?

JOE. I'm just going to, Mr. Flumdetter.

BLUTTS [*seizing* MR. FLUMDETTER *by the arm*]. But you haven't heard my special proposition yet. My company made a survey of the leading druggists in the United States, and we picked 400—only 400 out of 27,283—whom we presumed reputable to introduce our paper to the public. You are one of them.

MR. FLUMDETTER. Joe, will you show this gentleman out?

BLUTTS. Now to those 400 we are making a special proposition as a special introductory offer. We're giving you absolutely free—

JOE [*to the three* BOYS]. Come on, fellows.

　　　[*They proceed to forcibly eject* BLUTTS.]

BLUTTS [*continuing to speak while the four* BOYS *push him across stage and out of the door*].—five packages of "Mellifluous" art blotting paper, with your name stamped on it to give out to customers. Ordinarily it retails at forty-three cents a package, and you are getting it without any detriment; and besides this we are according rates on the paper itself. It is to retail at a dollar and a half a box, and our ordinary wholesale price will be a dollar and a quarter; but, however, your initial order will cost you only one dollar a box if you choose, and I know you will, to order at least 50. That's a clear profit of fifty cents to you, and—

[*By now he is well out, and* JOE *and the* BOYS *return, wiping their hands.*]

BILL [*to* MR. FLUMDETTER]. Phew, but it's hot!

MR. FLUMDETTER. It certainly is.

TOM [*to* MR. FLUMDETTER]. Bet this kind of day helps the ice cream sales.

LEN. Have you installed an electric refrigerator, or do you still use ice to keep the cream?

MR. FLUMDETTER. Oh, it's electric.

TOM. You certainly are modern, Mr. Flumdetter. I'll bet there aren't many towns this size that would have things like that installed.

MR. FLUMDETTER. That's right.

TOM. It certainly is the weather to make you feel like something cool.

MR. FLUMDETTER. Yes, it is. Have some peanuts? [*He offers a couple to the* BOYS *who take them.* MR. FLUMDETTER *exits Right.*]

[JOE *is busy fixing the pump. The* BOYS *go over toward the Left door and talk in low tones.*]

BILL. Old skinflint! Two cents' worth of peanuts!

TOM. I've got to have ice cream or die. I've never been so hot in my life!

BILL. A chocolate cone! Oh boy!

TOM. I haven't a cent.

BILL. Neither have I.

LEN. Well, let's get cones. We deserve them anyway, the tight-wad!

BILL. How?

LEN. It oughtn't to be hard. There are three of us.

BILL. Well?

LEN. Well, Bill, you keep crabby-knots busy. Tom can see Joe doesn't interfere, and I'll get the cones.

TOM. Do you think it would work?

LEN. Why not? Wait until the store's empty—or we can do it now, before anybody comes in. Bill, you go back in to Flumdetter and say you've got a pain, and ask him what's good for it. Take a while to tell him what's wrong with you. Tom can get Joe out of the shop by telling him that a bunch of gypsies just went around the corner. That'll get him to go round the corner to see them, and while he's doing that I can get the cones and sneak up the block and around the other corner.

BILL. Good. Make mine chocolate.

TOM. Mine too. Let's go!

BILL [*who has glanced out the window*]. Wait a minute. [*Loudly.*] Someone's coming—and how! [*He starts to comb his hair. The* BOYS *watch* SUE *and* JANE *approaching off stage Left.*]

TOM. Hey! Hey! Pipe the swell dames! Watch papa perform now.

JOE [*looking up over the fountain*]. You should worry. They all fall for you anyhow.

[SUE *and* JANE *enter Left.*]

BILL [*trying to be casual*]. My gosh, it's hot this afternoon.

TOM. It isn't the heat. It's the humidity.

LEN. Yes, that's what I always—[*pretending to notice the* GIRLS *for the first time*]—Why, hello, girls!

SUE. Hello, Joe.

JOE. Hello, Sue. Come in to get cooled off?

SUE. You should know.

JANE. I've been perishing all day—I'm simply paralyzed with heat. Give me a glass of water quick. [*Both sit at the fountain. The* BOYS *stroll around Center stage.*]

JOE. [*giving them both water.*] Here you are.

JANE. Thanks, Joe.

SUE. What are you going to have, Jane?

JANE. I want a cherry sundae.

SUE. I don't feel much like that.

JOE [*hopefully*]. How about whipped cream on chocolate?

SUE. Oh! Too sweet for my shape!

BILL. Nothing wrong with her shape!

SUE [*pretending not to hear*]. Oh, I know just what I want. Make me a sundae with butterscotch ice cream and lemon ice on a piece of cantaloupe. Then some chocolate and some coffee sauce, . . . oh, and some gooseberries and nuts.

JOE. O.K. Some whipped cream on it?

SUE. I guess not. [JOE *looks disappointed. He starts to speak, but thinks better of it.*]

JANE. I'll take a cherry sundae.

JOE. Cherry ice?

JANE. No. Vanilla.

JOE. Cherry ice is fresh today.

JANE. How thoughtful of you, Joe. [*His face brightens.*] But I guess I'll take vanilla just the same. [*He gives up, and fixes the sundaes.*]

SUE. Going to the movies tonight, Joe?

JOE. No. I gotta tend to the counter.

LEN. I don't. How about it, sister?

SUE. Fresh thing!

LEN [*facetiously*]. That's right. Nothing stale about me.

BILL [*to* JANE]. How's the cream?

JANE [*paying no attention*]. Joe, didn't you use cherry ice after all?

JOE. Gee, I did? I guess we were talking and I got mixed up. I'll give you another.

BILL. My treat!

JANE. Thank you, Joe, but I'll keep this one.

JOE. Sure it's all right?

JANE. Absolutely.

[NEVADA *reënters and comes up to* JOE.]

NEVADA. Mistah Joe, ah done made a mistake again. Seems like ah'm havin' the worst trouble. Seems like ah got the right thing and then changed it. You see the missus sent me fo' vanella, and ah got thinkin' how vanella was mah favorite cream, so ah got it, and then ah got to thinkin' that ah must have got it 'cause ah like it, so ah came back and got chocolate, but seems as ah was right all the time. So now ah gotta change again, and will you please make it quick, Mistah Joe, 'cause the leddies is in an awful uproar, and the missus, she's mad.

JOE. Are you sure you're right, Nevada? This is the last time I'll change it.

NEVADA. Yas suh! Don't catch me makin' no more mistakes. Ah got it clear this time. The Missus done want chocolate.

JOE. You've got chocolate there. You just said you wanted vanilla instead.

NEVADA. Yas suh, vanella. That's what ah said.

JOE. Well, you said chocolate afterwards.

NEVADA. Did ah? Then chocolate must have been it.

JOE. Well, that's what you've got.

NEVADA. Ah have? Then why did ah come back here? Guess Ah'm sort of mixed up.

[THE MAN FOR MANAYUNK *enters Left*.]

MAN FOR MANAYUNK [*to* JOE *apologetically*]. Could you please tell me how to get the trolley for Manayunk?

JOE. Just a minute. . . . Now are you sure you want chocolate, Nevada?

NEVADA. Yas suh! Funny mah thinkin' ah had to come back heah. That's a good one on me. Sure am glad ah didn't change. Good-by. [*Exit Left*.]

JANE. Isn't she a scream?

JOE. She's a nuisance.

SUE. Like some other people.

LEN. I hope you don't mean me.

SUE [*sarcastically*]. Oh no! Are you ready to go, Jane?

JANE. Yes. I'm paying for them today, Joe.

JOE. Think nothing of it. They're on the house.

SUE. Joe, how sweet of you!

JANE. Thank you, Joe. Bye-bye! [*They exit Left*.]

MAN FOR MANAYUNK [*to* LEN]. Could you please tell me how to get to Manayunk?

LEN. I'm in a hurry. Ask Joe. Come on, fellows.

BILL. Right! Which way are they going, Tom?

TOM. Down the street.

LEN. That's a good sign. So long, Joe!

JOE. So long! Hope you make them. [*The* BOYS *exit Left.*]

MAN FOR MANAYUNK. Sorry to be such a nuisance, but can you inform me how to get the Manayunk trolley?

JOE. When you go out, turn left and go three blocks. Then turn right, and—

[*He is interrupted by* MR. WASSERMANN, *who rushes in with his small daughter,* LILIAN.]

MR. WASSERMANN [*Center*]. Quick! Quick! My little Lilian is dying.

JOE. I'll call the doc. [*Calling off Right.*] Mr. Flumdetter! Mr. Flumdetter!

[MR. WASSERMANN *begins to slap* LILIAN *on the back.*]

MR. FLUMDETTER. Yes? [*He enters, Right.*] Ah, Mr. Wassermann! What can I—?

MR. WASSERMANN. About an hour ago, I left Lilian playing with a large brown button, and when I came back the button was gone. Do something quick or she'll choke.

MR. FLUMDETTER. Can she breathe now?

MR. WASSERMANN. Can you breathe, Lilian?

LILIAN [*at the top of her voice*]. No!

MR. WASSERMANN. See! She'll die.

LILIAN [*crying*]. I don't wanna die! I don't wanna die!

MR. FLUMDETTER. Never mind. You won't die. I'll give you some castor oil. [*He exits Right and returns immediately with castor oil bottle and spoon.*]

LILIAN. Don't want castor oil!

MR. WASSERMANN. Come, come, Lilian! You must drink it down like a little man.

LILIAN. Don't wanna be a man.

MR. FLUMDETTER. Here, Lilian, open your mouth.

[MR. WASSERMANN *holds her nose while* MR. FLUMDETTER *pours the oil.* LILIAN *struggles violently, and finally spits it out.*]

Mr. Wassermann. Lilian! Now you'll have to take another dose!

Lilian. Why?

Mr. Wassermann. To get rid of the button.

Lilian. What button?

Mr. Wassermann. The one you swallowed.

Lilian. I didn't swallow no button.

Mr. Wassermann. Where's the one you were playing with?

Lilian [taking it from her pocket]. Here it is!

All [weakly]. Oh!

Mr. Wassermann [uncomfortably]. Come, Lilian!

Lilian. Don't wanna come! [Her father yanks her out Left.]

Joe. What a guy!

Mr. Flumdetter. Well, of all the—!

Man for Manayunk. Please, could you tell me how to get the trolley for Manayunk?

Joe. Why you go three blocks to the left to an iron man, then turn right and—

[The boys reënter from Left slowly and sheepishly. len has a black eye.]

Joe. Where'd you get the shiner, Len?

Bill [singing]. "Sweet Sue, Just you."

Len. I'm off women!

Mr. Flumdetter. Want some arnica on it?

Len. Yeh.

[mr. flumdetter exits Right and returns immediately with arnica bottle.]

Tom. Some sheik, he is!

Len. Well, you didn't do much better.

Mr. Flumdetter. Close your eye, Len. [He rubs arnica on it.]

Len [jumping about]. Ouch! Oh!

Mr. Flumdetter. Just a minute. Stand still!

Len. Owwwwwwh!

Mr. Flumdetter. There! That'll fix it.

Len. Fix it? You're killing me.

Mr. Flumdetter. Don't be so forward next time. [He exits Right].

MAN FOR MANAYUNK [*to* JOE]. Would you tell me how to reach the Manayunk trolley?

JOE. Why you go three blocks to the left, and then turn right and go four blocks. Then—

LEN [*speaking sotto voice to* TOM *and* BILL *immediately after the exit of* MR. FLUMDETTER *and at the same time as the speech of the* MAN FOR MANAYUNK]. Now's the time! Bill, you go in with Flumdetter. You get the others out, Tom. I'll meet you around the corner. Act quick!

BILL. Right! [*He exits Right.*]

TOM [*looking out of the door Left and calling*]. Hey! Look at the gypsies!

JOE [*interrupted in his explanation of the way to the* MAN FOR MANAYUNK, *he now stops abruptly and rushes to the door followed by* MAN FOR MANAYUNK]. Where?

TOM. They just went around the corner. Come on!

JOE [*following* TOM *out the door*]. Were there many?

[LEN *is left alone and goes over to the fountain. He has the lid off the can and has picked up the dipper when* BILL *whistles warningly from off Right.* LEN *has just time to drop the dipper and jump over in front of the fountain when* BILL *and* MR. FLUMDETTER *come in.*]

MR. FLUMDETTER. I have just the thing for that pain out here. . . . Where's Joe?

LEN. He went to look at some gypsies.

MR. FLUMDETTER. Humph! Gypsies aren't as bad as some others I know. [*From behind the counter he pours out of a bottle into a glass, and gives it to* BILL.] Here! This will fix you up.

BILL [*hesitatingly*]. It smells awful.

MR. FLUMDETTER. You won't mind it. It's just a little bitter.

BILL. My pain seems to be much better.

MR. FLUMDETTER. Nonsense. Drink it down.

BILL. Well, don't you think that as I *do* feel better, it would be foolish to take it, for it might start it up again?

MR. FLUMDETTER. Hurry up and take it.

BILL [*resigned*]. Well! [*He makes a face and gulps it down, then explodes.*] Oh! Water! Help! [MR. FLUMDETTER *hands him a glass he and drinks it down.*] What a taste!

[TOM *and* JOE *enter Left.*]

TOM. There weren't any, after all.

MR. FLUMDETTER. Joe, I've told you so often never to leave the fountain under any circumstances, that I should think—

LEN [*at the window*]. My jumping goldfish! Look what's coming!

MR. FLUMDETTER. That woman! Excuse *me!* [*He goes into the back room.*]

BILL. It's the battleship Maine under full steam!

JOE. Shh!

[MRS. VAN DER VEER DE LANCY *enters Left, with a small white poodle under her left arm. She is turning the poodle's head so as to make it face front.*]

MRS. VAN DER VEER DE LANCY. Come, come, Clarissa! I will *not* have you associating with that vulgar Airedale.

JOE. Good morning, Mrs. Van der Veer de Lancy.

MRS. VAN DER VEER DE LANCY [*seating herself at the center table, and placing* CLARISSA *on the stool next to her*]. How do you do! I'd like a raspberry puff, and Clarissa will have— what will you have, Clarissa?

CLARISSA. Bow wow!

MRS. VAN DER VEER DE LANCY. The little dear! Aren't you cute! She'll have coffee sauce on strawberry cream. [BILL *whistles.*] Don't mind that man, Clarissa. [BILL *whistles again.*]

TOM. Has Clarissa had her manicure this mawning?

LEN. No. She's been too busy getting a permanent wave.

MRS. VAN DER VEER DE LANCY [*severely*]. Young man! Will you please not annoy Clarissa. She bites.

LEN. Yeh? Come, Clarissa, let's see your pretty teeth.

MRS. VAN DER VEER DE LANCY. Young man, behave yourself!

[*While she is scolding the* BOYS, JOE *pops a cherry at* CLARISSA *and hits her on the nose. She barks, and* MRS. VAN DE VEER DE LANCY *turns to her.*]

Mrs. Van der Veer de Lancy. Did naughty man hurt mama's 'ittle darlin'? [*She picks her up.*]

[JOE *serves the raspberry puff and sundae.*]

Mrs. Van der Veer de Lancy. Here's your sundae, Clarissa. Now thank the nice clerk.

Clarissa. Bow wow!

Mrs. Van der Veer de Lancy. That's a good girl.

Nevada [*entering Left*]. Ah's back again, Mistah Joe. Mah feet is done neah worn out. This be the beatenest afternoon ah ever did spend. Seems like ah can't get nothin' straight.

Joe. What is it this time, Clarissa? Vanilla?

Mrs. Van der Veer de Lancy. Sir!

Joe. Pardon me. Nevada.

Mrs. Van der Veer de Lancy. Will you give me five quarts of chocolate cream to take with me?

Nevada. Yeh. Ah've got to have five quarts of vanella. You give this leddy mah chocolate. [*She puts ice cream package on counter.*]

Mrs. Van der Veer de Lancy. Why, it's too soft by now.

Nevada. Well, ah've got to have vanella. The leddies up to the house is most impatient. Youah fault too, Mistah Joe. You got me all mixed up last time. Now ah'm sure it's vanella. You see the missus done sent me fo' vanella, and ah got to thinkin' how choc—ah mean vanella—was mah favorite ice cream, and—

Joe. I've heard all that before. This time I'm going to phone and make sure. [*He goes to the phone and picks up the receiver.*]

Nevada. The missus is sure sore. Ah hates to think what she'll say.

Mrs. Van der Veer de Lancy [*impatiently*]. May I have my chocolate cream?

Joe [*at phone*]. Green 102. . . . Just a moment, Mrs. Van der Veer de Lancy— Hello! Yes. Is this Mrs. Jones? . . . This is Flumdetter's Drugstore. Your maid is back again. Just what kind of cream *do* you want? . . . [*He holds*

his ears.] . . . Oh! . . . [*Repeating movement.*] . . . Oh!
. . . All right—five quarts of vanilla. . . . I'll see she gets
it. . . . Good-by. [*He hangs up the receiver.*]

MRS. VAN DER VEER DE LANCY. I'm waiting for that chocolate cream.

[*Enter* MAN FOR MANAYUNK *at Left.*]

JOE. I'm getting it now, Madam.

BILL. Would Clarissa like a cigarette?

LEN. No. It's too unladylike.

JOE [*to* MRS. VAN DER VEER DE LANCY]. Here's your ice cream.
[*As she is watching the* BOYS, *he moves the ice cream package*
NEVADA *returned, toward her.*] I'll get yours now, Nevada.

MAN FOR MANAYUNK [*to* NEVADA]. Will you please tell me
the way to Manayunk?

NEVADA. Ah ain't rightly sure. Ah reckon you bettah ask
someone else.

MAN FOR MANAYUNK [*to* MRS. VAN DER VEER DE LANCY.]
Madam, how can I get to Manayunk?

MRS. VAN DER VEER DE LANCY [*crushing him with a glance
through her lorgnette*]. Whearrrr?

[*The* BOYS *start to pinch* CLARISSA, *who barks.*]

MRS. VAN DER VEER DE LANCY [*turning on the* BOYS]. Brutes!
Pick on someone your own size!

LEN. But Clarissa is so vicious!

JOE. Here's your ice cream, Nevada. It's the last drop of
vanilla, too. [*He sets five bricks of ice cream on the counter.*

NEVADA [*noticing* CLARISSA *for the first time, and in amazement*]. That sure am some dawg! Or am it a dawg?

MRS. VAN DER VEER DE LANCY [*to* BOYS]. I'll summon an
officer.

BILL. Shucks, lady.

MRS. VAN DER VEER DE LANCY. Guttersnipes! Rowdies!

NEVADA. Well, ah better be hurrying back. Let's see! This
here's mine. [*She picks up* MRS. VAN DER VEER DE LANCY'S
(*chocolate*) *package and exits Left.*]

BILL [*to* MRS. VAN DER VEER DE LANCY]. My, my, lady. You shame me!

MRS. VAN DER VEER DE LANCY [*calling*]. Mr. Flumdetter! Mr. Flumdetter! Will you please come here, please!

LEN. Well, I guess we'd better be leaving, boys. So long, Joe. [*They sidle toward the door at Left.*]

BILL. Lady, don't forget to tell Clarissa about halitosis! [*They exit Left.*]

MAN FOR MANAYUNK [*following* BILL *as he crosses to door Left*]. Please, won't you tell me how to get to *Manayunk!* [BILL *and* MAN FOR MANAYUNK *exit Left.*]

MRS. VAN DER VEER DE LANCY [*as* MR. FLUMDETTER *enters*]. Never mind, Mr. Flumdetter. I have routed the ruffians.

MR. FLUMDETTER. I'm sorry this happened, Madam.

MRS. VAN DER VEER DE LANCY. You should not allow such persons on your premises. Come, Clarissa. [*She picks up the vanilla package and turns to* JOE.] Charge this.

JOE. Yes, thank you.

MR. FLUMDETTER. Good day, Madam.

MRS. VAN DER VEER DE LANCY. Good day! [*She exits Left.* MR. FLUMDETTER *turns to* JOE.]

MR. FLUMDETTER. Have you fixed that pump yet, Joe?

JOE. I was just starting to do it. I'll finish it now.

[MR. FLUMDETTER *exits Right.* JOE *works over the pump. The* BOYS *enter Left.*]

BILL. So the army and navy's departed.

JOE. Yep.

[LEN *winks at* BILL *and* TOM *and picks up a soft rubber ball which he throws at a spot on the Right wall up stage. It hits.*]

LEN. Can you do that, Bill?

BILL. Let's see it. [*He throws the ball and misses.*] Rotten. I'm out of practice. How about you, Tom?

JOE. I can do it if he can't.

TOM. Let's see you.

JOE. All right. Give me the ball.

BILL. Here! [JOE *hits the spot.*] Pretty good!

LEN. Bet I can hit that book over there.

JOE. So can I.

LEN. Let's see you.

JOE. Here goes. [*He hits it.*]

BILL. Hot stuff!

LEN. Let me try it. [*He also hits the book.*]

TOM. You hit it even squarer. Guess you better surrender, Joe.

JOE. Say, I can hit a mark further than he can.

BILL. I doubt it. Len's darn good.

TOM. Well, try and see.

LEN. We've hit as far as we can throw in here.

TOM. And you hit squarer.

JOE. If we had more space I'd show you.

BILL. Lots of room outside!

JOE. I can't leave.

TOM. I wouldn't either, if I were you.

JOE. Say, I'm not afraid of *him.* [*Jerking his head toward Right, to indicate* FLUMDETTER.] Don't get that in your bean.

LEN. I'll bet I can hit the knocker on Foley's front door from the corner.

JOE. You *can*not.

LEN. Two bits says I can.

JOE. Two bits says you can't.

LEN. Well, I'll go do it. As you can't leave, I suppose you'll take Tom's word for it.

JOE. I *will* not. [*He goes to the door and looks up and down the street.*] Don't see anyone coming. Come on, quick!

[*He goes out followed by* LEN *and* TOM. *The last two wink at* BILL *who remains. As soon as they are gone,* BILL *looks in at* FLUMDETTER *off Right, then goes over to the fountain. He dishes out three cones, and is about to start off when* FRANK *and* KITTY *enter Left. He drops the cones under the counter.*]

FRANK. Why, Bill! When did you start working here?

BILL. Oh, I'm just watching the place for Joe. He's out throwing at targets with Len. I'll get him.

FRANK. No hurry.

BILL. O.K. [*He exits Left.* FRANK *and* KITTY *sit at the center table.* FRANK *puts his arm around her, and she giggles.*]

FRANK. Gee, but you look cute today.

KITTY. Do you really think so?

FRANK. You bet I do. Give me a kiss!

KITTY. Be yourself.

FRANK. Just one.

KITTY. No. Besides, someone might see us.

FRANK. No one around. [*He bends over her.* JOE *comes in at the door Left and coughs. They part guiltily.*]

JOE. Pleasant day!

FRANK. Hello, Joe. How's business?

JOE. O.K. Hello, Kitty.

KITTY. Hello, Joe.

FRANK. Bill said you were having a contest with Len. Who won?

JOE. I did—but Len couldn't pay his debt.

FRANK. Good for you—that you won, I mean.

JOE. What'll you have, Kitty? [*Going behind counter.*]

FRANK. The sky's the limit!

JOE. Whipped cream's awfully good today.

KITTY. Guess I'll have a banana split.

FRANK. Small coke for me. I'm not feeling awfully hungry.

JOE. I've a swell new idea, Kitty. Bisque instead of vanilla in a banana split. [*He starts to make banana split with bisque ice cream and whipped cream on top.*]

KITTY. Oh, I guess I'll be old-fashioned.

FRANK. That's right! "An old-fashioned girl in a gingham gown—" You know the rest.

KITTY [*simpering*]. Oh, Frank! Isn't he awful, Joe?

JOE [*looking in ice cream can*]. Oh my gosh, Kitty! There isn't any vanilla left.

KITTY. Oh, well, I'll take bisque.

FRANK. What'll you do for the rest of the customers?

JOE. I'm putting the pineapple over in the vanilla place now. They look about the same. . . . Here, how's this look? [*Putting sundae in front of her.*]

KITTY. Just wonderful. You sure can mix a sundae, Joe.

JOE [*modestly*]. Well, I've had plenty of practice.

FRANK. Joe, will you get me a pack of Camels?

JOE. Sure thing.

[*While he turns to get them,* FRANK *slips his arm around* KITTY. MISS BLUM *enters, Left. She stops, scandalized, and coughs.* FRANK *removes his arm guiltily, and* MISS BLUM *crosses to the fountain.*]

JOE. Here're your cigarettes, Frank. . . . Yes, Miss Blum?

MISS BLUM. I want a dish of vanilla ice cream. I've been waiting over at Mrs. Jones' for exactly 43 minutes. That girl Nevada made a mistake.

JOE. Yes. She's been in here a couple of times. She's stupid. . . . Er— Don't you want some chocolate syrup on your vanilla cream?

MISS BLUM. No thanks! I always take it plain. It's more healthful.

JOE. Chocolate's very nourishing.

MISS BLUM. No. No. Just vanilla.

JOE. We've some wonderful new pineapple sauce I'd like you to try.

MISS BLUM. Not today.

JOE. All right. [*He gives her a dish of pineapple cream.*]

FRANK. Can we have some water?

JOE. Sure thing! [*While he is waiting on them,* MISS BLUM *starts to eat. She takes a spoonful and makes a face.*]

MISS BLUM. You've given me pineapple. [KITTY *giggles.*]

JOE. Why, Miss Blum, you can see for yourself that this is the vanilla can.

MISS BLUM. But it's pineapple.

JOE. That's funny. Wasn't yours all right, Kitty?

KITTY. Yes, indeed! Come on, Frank. [*They cross to door Left, laughing.*]

FRANK. So long, Joe!

JOE. So long! Good-by, Kitty. [FRANK *and* KITTY *exit Left.*]

MISS BLUM [*taking another mouthful*]. I wonder what can be wrong with me. I'm sure that this is pineapple.

JOE [*hopefully*]. Have you been eating any pineapple lately, Miss Blum?

MISS BLUM. Why, I did have some pineapple punch at Mrs. Jones', but—

JOE. Well, that must be the reason.

MISS BLUM. I don't see—

JOE. The taste must last.

MISS BLUM. Well, I can't stand this. I guess I'll have some candy instead. Let's see! Give me some gumdrops—about a nickel's worth.

JOE [*sarcastically*]. I'm not sure that we have that many. I'll see.

MISS BLUM. They're fresh, aren't they?

JOE. Yes, indeed. "Always fresh"—that's our motto.

MISS BLUM. I like them big and fat and juicy. See! Give me that one. [*She points out gumdrops as he puts them in a bag.*] And that. . . . Not that one—it doesn't have enough sugar on it. . . . That's right. Now how much do I owe you?

JOE. Twenty cents.

MISS BLUM. Well, here it is. But I must say I never tasted such ice cream.

[*A crowd of small* BOYS *rush in, storming the fountain.*]

FIRST BOY. Give me a double chocolate ice cream cone!

SECOND BOY. I want salted peanuts.

THIRD BOY. I wanta popsickle.

FOURTH BOY. Mavis for me.

SECOND BOY. 'Tato chips, too.

FIRST BOY. And don't be stingy with the ice cream.

FOURTH BOY. You owe me a bite of your popsickle, Freddie.

THIRD BOY. I'm going to charge mine.

FIRST BOY. Bet your pop won't let you!

SECOND BOY. We want service!

MISS BLUM. Oh, what dirty hands!

FIRST BOY. Rats!

SECOND BOY. Aw, go kiss a cow!

MISS BLUM. What urchins!

ALL [*dancing around her*]. "Sticks and stones will break my bones, but names will never hurt me!"

> [MISS BLUM *exits Left hurriedly. The* BOYS *start grabbing things right and left.*]

FIRST BOY. Give me this!

SECOND BOY. Where's my popsickle?

THIRD BOY. Hey, these are my potato chips.

JOE. Stop! Give me your money first.

FOURTH BOY. I will not!

FIRST AND SECOND BOYS. Jipper!

MR. FLUMDETTER [*rushing in*]. Here, here! What's the idea?

FIRST BOY. Let's mob 'em!

SECOND BOY. Pile on lumber! [*They charge* JOE *and* MR. FLUMDETTER. *There is a general broil. Stools and tables are upset.*]

MR. FLUMDETTER. I'll get the police.

THIRD BOY. Go eat a lemon.

FOURTH BOY. You're all wet!

JOE. Beat it! [*He and* MR. FLUMDETTER *eject the* BOYS.]

FIRST BOY. Ouch, my shins!

SECOND BOY. Leave go of me!

MR. FLUMDETTER. Stop biting!

THIRD BOY. I'm going to tell my mama!

FOURTH BOY. You're hurting me, you big brute!

SECOND BOY. Bully!

> [MR. FLUMDETTER, JOE *and the* BOYS *have all gone out Left by now, and the shop is deserted.*]

MR. FLUMDETTER [*calling off stage Left as he follows the* BOYS]. Stop! Stop! Catch 'em, Joe!

> [*The three* BOYS *enter Left.*]

LEN. What a mess! Looks like there's been a fire.

BILL. Wonder where Joe is. Say, you don't suppose they've all gone somewhere, do you?

TOM [*at the inner door*]. No one here.

LEN. What luck! You two go wait in the doorway. I'll get the cones. If you see anyone coming, whistle.

BILL. Right! And don't be stingy.

[TOM *and* BILL *go over to the door.* LEN *goes to the fountain and dishes out the cones, loading them well. It takes him a few minutes, and* BILL *and* TOM *are a bit lax in their lookout.* LEN *starts to the door with the cones when* TOM *suddenly gives a start.*]

TOM. Watch it! Joe's coming!

LEN. Where?

TOM. He's right here. He sees me. Hide 'em. [LEN *looks around in despair. He pops one cone in his mouth, but shudders with cold.*]

BILL [*calling*]. Well, what's been going on, Joe? [*Sotto voce.*] Hurry up!

[LEN, *in a fit of agony, stuffs another cone into his mouth as* JOE *comes in sight. He looks about him wildly, sees no hiding place, and thrusts the third cone into his trousers pocket.* JOE *enters, just in time to see him. He pretends that he has not noticed it.*]

JOE. Oh, nothing but a little rough and tumble with some kids. Phew, but it was hot work! Flumdetter's still chasing them.

TOM. I thought there'd at least been a cyclone! [LEN *is groaning and shivering.*]

JOE. What on earth's the matter with you, Len? You act as if you had a chill.

LEN [*swallowing the last of the ice cream in his mouth with a supreme effort.*] Ugh! Waugh! I—I—well—

JOE. Gosh, he looks really sick! [*He feels* LEN's *head.*] He's got a bad chill! I'll get a hot-water bottle. You go for a doctor, Bill. Here, sit down here. [*He shoves him into chair Center and rushes behind counter and fills hot-water bottle.*]

BILL. Oh, I think he'll be all right.

JOE. Nonsense! It looks like a serious case. Run! Can't you see he's sick? [JOE *returns to* LEN *at chair Center.*]

LEN. I'm not—og—I—I don't nnnneed a hhhhhot-waterrrr bbbottle. [*He rises to leave.* JOE *reaches him and pushes him down in a chair.*]

JOE. Sit down! Here! [*He puts the hot-water bottle on his lap.*] Bill, won't you run for the doctor?

BILL [*horror-stricken*]. I—I—

JOE [*to* LEN]. It won't do you any good unless you press it close. See—like this! [*He pushes the bottle firmly against the pocket which contains the cone.* LEN *squirms as drops begin to fall from his trousers. He tries to get up, but* JOE *holds him down, pressing the bottle even more firmly.*] I know it's hot, but this is for your own good.

LEN. I—I—I've gggot to gettt home. I—

JOE. Don't be foolish. You're too sick to move.

LEN. Tom, I— [*By this time there is a puddle on the floor.* JOE *sees it and pretends to start with surprise.*]

JOE. What on earth—! [*As he starts, he lets go to* LEN, *who jumps up and runs for the door followed by* BILL *and* TOM. *A stream flows behind him as he runs.*] Why, what the—! Len! Wait a minute, Len! [*Overcome with laughter, he follows them out the door Left. The store is deserted.* NE-VADA *reënters, Left.*]

NEVADA. Mistah Joe, ah must have got Mrs. Van der Veer de Lancy's bag by mistake, 'cause when ah got home ah had chocolate. . . . [*She sees there is no one in the store.*] Hey! Where's Joe? Mistah Joe! Mistah Joe! Hey, anybody! Man Lawd, what a mess this place be! Well, ah've got to have ice cream. Guess ah'll have to help mahself. [*She goes back of the fountain.*] Let's see. Chawclit, pineapple —funny there ain't no pineapple—, coffee, bis-que, lemon, vanella—here it is, vanella. Ain't no one here? Mistah Joe! Guess ah'll just have to help mahself. [*She sticks her finger in the can and licks it.*] Huh! Tastes like pine-apple. Must be vanella, though—says so. Gosh, Missus must be gettin' sore. Ah'd bettah hurry. [*She dips out the cream for herself.*] Here goes! [*She starts to leave.*] One thing, ah sure must be right this time. Ah got it mahself. [*Exit.*]

CURTAIN

THE BRAND

BY

FORREST I. BERKLEY-BOONE

A ROYALTY PLAY

THE CAST

Jim Lowe, *tenant farmer*
Ed Lane, *sheriff*
Dave, *his deputy*

THE SCENE

A settler's cabin, in the western Dakotas on the edge of the Bad Lands: late afternoon.

A table is down Right, with a chair on each side. A bed stands on the right against the back wall. Against the left wall of the room is a cupboard. In the center of the back wall is the door which is closed. In the wall left of the door is a window, with dirty curtains, the property of some former owner.

———————•———————

At the rise of the curtain, Jim Lowe *is lying on the bed. A noise at the window, the wind, perhaps, startles him. He jumps up, crosses to table and picks up a revolver. Carrying it ready, he goes to the window and cautiously looks out. Apparently he sees nothing. Going over to the corner he picks up a lantern. He carries it to the table. As he is working on it the face of* Ed Lane *appears at the window.* Jim *strikes a match, but he is so nervous that he is unable to secure a light from it. He strikes another. The face disappears.* Jim *lights the lantern. As he finishes, a knock comes at the door. Startled, he grabs the lantern and gun. He waits. The knock comes again. Quickly he puts the lantern on the floor in the middle of the room and then opens the door, concealing himself behind it as it opens.*

Jim. Come in!

236

[LANE *enters, pushing the door open with his arm. He is a clean, big fellow, about* JIM'S *age. As soon as he is in the room,* JIM *jumps out from behind the door with his gun leveled.* LANE *backs off hurriedly.*]

LANE. Hey! What'cha tryin' to do, kill me?

JIM [*lowering his gun*]. Oh, I didn't know who—I thought— Well, you never can tell who's comin'— [*They survey each other for a moment.*] Well, what d'ya' want?

LANE. Your name's Jim Lowe, ain't it?

[JIM *raises the gun up with a jerk.*]

JIM. Yeh, that's *my* name. What's *yours?* And what d'ya want?

LANE. My name's Lane. I gotta farm down here a ways. I was just comin' past and thought I'd drop in a bit.

[JIM *moves back, lowering the gun a little and indicates a chair.*]

JIM. The *name's* familiar. Set down, Lane. [LANE *sits at right of the table.*]

LANE. I was passin' through town an' some of the boys 'lowed you might wantta buy some cattle, you bein' new here. I gotta bunch to sell.

JIM. No, I don't reckon I want any. I'm kinda figgerin' on movin' away.

LANE. Movin'? 'Way the boys talked you hadn't been here more'n a month.

JIM. Month next Tuesday.

LANE. You must be awful anxious to move.

[*In the window the face of* DAVE, *the deputy sheriff, peers in.*]

JIM. Well, don't seem as if there's anything here to interest a man—a he-man, anyhow.

LANE. No, I guess there ain't now. Seems as if the whole durned place's gone to sleep. I tell ya', Lowe, it'd done your heart good to ha' seen this country about fifteen, twenty years back. It was a man's country then.

JIM. Yeh?

LANE. It sure was. Them was the days. 'Recollect one time ol'

Hans Thorne . . . [*He gets up and going to the window, pulls back the curtain and points. It is half pointing and half waving.* JIM *eyes him sharply.*] . . . you can see his light over there beyond the mill. 'Recollect ol' Hans had a peach of a fight. Seems him an' another feller had had a scrap an' Hans got a lickin'. Never forgot it, he didn't. Been about ten years before too. [*He comes down to the table.*] Well, he met this feller. Hans' hed been drinkin' an' he remembered the old grudge. Wasn't no ways uncommon for a man to carry a gun in them days, an' they was both totin'. [*He sits down at the table.*] Well, it was all over in half a second. Some o' the boys carried what was left o' the other feller into a saloon, 'n' Hans set the crowd up to the drinks. Kinda celebratin' the victory, I guess.

JIM [*moving around behind* LANE *and watching him*]. What'd they do to him?

LANE. Hans? . . . nuthin'. [*He chuckles.*] Jury decided the stranger he'd been killed in a foolish attempt to stop a movin' piece of lead. [*He laughs.*] I claim that was a clear case of juri-prudence.

JIM. Sure was.

LANE [*he sighs*]. Guess them days is gone fer good. Lowe, you sure missed half your life not bein' here when the country was lively.

JIM. Well, I don't reckon I missed a whole lot at that. I was in some pretty hot places 'bout that time myself. [*He pulls the chair left of table out and for the first time, sits.*]

LANE. That right?

JIM. One time I seen a man took right out of jail and hung on a tree—with the sheriff hangin' beside him. Sheriff had been in cahoots with a couple o' claim jumpers.

LANE. What happened to the other jumper?

JIM [*laconically*]. Got away.

LANE. Wonder where he went?

JIM [*sharply*]. How d' I know?

LANE. Sounds like the wild and woolly west all right.

JIM. Yeh, it was. Happened in the Black Hills.

LANE [*visibly impressed*]. You said you seen it? You mustta been out there?

JIM. Yeh . . . for awhile.

LANE [*admiringly*]. I always wanted to go out there but I never got enough nerve. Purty tough, I guess. How was it, did ya' get much gold?

JIM. Well, not an awful lot. 'Nuf to go on a bust once in awhile. Here's the only thing I got left of it now. [*He holds out his hand. On the middle finger is a heavy ring.* LANE *gets out of his chair and leans over to inspect it.*]

LANE. Well, durned if that ain't the queerest ring I ever seen. How'd ya' get it that way? Got your initial right on top, ain't it?

JIM. That ring's made out of one solid nugget. Just took it and whittled out the inside and then took my knife and whittled out around the "J" and made it stand out.

LANE. That's sure a funny ring.

JIM. There ain't another ring in the country like that one.

LANE. No, I reckon there ain't. Well, I missed out on that.

JIM. Seems to me I heard something outside. Did you?

[*He goes to the window, his back to the table.* LANE *reaches for the gun, holds it under the table and extracts the cartridges. Then he lays it down.*]

LANE [*while he is doing the business*]. Can't say I did.

JIM. Sounds like somebody.

LANE [*carelessly moving over to the window*]. We *did* kinda have a mite of excitement to-night though.

JIM [*with affected carelessness*]. Ya' don't say so?

LANE. Oh, not a great sight, I guess. Feller come staggerin' into town with one side o' his head and face all bloody. Said he'd been in a fight. [*Pause.*] Hadn't you heard about it?

JIM [*crossing to chair Left, and sitting*]. Ain't been anybody around since noon. Was he hurt bad?

LANE. I thought I seen a saddled horse there in the yard.

JIM. That's mine.

LANE [*quizzically*]. Ya' keep a saddled horse round all the time?

JIM [*embarrassed by the question*]. Why . . . I kinda figgered . . . I kinda figgered on riding into town to-night, maybe.

LANE. Oh, yeh.

JIM. But about this feller. Was he hurt bad?

LANE [*leaning on the wall between the window and the door*]. Oh, no. Leastways, I don't calc'late he was. Cussin' mighty.

JIM. An' what might his name ha' been?

LANE. Stranger to me. Name might ha' been Riley for all I know.

JIM [*in a tense voice, leaning forward*]. How'd it happen? What'd he tell about it?

LANE. Some quarrel between them I reckon. 'Way he tells it, he was walkin' along the road some'r's about dusk an' th' other feller jumps out from behind some brush and fetches him 'longside the head with a club. Knocked him down an' then stood there and laughed at him.

JIM [*fiercely*]. He said that, did he?

LANE. Yeh. Ya' know, it's funny, but he won't even tell the feller's name.

JIM [*grimly*]. An' then what'd he do?

LANE. He says he got up and they rassled around for the club. An' finally he gets it and throws it away.

JIM [*between his teeth as he rises*]. Y-e-a-h?

LANE [*standing down Right at table*]. Well, I guess he give it to him plenty then. Said he knocked him down an' made him beg for mercy. . . .

JIM [*leans over the table and snarls*]. He did, did he?

LANE. Leastways that's what he said.

JIM. He's a liar!

LANE [*quietly*]. Didn't he lick ya', Jim?

JIM. No, he didn't, the liar! He never could!

LANE [*his voice getting hard*]. Lick you, Jim?

JIM. Yeh, *me*— [*He realizes and ends lamely.*]—that is, su'posin' it was me.

LANE. What'd ya say his name was?

JIM. Ken Dutton.

[LANE's *voice sudden cracks like a whip.*]

LANE. How'd you know? There ain't been anybody 'round since noon. [*Softly.*] What'd you do it for, Jim?

JIM. Who said I did it?

LANE [*coming up behind table*]. You did. Ain't no use denyin' it.

JIM [*slowly*]. No, I guess there ain't. [*Fiercely.*] Yeh, I did it! I told him fifteen years ago I'd put my brand on him. I've done it. I'm sorry I didn't hurt him worse.

LANE [*leaning toward* JIM. *Still softly*]. What'd ya do it for, Jim?

JIM [*broken*]. It don't matter. Now I gotta go away. He'll get me. [*Suddenly he smashes his fist on the table.*] But I branded him all right!

LANE [*tensely*]. What'd ya do it for, Jim?

JIM. It ain't none of *your* business. He'll get me. I gotta go.

LANE. No, Jim. He won't get you. Now, Jim, I wanta ask you a question. Was you the other claim-jumper?

[*Startled,* JIM *leans back. An expression of fear crosses his face.*]

JIM. Who are you? What business you got askin' me that?

LANE. Ca'm down, Jim. I never seen him in my life before.

JIM. What d'ya wanta know for, then?

LANE. You don't look much like a claim-jumper, Jim.

JIM [*in a flood of bitterness*]. I ain't! He was the claim-jumper!

LANE. An' who was you?

JIM [*bitterly*]. I was a vigilante. I don't look much like it now, do I?

LANE. How'd it happen?

JIM. He knew me. An' ten years after I met him on the street in Cheyenne. He'd swore he'd get me. He nearly got me that night. I got a bullet in my shoulder now.

LANE. He ambushed ya?

JIM. Yeh. That kinda scared me. But I couldn't find him. He didn't dare try it there again. But purty near a year after, he found out where I lived. I was away, but he killed all my stock an' burnt my house. The law couldn't ketch him. I got scared an' started runnin'. I've moved three times since then. An' every time, he found me. He found me to-night.

LANE. Yeh?

JIM. I seen him a mite before he seen me. He didn't have time to pull his gun out of his pocket. I hit him, twice an' then he fell. He got up though, an' I hit him again. He fell an' I just got scared and started runnin'. [*Almost pleading.*] I never had no club, though, Lane. Just my bare fist.

[LANE *looks at him, sees he is telling the truth.*]

LANE [*regretfully*]. Jim, I hate'a do it . . . but I got to. I arrest you for . . .

[*The effect is instantaneous.* JIM *springs and grasping the gun, snaps.*]

JIM. Put yer hands up!

[LANE *complies. Covering him with the gun,* JIM *picks the lantern up from the floor and holds it cautiously up.*]

JIM. Now, who are ya'? Ya sneakin' spy! [*Suddenly the truth dawns on him.*] Say, I'll bet y'ur the sheriff, ain't ya'? [*He sees his answer in* LANE'S *face. Slowly he backs to the door. He puts the light down, to the right of door, just out of the way. His pent-up emotions flow through his voice.*] He hired the law t' kill me, didn't he? He can't hisself, so he hires you. He chased me fer ten years, now you're after me. Ya' think ya' kin get me, don't ya'? [*He pulls the gun up.*] Ya' ain't, sheriff. Yer at the end o' yer string right now. I'm leavin' ya' fer him to see. I'm a' leavin', sheriff. [*He pulls the trigger. It doesn't fire. Again. He sees that he has been tricked and opens the door. But his path is blocked by a very business-like rifle in the hands of* DAVE.]

DAVE. No, I reckon not. *This* gun goes off when I pull the trigger. Get back in there!

LANE. Didja get all he said, Dave?

DAVE. Every word, sheriff.

LANE. Always be sure yer gun's loaded, Jim. [*He rolls the cartridges out on the table.*]

JIM. What right ya' got, comin' in here?

LANE. I hate to do it, Jim. I arrest you for the murder of Ken Dutton.

JIM. Murder? . . . Murder?

LANE. He died two hours ago, without speakin'. [*Pause.*] You nearly got away with it, Jim. Nobody knew ya' knew him.

JIM. Murder! [*He is breaking, but with a touch of bravado.*] But . . . I put my brand on him!

LANE. Yeh, you did. Dutton was killed by a blow on the temple. Right there was the mark of your ring with your initial. Yeh, Jim, you branded him. If it hadn't been for that, you'd a' got away.

[LANE *is still standing by the table. The* DEPUTY *close to the open door. The light is close to him. Defiantly* JIM *walks up to the* DEPUTY *and extends his hands for the cuffs. The* DEPUTY, *reaching to his belt for them, is off guard just a minute. It is enough. With a leap,* JIM *kicks the lantern out. It is pitch black. For a few seconds there is the sound of struggling, then the door slamming, and finally:*]

LANE. The light! The lantern!

[*Quickly* DAVE *strikes a match, and lights the lantern. The door is closed. Gun in hand,* LANE *runs to the door and opens it. From out of the night comes the muffled sound of a horse's hoofs, running at full speed.* DAVE *slumps.*]

DAVE. That horse! It's my fault, Lane. He'll be in the Bad Lands in the mornin'.

[LANE *walks over to the door and looks out into the night. Then he hooks his fingers in his belt and leans against the*

*door frame. A minute he leans there, then he turns. There
is a half smile on his face as he says, quizzically:*]
LANE. Well, Dave . . . I didn't figgur t' run fer re-election,
. . . anyhow.

CURTAIN

MRS. MAGICIAN'S MISTAKE

BY

VIRGINIA DIXON

A NON-ROYALTY PLAY

THE CAST

MAGICIAN
KALLYHOO, *his friend and pupil*
TOM PERKINS, *who lives next door*
MRS. MAGICIAN
MRS. FRIEND
As many children as you want

THE SCENE

A room in the house of MAGICIAN.
*Along the back wall are shelves with large black bottles and
boxes. These are labeled by chalk letters with "Hen's
Teeth," "Guinea Pig Tails," "Magic Carpet Yarn," "Elixir
of Youth" and "Recipes." One very big bottle at least three
feet high, with a label, "The Most Magical Magic of All,"
stands in the middle of the back wall on a pedestal. A large
table faces the audience down Right Center, on top of which
are large wooden chopping bowls, spoons, alcohol lamp, and
test tubes in stands. Two stools are placed on either side.
On the left stage a large rocking or Morris chair faces a
sofa or bench which is flat against the left wall. Just above
this sofa is the single door to the room. The room is a
peculiar combination of the realistic and the magical.*

THE CHARACTERS AND COSTUMES

MAGICIAN, *wears a black gown and black pointed hat with
crescent moon and star decoration.*
KALLYHOO *wears a black gown and skullcap, indicating he
isn't quite as magical as* MAGICIAN.
TOM PERKINS *and the other* CHILDREN *wear ordinary
clothes.*

MRS. MAGICIAN *and* MRS. FRIEND *are dressed as little girls,*
"playing lady," would be dressed. Their skirts are too long;
their hats are too big. Each carries a handbag.

———————•———————

At the rise of curtain MAGICIAN *sits moodily in rocking chair,*
head in hands, staring into space. KALLYHOO *knocks at door.*
MAGICIAN *starts, turns around toward door.*

MAGICIAN. Come in. [KALLYHOO *enters.*] Oh, it's you, is it
Kallyhoo? I'm glad to see you. Come in and sit down.

     [KALLYHOO *sits on sofa and looks at* MAGICIAN *curiously.*

KALLYHOO. Well, Magician, what's the matter with you this
fine beautiful day? You look so grumpy and gloomy. What's
the trouble?

MAGICIAN. You're right, Kally, I am miserable, just plain
miserable. I haven't anything to do. Mrs. Magician has
gone out in the car with a friend of hers, and I'm all alone
and I haven't anything to do and I can't think of any more
magic to make. I've got dozens of wishing rings and magic
carpets, and good luck charms out in the storeroom there.
Nobody seems to need any more of those things, and I just
can't think of any good new magic ideas.

KALLYHOO. Oh, never mind. Let's just play this afternoon.

MAGICIAN. I've got to work today. It isn't Saturday, you
know.

KALLYHOO. Come on and go fishing with me.

MAGICIAN. What's the fun of going fishing if I take my magic
fish hooks along? Every time you put one into the water,
there's a fine big fish on it—and by and by you get so tired
pulling them in. Besides I don't think magic fish taste as
good as the regular kind, and I never can catch any of those.
—No, I don't want to go fishing.

KALLYHOO. Well.—Let's both think of something new to make.
Let's think *very* hard and maybe something will come.

     [*They both hold their heads in their hands, and think*
very hard, eyes closed for a minute.]

KALLYHOO. I have it. [*Suddenly he jumps up, excited, and*

crosses to center of room.] I know what you must do. You'll make hundreds, yes thousands of people very happy. It's wonderful. [*Dances up and down.*] It's really remarkable. Why haven't you stupid magicians thought of it before? How thrilled everybody will be,—children, mothers and fathers,—teachers, everyone. [*He dances over to* MAGICIAN, *pulls him to his feet, and dances him around, Center, even though he protests.*]

MAGICIAN. Kally, stop it. [*Pulling away from him to Left Center.*] Whatever is making you act so crazy? Stop your prancing, and let go of me and tell me what's in your mind.

KALLYHOO. Oh it's too lovely, too beautiful. All little children will love you, love you, and we'll all be happy, happy, happy, happy. [*Starts in his dance again.*]

MAGICIAN. Stop it, I say, and tell me what this grand idea of yours is. Hurry. [KALLYHOO *stops his dance, goes over to* MAGICIAN *mysteriously, and whispers in his ear.* MAGICIAN *looks puzzled, then interested, then starts in dancing too.*] Oh, it *is* wonderful. What a beautiful idea. We must find a way to do it. How beautiful, how thrilling! All the little children will love us. Kally, you're splendid. Now we must think again how to do it. [*He sits on stool left of table.*] Come sit down and let's think. [KALLY *goes to stool at right of table and sits.*] Ready,—one, two, three. Think.

[*They both think very hard for a few seconds with their heads resting on both hands which rest on their knees.*]

MAGICIAN [*thoughtfully*]. It will be very hard,—to make magic medicine that will make children know their lessons without studying them,—but Kally,—it's such a *good* idea, we must do it.

KALLYHOO. Just think. No more study hours, no more home work,—all the time just to play and *recite* lessons in. And won't the teachers be pleased, too, and the fathers and mothers?

MAGICIAN. It will be hard to make such a very magic medicine, but I think we can do it.—Let me see, what have I got to put in it? [*He gets up and goes to shelf and looks anxiously at all the bottles and boxes, shaking some, looking into others.* KALLYHOO *follows him and does everything that* MAGICIAN *does, just after him.*]

MAGICIAN [*meditating*]. No,—that won't do, I know. [*As he puts down one box.*]

KALLYHOO. No, that won't do, I know. [*He puts down box.*]

MAGICIAN. It's got to be something very strong, of course, but not harmful.

KALLYHOO. Oh, yes, very strong of course, but not harmful.

MAGICIAN. And then, you know, it must be intellectual. [*He looks off into space, lost in deep thought.*]

KALLYHOO. Oh, yes, certainly very intellectual. [*He looks off into space.*] Don't you think we might start in with just *arithmetic* at first and gradually work it up to include *all* subjects? That would be a help to almost everyone, I know. We could begin by taking all the *answers* in the back of the arithmetic book, chop them up fine, mix them with vinegar and salt, beat well and bake in a quick oven for forty minutes. Then all anyone would have to do would be to eat a little of this arithmetic cake when he got up in the morning, and presto,—there you are, all the answers to all the arithmetic problems for the day. [*He beams at* MAGICIAN *who looks a bit disgusted.*]

MAGICIAN. Really, Kally, that's just like you. You always go ruin even your good ideas by making stupid suggestions. No, it won't do *at all*. This new magic of mine is going to be for everything *all at once*. Now don't interrupt my thinking again unless you have a *really* good idea. [*Starts thinking.*] Ah,—ah-h-h . . . [*Very slowly.*] I believe . . . I . . . have . . . it. [*Goes back to big bottle on shelf. Lifts it down very carefully, shakes it,—looks into it dubiously,—shakes it again, brings it over to table.*] I've got it! [*He paces up and down with* KALLYHOO *following him.*] I need the old arithmetics with the answers,—you did give me an idea, Kally, even if you are rather dumb. I need arithmetic answers, maps of all the continents, an ancient history, a European and an American history,—a grammar, and a speller. You get them from the cupboard.

[MAGICIAN *goes to his stool.* KALLYHOO *goes and brings books from the shelves to table.*]

MAGICIAN. Put them in that biggest chopping bowl and chop them up very, very fine. [KALLYHOO *starts into work.* MAGICIAN *darts to closet again and brings back a card.*] While we're at it, Kally, we might just as well put in a few A + 's in deportment too, I guess. [*Gives card to* KALLYHOO *who chops it up and adds it to mixture.* MAGICIAN *goes back and forth to shelf, bringing bottles and boxes to table.*]

KALLYHOO. There.—I think that's a pretty good job. I had to be very careful not to split any of those infinitives in that grammar book. Some teachers are so fussy. This is quite an important job,—the mixing always is, they tell me.

[MAGICIAN *inspects it. Nods approval.*]

MAGICIAN. Now, be careful, and don't spill it, and bring it over to my end of the table. [KALLYHOO *obeys.* MAGICIAN *looks at it critically, then begins adding a dash of this and a sprinkle of that out of his various bottles and boxes.*] Now, what do you think? Hadn't we better put in just a pinch of Latin and algebra and a drop or two of nature study,—just to be on the safe side?

KALLYHOO. Splendid idea. I'll go get some. [*Goes to cupboard and brings back a few pages which he tears up and puts in.*] Oh, I'm so excited,—but how are we going to make it *work?*

MAGICIAN. Never you mind. Don't you suppose I've thought of that? That's where my superior intelligence and greater understanding come in. You *have* the idea,—*I* make it work. See that big bottle? [KALLYHOO *nods.*] It's the most magical of all magic in the whole entire world. And there's only a tiny drop of it left. But it's so magical it can do anything, and I'm going to use the last drop of it to make it so that little children can forever after always know all of their lessons. Now, are we ready? [*He picks up big bottle, turns it upside down, shakes it carefully, turns it rightside up and*

*looks inside, then turns it upside down and squeezes it very
hard.* KALLYHOO *takes up big mixing spoon and stirs the
stuff in the bowl vigorously.* MAGICIAN *lights spirit lamp and
together they place bowl over it.*]

MAGICIAN. Stir it, Kally. It won't take but a few seconds because my magic is so very strong. The last drop of the most
magical stuff in the world, but nobody will ever be bothered
again with remembering dates, and how to spell hard words,
or anything. It's worth sacrificing the last drop for that.

[*They carefully lift the bowl on to the table again.* MAGI-
CIAN *peers in, and lifts spoon up. A stringy black substance
—like molasses—is dipped up.*]

KALLYHOO. It looks *very* powerful. I'm sure it will do anything. Shall *we* try it?

MAGICIAN [*almost out of patience*]. Kally, why don't you
use your brains? Would it be a fair test to try it on you
and me? We know so much already that we wouldn't know
whether it was working or not. Go get that stupid Tom
Perkins who lives next door. [KALLYHOO *hurries out, calling,* "TOM, TOM."] Tom is so dumb he can't learn anything. He doesn't even go to school. And he knows just as
much as if he did. [*He stirs the mixture.*]

KALLYHOO [*off stage*]. Here he is. Now I have him.

[*Almost instantly he comes back with stupid* TOM.]

KALLYHOO. Here he is. He doesn't know anything.

MAGICIAN. How do you know he doesn't know anything?

KALLYHOO. I asked him and he said he didn't.

MAGICIAN [*kindly*]. Tom, would you like to be the bright-
est boy in town?

TOM [*stupidly*]. I don't know.

MAGICIAN [*a little surprised*]. What, don't you want to know
as much as the bright little boys and girls?

TOM [*still stupidly*]. I don't know.

KALLYHOO [*triumphantly*]. You see, he doesn't know anything. Now if this stuff works on him—

MAGICIAN. I'll give him a taste of it, and we'll see.

KALLYHOO. A taste of it. He'll need half of it.

MAGICIAN. Tom, open your mouth. [*He takes spoonful of mixture and gives it to boy who swallows it.* MAGICIAN *and* KALLYHOO *look at him anxiously. He makes a terrible face, then coughs, looks at one, and then the other, coughs.*]

TOM. I have reached this conclusion, namely, that the difference between the total product of a given piece of land and the product resulting from an equal expenditure on the margin of cultivation is the measure of the specific contribution of that land to the social income. As Marshall remarked there is a fundamental difference between those incomes yielded by agents of production which are to be regarded as rents or quasi-rents and those—

[MAGICIAN *and* KALLY *start in amazement.*]

KALLYHOO. Give him some water quick.

MAGICIAN. That mixture is too strong. Get some water. We can't have him going on like that.

[KALLYHOO *gives boy a drink, followed in quick succession by two more.* TOM *gulps them down quickly.*]

TOM. Hi, Mr. Magician, what are you feeding me? That stuff burned terribly. Give me more water. [KALLYHOO *gives him two glasses.*] There, that's better. Well—I guess I better be running along now. I've got some reading to do before dinner. [*He disappears out door.*]

KALLYHOO [*gasping*]. Wasn't that *awful?* It's a good thing we tried that strong stuff on such a very stupid child. What would it have done to an average bright one?

MAGICIAN. Yes, it was lucky.

KALLYHOO. Now let's put some water in this stuff and dilute it so that we can use it with safety.

MAGICIAN. I hope we didn't give Tom too much water and spoil all the good it did him. Here, I'll do it, and you go get all the children who were kept in after school this afternoon and bring them here. Tell the teacher we'll take care of them.

[KALLYHOO *goes out and* MAGICIAN *proceeds to dilute mixture and add a little of this, that, and stir. Very shortly voices are heard off stage and* KALLYHOO *comes back very soon with mob of* CHILDREN.]

KALLYHOO. Here we are, and everyone has made some sort of mistake in the lesson today. [*He lines them up in a row, according to size, inspects them carefully, makes a change or two.* CHILDREN *stand quietly, a little bit scared.*]

MAGICIAN [*steps out and looks them over*]. They don't *look* stupid, [CHILDREN *giggle*] but if you say they are, why, of course, you know. Well, we'll soon fix them up. [*Goes to table, takes bowl and gives it to* KALLYHOO *to hold. They go to* FIRST CHILD. MAGICIAN *gives him a spoonful.*]

FIRST CHILD. Columbus discovered America in 1492.

[MAGICIAN *gives* SECOND CHILD *a spoonful.*]

SECOND CHILD. D-e-c-*e*-i-v-e.

[MAGICIAN *gives* THIRD CHILD *a spoonful.*]

THIRD CHILD. Asia is the largest of the continents. China and Siberia are—

[MAGICIAN *gives* FOURTH CHILD *a spoonful.*]

FOURTH CHILD. $11 \times 11 = 121$

[MAGICIAN *gives* FIFTH CHILD *a spoonful.*]

FIFTH CHILD. "It was the schooner Hesperus"—

[MAGICIAN *gives* SIXTH CHILD *a spoonful.*]

SIXTH CHILD. Amo, amas, amat—

[MAGICIAN *gives* SEVENTH CHILD *a spoonful.*]

SEVENTH CHILD. First William the Norman, then William his son—

[MAGICIAN *gives eighth child a spoonful.*]

EIGHTH CHILD. "Maitre corbeau sur un arbre perché—"

[MAGICIAN *gives* NINTH CHILD *a spoonful.*]

NINTH CHLD. If a banana and a half cost a cent and a half, a dozen bananas—

[MAGICIAN *gives* TENTH CHILD *a spoonful.*]

TENTH CHILD. Paris is the capital of France—

MAGICIAN. It works, hooray!

KALLYHOO. It's wonderful! It's marvelous!

MAGICIAN. It's the best piece of magic I've ever done.

KALLYHOO. Just think what you've done for all the children in the world. There'll never never never be any more home work or lessons.

[*Great hubbub among the* CHILDREN *still shouting their bits of knowledge. Much running around, saying their sentences to each other.*]

MAGICIAN [*calming the uproar*]. Children. Let's all go back to school and surprise the teacher. No more stupid children.

KALLYHOO. Just a spoonful every night before you go to bed.

[*They line the* CHILDREN *up two by two and they all go out chattering and laughing and giggling, but still saying their sentences. Almost immediately* MRS. MAGICIAN *and her* FRIEND *enter.*]

MRS. MAGICIAN. Well, now, didn't we have a nice drive? I did so want George to come along this afternoon. You know he really works *too* hard, and this magic business is so wearing.

MRS. FRIEND [*Sits on sofa, Left*]. It would do him good to get away from his work now and then.

MRS. MAGICIAN. Will you *look* at the mess he's left this place in. [*She hastily tidies up room, collecting boxes and putting them in their places,—piles up utensils on table.*]

MRS. FRIEND. It looks as if he'd been very busy today. What fun it must be,—being a magician.

MRS. MAGICIAN [*still busy, clearing up*]. It's interesting all right. But look at this room. I'm always having to pick up after him.

MRS. FRIEND. You know it was lucky you had that magic puncture fixer this afternoon when we had the flat tire. All you had to do was to rub it on, and the tire was mended.

MRS. MAGICIAN. Yes, it is convenient. But magic is so messy. He leaves everything for me to pick up. I wonder what this is? [*Going to bowl and sniffing.*] It doesn't smell very nice. I wonder if it's spoiled? [*Continues to pick up and clean up.* TOM *enters, looking almost as stupid as he did at first. He comes into room, looks around questioningly, as if he were trying to remember something.*]

MRS. MAGICIAN. Well, Tom Perkins, what do you want?

Tom [*dully*]. I don't know. [*He continues to look around, then starts towards table where bowl of magic mixture is, with some gleam of intelligence in his face.*]

Mrs. Friend. Such a nice looking boy,—too bad he's so stupid.

Tom. I want some.

Mrs. Magician [*not unkindly*]. Some what, Tom?

Tom. I don't know— [*Troubled.*] It made me very happy.

Mrs. Friend. Whatever is he talking about?

[Mrs. magician *continues her tidying up. She goes to bowl again and sniffs again.* tom *follows her and points to bowl.*]

Mrs. Magician. Tom, what do you want? [*To* mrs. friend.] I declare this is dirty looking stuff. I think I'd better throw it out. [*She picks up bowl.* tom *rushes at her.*]

Tom. No, no,—it's good, good. Don't throw it away.

[Mrs. magician *and* mrs. friend *look at him in amazement. He continues to make protests.*]

Mrs. Friend. I think he gets worse instead of better. His mother and father ought to take better care of him. [*She rises.*] Here, Tom. Be quiet. [*She pushes him away.* mrs. magician *lifts up bowl and starts to door with it.*]

Tom. Don't, don't. It's good.

[Mrs. friend *grabs him as he tries to stop* mrs. magician. *She throws the magic out of the door.*]

Tom. Don't. Don't. It's good to eat.

mrs. magician. Good to eat. Did you ever?

[Mrs. friend *lets go* tom.]

Tom. She throwed it away. She throwed it away. [*He runs out door.*]

Mrs. magician. Whatever made that child act that way? There, this place looks better. If you'll sit down a minute, we'll have a cup of tea.

Mrs. Friend. I'm so sorry, but I'll have to run along. I had such a nice afternoon. Let's go again sometime soon. [*She goes out.* mrs. magician *still putters around as voices of* children *and* magician *are heard, returning. They all troop in beaming, and noisy.*]

MAGICIAN. My dear, such an afternoon—the best piece of magic I've ever done. You'll be so glad when you hear about it. Kally helped too,—and all these children here, made happy for ever more, as well as all the children in the whole world. Such a piece of magic as I've been up to. Do you know what I've done?

MRS. MAGICIAN. I'm sure it *must* be lovely. Everyone looks so pleased. I'm so glad you've done something nice for the children. Tell me all about it.

FIRST CHILD. I know *all* my history lesson.

SECOND CHILD. I can spell *all* the words in the spelling book.

THIRD CHILD. Geography isn't hard any more at *all*.

FOURTH CHILD. Do you want to hear me say my tables?

FIFTH CHILD. I know *all* my poem by heart.

[MAGICIAN *motions* CHILDREN *to be quiet.*]

MAGICIAN. I've just stirred up a new kind of potion. If a child takes one teaspoonful of it before he goes to bed, he'll know all his lessons the next day without studying them a bit. Isn't that wonderful?

[*The* CHILDREN *all rejoice.*]

MRS. MAGICIAN. George, how thrilling! Beautiful! Georgeous! How did you ever do it? Tell me.

MAGICIAN. Just you look at this. [*He starts to go to bowl, sees it empty, looks startled and then angry.*] Who's been meddling with my things? Who touched that bowl? Who threw out that mixture?

[CHILDREN *all look scared and start weeping.*]

MRS. MAGICIAN. What's the matter with you? I threw out that dirty looking stuff in the bowl. Never have I seen this place look worse than it did this afternoon when I came in with Mrs. Friend. She was polite about it, of course, but I should think you could learn to make your magic without making such a mess all over the place.

KALLYHOO. You,—you threw it away?

MRS. MAGICIAN. Of course I threw out that stuff.

[MAGICIAN *seems half stunned.* KALLYHOO *sinks dejectedly into sofa Left.* CHILDREN *cry softly.*]

MAGICIAN [*in severe tones*]. Mrs. Magician, do you know what you have done? You have just sent thousands of little children back forever into the bondage of home work and lessons. After I spent all this afternoon getting them out of it, too. See what this mania of yours for cleaning up has done. [*Sinks into chair Left, despondent.*] Children, go get your books.

CURTAIN

BREAKFAST

BY
G. WHITFIELD COOK

A ROYALTY PLAY

THE CAST

A Pompous Husband
A Well-meaning Wife
A Son
A Daughter
A Small Daughter Who Won't Eat Prunes
A Maid

THE SCENE

A dining-room at breakfast time.

A double door Right leads into the hall. Along the back wall a sideboard stands in the center. On the left wall is the door leading into the pantry and kitchen. A rectangular dining table is in the center of the room. Chairs with arms are at each end where places are set. On the up-stage side are two chairs and places set. On the down-stage side there is one chair and place set in the middle. A mirror hangs on the right wall below the door. There is in the atmosphere that unsettled, hurry-scurry feeling that pervades the air of American households at the time of day when prunes, oatmeal and three-minute eggs are the dominating influence.

THE CHARACTERS AND COSTUMES

John, *the pompous husband, is the dignified type of father and husband. Inclined to width rather than length. There is something a little ridiculous about his would-be pomposity. One can see that he knows life from every angle, on absolutely every angle. He will tell you that himself.*

Isabel, *the well-meaning wife, is a quiet woman, yet there is determination in her face. Upon her shoulders falls the diffi-*

*cult task of managing the family and at the same time let-
ting her husband think he is managing it.*

GEORGE, *the son, is a vigorous person with all the earmarks
of a high-school sophomore.*

WINIFRED, *the daughter, is clad in a decidedly chic dress and
large pearl earrings. She is a very blasé high-school senior
who affects a bored, world-weary manner which is extremely
odd.*

EDNA, *the small daughter who won't eat prunes, is a girl of
about seven years. We can see that she has a great deal of
her father's pomposity, even at that tender age.*

———————

At the rise of the curtain ISABEL *is sitting at the left end of the
dining-room table eating something . . . probably prunes,
for the family is addicted to prunes. A* MAID *enters from
the kitchen Left and sets a dish of prunes at each of the two
places up stage and at the one down stage and a glass of
orange juice at the place set on the right. She goes out
Left. For a moment the wife is alone on the stage. We must
not begrudge her this moment, for it is about the only peace-
ful one she has during the entire day.* JOHN *enters from the
hall, Right. He carries under his arm a book and the morning paper. In silence he takes his place at the right end of
table opposite his wife, puts down his book, and opens his
paper and drinks his orange juice while he reads. There is a
moment of domestic silence. Then the* MAID *enters from Left
and stands at the right of table by* JOHN.

MAID. Oatmeal?

[*This is launched at the* HUSBAND. *That good man, however, is quite oblivious to such insignificant subjects. He remains hidden behind his paper.*]

MAID [*rather ferociously*]. Oatmeal?

[*Silence.*]

WIFE. John, dear, oatmeal? [*Silence.* MAID *registers disgust.*]
John, will you please come out from behind that paper!
[JOHN *hears and obeys.*] Will you have some oatmeal?

HUSBAND [*feeling extremely sorry for himself bullied around like this*]. Of course not. [*He resumes his reading.*]

    [MAID *crosses to Left.*]

HUSBAND. Er, I think I will have some after all. I believe you once told me, Isabel, that oatmeal is good for one.

    [*The* MAID *exits Left.*]

WIFE. So glad to see you are beginning to eat what is good for you, dear. It's a good example for the children.

    [*The* HUSBAND *folds his paper and assumes an extra look of importance.*]

HUSBAND. Exactly. That's why I am eating oatmeal. I realize that it will be a good example for the children. Which leads me directly to a subject that I wish to discuss with you.

WIFE [*always dutiful*]. Yes, dear?

HUSBAND. It is in regard to the children.

WIFE. Yes, dear.

HUSBAND. For a long time I have felt that we should take some drastic action in regard to the behavior of George and Winifred. Now George seems to lack almost everything, courtesy, common sense . . . why, I understand he refers to me as the . . . ah . . . old man.

WIFE. But, dear, you must have patience with him. Remember he is only a boy. Besides, there's . . .

HUSBAND. That is no excuse, Isabel, you are not firm enough with him. I don't want to say anything against you, but I don't think . . .

WIFE. Well, if I am not bringing up the children properly, perhaps you had better take all the responsibility.

HUSBAND. Exactly what I propose to do. And I shall begin this very morning. [*The* MAID *enters from the Left bringing his oatmeal to him and then exits with empty glass.*] Isabel, I have been reading this book. [*He holds up the book he brought in with him.*] A very excellent book on "The Best Methods of Raising Children." I intend to follow these methods sincerely; and I know there will be results. [*He begins to eat his oatmeal.*]

WIFE [*despairingly*]. Oh, John . . .

HUSBAND. What's the matter?

WIFE. Oh, John, you are always following methods laid out in some foolish book written by some foolish man.

HUSBAND. Why, Isabel, you know . . .

WIFE. Oh, I know! Remember what happened when you followed the methods told of in a book entitled "How to Grow Hair in Twenty-four Hours"? And the time you followed the rules from "How to Become a Social Lion"? You are always reading books on how to do something. Silly, impractical books! And this is the silliest of them all.

HUSBAND [*a bit hurt*]. You haven't even read the book.

WIFE. Well, I know! As though anybody could tell anybody else how to bring up children.

HUSBAND. Isabel, I am going to show you that this book is correct in its ideas.

WIFE. Oh, all right.

HUSBAND. This book lays down three laws and only three that must be followed. First, the parent must be strict. Second, the parent must show interest in the affairs of his children. And third, the parent must set a good example. I have already set a good example by eating oatmeal, which I detest. And I intend to set another by refraining from drinking my usual second cup of coffee.

WIFE. But you've never gone without your second cup!

HUSBAND. I'm determined to show these children the virtue of will power.

WIFE. Well, you can try your methods as much as you like. *I* won't stop you.

[*There enters from the hall Right* EDNA. *She walks sedately to the table and sits at the place set on the down-stage side.*]

HUSBAND [*in his best fatherly manner*]. Good morning, Edna.

SMALL DAUGHTER. Morning, Papa. [*She notices the prunes in front of her.*] Oh, Mamma, prunes again? [*She makes an extremely unbeautiful face.*]

WIFE. Yes, dear, and you must eat them.

SMALL DAUGHTER. Well, I won't. [*She swings around in her*

chair facing her father and is profile to the audience.]

WIFE [*calmly. This is no new occurrence for her*]. Oh, yes, you will, darling.

SMALL DAUGHTER. I *won't.*

WIFE. Now, Edna, you . . .

HUSBAND. Isabel! [*He conveys to her that he wants her to be silent and allow him to try his methods.* ISABEL *sighs.*]

HUSBAND [*talking slowly to* EDNA]. Now, Edna, do you know how good prunes are for little girls? They make little girls grow big and strong. A girl who doesn't eat prunes can't be well. And you want to be well, don't you? [EDNA *isn't sure that she does and swings around facing her mother.*] Whenever you see prunes you should say to yourself, "Little prunes make big girls." Now, just taste these prunes and see how good they are.

SMALL DAUGHTER. I don't *like* prunes.

HUSBAND. But they're so good. Why, I like them immensely.

SMALL DAUGHTER. You never eat them, papa.

HUSBAND [*indignantly*]. Well, that doesn't mean I don't like them. I do. [*He eats one of* EDNA'S *prunes.*] They're so good.

SMALL DAUGHTER. Well, if you like them, you can have them all.

[*The* WIFE *snickers and the* HUSBAND *throws her a withering glance.*]

[*At this point* GEORGE *can be heard coming downstairs, and soon he appears in the doorway Right, combing his hair and whistling the latest jazz tune. He goes to the mirror on the wall Right and gazes at his locks as he combs them. Not for one moment does he stop his loud whistle.*]

HUSBAND. Good morning, George.

SON [*in between notes of his tune*]. Mornin'.

HUSBAND. George, is there any particular reason why you must comb your hair in the dining-room?

SON. Ask me another.

HUSBAND. Answer me!

SON. The answer is "No."

HUSBAND. Then I wish you would do it upstairs. The dining-room is not the place.

[*The* SON *dashes to his place on the left up-stage side of the table near his* MOTHER. *He starts eating his prunes, continuing his whistling between mouthfuls.*]

HUSBAND. Please don't whistle at the table.

SON. All right. But isn't that a swell tune?

HUSBAND. I didn't notice it.

SON. It goes like this. [*He starts the tune again, but is quickly interrupted by his* FATHER.]

HUSBAND. Not now, George. I can hear it some other time.

SON. Gee, Chic Johnson's orchestra can play it fine.

[*The* MAID *brings in the cereal for* GEORGE *and takes out his prune dish. The* SMALL DAUGHTER *is still looking away from her prunes, and making folds in her dress.*]

WIFE. Edna, you must eat your prunes. You can't have anything else to eat until you've eaten all of them.

SMALL DAUGHTER. Mamma, I can't eat 'em.

WIFE. Oh, yes, you can. [*She takes* EDNA'S *spoon and dishing one out, holds it towards* EDNA.] Here. Here's a nice soft one.

[*The* SMALL DAUGHTER *turns her head away.*]

SON [*looking disgustedly at* EDNA, *and wondering why there are such things as little sisters*]. Gosh, why don't the little simp eat 'em?

WIFE. Now, George.

SON. Well, why don't she?

HUSBAND [*correctingly*]. Why *doesn't* she?

[*The* SON *takes no heed.*]

SON [*after a moment during which he hastily eats cereal*]. Say, Dad, do you think I could have a saxophone?

HUSBAND. Saxophone?

SON. Yeh, Chic Johnson told me yesterday that I had an ear for music and that I oughta get a sax or somethin'. I've always thought I'd like to have a sax.

HUSBAND. I think a violin would be better, George.

SON. Naw! Violins are no good. I want somethin' that can make some noise.

HUSBAND [*hearing the imaginary strains and squawks of a saxophone*]. Well, we'll see.

WIFE. Where in the world is Winifred? It's getting late.

SON. She's curlin' her hair, and probably burnin' it all off, too.

WIFE [*going to doorway Right, and calling*]. Oh, Winifred! Winifred!

DAUGHTER [*still upstairs*]. I'm coming!

WIFE. Well, do hurry. It's after eight! [*She resumes her seat and continues to coax the* SMALL DAUGHTER *to eat prunes.*]

HUSBAND [*assuming his most pompous, grave manner*]. George, for a long time I have wanted to talk to you. About various matters. But particularly about your attitude. Your attitude, my boy, is not nearly as good as it might be. [*The older* DAUGHTER *enters Right.*] You are careless. You overlook the little niceties . . . [*The* SON *sees the* DAUGHTER *and lets out a whoop.*]

SON. Whoopee, she's got on earrings!

[*The family stare at the* DAUGHTER *as she takes her seat right of up-stage side by her father.*]

SON. And look at the size of 'em!

DAUGHTER. Shut up.

WIFE. Really, Winifred, if you knew how ridiculous you looked . . .

SON. Ridiculous! Why, she's absolutely funny! And with her hair all frizzed up . . .

DAUGHTER. Oh, be still! [*She eats one prune.*]

HUSBAND [*deciding that this is a good opportunity to try out the method involving firmness*]. Winifred! Take those things off!

DAUGHTER. Don't be silly, father.

HUSBAND. I am not silly. I mean what I say. Take them off. I won't have any daughter of mine going around the streets looking ridiculous.

DAUGHTER. You act as if you had never seen earrings before. Why, lots of the girls wear them.

WIFE. But they don't suit you, Winifred.

SON. I'll say they don't.

DAUGHTER [to SON]. Oh, you're so smart, aren't you? Well, you'd better be careful. Remember that I can tell a thing or two about you.

[The SON remembers that she can and subsides into silence.]

HUSBAND. Are you going to remove those things?

DAUGHTER. Oh, if you insist. [She hesitates.] But all the girls wear them.

[The HUSBAND looks very firm and she reluctantly removes the earrings.]

[The MAID enters from Left, serves coffee to HUSBAND and WIFE, and cereal to DAUGHTER, and takes away the cereal dishes from HUSBAND and WIFE.]

SON [to DAUGHTER]. Dad says I can have a sax.

HUSBAND. I said I would see.

SON. Oh, well . . .

DAUGHTER. That'll be fine. Harold plays the saxophone beautifully.

SON. Who's Harold?

DAUGHTER. He took me to Fuller's dance last night.

HUSBAND. What's his last name?

DAUGHTER. I think it's Meehan.

HUSBAND. You *think!!* Do you mean to tell me you're not even sure of his last name?

DAUGHTER [with great dignity]. Father, I trust you're a gentleman.

WIFE. He's really a very nice boy, John.

DAUGHTER. And aren't his eyes simply heavenly?

WIFE. Well, I didn't notice whether . . .

DAUGHTER. Oh, they are! Absolutely adorable!

SON [with disgust]. Oh, my gosh!

DAUGHTER. I always have liked brown eyes. I wish you had brown eyes, George.

Son. Oh, you do, do you? Well, I'll have 'em changed just for you!

Wife. Come, Winifred, eat your oatmeal.

Daughter. I'm not very hungry.

Son [*in mock earnestness*]. She's in love, mother. They're never hungry when they're that way.

[*The* Daughter *looks dreamily at nothing.*]

Husband. Now, really, Winifred, this is too much. Harold may be a very nice boy, but that is no reason why you should let him prevent you from eating your cereal.

Daughter [*dabbling with her oatmeal*]. He's wonderful!

Husband. Winifred! Do come to life.

Son. She's in love, I tell you.

Husband. Hush! You know, Winifred, you have worried me quite a bit of late. You act so silly over some of these boys.

Son. Henry Sills, for instance.

Daughter. What about Henry Sills?

Son. Uh-huh. Wouldn't you like to know?

Husband. Well, as I was saying . . .

Daughter. Oh, please don't give me a lecture.

Husband. I won't. But I must talk to you sometimes for your own good. I want you to have a good time, and all that, but I can't have you trotting all over with boys whose last names you don't know.

Daughter. I said it was Meehan.

Husband. You are slipping in your school work. Your last report card was the least satisfactory I have seen in a long time. And I have no doubt that all this galavanting around to dances and things is the direct cause of it. You are only a girl. Remember that.

Son [*mocking*]. Only a *little* girl.

Daughter. I guess I'm able to take care of myself!

Husband. That is just the point. You are *not* able to take care of yourself. You may think you are, but you are not old enough to judge. You are only a girl . . .

Wife. [*to* Small Daughter]. Come, Edna, you must eat all your prunes.

[SMALL DAUGHTER *shakes her head furiously.*]

HUSBAND. . . . Only a girl . . .

WIFE. Yes, I said you must eat all of them.

[SMALL DAUGHTER *puts one quickly in her mouth and turns toward her* FATHER.]

HUSBAND. Ahem! . . . As I said, you are only a girl.

WIFE. No, you can't leave even one.

[*The* HUSBAND *looks peevishly at his wife.*]

HUSBAND. Isabel, I wish you would not interrupt.

WIFE. Yes, dear, but Edna must eat all of her prunes, mustn't she?

HUSBAND. Yes, yes, of course! But I really think . . . [*His sentence trails off into nothingness, because he finds that he doesn't know what he really thinks.*] Well, to get back to the subject, Winifred. . . . You are only a girl.

DAUGHTER. Yes, I've been only a girl five times now.

[*The* MAID *brings in a tray of toast and eggs for all except* SMALL DAUGHTER.]

WIFE. You mustn't be impertinent to your father, Winifred.

HUSBAND. It's very rude.

MAID [*who feels she must voice an opinion*]. Rude, is it? Well, I remember what my maw used to do to us young 'uns when we was rude. She used to take us up and give us a good spanking. Yes, sir! And if you're asking me there's some young 'uns today that need just that!

DAUGHTER. Well, we weren't asking you.

WIFE. Sssshhh! [*Sweetly to the* MAID.] Will you bring us some water, Laura?

MAID [*filling glasses from pitcher on sideboard*]. Yes, sir, there never was anything that could take the place of a good spanking, no, sir . . . no, sirree . . . [*She goes out Right.*]

WIFE. Winifred, do be careful what you say. Laura is very sensitive, and maids are just about impossible to get.

SON. Say, Dad, do you know Henry Sills?

DAUGHTER. George, you shut up. [*She gets up and starts to leave by door Right.*]

HUSBAND. Winifred! Come and sit down!

DAUGHTER. I don't care for any more breakfast, thank you. I guess I've been humiliated enough for one morning! [*She walks haughtily out Right.*]

SON. Good-by, dear sister.

HUSBAND. Outrageous! Outrageous! Isabel, why didn't you make her obey?

WIFE. I thought this was your affair, dear.

HUSBAND. But you must help me.

WIFE. I wanted to let you try your new methods.

HUSBAND. Well, really, I think . . . [*He goes on with his meal. Then, after a pause.*] George, I want to have a few words with you. And I want you to listen to me. I have noticed for some time that you are becoming careless in many ways. You are becoming discourteous. [GEORGE, *having folded his napkin, jumps up, and crosses Right, combs his hair before the mirror.*] George!

SON. Yeh, I'm listening.

HUSBAND. Now, that's an example of the very thing I was speaking of. You are very discourteous. Please come back and sit down until I have finished speaking.

SON. I can hear you from here.

HUSBAND. George!

SON. Oh, all right. [*He comes and sits down.*]

HUSBAND. Courtesy, George, is a great asset. How do you suppose I would get along in business if I forgot courtesy? Would I get very far if I was rude to customers?

SON [*who has not been listening*]. For goodness' sake, mother, tell Edna to wipe her face.

WIFE. Edna, darling, use your napkin.

SON. You'd better label her prunes "FOR INTERNAL USE ONLY." She's decorating her whole mug with them.

WIFE. "Mug" is such a coarse word, George.

[GEORGE *has forgotten all about the little talk his* FATHER *was having with him, or rather without him; and he now jumps up and starts a little early morning dancing practice. He swings himself gracefully and jazzily toward door Right.*]

HUSBAND. George!

SON. You know, everybody tells me I'd make a swell professional dancer. Peg Benson told me the other day she bet I could pull down a couple of thousand in vaudeville.

WIFE. Who's Peg Benson, dear?

SON. Oh, a girl.

WIFE. Does she go to school?

SON. Uh-huh.

HUSBAND [*who has decided to try utter calmness*]. George, will you come here?

SON [*still thinking of the Benson creature*]. She has the funniest mop of yellow hair you ever saw.

HUSBAND [*with terrible calmness*]. George.

SON. And *great big* eyes.

HUSBAND [*rising calmly and going to his son's side Right Center*]. George, my boy, do you think I would?

SON. Would what?

HUSBAND. Get very far?

SON [*stopping his dancing and looking quizzically at his* FATHER]. Say!

HUSBAND. Well, do you?

SON. What aya talkin' about?

HUSBAND. Do you think I would get very far if I was rude to customers?

SON. Well, how should I know! [*He starts dancing.*]

HUSBAND [*who sees that calmness is a failure and that he must try strong forcefulness*]. George! Stop that! I want to talk with you.

[*At this point the* DAUGHTER *enters with her hat and coat on and her school books in her arm. She has the earrings on again. She walks calmly to the table, takes a piece of toast, says "Good-by" to anyone that would care to hear it, and walks out eating the toast. The* SON *bows elaborately towards her receding figure.*]

HUSBAND [*to the* SON]. I must talk to you about your attitude. I think . . . George! I ask you to listen to me.

SON. Go right ahead. I'm listenin'.

HUSBAND. I have noticed that you are not serious enough of late. You are too boisterous, too loud, too . . .

[*An automobile horn honks outside.* GEORGE *rushes to the door Right.*]

SON. Golly! They're honking for me!

HUSBAND. George!

SON. It's awful late, Dad, and I . . .

HUSBAND. George, I am not through with you.

[*The* MAID *enters Right and crosses to Left.*]

SON. Gee! I gotta get to school. They're honking for me. So long! [*He dashes out.*]

HUSBAND. George, I really . . .

WIFE [*calling after the* SON]. Don't forget your rubbers!!

[*A slam of an outer door is heard.*]

MAID [*turning at door Left*]. A good spanking! That's what they need. Yessir, and if they was my young 'uns that's jest what they'd get. Yessirree! Be strong and masterful. That's what I allus says, and I mean it. It's the only right way. You gotta be strong!

[*This unasked-for advice is to the* HUSBAND *the last straw. He boils over, but he does so sedately. He is always sedate.*]

HUSBAND. That's enough, Laura. I think I can manage my own children.

WIFE [*warningly*]. John!

MAID. Well, if you feel that way about it . . .

HUSBAND. I don't think I need any advice from you. Though I am sure you could give me a great deal.

[*The* MAID *exits Left swiftly.*]

WIFE [*rising*]. Now you have done it. Laura probably will leave this minute. And if she does, *you* can do the breakfast dishes. [*She exits Left.*]

[*The* HUSBAND *sighs deeply. Then he sees* EDNA *tracing the carving in the back of her chair and remembers that he has not fully tried his methods on her. He attacks the prune problem with rising hopes.*]

HUSBAND [*in an impressive voice*]. Edna, haven't you eaten your prunes yet?

SMALL DAUGHTER. Unt-uh.

HUSBAND. Well, you must eat them.

SMALL DAUGHTER [*not turning*]. I can't eat 'em.

HUSBAND. You must.

SMALL DAUGHTER. I don't like 'em.

HUSBAND. Remember . . . "Little prunes make big girls."

SMALL DAUGHTER. I don't like 'em!!

HUSBAND. Edna, I am going to tell you a story. Now listen attentively. Once there was a little girl . . .

SMALL DAUGHTER [*turning toward him*]. An' she had a 'lil curl. . . .

HUSBAND. No, no, no. Of course, she may have had a curl, but that is not the point.

SMALL DAUGHTER [*remembering the rest*]. Right in the middle of her forehead.

HUSBAND. The point is: she wouldn't eat her prunes.

SMALL DAUGHTER. Oh.

HUSBAND. And one day a big dragon came along and ate the little girl up. And that's what happens to little girls who don't eat their prunes.

SMALL DAUGHTER [*who is not as impressed as her father had hoped*]. And little boys, too?

HUSBAND. Little boys, too.

SMALL DAUGHTER. But, papa, how did the dragon know that the little girl wouldn't eat her prunes?

HUSBAND. Why . . . why . . . dragons just naturally know that sort of thing . . . I suppose.

SMALL DAUGHTER. Oh.

HUSBAND. Now will you eat your prunes?

SMALL DAUGHTER. I don't like 'em.

HUSBAND. Here. Here's a nice one. [*He holds a prune on her spoon right under her nose. She stares at the evil fruit for a moment then bursts out crying. The* HUSBAND *is thoroughly alarmed. He sits back in a daze.*]

[*The* WIFE *rushes in from the Left.*]

WIFE. What *is* the matter?

SMALL DAUGHTER. Mamma!

WIFE [*taking the* SMALL DAUGHTER *in her arms and sitting down*]. What is it, dear?

SMALL DAUGHTER. I can't eat my prunes and papa tried to make me and I can't and . . .

WIFE. That's all right, darling. You don't have to eat them.

HUSBAND. But, Isabel, you said . . .

WIFE. Sssshhh! Haven't you any sense? [*To the* SMALL DAUGHTER *who is still sniffling.*] There, it's all right, baby.

SMALL DAUGHTER. Papa said [*sniff*] that if little girls don't eat their [*sniff*] prunes a big dragon [*sniff*] will come and eat them up.

WIFE. How silly! He was just fooling you. [*Then for her* HUSBAND'S *special benefit.*] There *aren't* any dragons any more.

SMALL DAUGHTER. But that's what he said.

WIFE. Well, he didn't mean it. You just forget all about it. Here, where's your hanky?

SMALL DAUGHTER. I don't know. [*Long sniff.*]

WIFE. Well, run upstairs and get one. Quick.

[*The* SMALL DAUGHTER *exits Right.*]

WIFE. The idea of you putting those silly notions into her little head. I should think you would have had better sense. I suppose your foolish book told you to do that.

[*The* HUSBAND *sits meekly in his chair and says nothing. He is as near losing his sedateness as he will ever be.*]

WIFE. I hope you are satisfied with the things you have accomplished with that book.

[*The* HUSBAND *looks very meek indeed. The* WIFE *picks up the book from the table and reads the title.*]

WIFE [*reading*]. "The Best Methods of Raising Children." [*She can't suppress her laughter.*] John, how could you be so . . . funny!

[*The* HUSBAND *sighs and looks mournfully at a cigar which he has taken from his pocket as if he thought even that might turn against him.*]

WIFE. Laura is all up in the air, thanks to you. But I think she is going to stay.

HUSBAND. That's good. [*He puts the cigar back into his pocket. Then he sits a long time staring at his wife. At last he ventures to voice his thoughts.*]

HUSBAND. Isabel, I think . . . I think I'll have a second cup of coffee.

CURTAIN

THE THURSDAY

A BRITTANY LEGEND

BY

ALICE JOHNSTONE WALKER

A NON-ROYALTY PLAY

THE CAST

CRISTOUL
GARV
ROSALIE
GUÉZEL
PÈRE BRIZAC
MÈRE GALUDEC
THE FIRST KERION
THE SECOND
THE THIRD
THE FOURTH
THE FIFTH
THE SIXTH
THE SEVENTH

THE SCENE

A lonesome field in Brittany near the village of Carnac. It is twilight long ago.

In the center of the stage, which is a barren plain, arises two grim old Druidical stones. They are especially tall with a broad-faced surface facing front.

There is a log on the right side of the stage.

THE CHARACTERS AND COSTUMES

CRISTOUL *has a grotesque hump between his shoulders, which makes him bent and crooked, he has an air of patient courage about him, and a merry twinkle in his eye betrays a sunny temper.*

GARV *also is a humpback. His expression is discontented and peevish.*

278

THE KERIONS *live in Brittany. They are at home among the great Menhirs. The dolmen on the heaths are their houses. They move big stones as we move little ones. They are little men like dwarfs. They are all sorcerers. It is most unfortunate to get their ill will. They are dressed in coarse white material. A pointed hood frames their faces like a gnome's cap. The hood ends in a little round cape, six or seven inches wide. The stockings and trousers can be in one piece like night clothes. The stockings should end in a little point. A tight-fitting double-breasted coat comes nearly to the knees. It is girded with a rough cord. The* KERIONS *should vary in height like a flight of steps. The* FIRST KERION *being the tallest and the* SEVENTH *the shortest.*

THE BRETON PEASANTS *wear a broad-brimmed, low-crowned hat with wide silk or velvet ribbons dangling behind, a peasant's blouse of dark blue, with double row of silver buttons in front with very loose trousers to just below the knee.*

THE WOMEN *have full black skirts and tight fitting waists with lace caps, collars and aprons. Wooden shoes if possible for men and women.*

———————•———————

At rise of curtain the scene is empty and very quiet. The voice of CRISTOUL *is heard outside.*

CRISTOUL [*outside*]. Come, come! This log is not too heavy for thee. Bend thy back and pull! Ah, now I have it! [*Enter* CRISTOUL *from Left. He has a bundle of faggots on his shoulder and is dragging a huge log. As he enters he trips and falls*]. Aï! Aï! [*Sits up after a moment and rubs his head.*] That was a rude one! [*Slowly picks himself up and feels tenderly of his legs.*] Not broken yet, old broomsticks! You'll carry me many a mile more. [*Pretends to listen.*] What's that I hear? "Too stout a stick for a poor humpback to carry." A shame upon you for a pair of cowardly stumps! Whose hump is it, yours or mine? You are a pair of whiners you are. [*Stoops to pick up faggot.*] Hola! [*Listens.*

Calls.] Who comes? . . . Who comes? [*Looks off to Left.*]
Oh, 'tis thee, Garv.

GARV [*outside*]. Ugh! Ah! [*Grunts and sighs. Enter* GARV
from Left. He is carrying a scant bundle of faggots.] And
who should it be but poor Garv the humpback! . . . Oh!
That villain of a branch! It contrives to pierce a hole in my
poor back no matter how I carry it. Ouch! [*He angrily throws
down his faggot and rubs his shoulder.*] Art alone? [*He
peers around.*] I heard talking and thought mayhap it was
the Kerions, [*Lowers his voice.*] the little men. 'Tis a spot
they might fancy. [*Eagerly.*] Mark the thick grass. It seems
almost in the form of a circle . . . and these old stones . . .
[*Looks timidly about.*]

CRISTOUL. I was but talking to myself. I stubbed my toe just
now and had a famous tumble.

GARV [*seating himself near* CRISTOUL *at the foot of the big
stone*]. Thou with thy great hump shouldst not strive for
such heavy logs.

CRISTOUL. Garv, hast thou ever seen the little Kerions? Folks
say they live by these big stones. Never have I seen one.

GARV. No, not to say seen them, but old André who lives in
Carnac village has seen them.

CRISTOUL. What? Old black André who gathers cockles?

[*As they talk the heads of the little* KERIONS *begin to pop
up over the top of the big stone and around its sides. They
look down in complete silence at the humpbacks.*]

GARV. He says they like best the twilight time or the night,
the little rogues! Sometimes they play and dance here. He
has spied on them.

CRISTOUL. Name of a dog! Would I could see them! What are
they like?

GARV. André says they are odd little souls, queer caps and
droll faces.

[*The* KERIONS *turn and look whimsically at each other,
raise their brows and pat their hoods. They are eternally
cutting queer capers.*]

CRISTOUL [*chuckling*]. Would I could see them, the odd little imps! Let us tarry here.

GARV. Not I, Cristoul. 'Tis too likely they will come. 'Tis near nightfall. I marked not where I was sitting. [*Rises hastily. The heads of the* KERIONS *disappear.*] I do not much care about these old stones.

CRISTOUL. Why, what ails the old stones?

GARV [*apprehensively*]. André says they move themselves sometimes.

CRISTOUL. Move themselves!

GARV. Well, thou knowest they were once soldiers chasing good St. Cornely. . . .

CRISTOUL. To be sure I do; and has not my mother told me how he turned them all to stones before they drove him into the sea?

GARV. I see thou knowest the tale; who does not! Black André says these soldier-stones grow thirsty once a year on Christmas Eve and all tramp to the nearest stream to quench their thirst. Then is the time to look for the treasures they keep down in their holes. But if they get back while one is digging . . . Pat-a-tras! 'Tis the last of that poor soul.

CRISTOUL. I like that tale. Would all thieves could be so served!

GARV [*uneasily*]. Come, come along, Cristoul. 'Tis too dark here for me.

CRISTOUL [*tries to rise and makes a grimace of pain*]. No, I'll rest a bit longer, I will. 'Tis not Christmas Eve. [*Laughs.*] This stone won't move yet. Of what art thou afraid?

GARV. I, afraid? Not I, but . . . I like to get home while I can see the path. [*He gathers up his faggot and limps out Right.*] Good night, Cristoul.

CRISTOUL. Good night, Garv. [*Looks about him, stretches and apparently goes to sleep. The little* KERIONS *peep over the top of the stone again and look down on him.* CRISTOUL *throws back his head and begins to snore. Almost at once* GARV *steals in from Right and helps himself to branch after branch from* CRISTOUL'S *faggots, greedily adds them to his own slender armful and then tiptoes out.* CRISTOUL *opens his eyes and peers after* GARV. *Laughs indulgently.*] Now thou art happy, man. Thou hast a larger bundle of faggots to take home than I . . . Poor Garv! [*Rubs his back.*] This stone is not soft. I'll try my old log as a cushion. [*He moves to right side of stage and curls up with his head on the log, yawns several times and goes to sleep.*]

[*It gradually grows darker, seven* KERIONS *step out from behind the stone. They point to each other and double with silent laughter.*]

FIRST KERION [*poking the fat little* SECOND KERION *in the ribs*]. Thou art an "odd little soul."

SECOND KERION [*convulsed with laughter turns and jerks the pointed hood of the* THIRD KERION *over his face.*] Pull thy "queer little cap" over thy "droll little face," brother!

THIRD KERION [*clapping* FOURTH *and* FIFTH KERIONS *on their shoulders*]. Come, "odd little imps," make this sleepy human dance with us!

THE FOURTH *and* FIFTH KERIONS [*hopping up and down and silently clapping their hands.*] Ay, let the human dance with "the odd little imps"!

[*The* SIXTH *and* SEVENTH KERIONS *run up to* CRISTOUL *and give him little pokes until he begins to wake up. When he lifts his head and rubs his eyes, they run back to the others. The* KERIONS *stand in line on the Left, put their arms around each other's shoulders. The* FIRST KERION *at one end and the* SEVENTH *at the other retreat and advance across the stage before the bewildered* CRISTOUL. *They each call out a line at him in high piping voices in a sing-song fashion resembling a bugle call.*]

FIRST KERION. Wa . . . ake Mortal! [*Stamps.*]

SECOND KERION. Wake and dance. [*Stamps.*]

THIRD KERION. Seize thy chance. [*Stamps.*]

FOURTH KERION. Wake and prance. [*Stamps.*]

FIFTH KERION. Mid the stones of ancient France. [*Stamps.*]

SIXTH KERION. Rise and dance! [*Stamps.*]

[*The* KERIONS *form a ring in the Center and the* SEVENTH KERION *tries to draw* CRISTOUL *into it.*]

CRISTOUL [*reluctant and dazed*]. What is it, sirs? . . . I . . . dance?

KERIONS [*all stamp*]. Come and dance.

CRISTOUL. But . . . but . . . I'm a hunchback. I cannot dance.

KERIONS [*stamping*]. Come and dance!

CRISTOUL [*slowing rising*]. I might hobble around to please ye, sirs, but I'll spoil your dance.

FIRST AND SECOND KERIONS [*jerking him to his feet and into the ring*]. Come, come!

[*They form a ring with* CRISTOUL *limping along, awkward and reluctant.*]

FIRST KERION. What shall we sing, brothers?

SECOND KERION. Our new song, to be sure!

ALL THE KERIONS. Our new song, to be sure.

THIRD KERION [*to* CRISTOUL]. Listen, thou humpback, try to sing it. 'Tis hard.

[*They step back from* CRISTOUL *whose back is to the audience and raising their fingers, they solemnly begin to wag them.*]

ALL THE KERIONS. M . . . m. . . .

FOURTH KERION [*Interrupting*]. Why waste our new song on this human with a bunch on his back?

FIFTH KERION. He cannot learn it with his humped back.

SIXTH KERION. Nay, brothers, give him a chance.

SEVENTH KERION. The new song, brothers!

[*They nod their heads and, gravely wagging their fingers at* CRISTOUL, *repeat in chorus.*]

ALL THE KERIONS.

"The Monday, the Tuesday and the Wednesday!
The Monday, the Tuesday and the Wednesday!

[*Silence. They gaze at* CRISTOUL *who turns his head slowly from one side to the other.*]

CRISTOUL. "The Monday, the Tuesday and the Wednesday. . . ."

FIRST KERION. Why, he knows it already!

SIXTH KERION [*patting* CRISTOUL's *shoulder*]. What did I tell thee!

SECOND KERION. This fellow has wits though he be a human. Give us thy hand, man!

SEVENTH KERION. Into the ring with him. [*They take the half-scared, half-pleased* CRISTOUL *into the ring and slowly pace around.*]

THE KERIONS AND CRISTOUL.

> The Monday, the Tuesday and the Wednesday!"
> The Monday, the Tuesday and the Wednesday."

[*They begin a scale, repeating the refrain The Monday, the Tuesday and the Wednesday twice on each note of the scale until they arrive at the octave note. After they have sung the refrain twice, on the last syllable of Wednesday, "day," they drop abruptly to the note they started on, an octave lower.*]

[*They start the dance with slow pompous steps and grave decorum. They sing softly and slowly on the first and second notes of the scale but gradually sing louder and faster and dance faster and faster. By the time they have arrived at the eighth note of the scale, they are galloping madly about pulling and tugging poor lame* CRISTOUL *ruthlessly along. On the last "day" of the eighth repetition they stop with great suddenness. They crowd around* CRISTOUL *who is breathless.*]

FOURTH KERION. Well stepped out, thou humpback!

FIRST KERION. He dances like one of us. Little turtle back!

THIRD KERION. In spite of his crooked bones. [*He turns to form the ring again.*]

CRISTOUL. 'Twas a good dance. [*Fanning himself with his hand.*] But let me get my breath, good sir.

FIFTH KERION [*impatiently*]. No, no, come dance! [*Stamps.*]

ALL THE KERIONS. Come dance! [*They pull* CRISTOUL *into the ring and begin as before.*]

"The Monday, the Tuesday and the Wednesday,
The Monday, the Tuesday and the Wednesday."

[*They sing as before, dancing in a whimsical, quaint way
and stopping song and dance on the "Wednesday" that com-
pletes the octave.*]

CRISTOUL [*tired of the repetition, suddenly in the silence that
comes sings*]. "The Thursday!"

[*The* KERIONS *stare at him with wonder and delight.*]

FIRST KERION. What . . . what didst thou say, hunchback?
"The Wednesday, The Thurs . . . ?"

CRISTOUL [*boldly*]. "The Thursday!"

ALL THE KERIONS [*turning to one another*]. "The Thursday."
"The Thursday." Charming!

SECOND KERION [*begins to caper and dance and sing*]. "The
Monday, the Tuesday, the Wednesday and the Thursday!"
Mark how perfectly it goes. "The Thursday, The Thurs-
day!" It goes very well.

THIRD KERION. Wonderful little mortal!

FOURTH KERION. Our song is exquisite.

SEVENTH KERION. Our song is perfect.

ALL THE KERIONS [*in excitement*]. Our song is perfect.

FIFTH KERION. What a gift thou has given us, old bumpy
back!

FIRST KERION. A gift indeed! How can we reward him?

ALL THE KERIONS [*turn to* SEVENTH KERION *who is left alone
in the middle of the stage.*] How can we reward him?

[*Each little* KERION *holds his head in both hands and
thinks. There is a pause.*

FIRST KERION [*gives a violent start, tiptoes to the* SEVENTH
KERION *and whispers loudly in his left ear*]. A hat to make
himself invisible?

[*Pause. The* SEVENTH KERION *shakes head violently.
They all shake their heads violently. The* FIRST KERION *retires crestfallen. Pause. All think as before.*]

SECOND KERION [*approaches* SEVENTH KERION *softly and*

whispers distinctly pointing to the big stone]. Gold from our treasury?

[*The* SEVETH KERION *after a pause shakes his head slowly. All shake their heads slowly. Pause.* SEVENTH KERION *suddenly raises his head and lays a finger on his lips.*]

THIRD KERION. Brother, thou hast an idea! Out with it!

SEVENTH KERION [*takes his finger from his lip and points at* CRISTOUL]. Let us take off his hump! [*The six* KERIONS *hug the* SEVENTH KERION *rapturously.*]

THE SIX KERIONS. Brother, Brother! Well said! Well said! Let us take off his hump! [*The* KERIONS *fly at* CRISTOUL, *overturn him, discover a strap and buckle under his blouse and begin to unfasten it.*]

CRISTOUL. Stop, little sirs, what are ye doing to me? I did but say "The Thursday." [*He struggles.*]

SEVENTH KERION [*suddenly emerges from the heap of little men who are holding* CRISTOUL *down and brandishes* CRISTOUL's *hump. He laughs.*] He did but say "The Thursday," Brothers and lo, he has lost his hump!

[CRISTOUL *staggers to his feet. He is now as straight as a dart. He feels of his back, tries to look at it. He is dazed and amazed and stares from the laughing faces of the* KERIONS *to his neat hump. He walks up and feels the hump, shakes his head wonderingly.*]

CRISTOUL [*he suddenly drops on his knees and kisses the hands of the* KERIONS *nearest him*]. Let me thank ye, little sirs! Let me thank ye.

THE KERIONS [*laugh and pull away their hands. They tramp around him chanting*]. He did but say "The Thursday! The Thursday!" [*They flourish the hump like a banner and suddenly run off the stage to the Left, saying joyously.*] He did but say "The Thursday!"

CRISTOUL [*happy and excited feeling his back again*]. It has gone! I'm as straight as an I. I can jump! [*Jumps.*] I can skip! [*Skips.*] I look at the sky instead of the soil. Stars! Stars, do you see me? I believe I can fly. [*Laughs.*] Where is that log? [*Lifts log lightly to shoulder.*] I laugh at thee now, old log! [*Dances about with log on shoulder, sings.*] "The Monday, the Tuesday, the Wednesday and the Thursday." [*Voices are heard to Right.*] . . . 'Tis the village folk, [*Chuckles.*] and what a talk there will be now! [*Turns his back. Sets log on ground.*]

[*Enter several Villagers.* GARV, ROSALIE, GUÉZEL *and* PÈRE BRIZAC. *They hesitate a moment looking at* CRISTOUL'S *back.*]

ROSALIE [*runs up to him*]. Is it really thee, Cristoul?

GUÉZEL [*excitedly*]. Thou art straight as a tree! What has become of thy hump?

CRISTOUL. Hump? . . . Hump? . . . Whose hump?

GARV. Why thy hump, man. Thou hadst a hump like a camel. Much larger than mine!

ROSALIE. Do but listen to him! From a baby I have known thee, Cristoul and ever with a hump like a . . . a . . . a sack of meal between thy shoulders.

GUÉZEL. Whose hump indeed! Thy hump, man. What has become of it?

VILLAGERS [*in excitement*]. What has become of it?

CRISTOUL [*carelessly*]. Oh, *that!* Why . . . it flew away. [*Waves hand vaguely in the air.*]

VILLAGERS [*in open-mouthed astonishment*]. It . . . it . . . flew away? [*They attempt to imitate his gesture.*]

CRISTOUL [*with another jaunty gesture skyward*]. Yes, like that.

VILLAGERS [*looking up as though they would catch a last glimpse of the flyaway*]. Ah! [*Pause.*]

PÈRE BRIZAC. Oh, well! Thou art a lucky one, Cristoul, for 'tis surely gone. [*Turns him around and feels of him.*] Yes . . . 'tis flown away.

GUÉZEL. And had it wings, Cristoul?

CRISTOUL. That I cannot rightly say. Maphap it did. It seemed to float off in the air.

ROSALIE. I'll wager it had wings.

GUÉZEL. He says it floated off. Come, let us fetch Mère Galudec and ask her.

PÈRE BRIZAC, Yes, old Mère Galudec would know. [*Exit* ROSALIE, GUÉZEL, BRIZAC.]

GARV [*enviously, feeling of* CRISTOUL's *shoulders*]. Not a crooked bone! We are alone now, Cristoul, tell me the truth. How didst thou lose it?

CRISTOUL. 'Twas like this, Garv. I fell asleep here and I was awakened by the little Kerions . . .

GARV [*exclaims in astonishment*]. The little Kerions!

CRISTOUL. . . . who forced me to dance with them and taught me their song. What should the song be but "The Monday, the Tuesday and the Wednesday," over and over again.

GARV [*awestruck*]. Thou hast been dancing with the Kerions! Go on, man, what next?

CRISTOUL. Well, I became weary of the repetition of the three days so I added "The Thursday" to their song. They were extravagantly pleased and cast about them as to the recompense to give me. One of them said, "Take off his hump!" In a twinkling they had me on my back and had taken off my hump as easily as I pull off an old sabot. 'Tis the truth I am telling thee, Garv, and no lie.

GARV [*bitterly*]. Would I had stopped with thee.

CRISTOUL [*eagerly.*] That was what I thought, but courage, man. Are there not more days in the week?

GARV. . . . Name of a dog! Is there not Friday?

CRISTOUL [*clapping him on the shoulder*]. Even so. Stay here. Perchance the little men will return and invite thee to dance.

GARV. I will, I will! [*Pushes* CRISTOUL *to the Right.*] Leave me, leave me! Next time I see thee I will be straighter than thou. Ha ha!

CRISTOUL [*picks up log*]. Yes, thou wilt bring back a log twice the size of this. [*Walks off singing joyously to himself.*]

[GARV *steps around and peers in every direction. At last he hears something and darts behind big stone. Pause. Enter the* KERIONS *playing leap frog and forming with their lips the words "The Monday, the Tuesday, the Wednesday and the Thursday." After the* SEVENTH KERION *has entered and jumped over the other six, they form a ring and begin to sing their song.*]

KERIONS [*sing and dance as before*]. "The Monday, the Tuesday, the Wednesday and the Thursday," etc.

GARV [*steps from behind stone interrupting the dance*]. Let me dance too.

KERIONS [*look at him impatiently a moment*]. Come, come! [*Stamp.*]

GARV [*hobbling into the ring*]. Here I am.

KERIONS [*they face* GARV *with their backs to audience, raise their fingers and wag them at* GARV *as they teach him their song*]. "The Monday, the Tuesday, the Wednesday and the Thursday."

FIRST KERION. Cans't thou say those hard words, human?

GARV. "The Monday, the Tuesday, [*Rubs his head as though he could not remember.*] the Wednesday and the Thursday."

SECOND KERION. This human is not so stupid as he looks. Come dance!

[*They take* GARV *into the circle and dance as before with* CRISTOUL. *They sing the song through once.*]

GARV [*calling out in a loud voice*]. "The Friday!"

KERIONS [*let go hands and look furiously at* GARV, *sing.*] "The Monday, the Tuesday, the Wednesday and the Thursday." [*They speak, not sing.*] "The Friday." [*They clap their hands to their ears as though they could not bear the sound.*]

FIRST KERION [*in disgust*]. That goes badly!

SECOND KERION [*stamping*]. Very badly!

ALL THE KERIONS. It goes not at all!

SEVENTH KERION [*angrily*]. He has spoilt our song. Punish him!

ALL THE KERIONS. Punish him!

THIRD KERION. How shall we punish him?

ALL THE KERIONS. Give him the hump of Cristoul!

[*At these words, the hump comes flying through the air and lands in the Center of the stage with a bump. The* KERIONS *seize it and buckle it on to* GARV *in spite of his struggles. He rises angry and frightened.*]

GARV. Why, what have you done to me! I did but say, "The Friday."

KERIONS [*indignantly*]. He did but say "The Friday"!

SEVENTH KERION. Thou hast spoilt our exquisite song. Thou clodhopper! Thou spoilsport! Thou dromedary!

[*The* KERIONS *crowd around him and with shrill little voices and angry gestures repeat,* "Thou clodhopper, thou spoilsport, thou dromedary!" *Then with downcast looks they file out in a sad procession muttering,* "The Monday, the Tuesday, the Wednesday and the Thursday, THE FRIDAY! Brrrrrrrrr . . . rrrr . . . r!" [*They shiver with disgust as they speak the detested word "Friday." Their voices grow fainter but once more distinctly,* "The Friday. Brr . . . r . . . r . . . rr!" *comes back to the unhappy* GARV.]

GARV [*whining*]. Oh, this hateful hump! It won't come off! 'Tis twice as big! 'Tis that Cristoul's fault. [*He tries to look at his hump.*] He got me into this. How the village folk will laugh! Alas, here they come! Where can I hide myself? [*He goes to the front of the stage.*]

[*Enter the* VILLAGERS.]

ROSALIE [*holding up lantern*]. I tell thee his hump flew away. [*Goes up to* GARV.] Look for thyself, Mère Galudec.

MÈRE GALUDEC [*examining* GARV's *back*]. Hump gone! What fool's tale is this? 'Tis twice its former size.

[GARV *stands with his back to the* VILLAGERS *and tries to hide his face. The women crowd around.*]

GUÉZEL [*pulls at* GARV's *sleeve*]. This is not Cristoul, 'tis Garv! [*Amazed.*] What hast thou been doing to thy bump? [*Turns him around and tries to hide laughter.*] 'Tis twice as bumpy as before.

PÈRE BRIZAC. Name of a dog! Ha, ha, ha!

ROSALIE. Why, Garv . . . te, he, he!

GUÉZEL. What a hump! Oh, la, la, la!

GARV. Let me alone. What is there to laugh at! you nest of magpies!

[*Enter* CRISTOUL.]

CRISTOUL [*running*]. Garv. What luck, man? [*Sees* GARV *and laughs in spite of himself.*] Why, tell me what has happened.

GARV [*angrily*]. Laugh, laugh! I see thee laugh. It is thy fault if my hump has doubled. Meddler! I did but say "The Friday" and in an instant I heard naught but abuse. They said the word went badly and that I had spoiled all and must be punished.

CRISTOUL [*in grief*]. Alas, and was it thus!

GARV [*sneering*]. Oh, alas, and it was! Well thou knewest it would be so. At a word thy old hump appears from nowhere and in a trice the rascals fasten it on me. And it won't come off! It won't come off. . . . Laugh, laugh!

MÈRE GALUDEC. Rascals? What mystery is this?

CRISTOUL. 'Tis a shame, Garv, I grieve for thee. I do not wish to laugh but thou hast such a droll appearance with two humps.

GARV [*angrily beating with his stick to right and left as he limps away*]. Don't talk to me! I know thee now. Thou and thy Kerions.

THE VILLAGERS [*together*]. The Kerions, the Kerions! The little men!

MÈRE GALUDEC. The Kerions! Oh, la, la! Now is the mystery solved.

ROSALIE. 'Twas well done of the Kerions to give our Cristoul a straight back to match his honest heart.

GUÉZEL. And Garv is no crookeder outside than in. All the village knows him for a thief and a liar.

PÈRE BRIZAC [*awestruck*]. Thou hast talked with the Kerions, Cristoul, on this very spot?

CRISTOUL. On this very spot. [*There is a sensation on the part of the* VILLAGERS, *who draw away from* CRISTOUL.] They made me dance and sing with them and I added a word to their song that pleased the little men.

ROSALIE. Sing us the song of the Kerions, Cristoul.

ALL THE VILLAGERS [*frightened*]. Not here! Not by the big stones, girl!

GUÉZEL. Come with us back to the village. The little men would be angry if thou sangest their song here.

CRISTOUL [*gaily*]. Back then to Carnac and I who was ever the last, will run and leap and caper and beat you all to the village place. [*He laughingly pushes them into line for a race.*] One, two, three, go.

[*Off they all start laughing and pushing.*]

CURTAIN

PRODUCTION NOTE

To make the tall stone, take a large firm table and set a small firm table on it. Fasten a tall screen securely to the tables. Cover front and sides of screen with gray paper or cloth and shade with colored and white chalks to resemble stone. The smallest Kerions can stand on small table to look over stone and the others kneel or stand on edge of large table and peep around screen. Two step ladders could be used instead of tables.

The hump which Cristoul wears should be covered with the same material as his and Garv's suits. It should be fastened on by strips of the same material.

The music for "The Monday, the Tuesday, the Wednesday" may be the notes of the scale, or those words will be found, set to folk music in a volume of "Irish Country Songs" (Vol. II). Edited by Herbert Hughes.

SIX

BY

THEODORE SCHWARTZ

A NON-ROYALTY PLAY

THE CAST

WAGNER, *Clerk of Courts*
RAMSEY, *Counsel for the defense*
JOHNSON, *Associate Counsel for the defense*
JUDGE LA BARR
ANGELO MERIGO, *prisoner before the Bar*
THE JURY, *of twelve*
SHERIFF

THE SCENE

A courtroom.

JUDGE'S *bench on the center of the right wall. Door to* JUDGE'S
chambers down Right. CLERK'S *table Right Center directly in
front of* JUDGE'S *bench. Jury-box up stage Center, on raised
platform. A table Left stage with chairs about it. Water-
cooler up stage Left, near jury-box. Door down Left with a
light switch on the up-stage side of it.*

———————•———————

*At the rise of curtain the room is in semi-darkness. A dim form
is seen seated at left end of table Left, back to audience and
head bowed. Footsteps are heard approaching off stage Left.*
WAGNER *enters, overcoat and hat on. He switches on the
lights. Looks over his shoulder and sees the man at table.*

WAGNER [*regarding him in surprise*]. What! You here already, Ramsey? [RAMSEY *grunts without moving.*] Judge
come yet? [*Crosses Right, opens* JUDGE'S *door, and peeps in.
Comes back Center.*] I guess not. Ought to be pretty soon,
though. I phoned him that the jury in your case is in tonight.
[*Sits right end of table facing* RAMSEY.] They've been out
eight days now, haven't they? [RAMSEY *shakes his head and*
294

mumbles something.] You're right, it's seven days. Any idea what their verdict is?

[RAMSEY *rises and goes up stage, leaning against jury-box. His face is strained and tired.*]

RAMSEY. I was talking to Menzinger about an hour ago. He saw them when they filed out to The Sterling for dinner.

WAGNER. Menzinger is the one lawyer in this country that can tell the verdict of a murder jury by just looking at them. What did he say about yours?

RAMSEY. Of course he may be wrong.

WAGNER. He usually isn't. What did he say yours would be?

RAMSEY [*slowly*]. Guilty of murder in the first degree!

WAGNER [*whistles softly, then shrugs shoulders*]. Oh, well, I expected it. Sheridan had a pretty tight case against your man.

RAMSEY. And Menzinger added that he could see the electric chair look in their faces. He may be wrong there too.

WAGNER [*smiling*]. You're an optimist aren't you, Ramsey? Menzinger wrong about a murder jury? Hasn't been yet. You'd better start thinking of an appeal.

RAMSEY. No chance for a successful appeal. Oh, we'll make one, but it will be just for the sake of appearances. [*Pauses, eyes* WAGNER.] Keep that under your hat, though. I shouldn't have said it.

WAGNER. Now, I'll tell you something. This is just between you and me, see? I was talking to Donovan, the officer in charge of the jury, and he told me confidentially that after the second day there was only one man holding out against a first degree for Merigo.

RAMSEY [*eagerly*]. Who was it?

WAGNER. Blake. John Blake. I guess he held out until tonight.

RAMSEY. Blake? The old man, number six, who sits right here in the first row? [*Touches chair at left end of first row in jury-box.*] So Blake held out, did he?

WAGNER. Yep. He must be a nervous wreck, after six days of it. You'll see signs of it when he comes out.

RAMSEY [*meditating*]. I wonder how he came to give in finally?

Did he change because he was finally convinced Merigo killed
Ponterico, or because he couldn't stand the grind any longer?
He's pretty old, you know.

WAGNER. Can't tell. They very probably talked him ragged.
One man doesn't have a chance when a jury's out as long as
this one.

RAMSEY. Then the possibilities are that Blake still thinks
Merigo is innocent.

WAGNER. Well, he agreed with the rest finally, didn't he?

RAMSEY [coming down Center]. Yes, but he was under a strain.
That makes a difference.

WAGNER. Not in the verdict.

RAMSEY. No, not in the verdict. [Pause.] I don't know about
that appeal, now that I think of it. Johnson may be able to
find an error. He's studying it now. He's pretty sharp at that
sort of thing.

WAGNER. And if you can't get a re-trial, what then?

RAMSEY. Wait a minute. How do you know the jury is bringing
in a verdict of guilty? May not need a re-trial.

WAGNER. You're catching at every little straw, aren't you?
Suppose they do convict. What then?

RAMSEY. We'll poll the jury, of course.

WAGNER [sarcastically]. Of course you'll poll the jury! You'll
have me ask them to vote individually, and one by one they'll
say, "Guilty of murder in the first degree." And your man is
still on his way to the chair. What's the use, anyway? You
haven't a chance in a million of a jury disagreeing now on
the poll. There isn't a case in history, is there?

RAMSEY. There may be one or two cases, and I haven't heard of
them. But there's just one chance in a million that this jury
will disagree—and I'm going to ask for a poll.

WAGNER [with a gesture of resignation]. All right, poll away
to your heart's content. [Starts out Left.] I guess I'd better
go down and get the records. Things will be getting under
way pretty soon.

[JOHNSON enters Left. He also appears to be under a
strain.]

WAGNER. All set to hear some bad news, Johnson?

JOHNSON [*crossing to left end of table*]. What bad news?

WAGNER [*to* RAMSEY]. Break it to him gently.

  [WAGNER *exits Left.*]

RAMSEY [*crossing to right end of table*]. Find anything?

JOHNSON. Nothing that'll do us any good. Little technicalities; one in the cross-examination of Merigo, and one in La Barr's charge to the jury. Not enough to get a re-trial on. [*Crosses above table toward* RAMSEY.] What's the bad news Wagner was talking about?

RAMSEY. Nothing definite. Menzinger says the jury looks as if Merigo takes the chair.

JOHNSON. Did he see the jury? [RAMSEY *nods.*] Then if he's right, we're through. [*Sits at up center of table disconsolately.*] Well, we did the best we could for him, but the gun and the testimony of the Francioni woman licked us. Of course, we call poll the jury, but that— [*Shrugs his shoulders.*] We can pray and get better results.

  [RAMSEY'S *face suddenly becomes animated.*]

RAMSEY [*excitedly*]. Wait, there's just the ghost of a chance! [JOHNSON *swings around facing him.*] Look. [*Comes across to* JOHNSON *and leans over to him, speaking softly.*] Wagner just told me that Blake was the one man who held up the verdict of guilty for a week. When he gave in tonight, it was very probably because of the strain he was subjected to by the others. He may still believe Merigo is innocent. There may be just a particle of doubt in his mind, and that's enough.

JOHNSON. Well?

RAMSEY [*speaking rapidly*]. There are two things for us to work on. In the first place, Blake is a nervous wreck by this time. That makes him weaker and easier to break if we can get enough pressure on him. In the second place, we can figure this way. Say he was forced to agree to a verdict of guilty by the strain. Now, if he's not absolutely convinced, the chances are that with pressure on the other side, he'll turn his decision.

JOHNSON. You're figuring that he might disagree when the jury is polled, then?

RAMSEY. What do you think of it?

JOHNSON [*doubtfully*]. Well, a poll does put a man under a strain, but I doubt if it's powerful enough for that.

RAMSEY. That's just my point. We'll have to make it powerful enough. Here's what I want you to do. Meet Merigo as soon as the sheriff comes into the courthouse with him, and tell him that you've heard the jury has agreed on a verdict of *not* guilty.

JOHNSON [*startled*]. Why, that's cruelty when you're sure that's not the verdict.

RAMSEY. I know, but we've got to do it. The idea is this. I want Merigo to come into this courtroom smiling. Tell him to watch the man sitting at the end of the front row. I want Blake to see Merigo come in smiling. It's hard to send a man to the chair when he's smiling trustfully at you.

JOHNSON. But he'll sink under when he hears the verdict of guilty!

RAMSEY. Great! I hope he does. It's just what I want. Something else for Blake to see. It will make him and the rest of the jury realize what they've done to Merigo. They'll see this business in terms of Merigo, for once. And then, when we poll them individually—well—anything might happen.

JOHNSON. You don't expect that anyone else on the jury besides Blake will be affected?

RAMSEY. No, not enough to make them renege. This is for Blake's benefit. He's the only one that would disagree on the poll.

JOHNSON [*rising and going toward exit Left*]. All right, if you think it best. I'll get Merigo now. [*Stops at door, troubled, and turns to* RAMSEY.] But I hate to pull anything like that on the poor wop. He's been through enough these two weeks. [*Comes a few steps toward* RAMSEY.] Can't we try something else?

RAMSEY. Nothing whatsoever.

[RAMSEY *sits heavily at table Center, facing down stage.*]

JOHNSON. But it's so futile! I know you have a reputation for never giving up, but why subject Merigo to that terrific shock when the chances aren't even faintly with us? I don't know of a jury in common law history which has disagreed on the poll. We can't change history.

RAMSEY [*stolidly*]. No, we can't change history. But we can poll this jury.

JOHNSON. All right, you have charge of the case. I'll tell him I've heard the jury has acquitted him; that he's scot-free. [*Exit Left.*]

[*The door to the* JUDGE'S *chambers Right opens, and* JUDGE LA BARR, *overcoat on and hat in hand, enters. He is dressed in evening clothes. Crosses Center.*]

LA BARR. Good evening, Ramsey. I hear your jury is in.

RAMSEY [*standing up*]. Oh. Good evening, your honor. Rather an inconvenient time for you, isn't it?

LA BARR. Not at all. I'm glad to have something to do between now and ten. You're going to the Woodward affair too, aren't you? [RAMSEY *shakes his head in negation.*] By the way, have you heard anything of the probable verdict?

RAMSEY. Not a thing.

LA BARR [*turning Right*]. Well, it will be very interesting to find out.

RAMSEY. Yes, it will be very interesting.

[WAGNER *enters left, great court-record under his arm and crosses Right.* LA BARR *turns to him at door Right.*]

LA BARR. You'll call me when everyone's ready, won't you, Wagner?

WAGNER. Yes sir!

[*Exit* LA BARR *Right.*]

[RAMSEY *looks after* LA BARR *musingly, then sits at table again.* WAGNER *places court-record on* CLERK'S *table in front of* JUDGE'S *bench.*]

WAGNER [*casually, for sake of conversation*]. So you're going to poll the jury.

RAMSEY [*irritably*]. Have you ever seen a murder jury with a verdict of guilty get by without a poll?

WAGNER. I was just asking. Doesn't matter to me. But it's a strain on the jury, you know. I remember two years ago in the Hoffman case, one of the jurors keeled over after he was polled. It's not an easy thing for a man to stand up before a prisoner and say to him, "Prisoner, I find you guilty of murder in the first degree, and hereby sentence you to death by electrocution." Try it once yourself.

RAMSEY. The juror doesn't say that.

WAGNER. Of course not, but that's what it amounts to, isn't it?

RAMSEY. Yes, it amounts to that.—and hereby sentence you to death by electrocution. [*Shudders.*] It's a terrible thing for one man to say to another.

[JOHNSON *enters Left.* RAMSEY *turns to him inquiringly.*]

RAMSEY. Did you do it?

JOHNSON. Yes.

RAMSEY. Where is he?

JOHNSON [*pointing left over his shoulder*]. Coming. The sheriff's bringing him.

[ANGELO MERIGO *enters Left, smiling happily. He is followed by the* SHERIFF. MERIGO *goes eagerly toward* RAMSEY, *and starts to speak.* RAMSEY *motions him to be silent, and places him at right end of left table, facing right.* RAMSEY *stands back of his chair patting* MERIGO'S *back assuringly.* MERIGO *smiles up at him with child-like trust. The jury enters Left in file, crosses up stage, and enters jury-box at left end.* BLAKE, *a man of about sixty, white-haired and frail, comes sixth in file. He hesitates as he passes* MERIGO *and sees his smile. Shakes his head sadly. He remains standing in his place for a moment after the others have sat, and looks down on* MERIGO *compassionately.* JOHNSON *and* RAMSEY *exchange significant glances. Then* BLAKE *sits.* RAMSEY, *his eyes on* BLAKE, *moves up stage Center.* WAGNER, *who has been watching* MERIGO, *goes to* RAMSEY *up Center. The* SHERIFF *stands back of* MERIGO.]

WAGNER. What's that wop smiling about? [RAMSEY *shrugs his shoulders.*] He gives me the creeps.

RAMSEY. Better call the judge.

[WAGNER, *after taking another look at* MERIGO, *crosses Right. Knocks at door Right.* WAGNER *takes up gavel on bench and strikes it two or three times. Everyone rises. After a moment,* JUDGE LA BARR *enters Right and takes his place at the bench.*]

WAGNER. The court is now open. [*Strikes gavel. Courtroom sits.* RAMSEY *right end of up-stage side of table Center.* JOHNSON *next to him.* WAGNER *turns to* LA BARR.] The jury in the Merigo case is in, your honor.

LA BARR [*turning to jury*]. Gentlemen of the jury, have you arrived at a verdict?

FOREMAN OF JURY [*rising*]. Yes, your honor.

[WAGNER *crosses to jury-box, and receives written verdict from foreman. Takes it to* LA BARR, *who opens it and reads.*]

LA BARR [*impressively*]. Gentlemen of the jury, hearken unto your verdict as you have rendered it and as the Court hath recorded it. [*Reads.*] We, the undersigned jurors, in the case of the Commonwealth of Pennsylvania versus Angelo Merigo, do find the defendant guilty of murder in the first degree, and do fix the penalty at death by electrocution.

[MERIGO, *for an instant, doesn't understand. Swiftly the smile dies from his lips and a look of horror comes to his face. He becomes wild-eyed, and rises, grasping the table for support.*]

MERIGO [*crying out*]. No. No. [*The* SHERIFF *forces him down into his chair. He struggles like a man drowning, making incoherent sounds. Breaks away and falls on his knees at the feet of* RAMSEY, *clutching at his knees and pouring out a torrent of hysterical pleas.*] Tell 'em no! Tell 'em I dinn' kill Erico! I dinn' kill 'im. [*Turns to* JURY, *appealingly.*] 'Ones' 'a God I dinn' kill Erico! [*He sinks to a sitting position on the floor, his head resting on* RAMSEY'S *knee, his arms around* RAMSEY'S *leg. He cries, hysterical and terrified.* RAMSEY *and the* SHERIFF *lift him, a helpless hulk, and put him back in his seat. He lays his head on the table, crying softly.*]

[*The strain is manifesting itself on the faces of the jurors. When* MERIGO *cried out to them, they fidgeted, and turned away.* BLAKE, *at that plea, grasped his seat so intensely that the force lifted him slightly from his sitting position.* LA BARR, *on the other hand, if he was at all affected by the scene, did not show it. He ignored it, looking through some papers before him. Once or twice he looked sharply in the direction of the jury.* BLAKE, *after the collapse of* MERIGO, *looked appealingly at* LA BARR, *as though asking him to stop things from going any farther. After the courtroom has quieted down,* LA BARR *addresses the jury formally, as though no interruption had occurred.*]

LA BARR. The verdict, then, is guilty of murder in the first degree, and the penalty, death by electrocution. So say you all?

[*The* JURYMEN *mumble a low "yes" in unison—all except* BLAKE, *who is staring at* MERIGO. *All the members of the jury are perspiring, and mopping their faces frequently.* BLAKE *turns away and shudders slightly. Motions* SHERIFF *to get him a glass of water.* SHERIFF *does so during following speeches.*]

RAMSEY [*crossing to bench*]. Your honor, I should like to have a poll of the jury.

LA BARR [*nods to* RAMSEY, *turns to* WAGNER.] The clerk of court will poll the jury.

WAGNER [*to* JURY]. Gentlemen of the jury, your names will be called; you will rise in order and answer what your verdict is in the case of the Commonwealth versus Angelo Merigo.

RAMSEY [*as* WAGNER *is about to call names*]. Just a minute, Mr. Wagner.

[RAMSEY *crosses to* JOHNSON, *pushes paper and pencil toward him.*]

RAMSEY. Mr. Johnson, will you keep a separate record of the poll?

[JOHNSON *takes paper and pencil before him, and prepares to write. He stands at right end of table.*]

WAGNER [*standing Right Center at nod from* RAMSEY]. William McIntyre.

McINTYRE [*rising*]. Guilty of murder in the first degree. [*Sits.*]

RAMSEY [*turning to* JOHNSON]. One!

[JOHNSON *makes mark on paper.*]

WAGNER. George Savitski.

SAVITSKI [*rising*]. Guilty of murder in the first degree. [*Sits.*]

RAMSEY. Two!

[JOHNSON *writes.*]

[MERIGO, *without raising his head, groans. As each vote is made, he sinks a little lower, as though he were struck from behind.*]

WAGNER. Peter Duncan.

DUNCAN [*rising*]. Guilty of murder in the first degree. [*Sits.*]

RAMSEY. Three!

[JOHNSON *writes.*]

LA BARR [*motioning* WAGNER *to stop*]. Mr. Ramsey, is it absolutely necessary that you keep count?

RAMSEY. I would prefer to, your honor, if there is no objection.

[LA BARR, *after a moment's hesitation, motions* WAGNER *to resume the poll.*]

WAGNER. Lewis Sheridan.

SHERIDAN [*rising*]. Guilty of murder in the first degree. [*Sits.*]

RAMSEY. Four!

[JOHNSON *writes.*]

LA BARR [*obviously upset*]. Mr. Ramsey, would it be convenient for you to make your count silently? It seems that you are subjecting the court to an unnecessary strain.

RAMSEY. A life is at stake, your honor. There is no rule of procedure or statute which forbids an independent count. I must ask permission to continue.

[LA BARR, *in a quandary, motions* WAGNER *to resume poll.*]

WAGNER. Dennis Longman.

LONGMAN [*rising*]. Guilty of murder in the first degree.

RAMSEY. Five!

[JOHNSON *writes.*]

WAGNER. John Blake. [BLAKE *stares at him, but does not rise.*] John Blake!

[RAMSEY *and* JOHNSON *watch him tensely.* BLAKE *opens his mouth to speak, but remains silent. His eyes turn on* MERIGO *again.* MERIGO, *noticing the pause, turns and regards* BLAKE *hopefully.* BLAKE *tries again to speak, but fails. He puts his hands to his eyes, and shaking his head hopelessly, sinks lower into seat.* MERIGO *grasps convulsively at the hand of* RAMSEY.]

WAGNER. John Blake, you will rise and give your verdict in this case of the Commonwealth versus Angela Merigo.

[BLAKE, *not rising, looks up at* LA BARR *in mute appeal.*]

LA BARR. Mr. Blake, your verdict.

BLAKE [*hopelessly*]. I can't!

LA BARR [*after a slight pause*]. It is my duty to warn the jury that in case any one of its members disagrees or fails to give a verdict when polled, the jury shall be remanded to the jury-room by the court until such a time as it shall reach a verdict.

BLAKE [*desperately*]. I can't, your honor. I can't go back there! They'll drive me mad!

LA BARR [*tapping with the gavel*]. Your verdict, Mr. Blake.

BLAKE. But I can't! I can't send this man to the chair—and I'll go out of my mind if I have to spend another hour in that room with these men!

LA BARR [*relentlessly*]. Your verdict, Mr. Blake.

BLAKE [*after a pause, turns to* MERIGO]. It's no use. I can't hold out any longer. [*He rises. To* LA BARR.] Guilty of— [*Stops, then, wildly.*] But he's not. [*He sits.*]

LA BARR [*impatiently*]. The Court is waiting for your verdict, Mr. Blake.

RAMSEY [*rising*]. Your Honor—

LA BARR [*striking the gavel*]. Will you please refrain from interfering with the poll of the jury, Mr. Ramsey?

[RAMSEY, *after a moment's hesitation, sits, his eyes on* BLAKE.]

LA BARR. Mr. Blake, will you stand up? [BLAKE *rises unsteadily.* MERIGO *half rises, appealing to him with his hands.* BLAKE *regards him sadly for a moment.*]

BLAKE [*hopelessly, to* MERIGO]. I can't help it. They're forcing me. [*Steadies himself, pauses a few seconds, turns to* JUDGE,

and with an effort and a sudden determination.] Not guilty!
[*He sinks into his chair, staring before him rigidly.*]

[MERIGO'S *face lights up, and he starts up gratefully to go
to* BLAKE. RAMSEY, *smiling, holds him down.*]

LA BARR [*to* RAMSEY]. Do you wish to continue the poll, Mr.
Ramsey?

RAMSEY [*after a glance at* JOHNSON, *who nods*]. Yes, your
honor.

[RAMSEY *nods to* WAGNER, *who continues.*]

WAGNER. Alfred Munsey.

[MUNSEY *rises, and after fumbling about for a few seconds, sits again. He leans over to* THE FOREMAN *who sits in
front of him, and whispers in his ear.* THE FOREMAN, *in an
undertone, addresses a question to the others of the jury.
They all nod to him.* THE FOREMAN *rises.*]

THE FOREMAN [*to* LA BARR]. Your honor, the jury asks permission to return to the jury-room to reconsider the evidence.

LA BARR. Granted. The jury is remanded to the jury-room until
such a time as it shall have reached a verdict. Court dismissed.

[LA BARR *rises. The courtroom rises.* LA BARR *exits Right.
The* JURY *files out Left.*]

[MERIGO, *confused and not knowing what to make of it,
watches all this for a few seconds but does not wait for all
the* JURY *to finish filing out.*]

MERIGO [*eagerly*]. Mr. Ramsey, what's a matter? They let me
go home?

RAMSEY. No, not yet.

MERIGO [*edging away from the* SHERIFF *who puts his hand on
his shoulder, and holding on to* RAMSEY, *pleading*]. I don'
wan' 'a go back to jail. I'm 'fraid.

RAMSEY [*smiling*]. Go with him, Merigo. You'll be let out in
a little while.

MERIGO [*doubtfully*]. Ev'rything all right?

RAMSEY. Sure.

MERIGO [*trustingly*]. All right. [*He goes to* SHERIFF, *who takes
him Left. At the door,* MERIGO *turns to* RAMSEY.]

MERIGO. Good night, Mr. Ramsey.
RAMSEY. Good night, Merigo.
> [MERIGO *and* SHERIFF *exit.*]
> [RAMSEY *stands, smiling after him.*]

CURTAIN

THE VERY SAD UNICORN

A PANTOMIME

BY

G. WHITFIELD COOK

AND

VIRGINIA DIXON

A NON-ROYALTY PLAY

THE CAST

LITTLE PRINCE
PRIME MINISTER
SLAVE
FIRST SOLDIER
SECOND SOLDIER
THIRD SOLDIER
THE VERY SAD UNICORN
DAME PORRIDGE
ASTROLOGER
LITTLE GIRL
PURPLE DRAGON

THE SCENES

   I: LITTLE PRINCE'S *Throne Room*
  II: DAME PORRIDGE'S *Cottage*
 III: ASTROLOGER'S *Hut*
  IV: *A Place in the Forest*
   V: *A Battlefield*
  VI: LITTLE PRINCE'S *Throne Room*

THE COSTUMES

They may be the conventional ones suited to the type of the characters or they may be an elaborate stylized design, but in either case they should be very beautiful because of the simplicity of the settings. The Unicorn's costume should be yellow-brown with a sad expression painted on the face: an expression such as might belong to one constitutionally indisposed. It is necessary that he be able to grasp things with his hands. Most of the time he walks upright. Purple Dragon's costume may be made of some stiff material so he will look tough and angular. He does not need to be terrifically ugly, for, after all, he is rather a nice little dragon.

———————•———————

Scene I

LITTLE PRINCE'S *Throne Room*
A high throne up Right Center. A large blackboard up Left Center.
Entrances down Right and Left. LITTLE PRINCE *is seated on the high throne with a bib around his neck.* PRIME MINISTER *stands by him, feeding him with a spoon from a very large bowl labeled "Porridge." The bowl is held by* SLAVE. *The* THREE SOLDIERS *with broad short swords stand, one by the entrance Right, the second up stage Center, the third by the entrance Left.*
PRIME MINISTER holds out a spoonful of porridge
LITTLE PRINCE yawns
Turns his head away
PRIME MINISTER taps the LITTLE PRINCE'S shoulder
LITTLE PRINCE won't swallow the spoonful of porridge
PRIME MINISTER dips some more from the bowl
Holds the spoon again towards the LITTLE PRINCE
LITTLE PRINCE yawns
Makes a wry face
Leans his head on his hands
PRIME MINISTER holds out another spoonful
LITTLE PRINCE shakes his head decidedly
PRIME MINISTER hits him on the shoulder
LITTLE PRINCE shakes his head
PRIME MINISTER tweaks LITTLE PRINCE'S ear
LITTLE PRINCE shakes head
PRIME MINISTER sighs and orders porridge to be taken away
SLAVE marches out right
PRIME MINISTER removes LITTLE PRINCE'S bib
LITTLE PRINCE yawns

Looks very bored

PRIME MINISTER takes glasses from his pocket

Wipes them off with a large handkerchief

Puts them on

Goes to blackboard

Writes "2 + 2 = 4"

Stands off and points to it with a long stick

LITTLE PRINCE nods in agreement

He looks very bored

PRIME MINISTER writes "4 + 4 = 8"

LITTLE PRINCE yawns again

PRIME MINISTER writes again. This time "8 + 8 = 16"

LITTLE PRINCE gets up and begins to dance

PRIME MINISTER sees him

Claps hands angrily

PRIME MINISTER points sternly to throne

LITTLE PRINCE goes to it and sits down sadly

PRIME MINISTER taps blackboard with stick angrily

LITTLE PRINCE nods and pretends to be very much interested

PRIME MINISTER turns to write "16 + 16 = 32"

LITTLE PRINCE stands on his head

PRIME MINISTER looks at LITTLE PRINCE

He rages

He shrugs his shoulders and gives up

He claps his hands for SLAVE

SLAVE appears

PRIME MINISTER makes a gesture of playing guitar

SLAVE bows

SLAVE procures two guitars from behind throne

SLAVE gives one to PRIME MINISTER

He gives one to LITTLE PRINCE

SLAVE returns to side of throne

PRIME MINISTER plays guitar, a little phrase

LITTLE PRINCE plays the same

PRIME MINISTER plays a little more

LITTLE PRINCE does the same

PRIME MINISTER plays considerably more

LITTLE PRINCE examines one of his fingers minutely

PRIME MINISTER stops playing

He crosses and examines finger

Nothing is the matter

He is angry

He shakes the LITTLE PRINCE gently

He points to guitar

LITTLE PRINCE looks at him and shakes his head

PRIME MINISTER returns to center and plays

LITTLE PRINCE turns to SLAVE

He shows SLAVE a trick with his fingers

SLAVE laughs

LITTLE PRINCE laughs

PRIME MINISTER stops playing and rushes to throne

He sends SLAVE away

SLAVE goes out right

PRIME MINISTER points to guitar and returns to center

LITTLE PRINCE hides underneath the throne chair

PRIME MINISTER turns and sees that he has gone

PRIME MINISTER throws his guitar down

He beckons to TWO SOLDIERS

He asks for swords

THIRD SOLDIER drags LITTLE PRINCE out and brings him to
    the center

The TWO SOLDIERS go behind blackboard

They return with two swords

FIRST SOLDIER gives sword to PRIME MINISTER

SECOND SOLDIER gives sword to LITTLE PRINCE

They return to their places

PRIME MINISTER shows LITTLE PRINCE a fencing movement

LITTLE PRINCE repeats it badly

PRIME MINISTER shows LITTLE PRINCE a longer fencing
    movement

LITTLE PRINCE throws sword on floor

The THIRD SOLDIER picks it up and gives it back

PRIME MINISTER shows LITTLE PRINCE a very much longer
    fencing movement

LITTLE PRINCE does a little tiny one
PRIME MINISTER gets very excited fighting an imaginary enemy
LITTLE PRINCE returns to throne
Takes a book from behind throne and reads
Reads in dumb show, making many gestures
He yawns while the PRIME MINISTER still fights
PRIME MINISTER stops fighting
He sees LITTLE PRINCE asleep
The book falls
PRIME MINISTER exits Right very angrily
The SOLDIERS sleep standing up
A pause
Commotion off right
SOLDIERS awake, rush to door right and look off
THE VERY SAD UNICORN enters from right
Motions SOLDIERS out of the way
They back up gaping at UNICORN
UNICORN wipes his eyes with his paw
LITTLE PRINCE awakes
UNICORN holds out one of his maps to FIRST SOLDIER
On the back of it are the words printed very large
"Map of Rainbow's End"
UNICORN signifies he wants to sell it
FIRST SOLDIER shakes his head
UNICORN weeps harder
Looks around for handkerchief
FIRST SOLDIER takes one from his pocket
Hands it to UNICORN
UNICORN wipes his eyes
Holds the map up to SECOND SOLDIER
SECOND SOLDIER shakes his head very definitely
UNICORN weeps harder than ever
Goes to THIRD SOLDIER
Shows him map
He shakes fist at UNICORN
UNICORN continues to weep very very hard
THIRD SOLDIER motions UNICORN to move on

UNICORN continues to weep

THIRD SOLDIER takes him by one ear and leads him to exit Right

LITTLE PRINCE stands up

SOLDIERS stop and bow

LITTLE PRINCE points to UNICORN

UNICORN bows elaborately

LITTLE PRINCE nods

UNICORN gives roll of paper to LITTLE PRINCE

LITTLE PRINCE unrolls it

UNICORN signifies he wants to sell it

LITTLE PRINCE looks pleased and takes money from his pocket

PRIME MINISTER steps forward from the right

Takes money from LITTLE PRINCE

Looks at UNICORN and points towards door left

SOLDIERS come forward and push UNICORN off left

UNICORN weeps copiously

The SOLDIERS go off right

PRIME MINISTER takes book away from LITTLE PRINCE

Shakes finger at him

Goes off right

LITTLE PRINCE looks around

He looks out at audience and puts his fingers to his lips

He tiptoes off the throne, map under his arm

He takes PRIME MINISTER's stick from blackboard

Brings out a bundle of clothes from behind throne

Swings it on stick

Puts stick over his shoulder

Puts guitar over other shoulder

Picks up sword

Puts it in his belt

Starts tiptoeing after UNICORN to the left

Thinks of something

Stops

Goes to blackboard

Writes "good by forrever im going too find the end of the ranebow"

He goes off left
PRIME MINISTER returns from the right
Sees LITTLE PRINCE is gone
Waves arms in consternation
Claps hands for SOLDIERS
Runs frantically around the room
The THREE SOLDIERS appear from right
PRIME MINISTER points off stage left in direction LITTLE
    PRINCE went
The THREE SOLDIERS go out left after him
PRIME MINISTER begins walking up and down
He waves his arms frantically

LIGHTS OUT

SCENE II

DAME PORRIDGE'S *Cottage.*
*At the Right a fireplace with a big kettle on the fire plainly
labeled "Porridge." Shelves near it. Three chairs Center.
A large window at the back. A door Left. Also at the Left
are two wooden cradles. One very large, and one very small.*

DAME is stirring the contents of the pot on the fire
She stirs
She tastes
She does a little dance for sheer joy
Stirs
Tastes
Does another little dance step
UNICORN and LITTLE PRINCE appear wearily in the window
They gaze in
They sniff in unison
Sigh wearily
DAME turns and sees them
She nods merrily
They nod to her
She asks them in

They nod vigorously and move away from the window
DAME goes to door left
Opens it
LITTLE PRINCE comes in
She shakes his hand
UNICORN comes in
She shakes his hand
DAME motions to the chairs
LITTLE PRINCE sits in one
UNICORN sits in another
DAME gets three bowls from the shelves labeled "Porridge"
She gives one to each of the travelers and one to herself
She gets pot of porridge
Pours some into UNICORN's bowl
Some into her own bowl
And pours some into the LITTLE PRINCE's but
LITTLE PRINCE points to label on his bowl and shakes his head
DAME sits
UNICORN and DAME eat in unison
One spoonful
LITTLE PRINCE watches them wistfully
Two spoonfuls
LITTLE PRINCE watches them more wistfully
Three
Four
LITTLE PRINCE licks his chops
Five
Six
They are finished
LITTLE PRINCE picks up his bowl and starts to eat
DAME shakes her head and takes bowl away
Winks at UNICORN
The THREE SOLDIERS appear at the window in the rear
They put their fingers to their lips and stand peeking in
LITTLE PRINCE sighs
UNICORN sighs
LITTLE PRINCE yawns

UNICORN yawns
DAME smiles and points to cradles
LITTLE PRINCE gets into smallest one
UNICORN into biggest one
DAME goes to shelves
Gets two patchwork quilts
Puts one over each cradle
DAME sits on a chair
Folds her hands
Her head begins drooping to one side
She snores and sits up straight
UNICORN sits up in his cradle and looks at her
He lies down again
DAME's head begins drooping on other side
She snores and straightens up again
LITTLE PRINCE sits up and looks at her
He turns over and lies down again
DAME's head begins drooping again
She snores and snores
In unison the THREE SOLDIERS at the window look to the right
They look to the left
They move out of sight
A knock at the door
DAME rises from chair
LITTLE PRINCE and UNICORN still sleep in cradles
DAME moves to the door
Puts her ear against it
Another knock
DAME opens door slightly
It is pushed entirely open
The THREE SOLDIERS enter ferociously
FIRST SOLDIER points his sword at LITTLE PRINCE
Other two march forward and take hold of him
DAME runs over to fireplace
UNICORN jumps out of the cradle
DAME beckons to UNICORN
UNICORN goes to her quickly

She takes a big box from the shelves. It is labeled "Pills for
  Painful People"
She gives box to UNICORN
UNICORN goes to FIRST SOLDIER and offers him pill
He refuses pill
UNICORN goes to SECOND SOLDIER
He tries to put pill in his mouth
He can't
He tries to force pill in his mouth
He cannot
He goes to THIRD SOLDIER
He points suddenly upward
THIRD SOLDIER looks up, mouth opens
UNICORN tosses pill towards his mouth
THIRD SOLDIER closes mouth before pill gets in
The SOLDIERS pull LITTLE PRINCE out of cradle
They drag him towards door
DAME carries the bowl of porridge to LITTLE PRINCE
LITTLE PRINCE eats porridge
SOLDIERS look surprised
They look at LITTLE PRINCE eating porridge
They look harder
They look at one another
They look at him
They drop their swords
They drop their jaws
UNICORN tosses a pill into FIRST SOLDIER's mouth
FIRST SOLDIER gulps and suddenly becomes very meek
He kneels to the UNICORN
He begins to salaam
UNICORN tosses pill into mouth of SECOND SOLDIER
SECOND SOLDIER kneels and begins salaaming
UNICORN does same with THIRD SOLDIER
THIRD SOLDIER begins salaaming
All THREE SOLDIERS are now salaaming
LITTLE PRINCE finishes the bowl of porridge
DAME laughs

UNICORN laughs through his tears
LITTLE PRINCE laughs
They dance about
The SOLDIERS keep on salaaming
UNICORN, LITTLE PRINCE and DAME file out by the door waving good-by
They exit to left
The SOLDIERS keep on salaaming

LIGHTS OUT

SCENE III

The scene is in the ASTROLOGER'S *hut in which there is a blackboard Left, covered with figures all wrong, and a table, littered with pieces of paper Right. The old* ASTROLOGER *sits at the table, figuring.*

The door Center opens and LITTLE PRINCE, UNICORN *and* DAME *run in breathless and excited*

ASTROLOGER looks up, frowns and motions them away
LITTLE PRINCE goes to him and pantomimes that someone is chasing them
ASTROLOGER pushes him away
UNICORN goes up and pats papers with his paw
ASTROLOGER pushes him away angrily
He sits disconsolate, head in hands
DAME stands breathless and panting just inside the door too exhausted to move
The SOLDIERS appear at the window making faces
They grab at the people inside
DAME totters up to ASTROLOGER and motions him to look
ASTROLOGER looks at SOLDIERS but pays no attention to them
ASTROLOGER gets up and goes to blackboard
SOLDIERS try to climb in the window
LITTLE PRINCE, UNICORN and DAME are afraid
ASTROLOGER writes on blackboard, thinking deeply
He pauses between each mark

He writes sums all wrong, $2 + 2 = 3$; $4 + 4 = 7$; $8 + 8 = 15$
SOLDIERS are almost inside, waving swords and gesticulating
UNICORN goes to LITTLE PRINCE pleadingly
He points to wrong sums, to ASTROLOGER and to SOLDIERS
LITTLE PRINCE nods and goes to ASTROLOGER
He taps him on arm
ASTROLOGER looks at him
LITTLE PRINCE points to SOLDIERS climbing in
ASTROLOGER starts to continue doing sums all wrong
LTTLE PRINCE grabs chalk and writes, $2 + 2 = 4$; $4 + 4 = 8$;
    $8 + 8 = 16$
ASTROLOGER dances for joy
He shakes LITTLE PRINCE's hand
He shakes UNICORN's paw
He shakes DAME's hand
LITTLE PRINCE points to SOLDIERS
ASTROLOGER nods
He picks up wand
He makes magical pass in direction of SOLDIERS
SOLDIERS meekly fall back and out the window
LITTLE PRINCE, UNICORN and DAME shake ASTROLOGER's
    hand profusely
LITTLE PRINCE then shows ASTROLOGER map of the Rainbow's
    end
ASTROLOGER looks thoughtful, scratches head
He points in the direction out the door
LITTLE PRINCE pantomimes "Will you come too?"
ASTROLOGER nods
They go out center and exit to left

SCENE IV

A Place in the Forest

A small purple DRAGON is chasing a LITTLE GIRL around and
    around
She frantically tries to get away from him, running in a circle

UNICORN, LITTLE PRINCE, DAME and ASTROLOGER enter from right

DRAGON grows fiercer and fiercer

LITTLE PRINCE and UNICORN make feeble attempts to stop him

ASTROLOGER tries to stop him by waving wand

DAME tries to stop him by pantomiming "Shoo"

DRAGON brushes them aside and continues pursuing the LITTLE GIRL

LITTLE GIRL stumbles and falls

DRAGON goes up to her and starts to maul her

UNICORN looks up at LITTLE PRINCE pleadingly

He pats guitar with his paw

LITTLE PRINCE nods and quickly begins to play

DRAGON stops, lifts head, turns head towards LITTLE PRINCE

LITTLE PRINCE goes on playing with much gusto

DRAGON holds up a stick with a little white flag on it

He waddles over towards LITTLE PRINCE, then stops and sits down

He listens to music

LITTLE GIRL gets up, brushes off her dress

DRAGON begins to beat time with paw

UNICORN beats time with paw

LITTLE GIRL comes over and sits down

She beats time with her hand

DAME joins group and taps with her foot

ASTROLOGER pats time with his foot

LITTLE PRINCE stops playing

DRAGON wiggles over to him

He shakes LITTLE PRINCE's hand and pats guitar

LITTLE PRINCE pats DRAGON's head

UNICORN helps LITTLE GIRL straighten her sash and hair ribbon

DRAGON points to jaw and opens mouth

LITTLE PRINCE examines his teeth

LITTLE PRINCE beckons to UNICORN and LITTLE GIRL

They go and look at DRAGON's teeth

DRAGON holds his jaw painfully

LITTLE PRINCE pats DRAGON's head
He takes string from his pocket
Fastens one end to DRAGON's tooth
UNICORN, GIRL, DAME and LITTLE PRINCE move away from
    DRAGON
They all pull on string
One pull
Two pulls
Three pulls and the tooth comes out
DRAGON nods vigorously as a sign of his thanks
GIRL goes to DRAGON
Takes handkerchief from her pocket
Ties it under DRAGON's chin and up over his head with a perky
    little bow on top
DRAGON bows to her
PRINCE takes a shawl from his bundle of clothes
Goes to DRAGON
Puts it around DRAGON's neck
UNICORN goes to DRAGON
Pats his head comfortingly
DRAGON bows
PRINCE goes to LITTLE GIRL
Points to map and wants to know if she wants to go with them
LITTLE GIRL nods definitely
LITTLE PRINCE goes to DRAGON
Points to map and wants to know if he wants to go with them
DRAGON nods definitely
UNICORN, LITTLE PRINCE, LITTLE GIRL, DAME, ASTROLOGER
    and DRAGON line up in a straight row
They mark time for a moment
The DRAGON drops the LITTLE PRINCE's shawl
They march off left
The THREE SOLDIERS come in from the right
They look off left
They pull out their swords
They see the shawl
FIRST SOLDIER holds it aloft

Points to it
Other Two SOLDIERS stare at it
FIRST SOLDIER points towards the left
They all three march off left after the others

LIGHTS OUT

SCENE V

A Battlefield
LITTLE PRINCE, UNICORN, DAME, ASTROLOGER, LITTLE GIRL
and DRAGON *enter from Right, single file.*

LITTLE PRINCE has the map and is following it closely
They halt
DRAGON wipes his brow
DAME rubs back
ASTROLOGER fans himself
LITTLE GIRL sits down
LITTLE PRINCE looks at map, then at ground, then at map
    again
He beckons to UNICORN
UNICORN comes up, examines map, looks at ground and nods
    his head
They start to go on, getting in line and marking time
The THREE SOLDIERS enter right, running
They see the LITTLE PRINCE and his followers and stop
They put their heads together
The line of march is still marking time
SOLDIERS draw swords and rush at LITTLE PRINCE and com-
    panions
The line is in utter confusion
They all turn and face SOLDIERS
LITTLE PRINCE steps in front and draws his sword
He and the first SOLDIER fight together
LITTLE PRINCE knocks SOLDIER's sword from his hand
LITTLE GIRL runs and picks it up and backs SOLDIER off to
    right

She covers SOLDIER with sword
SECOND SOLDIER comes up
LITTLE PRINCE steps forth to meet him
SECOND SOLDIER and LITTLE PRINCE fight
LITTLE PRINCE knocks his sword from his hand
DAME comes forward and picks up sword
She backs SECOND SOLDIER off into left corner and covers him
SECOND SOLDIER stands quietly, hands up
THIRD SOLDIER advances waving his sword
LITTLE PRINCE steps forth to meet him
THIRD SOLDIER lets drive at him
They fight
LITTLE PRINCE knocks his sword from his hand
UNICORN comes forward and picks SOLDIER's sword up
He covers SOLDIER with sword, in center
LITTLE PRINCE wipes his own sword off
Procession forms again
LITTLE PRINCE goes first with map
Then UNICORN
Then FIRST SOLDIER
Then LITTLE GIRL with sword
Then SECOND SOLDIER
Then DAME with sword
Then THIRD SOLDIER
Then ASTROLOGER with sword
Then DRAGON
LITTLE GIRL, DAME, and ASTROLOGER brandish swords
They prick SOLDIERS with swords now and then
They march off right

SCENE VI

The Little Prince's Castle again

LITTLE PRINCE is asleep on the throne
The THREE SOLDIERS stand guard
PRIME MINISTER enters from right
SLAVE, holding large bowl, marked PORRIDGE follows him

They go to the throne
PRIME MINISTER wakes LITTLE PRINCE
PRIME MINISTER holds out a spoonful of porridge
LITTLE PRINCE yawns
LITTLE PRINCE eats porridge
The PRIME MINISTER is surprised
He holds out second spoonful
LITTLE PRINCE eats porridge
PRIME MINISTER is very surprised
Again
Again
Again
Again
SLAVE takes empty bowl away
PRIME MINISTER goes to blackboard
He taps with stick
Points to $2 + 2 = 4$
Then points to $4 + 4 = 8$
LITTLE PRINCE gets up and crosses to blackboard
PRIME MINISTER taps with stick
LITTLE PRINCE takes chalk
Writes $8 + 8 = 16$
Writes $16 + 16 = 32$
Writes $32 + 32 = 64$
PRIME MINISTER is surprised
He is very surprised
He drops stick
LITTLE PRINCE goes to throne
He takes guitar
He plays
He swings in rhythm
PRIME MINISTER looks surprised
He sways in rhythm a very little
He sways in rhythm a great deal
He sways in rhythm a very great deal
FIRST SOLDIER brings PRIME MINISTER a sword
SECOND SOLDIER brings LITTLE PRINCE a sword

PRIME MINISTER does a fencing movement
LITTLE PRINCE does a fencing movement
PRIME MINISTER does a fencing movement
LITTLE PRINCE fences with him
They fence
They fence
PRIME MINISTER is driven back
LITTLE PRINCE follows him
PRIME MINISTER turns and runs
LITTLE PRINCE swings his sword on his back
PRIME MINISTER runs out right
LITTLE PRINCE runs after him
The SOLDIERS laugh very much

CURTAIN

PRODUCTION NOTE

The scenery should be as simple as possible so that the action may be practically continuous. A simple set of curtains or screens may form the background. Each scene should be designated by the minimum number of properties. For instance, in scene one the throne, which should be built very high, and the blackboard are all that is necessary. Scene two has on the right a mantelpiece with a big kettle on the fire plainly marked "Porridge." Three chairs are center and two wooden cradles, one very large, the other small, are on the left. A large window and a door are in the rear center.

Scene three requires a table and stool and the blackboard and the center door.

Scene four need have one or two trees while scene five may be the empty stage.

These properties should be changed by two pages before the sight of the audience or in the dark and without the dropping of the front curtain. The action of the following scene may begin before the properties are entirely set. A signboard down stage right on which a placard denoting the scene is placed by one of the pages at the start of the scene, would be advantageous.

The success of this pantomime depends a great deal on the exact rhythm of all gestures and the precision and smoothness with which the gestures are executed. Absolute silence is essential. Even when movements that would normally make a noise are indicated, there is to be no sound.

THE FATAL QUEST

A BURLESQUE

ANONYMOUS

A NON-ROYALTY PLAY

THE CAST

HALF THE CURTAIN
THE OTHER HALF THE CURTAIN
BELLRINGER
KING
QUEEN
DUKE
PRINCESS

THE SCENE

A Throne Room

*This play needs no stage, no curtain and no setting although it
can be given as a regular play.*

*Two throne chairs should be placed in the center of the acting
area. The two "half the curtains" stand at the beginning with
their arms outstretched and covered with shawls or large
pieces of cloth over them, covering the throne chairs. After
the curtains have parted, by sidestepping, one to the Right
and the other to the Left, they stand throughout with their
arms at their sides till the curtains close again. The* BELL-
RINGER *sits on the down Right corner of the playing area.*

The characters of the KING, QUEEN, DUKE *and* PRINCESS *should
act out very vividly the pantomime of their lines. It is possible
to have the whole thing read by somebody off stage with the
characters merely pantomiming the action in sight.*

*The costumes should be a burlesqued treatment of the con-
ventional royal garments.*

———————•———————

ACT ONE

HALF THE CURTAIN. I am half the curtain.
THE OTHER HALF THE CURTAIN. I am the other half of the curtain.

CURTAINS. We are the curtains.

BELLRINGER. The bell rings for the first act.

CURTAINS. The curtains part.

KING. Enter the King.

QUEEN. Followed by the devoted Queen.

KING. He seats himself upon the throne, his sceptre in his hand.

QUEEN. The Queen stands gracefully beside him, gazing at him fondly. "My lord," she says in gentle tones, "why do we keep the Princess hidden from the eyes of men? Will wedlock never be hers?"

KING. The King waxes stern. "Fairy Queen," he says gruffly, "a thousand times have I repeated the Princess shall become the wife of no man."

DUKE. Enter the handsome Duke. "O King," he says in manliest tones, "I have this morning come from Your Majesty's borders. I have a message of greatest importance."

KING. "Speak!" says the King with marked interest.

PRINCESS. The Princess enters at left. At the sight of the handsome stranger, she is startled. Her embarrassment increases her loveliness.

DUKE. At first sight the Duke falls madly in love.

KING. The King rises in excitement. "Speak!" He shouts at the Duke, and begone!!!

DUKE. The Duke gazes at the Princess, his message forgotten.

PRINCESS. The lovely maiden blushes, and drops her eyes.

QUEEN. "My daughter," says the gentle Queen, "why do you intrude yourself here without permission?"

PRINCESS. The Princess opens her mouth to speak.

DUKE. The Duke holds his breath.

PRINCESS. "Alas," says the maiden, in tones melting in sweetness, "my angora kitten has strayed away and is lost."

DUKE. "Fair Princess," cries the Duke, in tones choked with feeling, "service done for you were joy; the kitten I swear to find." [*With high courage he strides away.*]

KING. "Stop him! Stop him!" shouted the King fiercely. "My servants shall find the cat for the Princess." Exit the King.

QUEEN. Followed by the devoted Queen.

PRINCESS. The Princess remains alone upon the stage. A sweet, far-away look in her eyes.

CURTAINS. The curtains draw close.

ACT TWO

BELLRINGER. The bell rings for the second act.

CURTAINS. The curtains part again.

PRINCESS. The fair Princess stands at the window. She hears the distant sounds of hoofs. "It is he," she cries, placing her hands upon her beating breast.

KING. Enter the King.

QUEEN. Followed by the devoted Queen.

DUKE. The Duke steps in buoyantly, puss in his arms.

PRINCESS. "My kitten, my kitten," cries the Princess joyfully. She takes her pet in her arms but her eyes follow the stalwart form of the Duke.

KING. The King is pierced with jealousy.

DUKE. The Duke falls upon his knees before the King. "O King," he says manfully, "I have found the kitten! I claim as my reward the hand of the Princess."

KING. The King trembles with wrath. "Begone!" he shouts furiously. "The hand of the Princess is to be won by no cat!"

DUKE. The Duke departs. As he passes the Princess, he grasps her soft hand. "I will return," he whispers in her ear.

PRINCESS. The Princess does not speak. But her clear blue eyes reveal the secret of her soul.

CURTAINS. The curtains draw sadly together.

ACT THREE

BELLRINGER. The bell rings for the third and fatal act.

CURTAINS. The curtains part for the last time.

KING. The King stands morosely, near the center of the stage.

QUEEN. The Queen stands sadly beside him. "My lord," she says in pleading tones, "relent. The Princess weeps day and night, nor will she be comforted."

KING. The King turns his back. "Hold your peace," he says in harsh tones.

QUEEN. The Queen weeps.

DUKE. Enter the Duke, his sword at his side, "O King," he says in harsh tones; and he says in a white passion, "for the last time I ask you for the hand of your daughter."

KING. The King spurns him. "Begone!" he shouts once more.

DUKE. The Duke draws his sword and stabs the King.

QUEEN. "My lord, my lord," cries the Queen passionately. She stabs herself and falls upon the King.

DUKE. "Ye Gods, what have I done?" cries the Duke in anguish. He drinks a cup of poison and falls dead.

PRINCESS. Hearing the cry, the Princess enters. She stops— transfixed at the horrible scene before her. "Heaven help me," she cries, waving her shapely arms. "I die of grief!" She falls dead upon the breast of her beloved.

KING. "Woe, woe—King of the land is dead."

QUEEN. "Alas, alas—the devoted Queen is dead."

PRINCESS. "The Princess is dead, and beautiful, even in death."

CURTAINS. The curtains unite forever.

The Curtain call.

HALF THE CURTAIN. No, once again.

THE OTHER HALF THE CURTAIN. We separate.

KING. The King is dead.

QUEEN. The devoted Queen is still dead.

DUKE. The manly Duke is still dead.

PRINCESS. The Princess is still dead, and still lovely.

CURTAINS. But this time not for long.

THE RIVAL PEACH-TREES

A SHORT FANTASY SOMEWHAT
IN THE CHINESE MANNER

BY

ALICE C. D. RILEY

* * *

Music by
DOROTHY RILEY BROWN
Songs: "Blow, Winds!" and "Love is a Lantern" to be sung to
music of songs published in "Tunes and Runes"—Riley-Brown
Published by Clayton F. Summy
429 South Wabash Ave.
Chicago, Ill.

* * *

Incidental and instrumental music by gramophone.
List of Columbia and Victor Records appended.

A ROYALTY PLAY

THE CAST

THE PRINCE—*50 years old*
THE PRINCESS—*his daughter, 15 years*
CHOCHO—*chief Lady-in-Waiting to the* PRINCESS—*15 years*
LADIES OF THE PRINCESS—*as many as desired—about 15 years*
LI CHANG—*Grand Vizir—60 years*
PLUMBO—*visiting Mandarin—50 years*
FOOCHA—*a poor but high-born student—25 years*
FU—*Page to the* PRINCE—*18 years*
FO—*Page to the* PRINCE—*18 years*
WANG—*Page to* PLUMBO—*18 years*
FIRST GUARD
SECOND GUARD
PEOPLE OF THE COURT
POPULACE
MUSICIANS, *pretending to play instruments*
A GIRL

THE SCENES

I—*The Court of the White Oleanders.*
II—*Room of the* PRINCESS, *one hour later.*
III—*The Court of the White Oleanders, immediately follow-
ing* SCENE II.
IV—*The Court of the White Oleanders, two days later.*

———————•———————

SCENE I

THE COURT OF THE WHITE OLEANDERS.

*The scene opens empty. The Chinese feeling is helped by hav-
ing the ushers in costume and carrying incense-sticks. Just*

334

before the play begins, darken the space set for the stage and start one of the gramophone records, mentioned in the list of music, off stage. Thus the PRINCESS *and her* LADIES *enter to music and it may run along through the first lines, gradually dying away. As* PRINCESS *and* LADIES *enter, they are running, laughing, chatting together. One of them pretends to be flying a kite.*

FIRST LADY. My kite—my kite!

SECOND. Look out! It will be torn on the oleander-trees.

THIRD LADY. Let out the string—let it *out!*

   [*Several pretend to help fly the kite.*]

CHOCHO. Your Highness is amused?

PRINCESS. Oh, yes! I love the kites, flying like silken birds. If I were not the princess, I should fly one, too. What smells so sweet?

CHOCHO. The oleander-bloom, Your Highness.

PRINCESS. Bring me a spray, my Lady Chocho.

CHOCHO [*clapping her hands*]. Ladies! Who will find the loveliest spray of bloom for the Princess?

LADIES [*all together*]. I will—I—I!

   [*They run about the stage, posing here and there as if smelling flowers. They stand on tip-toe and pretend to bend down the branches, exclaiming ad lib their "ohs" and "ahs."*]

PRINCESS. Careful, my Ladies! Do not harm the oleanders of the Prince, my Father. He would not be pleased.

LADIES. A tiny one, Your Highness?

PRINCESS [*smiling*]. Well, then, a very tiny one.

   [*They each pretend to pluck a very tiny bloom and run to her with it. She holds her sleeve to catch them.*]

LADIES [*as they drop their blooms*]. Dear Lady Princess—this! And this! And this! (Etc.)

PRINCESS. I thank you. These blooms are pure as are your maiden hearts; and fragrant as shall be the love you'll some-day give your husbands.

CHOCHO. Your Highness, we would not wed till you have made your choice, and set us good example.

PRINCESS. I do not wish to wed. I shall remain a maid. But you, my Ladies—see if you can catch these blooms I throw. Who catches will be wed within the month. [*One by one she pretends to toss into the air the blooms from her sleeve. The* LADIES, *with much laughter and running, pretend to catch. They may chatter to each other ad lib. In the midst of this,* CHOCHO *speaks.*]

CHOCHO. My Lady Princess, I see someone approaching. Shall I put on your veil?

PRINCESS [*looking off*]. Who comes? That sweet youth who stands before the blooms of my father's garden, worshipping as at a shrine! I'd like to see his eyes.

CHOCHO [*decidedly*]. 'Tis time to don the veil, Your Highness. [*She puts the veil she carries over the head of the* PRINCESS. *The* LADIES *all gather about her, holding their fans up before their faces and tittering.* FOOCHA *enters.*]

FOOCHA [*bowing as he discovers the* LADIES]. I hope I don't intrude. I search the Court of the White Oleanders.

PRINCESS [*through her veil*]. This is the place, sir; you see they're all in bloom.

FOOCHA [*bowing gallantly*]. I see such bloom the Empress Herself might ask it for her Hidden Garden!

PRINCESS. I see My Lord, tho' drest in simple fashion, is wonted to the manners of the Court.

FOOCHA. My Lady's falcon eyes see everything. 'Tis true this insignificant person was born to the Court, yet loss of favor and of fortune—! Behold me now, Sweet Lady, a simple student, bereft of all save knowledge, and art to make things grow.

PRINCESS. Student of horticulture?

FOOCHA. Yes, My Lady, and come by proclamation of the Prince to all who have something to offer for the new garden.

PRINCESS. You have something?

FOOCHA. Oh, My Lady, if you could see my garden in Humpback Street! Blossoms of fruit-trees—shaded from pink to rose, crinkled like plaited silk;—double blossoms, as 'twere six Mandarin skirts, set one above the other.

PRINCESS. If only I could see!

FOOCHA. I'd gladly offer for—for this garden—if— I've two of them— My Lady.—Might I dare offer one to you, as well as the one I thought to offer to the Prince?

PRINCESS. To me? Why! you don't even know who I am.

FOOCHA. I care not who you are, My Lady—I'd love to give you —anything.

PRINCESS. Why?

FOOCHA. Because—because your voice—oh, that voice! It is more lovely than any blossom in my garden. Do I offend you?

PRINCESS. No—but—you're good at pretty speeches, aren't you? Your tongue speaks—

FOOCHA. It is my heart that speaks. [*They are evidently much taken with each other. He leans towards her.*] Won't you lift your veil?

PRINCESS [*drawing back*]. No—no! Not—yet. I'm—nobody important. Could you care for a very unimportant person—a nobody?

FOOCHA. If she had a voice like yours—

[*The* LADIES, CHOCHO *leading, have been turned away, talking behind their fans, but evidently listening. Now* LADY CHOCHO *decides this has gone far enough. She turns with a cough.*]

CHOCHO. A—hem!

ALL LADIES. A—hem!

PRINCESS [*drawing back*]. I'm telling this gentleman about the new garden. [*Indicates foreground.*] This is the Prince's fifty-fifth—and last. He longs to go into meditation at the temple of the tombs of his Honorable Ancestors.

FOOCHA. The Prince is wise. A sweet spot for a garden. [*Goes to Center.*] You mean this lower terrace here, down these three steps? [*She nods.*] How is it watered?

PRINCESS [*indicating*]. The water comes from this pool. [*Center rear.*] It flows through this runnel— [*Line down from Center rear to point of steps.*]—to this lever here.

FOOCHA [*joining her at point of steps*]. Ah! This lever here at the top of these three steps?

PRINCESS. Exactly. These conduits carry the water either way —right or left. I'll show you. [*She pretends to go down the three steps and goes to Left.*] You see, if you should turn that lever right, the water would flow over here, to the left; and if you throw it left, the water would all flow right.

FOOCHA [*pretending to hold the lever*]. You mean, if I turn it left, so— [*He turns it, then runs down the three steps and leans down Right as if watching the water flow.*]

PRINCESS. Look out! 'Twill spurt! [*With a sudden cry he springs back, as if struck by a spurt of water. She calls to her* LADIES.] Turn it off—turn it off! [*The* LADIES *all rush to the point where the lever is supposed to be and pantomime turning it off.* FOOCHA *stands as if dripping water.*] Oh! you are wet—terribly wet! I'm so sorry!

FOOCHA. 'Tis sweet to have you sorry. I'm afraid I can't appear at the audience of the Prince.

PRINCESS. Oh, but you must. What shall we do? Chocho, what shall we do?

CHOCHO. If the Ladies danced their fan-dance of the wind; we might blow him dry.

PRINCESS. The very thing! Let's do it. Come!

[*The* LADIES *all run down the three steps.* FOOCHA *stands at Center, dripping. They all circle him, dancing and fanning as they sing:*]

BLOW WINDS

PRINCESS AND LADIES.

> Blow, winds, blow! Blow, winds, blow!
> Dry this gentleman,—and neatly.
> Wet apparel—dry it sweetly.
> Dry him fleetly and completely—
> Blow, winds, blow!

FOOCHA [*examining his clothes*]. Why—I'm—I'm dry!

LADIES [*tittering behind fans*]. Completely dry!

PRINCESS. As dry as Autumn before the rain-fall.

CHOCHO. As dry as dust in a slattern's house.

LADIES. As dry as compliments on an old man's tongue. [*Giggle behind fans.*]

PRINCESS. In short—you're dry.

FOOCHA. I'm grateful for the magic. I hope that I shall need you again. I shall never forget—

PRINCESS. Don't forget to come to the Audience of the Prince.

FOOCHA. Shall you be there? [LADIES *giggle behind fans.*]

PRINCESS. Perhaps. Promise you'll come.

FOOCHA. To you—I promise—anything. Till—later, then? [*He starts off, she runs after.*]

PRINCESS. Oh, please—what is your name?

FOOCHA. My name is Foocha—good-by! [*He goes.*]

PRINCESS [*looking after him*]. Foocha! Oh, Chocho, what a sweet young man!

CHOCHO [*dryly*]. You think so? I thought you didn't like him. [*The* LADIES *all titter behind their fans.*]

PRINCESS. You naughty Chocho. You're making fun of me. I don't care who knows it—I think he's—wonderful.

CHOCHO. Then shall I tell the Grand Vizir—

PRINCESS [*stamping foot*]. The Dragon eat the Grand Vizir— I hate him.

[*Notice off Right, as of a camel, groaning. All look Right.*]

CHOCHO. Now by the Dragon's tail, here comes the Grand Vizir.

LADIES. And his fat friend—Plumbo—on camel-back.

[*They all blow up their cheeks and take a few waddling steps in unison.*]

PRINCESS. Like bacon—a streak of fat and a streak of lean.

LADIES [*dancing a grotesque dance to the same music*].

> Fat and lean—fat and lean!
> See our Grand Vizir so crafty!
> See old Plumbo,—broad abaft-y!
> Don't their camels make you laugh-ty?
> Fat and lean!

CHOCHO. Look out! They are coming this way.

PRINCESS. They mustn't see us! The Grand Vizir would tell my father—

CHOCHO. We'll have to hide—

LADIES. In the oleander thicket.

CHOCHO. Hurry!

[*They all scramble into up-stage corners.*]

PRINCESS [*to the* LADIES *in opposite corner.*] Look out! I see your jackets.

[*Again they all scramble back, then become very still. They hold this throughout the following scene.*]

[*Enter* PLUMBO *and* GRAND VIZIR. *They pretend that they are riding camels. They do this by being themselves from the waist up, and the camels from the waist down. This means that they lift their legs high, reach out for a long, wiggling step, and repeat with the other foot. Meanwhile, the upper part of the body lurches in time with the steps, and the voices are shaken, as with the exigencies of a camel's gait. If this is properly produced, it becomes very amusing.*]

PLUMBO. By my best chop-sticks, this is awful!

GRAND VIZIR. Nonsense! The Emperor Himself might be proud to ride on these camels.

PLUMBO. Let him ride, then! He may have mine. Whoa! How do you stop the thing?

GRAND VIZIR [*having trouble also*]. I don't know. There, little one—there—there! [*Pretends to stroke his camel, who behaves badly.*]

PLUMBO [*beating his camel*]. Here, and there—you big brute! [*Both camels prance about. The riders appear terrified. When they are calm:*] Why the camels, anyway? What's the idea?

GRAND VIZIR. You must make a good impression on the Princess.

PLUMBO. I don't give two flirts of a kite's tail for the Princess.

GRAND VIZIR. Wait. You've not seen her. She's as beautiful as —these oleanders. [*His camel begins to misbehave.*] Whoa there—whoa!

PLUMBO. Look out! Mine's going to kneel down. What shall I do? I'm falling.

GRAND VIZIR. Beat him. [*Each struggles with his camel.*]

PLUMBO [*when his camel finally is still.*] Princess or no—beautiful or no—I'll not ride this camel again for her. Besides, if she's so beautiful—why does she always appear veiled? I don't trust it. That little lady Chocho is much more to my taste.

GRAND VIZIR. Put *that* out of mind at once. The Lady Chocho must marry me. She is the nightingale of my dreams. You are to marry the Princess—we'll get her old father out of the way by persuading him to go into meditation. You shall rule the Princess, and I will rule the kingdom. I have it all arranged. Whoa, there! Look out—my camel's—at it—again—[*He gallops about.* PLUMBO *is nervous.*]

PLUMBO [*shaking his head doubtfully*]. This won't agree with me. I don't like it—don't like it.

GRAND VIZIR. Which—the camel or the marriage?

PLUMBO. Neither. Why should she wish to marry me—a Mandarin from a far-away court?

GRAND VIZIR. Ah! That's where I come in. I shall persuade the Prince that the man who gives the most beautiful blossoming peach-tree for his new garden, should win the hand of the Princess.

PLUMBO. I have no peach-tree.

GRAND VIZIR. Ah! That's where I come in. There's one in a garden near here. A place in Humpback Street. We'll send your man to get it—

PLUMBO. Do you mean *steal* it?

GRAND VIZIR. One does not say "steal" to a Grand Vizir. Look out!—Your camel—beat him—beat him!

[PLUMBO *pretends to beat his camel. The* GRAND VIZIR *beats his. They exeunt in a whirl of excited cries and gallops. As their voices die away, the* PRINCESS *and her* LADIES *steal out and look after them.*]

PRINCESS. The old crocodile!

CHOCHO. Marry me, will he?" "That's where I come in." Not if I see him first.

LADIES. Look—look!

CHOCHO [*looking off*]. Fu and Fo are coming. The Audience is about to begin. We must go and join the Court. Come, Your Highness.

PRINCESS. Lift my veil.

[*Four of the* LADIES *take her square veil by its four corners, and lift it till the center floats like a curved shell above her.*]

[*Faint music—off.*]

PRINCESS. Hark! I hear the Court Musicians playing. We must run. Come!

[*With a flutter of fans they exit, the veil of the* PRINCESS *swelling in a great curve about her as they run.*]

[*Enter* FU *and* FO. FU *bears a chair,* FO *a parasol. The music may continue throughout this scene, very faintly.*]

FU. Is this the place?

FO. Yes. The Grand Vizir said: "The Garden of the White Oleanders."

FU. Well, here are the oleanders.

FO. And there—[*Indicating fore-stage.*]—is the empty court.

FU. Which is to become the fifty-fifth garden of the Prince.

[*Standing side by side, and still holding parasol and chair, they do a clogging step as they recite together:*]

BOTH.

> Five time ten is fifty—plus five is fifty-five.
> Fifty-five gardens for the Prince, as I'm alive!

FU. If the Grand Vizir had to carry this chair—

FO. Or this parasol—

[*They draw a great sigh together.*]

FU [*indicating his chair*]. Where shall I place it?

FO. Don't ask me.

FU [*placing it Right*]. If I put it here, Li Chang will say—

FO [*indicating Left*]. "Idiot! put it over there."

FU [*changing chair to Left*]. And if I place it over here—

Fo [*indicating Right*]. "Idiot! put it over here." He must show
  authority.

Fu. There's no pleasing him.

Both [*clogging as they recite*].

> We try to please the Grand Vizir
> By placing there—by placing here;
> But—knowing him—we sadly fear
> We cannot please the Grand Vizir.

[*They end in a comic pose.*]

Fu [*placing chair Right*]. I'll try it here. So this is to be the
  new garden?

Fo [*folding parasol and laying it on chair*]. The fifty-fifth.

Fu. And the Grand Vizir is planning to fill it—

Fo. And his own pockets at the same time.

Both [*clogging and reciting*].

> Who would not like to be the man
> To fool the Prince—and gardens plan,
> And wire-pull, and scheme until
> His empty pockets he can fill?

[*End in comic pose.*]

Fu. I see you know his tricks.

Fo. All the world knows them—except the Prince.

Fu. Have you proof of his graft?

Fo. We go in cotton—he in padded silk.

Fu. He wears a coral button on his cap.

Both. Proof enough.

  [*The music swells louder. We hear the voice of the* Grand
  Vizir, *shouting:*]

Grand Vizir. Bring that parasol!

Fo. Yes-s-sss sir! [*He dashes off with the parasol.* Fu *moves
  the chair about nervously. Musicians enter, pretending to
  play.* (Columbia Record A3163 "Yao Yin" or Victor Record
  35777B "In a Chinese Garden.") *Next comes the* populace,

laughing and talking together. Then the PEOPLE OF THE COURT, *to whom the* POPULACE *bows. Finally the* GRAND VIZIR, *shouting:*]

GRAND VIZIR. Fu—that chair, idiot! Put it over here. [*Indicates opposite place.*

FU [*running with the chair*]. Yes-s-sss, sir! [*Places chair as directed.*]

POPULACE [*shouting*]. "Hail to the Prince!"

[*The* MUSICIANS *take their places near chair. At a music cue, enters the* PRINCE, *with* FO *holding the parasol over him. The* PRINCESS *and her* LADIES *enter. She is still veiled. Two of the* LADIES *carry a chair for the* PRINCESS *which is placed for her. All but the* PRINCESS *kowtow. She bows deeply to her father. When he arrives at his chair, he waves his fan.*]

PRINCE. Hail, O My People!

ALL [*rising*]. Hail! Hail! [*He seats himself. The* GRAND VIZIR *is fussing about, placing people. Music continues softly.*

PRINCE. My Beloved People, my proclamation summoned you here today to take part in the planning of this, my last and fifty-fifth garden. Has any one a plan to suggest?

[*Music stops.* FOOCHA *enters at rear, unnoticed.*]

GRAND VIZIR [*quickly*]. Ah! That's where I come in. The new garden will lie in this court before us. I've planned a blossoming peach-tree to the right,—another to the left.

PRINCE. But I wish something new—unusual. I have already peach-trees.

GRAND VIZIR. But not like this, Augustness. This is brought to you by my friend, the Mandarin Plumbo, from a far-away court. May I present him to Augustness? [*He shoves* PLUMBO *forward.*]

PLUMBO [*as he reluctantly goes forward, mutters*]. This won't agree with me.

PRINCE. Welcome to Our Kingdom. Is it true that you have a wonderful peach-tree which you desire to present us?

PLUMBO [*looking helplessly at* GRAND VIZIR]. Augustness—I—I —I—

GRAND VIZIR. Sire, it is true that he has the most marvelous tree in all the world.

PRINCE. Then I must have it.

GRAND VIZIR. It shall be yours if—

PRINCE. What price?

GRAND VIZIR. Not gold, Augustness.

PRINCE. Ah, more precious still? What does he want,—position—power?

GRAND VIZIR. Augustness, he seeks a wife.

PLUMBO [*muttering to himself*]. This won't agree with me.

PRINCE. A wife? He does well. The women of my kingdom are the most beautiful—the most virtuous—

GRAND VIZIR. He seeks the most beautiful—the most virtuous —in short—the Princess.

PRINCE. A price indeed!

PRINCESS. The tree comes high.

GRAND VIZIR. Augustness wishes to retire into meditation?

PRINCE. I do. I would retire to the temple of the tombs of my Honorable Ancestors and meditate.

GRAND VIZIR. Precisely. With the Princess married to the Mandarin Plumbo, Augustness may retire.

PRINCESS. I do not wish to marry.

GRAND VIZIR. Women must marry.

PRINCESS [*before the* PRINCE]. O Honorable Father, forget I am a woman—do not force this marriage—

GRAND VIZIR. Augustness, except the Princess, there is not a person here who would not sacrifice for you. [*Turns to the crowd.*] Do I speak true?

ALL. Hail to the Prince! Long live the Prince!

PRINCESS. And would I not sacrifice— ?

GRAND VIZIR [*pushing forward* PLUMBO]. Good! Here is Lord Plumbo.

PRINCESS [*drawing back*]. O August Father—anything but this—

PRINCE. Beloved Daughter, the Princess Royal *must* marry.

PRINCESS. Then if I must—I must. But if I am to be given in

exchange for a peach-tree, it may be possible—just possible, Augustness—that someone has a better tree.

GRAND VIZIR. Impossible!

PRINCE. Let the Princess speak.

PRINCESS. Hear me, O People of my Father's Kingdom. Because my August Father so much desires the most beautiful peach-tree in all the world for his new garden; I here and now promise to marry the one who shall bring for this garden the loveliest tree. Do any of you offer?

GRAND VIZIR. The Mandarin Plumbo has already offered.

PRINCESS [looking about the crowd anxiously]. And no one else? [She discovers FOOCHA, standing alone and silent.] Has no one here a tree to offer? I see a stranger here—a youth. [Indicates FOOCHA.] Have you, sir, a tree?

FOOCHA [stepping forward]. I have a tree. I should be happy to give it to the Prince without demand—

PRINCE. You've heard my daughter's offer,—she may not take it back.

FOOCHA. Then I am proud to offer.

GRAND VIZIR. Fellow, how dare you!

PRINCESS [quickly]. I said "anyone." Father, you will allow this youth—?

PRINCE. Of what family do you come, young man?

FOOCHA. Of the family of Fuh-keen, Augustness.

PRINCE. An old and honorable family.

FOOCHA. Though now out of favor and fortune. I am poor, but a student, Sire.

PRINCE. And you really have such a tree.

FOOCHA. A tree as gay as the sun and as mysterious as the moon. A tree that laughs and dances—even sings.

GRAND VIZIR [with a menacing step toward him]. It is not true —you've no such tree.

PRINCE. Silence! [To FOOCHA.] Where did you get this tree?

FOOCHA. Myself I grew it—child of my own experiments and care.

PRINCE [to PLUMBO]. And did you, also, grow your tree, Lord Plumbo?

PLUMBO. I—Augustness—I—

GRAND VIZIR. It is his own, Augustness.

PRINCE. Good! The race is even. Listen. You each—you, Foocha and Lord Plumbo, shall yourselves plant your own trees— those of your own growing. Let them be planted by four o'clock today. I shall not know which tree belongs to whom. My Grand Vizir shall divide equally the water between them. Two days hence, see that you all assemble here, and I shall judge the trees. The owner of the tree I choose shall marry the Princess. The owner of the other tree shall be banished the kingdom. Have I judged well, my people?

ALL. Long live the Prince!

GRAND VIZIR. Augustness, when Lord Plumbo marries the Princess, have I your honorable permission to marry the Lady Chocho?

   [*Much commotion behind fans.*]

PRINCE. If Lord Plumbo win, you shall marry the Lady Chocho. [*Rises.*] Let music play.

   [*Music begins softly.* MUSICIANS *have pantomime of playing. He starts the procession off. The* PRINCESS *and her* LADIES *next, then* GRAND VIZIR *and* PLUMBO, *then* COURT *and* POPULACE. FOOCHA *is left on alone. Suddenly, the* PRINCESS *comes running back.*]

PRINCESS. Oh, Foocha, I should not let you risk so much for me.

FOOCHA. Your Highness, I would risk my life. But I did not dream, when I talked to you so freely, that you were Princess Royal.

PRINCESS. And do you love me less for that?

FOOCHA. 'Tis not a question of my love, but of my position. I'm a poor student—I am not worthy to wed a Princess.

PRINCESS. And if I were a poor maid—then would *I* not be worthy? You *must* not let him win. Go! Bring your tree! I pray it be as lovely as you think!

FOOCHA. Although I have not seen your face, it could not be lovely enough for—you. I go! [*He runs off. She stands, watching him off, then speaks:*]

Princess.

Oh, great Quan Yin, protect him and his tree;
Bring him good luck—and give his heart to me!
[*She exits the opposite side.*]

Scene II

The Property Man sets a screen for background, places a table and chair, and displays to the audience a placard reading:

ROOM OF THE PRINCESS ONE HOUR LATER

He then retires to his corner and reads, etc.
[*Enters the* princess, *followed by* chocho. *The* princess *lifts off her veil and throws it on the floor.* chocho *picks it up, folds it carefully, and hands it to the Property Man.*]

Princess [*throwing off her veil*]. O Chocho, what a beau-u-u-ti-ful young man!

Chocho [*practically*]. Keep your eye on the Grand Vizir, My Lady; he's up to mischief.

Princess [*still in her dream*]. Such perfect manners!

Chocho. Li Chang knows that with Plumbo as Prince Consort, he, himself, will have the real power. He means to win.

Princess [*coming to*]. No, no! Foocha must win. I must be sure of that.

Chocho. You can't be sure of that. If Li Chang brings the better tree, and the Prince chooses it; you'll have to keep your word. You can't be sure.

Princess. I *must.* Open my dressing-case. I must make myself beautiful.

[*These dressing-cases are of wood, cubicals about 12 × 12 × 14, a little higher than wide or deep. They open by lifting the lid which is faced inside with a mirror. One adjusts this by sliding the bottom edge forward. Double doors at front open, disclosing tiny drawers, in which are kept all toilet articles like rouge, eyebrow pencil, combs, hair-ornaments, etc.* chocho *lifts this small box—pretended—*]

to the table and opens and adjusts. The PRINCESS *seats herself before it. The table and chair are real; the rest imagined.*]

CHOCHO. There! Is the mirror right?

PRINCESS. Tip it a little more. [CHOCHO *adjusts.*] There!
Mercy, what a fright I am! To think *he* saw me like
this!

CHOCHO. He didn't see you. Remember you were veiled.

PRINCESS. Thank all my household gods! In which drawer is
my rouge?

CHOCHO [*pretending to open one*]. There it is, My Lady.
[*Knock heard off Right,—edge of screen.*] Some one is knocking.

PRINCESS [*making up before pretended mirror*]. See who it is.
  [CHOCHO *goes Right and pretends to open a door. She
bows.*]

CHOCHO. Sir Grand Vizir, you take us by surprise.

VOICE OF LI CHANG [*off*]. I wish to see the Princess.
  [CHOCHO *looks back over her left shoulder at the* PRINCESS,
who signals: "Yes."]

CHOCHO [*bowing*]. Pray enter, Sir.
  [LI CHANG *enters.* PRINCESS *rises and comes down Left
Center.* CHOCHO *pretends to close door and comes down to
Right Center.* LI CHANG *has come down to front Center. Thus
he is between them.*]

LI CHANG [*bowing*]. I thank Your Highness for receiving my
miserable and worthless person.

PRINCESS [*returning the bow*]. Sir Grand Vizir, I make you
welcome to my miserable room. To what do I owe the over-
whelming joy of this visit?

LI CHANG. I bring to Your Highness and to the Lady Chocho
an invitation for this afternoon.
  [*The two women exchange significant glances.*]

PRINCESS. For this afternoon? Then the Grand Vizir wishes
us to be present at the tree-planting?

LI CHANG. No, no! Oh, Your Highness,—not that! How could
Your Highness believe that I would ask her to humble herself to watch so miserable a spectacle! No. The invitation I

bring is most amusing. My Lord Plumbo, the visiting Mandarin, has with him a magnificent camel train. The Flowery Way is all in bloom,—a sight worth my best snuff-bottle. I will have the camels brought round at once and— [*False start Right.*]

PRINCESS. Wait. Thank the Lord Mandarin for me and say that we regret that we cannot accept the loan of his most magnificent camels.

LI CHANG. What! Your Ladyship refuses? [*She bows.*] Impossible! You should see the camels. Their trappings are of cut velvet—

PRINCESS. I regret the cut velvet but—I remain here.

LI CHANG [*worried*]. Surely Your Ladyship is not intending to be present at the tree-planting this afternoon? I assure Your Highness that would be most improper.

PRINCESS [*haughtily*]. I do not need even the Grand Vizir to tell me, The Princess Royal, what is proper and what is not. [LI CHANG *bows his apologies.*] The sun this morning has given me a headache. I shall rest.

LI CHANG [*eagerly*]. And the Lady Chocho?

PRINCESS. The Lady Chocho remains with me. [*He bows.*] Make our apologies to the Mandarin Plumbo. I regret the camels.

CHOCHO. And the cut velvet.

PRINCESS. Tell him. The audience is ended. [*He bows himself out.* CHOCHO *runs to close the door on him, then back to her mistress.*] Fancy *those* camels!
  [*They giggle.*]

CHOCHO. Fancy—cut velvet!
  [*They giggle.*]

PRINCESS. Naughty Chocho! Remember—you are "the mocking-bird of his dreams."

CHOCHO. He is the carrion crow of mine.
  [*They giggle.*]

PRINCESS. What is he up to now?

CHOCHO. Mischief. We must hurry. He needs watching.

PRINCESS. Run quickly and fetch our disguises.

[CHOCHO *exits Right. The* PRINCESS *seats herself and combs—or pretends to comb, her hair. Meanwhile, she sings:*]
PRINCESS

LOVE IS A LANTERN

Sung by the Princess

Love is a lantern, swung to the sky;
Softly it glows as my dear goes by.
Shadows between us blackly I see;
So light his way till he come to me—he come to me.
So light his way till he come to me.

[CHOCHO *returns bringing two dark cotton coats, such as coolies wear.*]
CHOCHO. Your Highness, do these suit you?
PRINCESS [*taking one*]. How ugly! Still, it's blue—blue always did become me. We'll try it on. [*She rises.* CHOCHO *helps her off with her handsome coat from Scene I, which she hands to the Property Man, who puts it away. Then she helps her on with the dark coat. Let them talk ad lib during this:— "The right sleeve, please!" or anything.*] There! How do I look, Chocho?
CHOCHO [*practically*]. *Not* like a wash-maid with those embroidered hose. You must go barefoot.
PRINCESS [*taken aback*]. Barefoot—oh!
CHOCHO. Barefoot. Sit down and let me take off your hose. [*Kneels.*]
PRINCESS [*sits, much amused*]. The barefoot Princess! [*Lifts right foot to* CHOCHO.] There! Right foot. [CHOCHO *takes off that stocking.*] Now, left foot.
[*Same play left.* PRINCESS *wiggles her toes and giggles.*]
PRINCESS. How *can* I walk on them!
CHOCHO. It has been done. Try it.
PRINCESS [*humming and dancing*]. And you go change. [CHOCHO *ducks behind the screen.*]

"Love is a lantern swung to the sky,
   Softly it glows as my dear goes by." Etc., etc.

[*Sits to finish her make-up.*] Chocho!

CHOCHO'S VOICE [*behind screen*]. Yes, My Lady?

PRINCESS. What did you hear while you were out?

CHOCHO'S VOICE. I heard the camels groaning.

PRINCESS. Nothing of Foocha?

CHOCHO [*appearing from behind screen, her coat changed and barefoot*]. Nothing, My Lady. Are you ready? [*Looks her over.*] Not enough rouge.

PRINCESS [*dabbing it on thick*]. There! How do I look?

CHOCHO. Wonderful! If Li Chang should recognize you—

PRINCESS. No danger. He'll not look at a wash-maid above the feet; and he has no occasion to recognize my great toe. Come! [*She starts off.*]

CHOCHO. But I must take something for us to wash,—these towels you've thrown on the floor. [PRINCESS *is off.* CHOCHO *runs to make-up case and hastily pretends to make herself up.*]

VOICE OF PRINCESS [*off*]. Hurry, Chocho!

CHOCHO [*snatching up supposed towels from floor.*] As soon as I get these towels—coming! [*She exits hastily.*]

SCENE III

Property Man strikes screen and takes off screen, table and chair. He now displays placard reading:

TERRACE OF THE WHITE OLEANDERS

[*The* PRINCESS *enters, walking gingerly, followed by* CHOCHO.]

PRINCESS. Ouch! This sharp grass hurts my feet! [*She stops to nurse one.*]

CHOCHO. If Your Ladyship will—

PRINCESS. Sssh! You must not call me that. Someone will hear you. I'm just a wash-maid now. Are we in time?

CHOCHO [*looking off Right*]. Barely. An oxcart comes along the Flowery Way. That will be Plumbo's tree.

PRINCESS [*looking Right*]. Let me look! Oh! A big one—and a beauty.

Chocho. Yes. Come to the pool. We must get to work. Remember we are wash-maids.

Princess [*still looking off*]. A million branches, each with a million peach-blooms; all double-petaled and blushing like a maid—

Chocho. Come and begin your washing.

Princess. Oh! Oh! What ever shall I do? Foocha's tree can never equal that. What shall I do?

Chocho [*on her knees at the pool, washing*]. Come here and learn to wash.

Princess [*almost in tears*]. By my best brocaded trousers, if I have to marry Plumbo—! Oh! He waddles!

Chocho. There are worse crimes than waddling.

Princess [*wailing*]. But I'll have to waddle too. [*She waddles to pool, opposite* chocho.]

Chocho. Quick! Kneel down. You must learn to wash if you're to pass as wash-maid.

Princess. I have to wipe my eyes.

Chocho. Here! [*Pretends to pass up a towel with which the* princess *pretends to wipe her eyes*.] Hurry! Kneel down! [princess *does*.] Now, dip your towel in the pool.

Princess [*doing so, then looking at it*]. Oh! These horrid spots of red! I'll never get them out.

Chocho. Only My Lady's rouge. It will come out. You take the soiled spot so—[*Demonstrates.*]—between your knuckles, and rub it so—

Princess [*trying awkwardly*]. So?

Chocho. No, no! Between your knuckles—so.
[*The* princess *tries*.]

Princess. Ouch! It takes off all the skin.
[*Voices off Right.*]

Chocho. Be careful! They are coming.
[*They bend over pool, pretending to wash*.]

Plumbo's voice [*off*]. Whoa! whoa! I can't get off this camel —whoa! whoa! [*Great noise off. The women look off and laugh softly together*.]

Chocho. See! The Lord Grand Vizir runs to help him off.

LI CHANG'S VOICE [*off*]. Make him kneel!

PLUMBO'S VOICE [*off*]. Make him kneel yourself. You got me into this camel business.

[*Suddenly, in the midst of their laughter, the two women stop and hurriedly begin to work.* LI CHANG *and* PLUMBO *enter, followed by* WANG.]

PLUMBO. I'm all upset. This won't agree with me.

LI CHANG. Such a figure of a lover! I wish I had entered this affair in my own name.

PLUMBO. You, indeed! You the figure of a lover—! [*Laughs.*]

LI CHANG. Only he who carries the whip can afford to laugh.

PLUMBO. I beg your pardon. I withdraw, in your favor, from the contest for the hand of the Princess.

LI CHANG [*weighing it*]. No. It is too late to change. Besides, I've chosen elsewhere.

PLUMBO. Ah? The Lady Chocho?

LI CHANG [*grinning foolishly*]. Plump little Partridge!

PLUMBO. I thought 'twas "nightingale."

LI CHANG. Delectable Chocho! No, you must wed the Princess.

PLUMBO. If *he* should have the better tree?

LI CHANG. Who—that fool Foocha? Didn't we take his best? He shall not have the better tree—that is where I come in.

PLUMBO. The Prince said: "Trees of your own growing and planting." I never grew nor planted anything.

LI CHANG. What need to grow when you may take? We shall beat him with his own tree. Ha-ha! A pretty trick.

PLUMBO. A dishonest one.

LI CHANG. To a Grand Vizir, one does not say: "dishonest."

PLUMBO. Then call it diplomatic. He'll bring that other tree—the one with lovely buds; and doubtless he, himself, will plant it.

LI CHANG. I will allow you to plant yours. [*Laughs.*] Plant your tree, Plumbo.

PLUMBO [*indignant*]. To a Mandarin, one does not say: "plant your tree."

Li Chang. Your servant, Wang, shall plant it. 'Tis the same thing. I'll turn the water on. Together we shall manage.
[*The women are listening carefully.*]

Plumbo. You mean that you'll do something—er—diplomatic? No. I'll not—

Li Chang. You'll do just as I say. Consider! You're far from home. If you should—disappear [*gesture*]—just—disappear [*gesture*]—sh? [plumbo *shivers*, li chang *smiles*.] You'll do just as I say. [plumbo *bows*.] Good! come here [*Indicates off Right.*] and inspect *your tree*. It is a beauty. [*They exeunt Right.*]

Princess [*standing up*]. The warty old toad!

Chocho [*also standing*]. The crawling worm! Look at that tree—one mass of bloom!

Princess. And Foocha not here yet. Oh, dear!

Chocho [*looking off Left*]. He's coming now, his tree strapped to his back. See! [*They look off Left.*]

Princess. Poor dear! That heavy tree! 'Twill break his back.

Chocho. 'Tis not in bloom—his tree.

Princess. Bones of my Royal Ancestors! His tree is not in bloom. What shall I do, Chocho, what shall I do? [*Wrings her hands.*]

Chocho. You'll marry Plumbo.

Princess. I won't. [*Watching Left.*] He staggers with the weight. I'll help him. [*She exits Left.* chocho *stands guard, watching Right and Left.* princess *and* foocha *reënter, he bent double, as though carrying a tree on his back. Goes down three steps and to Left.*] Do let me help you, sir!

Foocha [*still bent, but struck by the voice*]. *That voice!* That lovely voice? Are you the Princess? I cannot see—

Princess. No, no! I'm just a maid who washes linen. Let me help you, sir!

Foocha [*going down to lower Left*]. I do need help. Are you strong enough to steady this tree, as I let it slide to earth?

Princess. Oh, I am very strong. [*Pretends to steady it.*] I have it. Now! Let it slide. [*Together they pantomime letting the pretended tree down, with effort.*] There! Now it's safe.

FOOCHA [*staggering and gasping as he tries to straighten up from his load.*] By all my household gods, that tree is heavy.

PRINCESS [*hiding her face behind her sleeve*]. Your servants should have carried it—

FOOCHA [*laughing grimly*]. I have no servants, maiden,— nothing but this tree, and my wits. They even stole my other tree—the one I meant to enter.

PRINCESS. Stole? Oh! [*She realizes it is* his *tree* PLUMBO *has entered*]. Then this is your second-best tree?

FOOCHA. No, not exactly. It is a rarer variety than the other. But that was in full bloom. This has buds. If only they will open during the two days—

PRINCESS. Oh, I hope they do!

FOOCHA. That voice! So much like *hers!* [*Tries to pull down her sleeve.*] Please let me look at you.

PRINCESS [*dropping her sleeve*]. I'm just a maid who washes linen.

FOOCHA [*starting as her beauty strikes his eye*]. Washes linen— YOU!

PRINCESS [*holding up her sleeve again*]. Please—!

FOOCHA. I thought your voice was like that of the Princess. Her voice is like a golden bell; but yours is like a lark's song in the dawn. No Princess ever was so beautiful—

PRINCESS. Please, sir—!

FOOCHA. Oh! give my heart the sunshine of your smile; and give my ears the music of your voice—

PRINCESS. But we should plant your tree—if you would wed the Princess.

FOOCHA. Talk to me not of Princesses or weddings; unless you'll wed with me.

PRINCESS. If you fail, you'll be banished.

FOOCHA. With you beside me, I should welcome that.

PRINCESS. And the poor Princess?

FOOCHA. The Princess will not care. She has her wealth, her rank, her power—

PRINCESS. While I have only—

FOOCHA. Me—if you will have me?

[CHOCHO *interrupts with a sharp hiss.*]

PRINCESS. They're coming. I must go.

FOOCHA. I'll let him win the prize.

PRINCESS. No, no! You must not fail. Promise you'll do your best? [*He nods.*] Beware of Li Chang—he'll play you tricks.

[*Again* CHOCHO *hisses. The* PRINCESS *runs up stage to the pool, the two women drop to their knees and pretend to wash linen. Enter* PLUMBO *and* LI CHANG, *followed by* WANG, *bent double under the weight of the other tree, which he pretends to carry on his back.*]

LI CHANG [*directing* WANG]. Here! Down these steps! One— two—three. [*Goes right front.*] Now over here.

WANG [*staggering*]. I cannot. It—is—heavy.

LI CHANG. Nonsense! I don't think so. Bring it here, I say. Let it down here. [*He indicates a spot Right front opposite* FOOCHA'S *tree at Left.*]

WANG [*swaying helplessly*]. Help! Help!

LI CHANG. I am no coolie. Let it down, I tell you.

WANG. Help!

FOOCHA [*springing to aid him*]. I'll help you. [*Does.*] There you are—safe. A lovely tree! So much like one I lost. In almost too full bloom.

O lovely tree! O miracle of spring!
Beware the Breeze, or Beauty may take wing!

[*To* PLUMBO.] This is your tree, sir? You grew it?

LI CHANG [*putting on horn spectacles*]. Who, pray, are you, that go spouting words as fountains spout their waters?

FOOCHA. My name is Foocha.

[PLUMBO *suddenly exclaims and draws* LI CHANG *to the Right, where they confer in whispers.* FOOCHA *pretends to begin to dig the hole for his tree. They finally go over to him.*]

PLUMBO [*indicating tree at Left*]. Sir, is this your tree?

FOOCHA. It is. The only one the robbers left me. It was a crime to dig it up just now—half-budded. My poor peach-tree!

Li Chang [*laughing*]. Ho-ho! His poor peach-tree! Without a single bloom.

Foocha. With water and sun, and two days' time—'twill bloom.

Plumbo [*gazing at tree*]. Its buds are various—see!

Foocha. One half its buds are pale, as if with fright; and half are blushing pink as maiden's cheek, when lover's step is heard. 'Twill have two shades of bloom,—one pale, one deepest rose.

Li Chang. Trees do not grow like that.

Foocha. This does.

[Li chang *and* plumbo *whisper together while* foocha *digs.* wang *digs indifferently.*]

Li Chang. Young man, where did you buy this tree?

Foocha. I did not buy—nor even steal it. I grew it. Perhaps you heard the Prince say: "Of your own growing." I grew this tree myself.

Li Chang [*pretending to take purse from his sleeve*]. See this purse, heavy with gold? Take it and—go.

Foocha [*digging*]. My tree is not for sale.

Li Chang [*dangling the purse*]. A purse of gold—very desirable.

Foocha [*digging*]. I do not desire it.

Li Chang. There's nothing more to be desired, young fool. Youth is romantic, eh? Your heart's set on the Lady? Ha! Were I a handsome youth like you, I would not wed with— [*whispers*]—ugliness.

[*The* princess *springs up but is at once jerked down by* chocho.]

Foocha. Ugliness? The Princess is not ugly.

Li Chang. Then why does she go veiled? Believe me, she's a monster.

Foocha. I don't believe it. She has a lovely voice. Besides, I've given my word. No. [*Digs.*]

Li Chang [*dangling the purse*]. Now *this*—this Golden Lady —no one yet has ever found her ugly. Take *her*—and go.

Foocha. No.

Plumbo. Why do you wish to wed the Princess?

Foocha. I do not wish. But I have given my word. I keep my word. [*Digs.*]

Li Chang. Idiot! You may not keep your head. [*To* plumbo.] Come aside, my friend, I have something to say to you.

Plumbo. This won't agree with me. [*They start off Right. He turns back on* wang *who isn't digging.*] You, fellow—dig! [*Exeunt* plumbo *and* li chang, *Right.*]

Foocha [*looking after them*]. So *that's* our Grand Vizir!

Wang. A crafty villain, if you ask me, sir.

Foocha. What do you know about him?

Wang. He made me dig up this tree—stole it from a little garden in Humpback Street—and now he makes me plant it again. It's heavy work and I'm a gentleman's gentleman. Digging is not my work. May his bones be scattered to the four winds of heaven!

Foocha. Humpback Street? [wang *nods.*] The garden with a blue-tiled gate? [wang *nods.*] I thought so. It is my garden,—and my tree.

Wang [*alarmed*]. Oh, sir, blame me not! I did not wish to steal it. I—

Foocha. Do not be alarmed. I well know whom to blame. You'd better dig, or you will get a beating.

[wang *digs. The* princess, *who has stood up as soon as the* grand vizir *went off, steals down to* foocha.]

Princess. Oh, sir, be careful. He means you harm. You'd have been safer, sir, to take his purse and go.

Foocha. Oh, Maiden-with-the-Golden-Voice, I cannot go.

Princess. You wish to wed the Princess after all?

Foocha. No, no! But I have entered in this contest and promised both you and the Princess. I must keep my word. If, 'gainst all odds, I win; the Princess may release me.

Princess [*decidedly*]. Never will she release you—be sure of that. But, if you wish to win I'll help you plant your tree.

Foocha. Not even that. The Prince said: "Grown and planted by yourselves." I shall play fair, whatever happens. Be careful, they are coming.

PRINCESS. I want to see you win. Good luck! [*She runs back to pool.* LI CHANG *and* PLUMBO *reënter.*]

LI CHANG [*to* PLUMBO]. Leave this to me. [*To* WANG.] Hurry with your digging. Make the hole wide and deep. DIG! [WANG *has been digging lazily.* LI CHANG *threatens as if to beat him.* WANG *starts to dig as fast as* FOOCHA *is digging.* LI CHANG *crosses to* FOOCHA.] Young Man, you still may take this purse and go. [FOOCHA *ignores him and goes on digging.*] Your tree will never bloom in two days' time. [FOOCHA *same play.*] And if it did, and had two shades of bloom, 'twould be a monstrosity.

FOOCHA [*stopping*]. Then why wish to buy it? [LI CHANG *dangles the purse.*] No. I stay here.

LI CHANG [*angry*]. May you die in torture! May the bones of your head be buried far from the bones of your body! May the tomb of your ancestors never know you!

FOOCHA. May the gods return that curse upon your own head! [*Digs.*]

PLUMBO [*who has been urging* WANG *on*]. Li Chang, is this hole deep enough?

LI CHANG [*crossing to Right*]. No. Dig, villain. [WANG *digs.*]

FOOCHA [*pretending to step out of the hole he has dug and measure with his spade*]. There! My tree is ready to plant. The sun-dial says nearly four o'clock. We were to have finished at four. The time is short. [*He pretends to slide his tree into hole and to shovel the dirt in round it.*]

PLUMBO [*excited*]. Four o'clock! I'll never finish in time. [*Runs across to* FOOCHA.] I'll give you gold if you will help my man.

FOOCHA [*pretending to stamp down the earth*]. Help him yourself. Here, take my spade. [*Pretends handing spade.*] The Prince said: "Planted by yourselves."

PLUMBO [*gasping as he digs*]. I'm planting. Come, Li Chang, and help.

[LI CHANG *has gone to the spot indicated as the "lever" in Scene I.*]

Li Chang. I'm helping.

Foocha. I'm ready for water. It's three minutes to four.

Plumbo [*gasping*]. My tree's not in yet.

Foocha. I'll slide it in for you. Here you are! [*He crosses to Right and slides the tree in.* plumbo *and* wang *receive it.* li chang *throws the lever over. Everybody shouts.*]

    [*The women have been standing up to watch, and now rush him from behind, throwing him down on his face. Struggle.* wang *climbs out of hole and runs down Right front where he squats, back to audience, watching.* foocha, *at the shouts of the women, rushes up the three steps and helps them hold* li chang. plumbo, *left in the hole, shouts "Help—help!" and runs in a circle, then pretends to swim. All is noise and confusion.*]

Plumbo. I'm drowning—drowning! Li Chang— Help!

Li Chang [*on his face, held down and beaten by the women.*] IDIOT, climb out!

Plumbo [*wailing and swimming*]. Help! Help!

Foocha [*forcing* li chang *down*]. Bully! Coward! Lie there!

Li Chang [*shouting*]. I'll have your head for this!

Plumbo [*swimming*]. Help! Help!

Foocha [*to women*]. Can you hold him? [*Indicating* li chang. *They nod.* princess *holds down his head,* chocho *his kicking heels.* foocha *runs down to* plumbo.] Here, sir; give me your hand. [*He pulls* plumbo *out, who stands, apparently dripping water, wringing it from his clothes, puffing and snorting. This whole episode played by* plumbo *for humor. The women begin to shout:*]

Women. Help! Help! We can't hold him.

Foocha [*dashing back to them and holding down* li chang]. I've got him. Run! Get to safety—quick!
    [*They exeunt Left, running.*]

Li Chang [*shouting*]. Torture! I'll have you tortured!

Foocha [*letting him up*]. I'll have you reported. The Prince said the water was to be divided equally. Throw that lever to my tree. Give my tree water. [*He throws the supposed lever over.*] What? No more water?

LI CHANG [*menacing him*]. Not one drop.

FOOCHA. But my tree *must* have water. [*Again he throws the lever.*]

LI CHANG. The pool is empty. Plumbo got it all.

PLUMBO [*Still gasping and wringing*]. Yes, I got it all. This won't agree with me. [*He picks up his coat which he took off when he began to dig, and trots off Right. Exits* PLUMBO. WANG *follows off.*]

LI CHANG [*leering at* FOOCHA]. I'll teach you to oppose me.

FOOCHA. Thief! First you steal my tree, and now you steal the very life of this poor tree; which should not have been moved. Take that! [*He knocks him down.*]

LI CHANG [*squirming away, still on ground*]. I'll have your head for this,—your head—upon a pike. [*By this he has reached a safe distance, and jumps up. He shakes his fist at* FOOCHA, *shouting as he exits Right:*] Guards! Guards! Help Help! [*He is off.*]

FOOCHA. Foocha, you're out of luck. "Upon a pike!" Hum! [*To tree.*]

> O Little Tree, of sweetly folded bloom,
> With courage you and I must face our doom.
> When on a pike my head lifts toward the blue,
> May summer show'rs refreshment bring to you!
> And let your petals, falling at her feet,
> Tell all my tale of loving to my Sweet.

[LI CHANG'S *voice off Right is heard:*]

LI CHANG'S VOICE [*off*]. This way—come this way! [*He enters, followed by two Guards.*] Here is the villain—take him! To the dungeon with him! March!

[*They start to take* FOOCHA. *He signals them "hands off."*]

FOOCHA. Keep your hands off me. I will follow. Lead.

[*They march off right.* LI CHANG *follows muttering imprecations under his breath.*]

SCENE IV

Property Man exhibits placard reading:

COURT OF THE WHITE OLEANDERS TWO DAYS LATER

[*Enter* LI CHANG *and* PLUMBO.]

LI CHANG. You see! Your tree is perfect—in full bloom.

PLUMBO. You *call* it mine. I paid you for it.

LI CHANG. I call it yours and so will you,—remember that. His tree? Scarcely a bud has opened.

PLUMBO. But those that have are wonderful. Had his had water, it would have surpassed mine an hundred fold.

LI CHANG. You see how necessary was my scheming. The results justify my wisdom.

PLUMBO. You call it wisdom?

LI CHANG. Be careful that you call it nothing else. I could make you—disappear— [*Snaps fingers.*]—like that.

PLUMBO. Don't speak of it. When I look at his tree, and remember my shower-bath, I still feel— [*Loosens neckband.*] —choky.

LI CHANG. Then listen carefully to me. One thing I still fear, or one *person*,—the Princess.

PLUMBO. What could *she* do?

LI CHANG. She'll try to make the Prince choose the tree she thinks is *not* yours.

PLUMBO. Hummm! My popularity with the Princess—! This won't agree with me.

[CHOCHO *appears up Left, hiding.*]

LI CHANG. She must be deceived. She must be made to think your tree belongs to him; and I'm the man to do it. Then she will pull for yours. You'll win her hand and—

PLUMBO. *You* will rule the kingdom. This won't agree with me.

LI CHANG. I have it! What a scheme! I'll go and find the Princess [*Exits.*]

PLUMBO [*watching him off distastefully*]. You and your schemes—bah!

CHOCHO [*who has stolen down behind him*]. BAH!
  [*He yells and jumps. They laugh together. She is dressed as in Scene I.*]

PLUMBO. You scared me, Lady Nightingale—I mean, Partridge—pardon—?

CHOCHO. Chocho.

PLUMBO. Lady Chocho. By the Dragon's tail but you are lovely!

CHOCHO. Silly! This won't agree with you. Why did you say: "BAH!"

PLUMBO [*cautiously peering off*]. Sssh! I dare not tell you,— [*Smiles at her.*]—though I'd like to.

CHOCHO [*sidling closer*]. Whisper it. I'll never tell. [*He shakes his head.*] I think your tree is lovely.

PLUMBO [*frightened*]. W-w-who told you t-t-that was mine?

CHOCHO [*laughing*]. It looks so much like you,—so opulant —so rosy—so DOUBLE.
  [*They laugh together tenderly.*]

PLUMBO. I'm awfully upset, and that's the truth. This won't agree with me.

CHOCHO [*motherly*]. Poor dear! Tell me about it.

PLUMBO. I—I wish I were out of this place—alive.

CHOCHO. And me along with?

PLUMBO. Right along with.

CHOCHO. You mean, you don't wish to marry the Princess?

PLUMBO [*looking about nervously*]. Sssh! Not so loud. It makes me feel awfully—choky. [*Loosens neckband.*]

CHOCHO. Poor dear! Let me stroke it. [*She strokes his Adam's-apple with her finger tips. He fairly purrs.*] There! Does that feel better?

PLUMBO. Oh, this agrees with me—fine.

CHOCHO [*stroking*]. They say you have, at home, a lovely house?

PLUMBO. Lovely!

CHOCHO. How wonderful! [*Sighs.*] And that this house is full of chests which are full of coats full of embroidery and jewels,—all lovely?

Plumbo. Lovely!

Chocho. How wonderful! [*Sighs.*] And necklaces of turquoise and jade—all lovely?

Plumbo [*content as she strokes*]. Lovely! Lovely!

Chocho. Come down the Flowery Way and tell me all about them. [*They have already started Right.*] I adore jade—and turquoise—and—and— [*They are off.*]

[*The* princess *peeps out Left, watching them off. She is dressed as in Scene I, but is not veiled. When they are off, she enters.*]

Princess [*pretending to carry a heavy bucket of water*]. The way is clear. Come on! Hurry, Fu and Fo! [*They enter, tandem, each pretending to carry a heavy bucket of water.*] We must get our thirty daily buckets of water on this tree before the audience begins. These buds *must* open.

Fu and Fo [*together*]. Yes, Your Highness.

Princess [*pretending to empty her bucket at left-hand tree*]. There, Little Tree, take that drink!

Fu [*same business*]. There, Little Tree, take that drink!

Fo [*same business*]. There, Little Tree, take that drink!

[*Standing in line, they all draw a prodigious sigh.*]

Princess [*to* fu *and* fo]. Take my bucket. [*Pretends handing it.*] Has the tree had enough?

Princess [*looking carefully at both*]. Really, I can't decide. Has the tree had enough?

Fu and Fo [*chanting and dancing*].

> Tell me, now, what do you think?
> Has it had enough to drink?
> Thirsts sometimes become rapacious
> Passing reason. Oh, my gracious!
> Folk who do such heavy drinking
> Ought to take it out in thinking.

[*They strike a comic pose.*]

Princess. The tree is not rapacious. You are lazy. [*Circles the tree as if looking for bloom.*] Any blossoms? One—two —three. Do you see any more?

Fu and Fo [*chanting and dancing*].

> Seeing things is in the eye.
> Some can see and not half try.
> Some miss seeing, I suppose,
> What's right underneath the nose.

Princess. Do you mean me? What am I missing?
Fu and Fo.

> From the itching in our thumbs
> Something snaky this way comes.
> You'll observe, when he is here,
> Something like a Grand Vizir.

[*They dance a final flourish and exeunt Right.*]
[*The* princess *shows alarm, pretends to run up steps, starts off Left, but runs into* li chang, *who enters there.*]
Li Chang [*bowing*]. Your Highness!
Princess [*regaining her composure*]. My Lord Grand Vizir! I hope your Honorable Health is satisfactory.
Li Chang. Satisfactory to whom, My Lady? *I'm very well.* I *hope* that's satisfactory to *you*, My Lady.
Princess. I am enchanted to hear it. I must be going. [*False start.*]
Li Chang [*stopping her*]. I hope, before Your Highness goes, that she will view with me the rival peach-trees.
Princess [*pretending surprise*]. Oh, yes, the rival peach-trees! I had forgotten. Are they here? [*Pretends to see them first time.*] Oh! Two trees!
Li Chang. Your Highness has an interest in these trees.
Princess. Since I'm to wed the owner of the winning tree in today's contest, I have.
Li Chang. Which does Your Highness think will win?
Princess [*looking carefully at both*]. Really, I can't decide. What thinks the Grand Vizir?
Li Chang [*bowing*]. I think the winner's the luckiest man in all the kingdom. The other's out of luck. [*He grins.*]
Princess [*looking full at him*]. I see you're thinking of the

young man. They tell me you had him thrown in chains. What for?

LI CHANG. Such ugly tales are not for pretty ears. [*Again he bows.*]

PRINCESS. Then it *is* true. Why is he in a dungeon?

LI CHANG. He tried to murder me.

PRINCESS [*pretending horror*]. Murder the Grand Vizir! How horrible!

LI CHANG. His gang of cut-throats was with him,—great, giant women, savager than he. I barely escaped with my life.

PRINCESS [*pretending great alarm*]. Oh, My Lord Grand Vizir, I hope you are not hurt!

LI CHANG [*taken in*]. They did their best to kill me. The most vicious one beat my head almost to pulp with her great, sledge-hammer fists. [*This was she. The* PRINCESS *buries her face in her sleeve and shakes with laughter.*] My Lady weeps? My Lady's very kind. [*He is almost maudlin.*]

PRINCESS [*still hiding her face*]. Oh, My Lord, if you *had* been killed! [*Takes down her sleeve.*] Of course, you killed *her*.

LI CHANG. I fought so bravely the whole mob of them, that they ran away—all but this young villain. Him I threw in prison. I'll have his head upon a pike. Even two days have not healed all my wounds.

PRINCESS. I commiserate your Honorable Person. The contest ends today?

LI CHANG. Within the hour. Through the villainy of this young fool, one of these trees has had no water, and I fear— [*Notices for the first time that the tree has been watered.*] Hello!

PRINCESS. No water? How unfair!

LI CHANG. I deprecate unfairness.

PRINCESS. I'm sure you do. The Grand Vizir is noted as re- gards his fairness.

[*He looks quickly at her with suspicion, but she looks very innocent. Again he inspects the tree.*]

LI CHANG. Someone has watered it. Now who?

PRINCESS. Since the youth, Foocha, is in prison, this must be Lord Plumbo's tree?

LI CHANG [*delighted to have deceived her*]. *It must.* Oh! I forgot. I should not have spoken. I have no right to let you know—

PRINCESS [*demurely*]. As I said before, the Grand Vizir is noted as regards his fairness. Your friend, the Mandarin, is playing in hard luck.

LI CHANG. This tree hasn't a chance.

PRINCESS. Still, the blooms which *have* opened are marvelously lovely. It is a pity!

LI CHANG. Especially as its failure and the cause may strain diplomatic relations between his country and ours. Perhaps Your Highness could persuade the Prince to give extra consideration to Lord Plumbo's tree—?

PRINCESS. Never! I will not plead the cause of My Lord Plumbo. He must take his chances. The hour of the audience is here. I go to don my veil. [*She exits.* LI CHANG *stands rubbing his hands with glee.*]

LI CHANG. Ha! Li Chang, you clever fox! You'll rule the kingdom yet. Now for my darling Chocho!

[*He exits. The* PRINCESS *steals back, watching him off. She enters when he is gone, looks about, starts, and throws her veil over her head and withdraws up stage. The Guards enter, with* FOOCHA *in chains between them. They place him down Left.*]

FIRST GUARD. Young Man, stand there.

SECOND GUARD. No moving, or 'twill be the worse for you. [*To First.*] He's safe. Come on, let's roll the dice.

FIRST GUARD. Done!

[*They go up stage, Right, and kneel to play. They are barely in view of the audience, and become so absorbed in play that they see and hear nothing else.* FOOCHA *stands looking at his tree. The* PRINCESS, *veiled, steals down to him.*]

PRINCESS. Sir, you are in chains?

FOOCHA [*startled*]. Your Highness, I fear that I have failed you.

PRINCESS [*indicating left-hand tree*]. This is the tree you boasted of?

FOOCHA. I may not tell the story of these trees, Your Highness, but this poor tree—

PRINCESS. Someone has watered it.

FOOCHA [*smiling to himself*]. I think I know who did that.

PRINCESS. A woman? [*He nods.*] Whom you love?

FOOCHA. Forgive me, Your Highness! Love comes and goes at will. One can't command it. She is so lovely—

PRINCESS. Then what becomes of me?

FOOCHA. Again, forgive! I've failed you. Tomorrow'll see my head upon a pike.

PRINCESS. And she—this lovely maid—?

FOOCHA. If I could see her once before I—

PRINCESS. You shall, I promise that. [*Music is heard off.*] The Court approaches for the trial. I must go.

FOOCHA. Your Highness does forgive me?

PRINCESS. I—forgive—you.

[*She exits Left. The Music grows louder. The* GUARDS *rise and come to position either side of* FOOCHA. *The Courtiers enter gaily, talking and laughing together. Then a Girl who shouts:*]

GIRL. The Prince! The Prince!

[*Now the Populace surges in, shouting:*]

CROWD. Hail to the Prince—hail! Long live the Prince!

[*Finally* LI CHANG, PLUMBO *with* WANG, PRINCESS *with her Ladies and* CHOCHO, *finally the* PRINCE *attended by* FU *and* FO *with parasol and chair. The chair is placed, the* PRINCE *extends his fan, the music stops. All kowtow.*]

PRINCE [*with a great gesture*]. Hail!

ALL [*rising*]. Hail!

PRINCE. O My People, we are here to judge between the Rival Peach-trees;—that of the Mandarin Plumbo and that of the youth, Foocha. Let the two contestants stand forth. [PLUMBO *and* FOOCHA *stand forth.*] Where are the trees?

LI CHANG. Upon this lower terrace, Augustness.

PRINCE [*looking*]. But one is not in bloom,—or hardly in bloom.

LI CHANG [*watching carefully his effect*]. Augustness, we reget to set before your Honorable eyes so miserable—

PRINCE [*noticing* FOOCHA's *chains*]. The youth Foocha in chains? How is this? For what is he in chains?

LI CHANG. For murderously attacking me, Your Grand Vizir, Augustness.

PRINCE. What! This slim youth! Attack a man your size, Li Chang?

LI CHANG. He and two women, accomplices of his,—low creatures who beat and nearly murdered me.

PRINCE. Dastardly! These women, what did they look like?

LI CHANG. Giants in size. I could not see their faces. They threw me down and beat me mercilessly. They nearly murdered me. Then *he* held me down while they escaped. His head upon a pike, Augustness!

PRINCE. Who are these women, Foocha?

FOOCHA. I cannot say, Augustness.

PRINCE. This looks bad for you, young man. I will investigate this later. First, these trees. There is no choice at all between them. Do you agree, my daughter?

PRINCESS. Augustness means that he chooses the—?

PRINCE. The right-hand tree.

CROWD [*led by* LI CHANG]. Long live the Prince! [LI CHANG *beams.*]

PRINCE. Does any here know reason why the right-hand tree should not be chosen?

PRINCESS. August and Honored Parent, may I speak?

PRINCE. Speak on.

PRINCESS. It is true that the right-hand tree is the more perfectly in bloom, but there are circumstances—

LI CHANG [*quickly, to* PRINCE]. Augustness chooses the right-hand tree?

PRINCE. Let the Princess speak. [*To her.*] Speak on.

PRINCESS. I do not say that the Grand Vizir has done anything so dishonorable as to tell me which tree is which; but I inadvertently came upon him lamenting the left-hand tree. He said it had had unfair treatment, and that he feared,— since it belonged to our distinguished visitor,—diplomatic difficulties, because all its water had been diverted to the other tree.

LI CHANG [*who has been growing more and more distraught*]. Augustness, we make no special plea. Augustness has chosen the right-hand—

PRINCE. Not so fast. I hate injustice. If this tree has been deprived of its fair share of water—? I left that in your hands, Li Chang. What has happened?

LI CHANG. I have already told you how this villain— [*Indicates* FOOCHA.]

PRINCESS. Ask Wang, the servant of Plumbo, what has happened?

PRINCE [*beckoning*]. Here, fellow!

WANG [*in terror*]. Oh, Augustness, be merciful! [*He throws himself on his face.*]

PRINCE. No one accuses you. Speak. What happened?

WANG. I dare not speak, Augustness.

PRINCE. I promise you protection. Speak. [WANG *grovels in terror.*] Come, must I call the torturers? Speak out.

WANG. Augustness, I speak truth. This tree you see upon the right—

LI CHANG. Your Highness, this fellow is not to be trusted. If I may tell you—

PRINCE. Quiet, Li Chang. You, fellow—go on—the tree upon the right—?

PLUMBO [*murmurs to himself*]. This won't agree with me.

WANG. Sire, I was made to steal it from a little garden with a blue-tiled gate in Humpback Street. This Foocha says the tree is his.

PRINCE [*to* FOOCHA]. Does he speak true?

FOOCHA. He does, Augustness. This right-hand tree was the one I promised to bring Your Highness; but when I reached my garden, they had been there before me.

PRINCE. They?

FOOCHA. Wang and his master, and—Your Grand Vizir.

LI CHANG. It is not true. This fellow—

PRINCE [*sharply*]. Quiet, I tell you! Who turned the lever for the watering?

LI CHANG. I did, Your Highness; but when I was attacked—

PRINCE. Huumm! I see this other tree has just been watered. Who did this?

[*There is a pause, then the* PRINCESS *and* FU *and* FO *step forward, they either side of her.*]

PRINCESS. I did it, Father.

PRINCE. You, Daughter? You are concerned in this?

PRINCESS. Deeply concerned, since I'm to wed the owner of the winning tree. I think, at least, he should be honest.

PRINCE. Who is dishonest?

PRINCESS. Ask these Pages.

PRINCE [*to* FU *and* FO]. Speak!

FU AND FO [*chanting and dancing*].

> Seeing things is in the eye.
> Some can see and not half try.
> Some miss seeing, I suppose,
> What's right underneath the nose.
> Let the Lady Princess see
> Magic work upon this tree.

PRINCESS. May my Ladies try what they can do, Augustness, for this Little Tree? [*He signals yes.* LI CHANG *begins to slowly back off stage.*]

> Come, Ladies, swing your fans and let us see
> How near to summer breezes we can be,
> In coaxing buds to blow upon this tree.

[*She draws her fan from her sash, they do same. Music begins off—*MUSICIANS *pretend to play.* LADIES *sing and dance as they circle the tree, fanning with one movement. The* CROWD *shows interest, then surprise, then amazement, and finally bursts into shouts as the song ends and the tree is supposed to bloom.*]

PRINCESS AND LADIES.

BLOW WINDS!

Blow, winds, blow! Blow, winds, blow!
Light as down your touch impresses,
Light as Lover's soft caresses,
Shake out folded blossom-dresses!
Blow, winds, blow!

[*The "Ohs" and "Ahs" end in a shout:*]

CROWD. Hail, Lovely Tree!

PRINCESS. Is it well, Honorable Father?

PRINCE. It is well. Foocha wins the hand of the Princess Royal.
The Rival Peach-Trees both belong to him. Remove his
chains! [*The* GUARDS *pretend to do so.*] Lord Foocha, wed
the Princess!

[*The* PRINCESS *extends her hand to* FOOCHA, *who draws
back.*]

FOOCHA. Augustness, I cannot.

[*The* CROWD *murmurs threateningly.*]

PRINCE [*sternly*]. What? You refuse the hand of the Princess?

CROWD [*shouting*]. Behead him! Behead him!

PRINCE. What does this mean? You entered the contest freely.

FOOCHA. I did, but the Princess knows that I now love another,
—a simple wash-maiden.

PRINCESS [*throwing off her veil*]. No, Foocha, not another. I
am the wash-maiden,—see!

FOOCHA. My Love! [*She goes to him.*]

PRINCE. Hold! First this crime. Li Chang accuses Foocha and
his accomplices of attempting to murder him. Foocha is
here, but where are the mighty Amazons who attacked and
nearly killed my Grand Vizir? Foocha, command your Amazons to stand forth. [FOOCHA, PRINCESS *and* CHOCHO *step
forward.*] What! You attacked him?

ALL THREE. We did, Augustness, when he stole the water.

[*The* PRINCE *bursts into laughter. The* CROWD *laughs*

with him. LI CHANG *starts to escape but at a gesture from the*
PRINCE *is stopped by the* GUARDS.]

PRINCE [*rising*]. The tangle is untied. I speak in judgment. My
Daughter, the Princess, is now your ruler, and Foocha, as
Prince Consort, shall wear my robes of state. My Lord
Plumbo shall wed the Lady Chocho and become our valued
neighbor. Li Chang and I retire from the world, he to repent
his sins, I to meditation; while in this garden shall ever
bloom the Peach-trees of Foocha. Hail to the Bride and
Groom!

CROWD. Hail! Hail!

PRINCE. The wedding feast awaits us. Come! Let Music play!

[*He leads off, followed, by* LI CHANG, *his face hidden in
his sleeve. Then* FOOCHA *and the* PRINCESS, PLUMBO *and the*
LADY CHOCHO, *and the rest. The Music continues until all are
off.*]

CURTAIN

PRODUCTION NOTE

The stage is open and has a neutral background. If played
out-of-doors, no background save nature is needed.

In costumes, color and design are the important things. Chinese women often wear dark plain trousers with very gorgeous
coats. Therefore, in Scene II, only the coats need be changed.
Fans, china, book-illustrations,—all will furnish ideas for costume designs.

The Property Man wears plain dark trousers and coat, and a
skullcap.

The changes of scene may be indicated by having the
Property Man display placards bearing the titles of the scenes.
It is he who sets up and takes away the screens, table, chairs,
etc.

All small properties are imagined; and are indicated by
pantomime. If the pantomime be very definite, and always in

the same place for the same article, there will be no difficulty in creating the illusion for the audience.

Music

Music for all three verses, "Blow Winds!," "Tunes & Runes," page 44.
Music for "Love is a Lantern," "Tunes & Runes," page 33.

Records

Chinese March—Yao Yin—Columbia—A 3163
Danse Orientale (Glazounow)—Victor 1335-B
"In a Chinese Temple Garden"—Victor 35777-B (Persian Market-A)
Chinese Record—Victor 42489-A & B

THE NEXT-BEST MAN

A Two-Act Comedy

BY

LEON M. PEARSON

A ROYALTY PLAY

THE CAST

Mrs. Upjohn
Robert (Speedy) Pace
Emma Jane Upjohn
James (Sock) Stockton
Miriam Upjohn
Reginald Vandervoort Riggs
Constance Bliss
Joseph Brady

THE SCENE

The Parlor in the Home of Mrs. Upjohn.

There is a door down right which leads to the pantry. The entrance to the parlor is through a large double door up center. To the right of this is the front door and to the left is the rest of the house. Down stage right is a small table and an arm chair by it. Another chair is to the right of the center door. Still another chair is down left. Right center is a large armchair and left center is a small couch. The room gives a sense of comfort and quiet.

———•———

At the rise of the curtain

Mrs. Upjohn *enters from the door at right, carrying china tea dishes, which she places and arranges on the table downstage right.* Mrs. Upjohn *does not look more than forty. She moves about with a youthful agility, and, as she arranges the tea things, she smiles, thinking beyond cups and saucers.*

Speedy *sounds the brass knocker at the outside door off center to right. She leaves the room by the double doors at the back, and, for a moment, the stage is empty.*

378

When she returns center from right she is followed by ROBERT ("SPEEDY") PACE, *who is a pleasant young man of twenty-one, stocky in build and quiet in manner.*

MRS. UPJOHN [*goes to table down stage right—arranges tea things*]. Sit down, Robert. I was just arranging the tea things. Did you want to see Miriam?

SPEEDY [*standing in front of sofa*]. Well, there's no hurry, Mrs. Upjohn. Matter of fact, I'd just as soon talk to you.—That is—just now—I mean. Or any time of course.

MRS. UPJOHN [*lightly*]. Thank you, Robert.

SPEEDY [*still stumbling*]. You see, I came now instead of later because I wanted to— Well, as a matter of fact, I came to—mow the lawn.

MRS. UPJOHN. Does it need it again?

SPEEDY. Yes, and I need the exercise. You see, it's sort of hard for a fellow who's been in athletics in school and college to get used to this office life,—and golf doesn't appeal to me. I like something more strenuous.

MRS. UPJOHN [*still lightly*]. Well, you might run over the tennis court a few times with the roller.

SPEEDY. All right! That's what I like.

MRS. UPJOHN. We've got a lot of ashes in the cellar. You may take them out to the dump.

SPEEDY [*laughing*]. Sure!

MRS. UPJOHN. And by that time, you'll be ready for a cup of tea.

SPEEDY. I'm not much on teas, but I wanted to come this afternoon because I wanted to— [*Hesitating*].

MRS. UPJOHN. Mow the lawn.

SPEEDY. Yeah, mow the lawn. Well, I wanted to see you, too. I think I ought to say something to you about myself and Miriam.

[*At this juncture,* EMMA JANE, *a vivacious bobbed-haired girl, enters suddenly at the center from left. She stops as suddenly*].

EMMA JANE. Whoa! Back! Excuse me! [*Exits center to left.*]

MRS. UPJOHN [*turning to* SPEEDY]. Yes, Robert?

SPEEDY [*a bit embarrassed*]. Miriam and I have been going around together for a long time,—ever since I began to care for girls, I guess. In fact, I never did have any other girl, —that is, not seriously. And so, well, I guess it's really about time I made myself clear,—that is,—what my intentions are. [*Pause*].

MRS. UPJOHN. Yes, Robert? [*Sitting in chair down stage right.*]

SPEEDY. Now I don't believe in elopements.

MRS. UPJOHN. So you've decided not to elope with Miriam?

SPEEDY [*laughs*]. I believe in taking plenty of time. [*Sitting on sofa.*] Marriage is the most serious step of your life. And I don't believe in divorces. So I haven't said anything to Miriam about marriage,—but I think she knows how I feel toward her.

MRS. UPJOHN. I think she does, Robert.

SPEEDY. So we're not engaged, or anything. I don't believe in hasty engagements, for two reasons; in the first place, a girl ought to be free to go around with anybody, so as to make sure she's getting the right man. And in the second place, a man ought not to ask a girl to marry him until he is ready to provide a home for her.

MRS. UPJOHN. Girls don't ask much at the start, Robert.

SPEEDY. No, but I don't believe what some people say that two can live as cheaply as one. And I believe in doing one thing at a time. You see, a diamond ring is pretty expensive. And that's the first step. I've got two hundred dollars in what I call the Ring Fund now, and pretty soon I'll be able to buy the ring,—that is, provided Miriam is willing. So—ah—well, I just wanted to let you know what my intentions are.

MRS. UPJOHN. That's very good of you, Robert. And I'm very glad to know. [*Crossing and sitting on sofa.*] Of course, I can't speak for Miriam, but I *can* give you a bit of friendly advice— You know that old saying about a bird in the hand?—Well, a ring on the hand is better than two hundred dollars in the bank.

SPEEDY. But you can't get a good diamond ring for less than—

MRS. UPJOHN. I know. I don't mean to interfere with your plans. But just think,—how much gold do you suppose Leander had in his pocket when he swam the Hellespont?

SPEEDY. You are a very unusual mother, Mrs. Upjohn.

MRS. UPJOHN. Perhaps I am.

SPEEDY. I'll have to think it over,—what you've said.

MRS. UPJOHN. All right. [*Rises.*]

SPEEDY. And now I guess I better go mow the lawn. [*He rises and removes his coat.*]

MRS. UPJOHN. All right, Robert. Come in for tea as soon as the crowd arrives.

SPEEDY. All right. I'll be brave.

[MRS. UPJOHN *exits right.* SPEEDY, *left alone, unknots his tie and removes his collar, both of which he folds and puts into the pocket of his coat. He lays the coat on the sofa and starts out. He stops, returns, takes up the coat, and looks about the room. Then, glancing again to the sofa, he folds the coat, and hides it behind a sofa cushion. He exits center to right, rolling up his sleeves.* MRS. UPJOHN, *enters from right, with more dishes, which she places in order on the tea table.* EMMA JANE *enters cautiously from the center from left.*]

EMMA JANE. At last!

MRS. UPJOHN. At last what? [*At table.*]

EMMA JANE. "Speedy" Pace has gone and done it! [*Goes to* MRS. UPJOHN.] Does Miriam know?

MRS. UPJOHN. No. Neither do you.

EMMA JANE. But I can guess.

MRS. UPJOHN. You can't guess right.

EMMA JANE. Aw, go on, mother. Answer me this. What did Speedy Pace ask your permission to do?

MRS. UPJOHN. Mow the lawn.

EMMA JANE. Well, if you're going to be mean, I won't play. [*She goes to the center door and looks out right. She turns back to her mother.*] Mother, will you kindly leave the room?

MRS. UPJOHN. Who's out there?

EMMA JANE. Friend o' my youth.

MRS. UPJOHN. Bring him in. I'm broad-minded.

EMMA JANE. So is he.

[*She gives a "Bob-White" whistle, which is answered from without, and* JAMES ("SOCK") STOCKTON *makes his entrance center from right. He is in white flannels and sneakers and carries a tennis racket.*]

MRS. UPJOHN. Hello, James. Is that the latest style in men's wear for afternoon tea?

SOCK [*crossing to* MRS. UPJOHN]. I've got a new name for Emma Jane, Mrs. Upjohn.

MRS. UPJOHN. What is it this time?

SOCK. You see they call me Sock. And she is so attached to me, I call her Garter.

MRS. UPJOHN [*going*]. Well, you've succeeded.

SOCK. In what?

MRS. UPJOHN. Driving me away. [*Exit right.*]

SOCK. Your mother's a good sport— Say, what about Speedy? Did he pop the question?

EMMA JANE. Hard to say. Mother's a clam. Said he asked her if he could—mow the lawn.

SOCK. Well, he's doing it.

EMMA JANE. If he asked her that, that was only the first scene. Can you imagine this?—Here, you be mother; I'm Speedy. [*She paces up and down the room with manly stride, head bowed in deep thought. Then, as with sudden determination, she stops before* SOCK, *and speaks in her deepest voice.*] Mrs. Upjohn, I've come to ask you a weighty question. May I— May I— I really hate to ask you— May I mow the lawn?

SOCK [*laughs*]. All right. Now I've got an act. You be your

mother. I'll be myself. No strutting around for me. I come
in at the door— [*He goes toward the door center and returns to her.*] Morning, Mrs. Upjohn. Happened to be
walking by on my way to the golf club, and I thought I
might just drop in and ask you for the hand of your daughter in marriage— All right? Thanks, old thing. [*Going
up stage.*] Ta, ta.

EMMA JANE [*loudly*]. No! Come back here, you scoundrel!—
On what do you propose to support my daughter?

SOCK. I propose to have *her* support *me*. That's why I call her
"Garter"!

[*He snaps his fingers in her face, and starts out center
again.*]

EMMA JANE. Hold, wretch!—Have you spoken to my daughter about this? What has she to say?

SOCK. Ask her yourself. I haven't the nerve. [*He abandons
the impersonation, and goes to the sofa, and sits.*] Come
here, Emma Jane, I've got to tell you something. [*She takes
a seat beside him.*] You know, when I was a kid I told
mother I wished I had been a girl, because then I would
never have to ask anybody to marry me. You see, you've
got to be serious about it; that's what makes it so bad. If
you could make a joke of it, then it would be a cinch. If
you could say, "Hello, old girl, let's go hitch up,"—that
would be dead easy. But they don't do it that way—in real
life. You have to say, "Will you marry me?" or "Will you
be my wife?" Those are the only ways you can say it.
And everybody has said it either one way or the other for so
many centuries that it's old stuff,—and you can't find any
new variation. See what I mean? [*She nods. He proceeds,
more slowly.*] So I've got to say it one way or the other,—
or both. I might try both. [*He turns to her.*] Will you
marry me and be my wife?

EMMA JANE [*solemnly*]. Yes and yes.

[*There is a pause.*]

SOCK [*sitting very erect*]. Is that all?

EMMA JANE. What more do you want?

SOCK. That wasn't so bad. [*Sinking back in sofa.*] But I hope I'll never have to do it again.

EMMA JANE. So do I!

SOCK. Well. That's the first step. Now the second step is, when shall we get married?

EMMA JANE. Whoa—back! You missed a step.

SOCK. Name it.

EMMA JANE. S.W.A.K.

SOCK. Meaning?

EMMA JANE. Sealed with a—

SOCK. Oh! My error! [*He kisses her twice.*] Doubly sealed. Now, the third step is—

EMMA JANE. —when shall we get married!

SOCK. Exactly.

EMMA JANE. Well?

SOCK. Any day suits me.

EMMA JANE. Seriously.

SOCK. Well, I've got a couple of hundred dollars in the bank.

EMMA JANE. That'll do.

SOCK. To furnish a home?

EMMA JANE. To furnish anything we don't get in wedding presents.

SOCK. Oh. . . . When shall it be? In a month?

EMMA JANE. I gotta have time to make a dress.

SOCK. Gosh, can't you make a dress in a month?

EMMA JANE. Sure, I guess so.

SOCK. All right. This is the fourth of June. So let's make it the fourth of— Fourth of July?

EMMA JANE. Why not? The beginning of the fireworks.

SOCK. Suits me. I'll have a holiday without asking for it.

EMMA JANE. All right. Sealed.

SOCK. S.W.A.—

[*Kisses her. Enter* MRS. UPJOHN *from right. She sees the kiss. She pauses a moment, then advances and sits on the sofa between them.*]

MRS. UPJOHN. People say that the morals of the young people are much looser than they were a generation ago. I'm not so sure of that, but I think you will agree with me that—

EMMA JANE [*leaping up*]. Mother, you got the wrong cue.

SOCK [*also rising*]. I think you're on the wrong track, Mrs. Upjohn. We're not just "young people." We're—we're—

EMMA JANE. Engaged!

MRS. UPJOHN. Indeed— Do you mean it?

SOCK. Yes.

MRS. UPJOHN. Well, well—and you only met—let's see—last month, wasn't it?

SOCK. First of April.

EMMA JANE. At Anna's April-Fool party.

SOCK. Two months ago.

EMMA JANE. Think of it!

MRS. UPJOHN. If I were still teaching school, I would send a report home to your mother marked "Unprepared."

SOCK. Two months is practically a hundred days. And I haven't wasted any time—

EMMA JANE. Mowing the lawn!

SOCK. Of course if you want me to be like Speedy Pace—

MRS. UPJOHN. I didn't say that.

SOCK. Well, I'm not.

MRS. UPJOHN. So I see— Children, I have just one thing to say to you, and then I must finish preparing for this tea.

EMMA JANE. Who's Miriam with? Not Speedy.

MRS. UPJOHN. No. Miriam is taking Mr. Riggs out for a walk.

EMMA JANE. Oh— Ho!

MRS. UPJOHN. Please don't interrupt— In deference to Miriam and her—uncertain position with Speedy—

EMMA JANE. Then he hasn't proposed?

MRS. UPJOHN. As I was saying—

EMMA JANE. 'Scuse, mother.

MRS. UPJOHN. This must not go any further than—friendship until Miriam and Speedy . . .

EMMA JANE. But mother, we're going to be married on the Fourth of July!

MRS. UPJOHN. You mean April Fool's Day.

EMMA JANE. No sirree.

[MRS. UPJOHN *looks to* SOCK.]

SOCK. That's right, Mrs. Upjohn.

MRS. UPJOHN. Celebrating the Declaration of Independence in fitting style, aren't you?—Now listen to me. James—I like you. And young lady, I like you, too. And I want you both to be happy. You *might* be happy if you were married in a month. But I am quite sure you would be happy if you waited until—well, at least until after your sister has led the way.

EMMA JANE. But there's no telling—

MRS. UPJOHN. Now, little girl, think twice. How would Miriam feel if her younger sister were to start making a wedding dress before *she* is even engaged?

EMMA JANE. Oh, Blah!

MRS. UPJOHN. And you may make fun of Robert all you like for *not* being "Speedy." But you could take some lessons from him in the school of courtship. Have you a Ring Fund?

SOCK. A what?

MRS. UPJOHN. You ask Robert what a Ring Fund is. [*They hear someone on the porch.* MRS. UPJOHN *rises and crosses to center.*] That can't be a guest already.

[*Looks off right.*]

SOCK. Guest? Gosh, I've got to change.

EMMA JANE. Me too.

[*Crosses to* MRS. UPJOHN *and looks out center to right.*]

MRS. UPJOHN [*at the door*]. No. It's Miriam and Mr. Riggs.

EMMA JANE. Oh, yes. [*To table down stage right.*]

[*These two appear at the door up center.* MIRIAM UPJOHN *is a fine-looking girl, with a manner more quiet than that of her sister, yet with a suggestion of latent high spirits in the quick smile and the bright eyes. At her side stands* REGINALD VANDERVOORT RIGGS, *a tall slender young man, who wears an air of sophistication and a cane, upon both of which he leans heavily.*]

MIRIAM. Well, here we are, back again the same day.

MRS. UPJOHN. How do you find the walking today, Mr. Riggs? [*To* SOCK.] This is his first day out of the house.

RIGGS. Not bad at all, thank you. Not bad at all.

MIRIAM. The rhododendrons are in bloom, mother, out at the Winston Gardens.

MRS. UPJOHN. You didn't walk that far!

MIRIAM. Oh, no, we rode.

RIGGS. Hired a vehicle.

MRS. UPJOHN. Oh, yes, of course.

RIGGS. Nice-looking man you have mowing the lawn.

MRS. UPJOHN. Oh, Robert. Yes, he's a devoted worker.

RIGGS. Yes, just so—very devoted. [*With a glance at* MIRIAM.]

MIRIAM. Well—I guess Constance and Joseph will be coming soon, won't they, mother?

MRS. UPJOHN. Yes. Wouldn't you like to rest a bit before the tea, Mr. Riggs?

RIGGS. I might, yes. A bit fagged, you know— [*To* MIRIAM.] Could you help me, Miriam? [*To* MRS. UPJOHN.] The stairs, you know.

MRS. UPJOHN. Yes, of course.

[*Miriam goes out with* RIGGS *center to left.—As soon as they have disappeared,* SOCK *goes to* EMMA JANE, *down stage right, limping, using his tennis racket for a cane, and says, with mock sophistication:*]

SOCK. I say, old thing, give me a hand. [*She puts her arm around him and supports him in a trip across the room.*] How would you like to hire a vehicle and run out to the Winston Gardens, eh?

EMMA JANE. And if you grow weary, Reggy dear, we could rest on a park bench.

SOCK [*as they turn up stage together*]. Will you help me, Miriam, the stairs you know. [*They walk up, pantomiming the business of taking arms.*] [*Coming out of it and crossing to* MRS. UPJOHN.] Say, Mrs. Upjohn, if we wait until

Miriam gets hitched up—does it make any difference who the man is?

MRS. UPJOHN. There'll only be one.

SOCK. Sure. But does it matter which one?

MRS. UPJOHN. I said there'll only be one and you know very well what I mean.

SOCK. This movie actor has covered more ground in two weeks than I have in two months, or Speedy in two years. [*Exit* MRS. UPJOHN—*down stage right.*]

SOCK. Listen, Emma Jane, no kidding. This man Riggs can be useful to us.

EMMA JANE. I'm all ears.

SOCK. If we have to wait for Speedy to propose, we may never get married. But this movie actor is working fast.

EMMA JANE [*crossing down stage left*]. "Mrs. Reginald Vandervoort Riggs." How does it sound?

SOCK. Awful. But that's not the point.

EMMA JANE [*turning*]. What point?

SOCK [*down stage right*]. "Mrs. James Arthur Stockton." How does it sound?

EMMA JANE. Better.

SOCK. Well—as my father used to say when he took the stick to me, "The end justifies the means."

EMMA JANE. But think of poor Speedy. He's so loyal.

SOCK. Yes. It would be sorta tough on him. [*Pause.*] But by golly, he needs a little dynamite.

EMMA JANE. Well—

SOCK. And then—"Mrs. T. J. Upjohn announces the marriage of her daughter Emma Jane—"

EMMA JANE. "Announces"?

SOCK. Yes.

EMMA JANE. "*Invites you to.*"

SOCK. Oh, that's right. I mustn't forget the wedding presents! —Say, how much do I give the preacher?

EMMA JANE. Oh, I don't know. The best man will take care of that.

SOCK. Who's going to be best man?

EMMA JANE. That's for you to say.

SOCK. I guess I'll ask Speedy. You can always depend on him. [MIRIAM *enters at center from left.*]

SOCK. That's right, isn't it, Miriam?

MIRIAM [*center*]. What?

SOCK. I say, you can always depend on Speedy.

MIRIAM. Yes,—to mow the lawn. [*Crosses to sofa.*]

EMMA JANE. Will you do something for me, Sock?

SOCK. What?

EMMA JANE. Do you have to ask what?—*now?*

SOCK. What do you mean—"now"?

EMMA JANE. After what's happened.

SOCK. Oh, my error. Well—?

EMMA JANE. Get my hat. Out at the court. [*He goes out center to right.*]

[*When he is gone, she turns down to* MIRIAM. *Standing close to her, she takes her sister's face in her hands, and kisses her.*]

EMMA JANE. I'm engaged to be married.

MIRIAM. Emma Jane! [*It is her turn to kiss her sister.*] Sock? [EMMA JANE *nods her head.*] Bless your heart. [*There is a hug.*] When did you do this?

EMMA JANE. Just a little while ago.

MIRIAM. Here? [EMMA JANE *nods.*] You're sure he means it.

EMMA JANE. Oh, yes.

MIRIAM. He's such a joker.

EMMA JANE. I know. But he means this.

MIRIAM. I like him.

EMMA JANE. So do I.

MIRIAM. You little monkey. [*Another kiss.*] How did you do it?

EMMA JANE. I didn't do anything.

MIRIAM. I know it— He's a lucky boy.

EMMA JANE. You're a sweet sister. Why don't you tell me I'm a mean old cat because I didn't wait for you?

MIRIAM [*turning aside to sit on the sofa*]. I wouldn't want you to wait for me.

Emma Jane [*sitting beside her*]. I'm going to, though.

Miriam. What do you mean?

Emma Jane. Wait until you marry before I do.

Miriam. What makes you think—? Oh, Speedy.

Emma Jane. It doesn't matter who it is—Speedy, or—anybody.

Miriam. But there's no one else who—

Emma Jane. Oh, yes there is. [*Mock sentiment.*] I can see the light o' love in the eyes of another man. [*Rises.*] He no sooner recovers from a compound fracture of the ankle bone than he falls and breaks his heart. [*Sits.*]

Miriam. Reggy.

Emma Jane. None other. But whether it's Reggy or Speedy, or Billy, or Henry, I'm going to wait for my sweet sister.

Miriam. I suppose Sock wants a little time to grow a bank account.

Emma Jane [*rising*]. Yes, partly that.

Sock [*entering center from right*]. Here's your hat, Emma Jane. [*He throws hat to her.*]

[mrs. upjohn *enters from the right.*]

Mrs. Upjohn [*sternly*]. Haven't you dressed yet? [*On this cue, * sock *sneaks out center to right.*]

Emma Jane. N-no, I've been very busy.

Mrs. Upjohn. Busy.—Scoot! [emma jane *turns in flight— exit center to left.* mrs. upjohn *turns to* miriam.] Have you seen Speedy this afternoon?

Miriam. Yes, he's mowing the lawn.

Mrs. Upjohn. I mean, have you seen him to talk to?

Miriam. No. I was with Reggy.

Mrs. Upjohn. Oh, yes, of course. [*She starts toward door right.*]

Miriam. Why, mother?

Mrs. Upjohn. Oh, nothing. I just wondered.

Miriam. Mother.

Mrs. Upjohn. Yes?

Miriam. Come here a minute. [mrs. upjohn *crosses to*

MIRIAM *at the sofa.*] Sit down. [*She sits.*] Do you think Speedy really wants to marry me?

MRS. UPJOHN. I'm sure of it. Why? Don't *you* think so?

MIRIAM. I'm not so sure.

MRS. UPJOHN. Why, dear? What's happened?

MIRIAM. Nothing. That's just the trouble— If you really want something, you generally ask for it, don't you?

MRS. UPJOHN. Yes.

MIRIAM. And if you don't ask for it, you don't want it very badly.

MRS. UPJOHN. Some people are less bold than others.

MIRIAM. Well then, if they lose, it serves them right. [*She rises and crosses to center.*]

MRS. UPJOHN. "If they lose?" Is there a chance of Speedy losing?

MIRIAM. I don't know, I'm sure.

MRS. UPJOHN. Speedy only wants to be considerate. I imagine the reason he doesn't propose is that he isn't quite ready to marry and he wants you to be free to go around with other men.

MIRIAM. But I'm not. That's just it. I go around with Speedy all the time, and the other fellows think we're secretly engaged. There hasn't been a man in this house for months except Speedy.

MRS. UPJOHN. Miriam, I'm going to make a prophecy. I prophesy that you will be engaged to be married within two weeks.

MIRIAM [*after an astonished moment*]. Has Reggy said anything to you?

MRS. UPJOHN. Reggy?

MIRIAM. Yes.

MRS. UPJOHN. I'm not talking about— What do you mean? Has he—

MIRIAM. Yes.

MRS. UPJOHN. Proposed?

MIRIAM. Yes.

MRS. UPJOHN. What did you tell him?

MIRIAM. I told him I couldn't accept him because I hadn't known him long enough— Then he asked me how many years I usually kept my suitors waiting. You see he thinks Speedy is waiting for me. It never occurred to him that I might be waiting for Speedy.

MRS. UPJOHN. Did you tell him?

MIRIAM. No, I didn't!

MRS. UPJOHN. No, of course not.

MIRIAM. Then I asked him if he thought we were well enough acquainted to be talking of such things. And he said he could readily understand how I might not be sure of him, but, for his part, he was too deeply in love to have any doubt about me. Oh, mother, he's glorious. Speedy never says things like that.

MRS. UPJOHN. Poor Speedy.

MIRIAM. Then he said he wasn't surprised that I didn't want to be the wife of a poor vagabond player. For I am poor, he said, no matter how much salary I get, I am poor in not having a wife and home. He says he spends more money in hotel bills for himself than it would cost to have a home for two—or more. And sometimes, he says, he leaves his soiled clothes to be laundered and sent on to him, and he moves on to the next place, and the laundry never reaches him. He made me feel so sorry for him that I know if he had asked me again, I would have accepted him on the spot.

MRS. UPJOHN. If you're looking for somebody to wash for, I'll discharge Violet.

MIRIAM. Oh, mother!

MRS. UPJOHN. Forgive me, dear. I know what you mean; and I know how you feel about Speedy. I can't decide for you. But I want you to remember something about Speedy. Speedy was an athlete in college, wasn't he?

MIRIAM. Yes, a runner.

MRS. UPJOHN. Did he excel in the short runs—what do you call them?—the dashes; or was it the long runs?

MIRIAM. He was a mile runner; why?

MRS. UPJOHN. Just so. Speedy is a long-distance runner. Reggy might beat him in the dash, but I'd bet on Speedy in the long run. [*She rises and crosses right.*]

MIRIAM. Mother. [MRS. UPJOHN *stops.*] Do you know what a runner is supposed to do near the end of a long run?

MRS. UPJOHN. No.

MIRIAM. Sprint! [MRS. UPJOHN *exits right and* MIRIAM *follows her. For a moment the stage is empty, and quiet. Then we hear the sound of a knocker at the front door.* MIRIAM *wearing an apron enters from the right, and crosses toward the center door. She stops, turns back, removes her apron, and stuffs it behind a sofa pillow. There her hand encounters a man's coat, which she brings forth, shakes out, frowning, and takes with her into the hall, leaving the apron in hiding.*]

[*Presently we hear voices in the hall, and* MIRIAM *appears again, ushering in* CONSTANCE BLISS *and* JOSEPH BRADY. *Our attention is drawn immediately to the young lady by reason of the startling colors in her costume, and we notice, too, that she is effusive in manner as she greets* MIRIAM. *The young man is comparatively diffident; he carries himself with a feminine manner, and gives meticulous care to the code of social conduct. He holds a brief-case under his arm, and a straw hat in his hand. With the other hand, he applies a white silk handkerchief to his brow delicately, with little pats. His shirt is colorful.*]

CONSTANCE. It's just too sweet of you, Miriam, to be the hostess for this little occasion. Of course it was really my idea, and by rights *I* should have given the tea, but on account of Mr. Riggs being— Well, he's not exactly crippled— What's the word I want. Joseph?

JOSEPH. One might say, *hors de combat.*

CONSTANCE. Yes, that's it exactly. Joseph *always* has the right word. He has helped me a lot on my scenario— Oh, but I mustn't talk about that yet. Anyway as I was saying, Mr. Riggs can't walk around much, and so I thought it would be awfully nice if we could get together here.

JOSEPH. It would hardly be proper for Constance to give a tea for Mr. Riggs when she hadn't met him.

CONSTANCE. No. And that was another reason. But of course it's nothing formal. This is just going to be an informal meeting of—of artists.

MIRIAM. You're making me awfully curious. I'm entirely in the dark.

CONSTANCE. Of course you are, dear. But I wanted to keep my little surprise until this afternoon, and then—and then— What should I say, Joseph?

JOSEPH. "And then *spring it*." Isn't that what you were going to say?

CONSTANCE. But I thought you would supply something not quite so slangy.

JOSEPH. I refuse to be treated as a walking encyclopædia! [*Crosses above sofa.*]

MIRIAM. You two are a pair. Now you'll have to excuse me for a minute. I haven't quite finished out here.

CONSTANCE [*sitting on sofa*]. Oh, dear, can't I help?

MIRIAM. No, thanks. Mother's helping me. [*She exits right.* JOSEPH *sits beside* CONSTANCE. CONSTANCE *rises and moves about the room.*]

CONSTANCE. I wonder where he is?

JOSEPH. Who?

CONSTANCE. Reggy, of course.

JOSEPH. Aren't you getting rather familiar with a man you haven't met?

CONSTANCE [*looking off right*]. I wonder if he's out in the kitchen with her?

JOSEPH. Ridiculous!

CONSTANCE. They were out riding together in an automobile.

JOSEPH. I think you'd better look over the manuscript.

CONSTANCE. Yes, I will. [*She sits beside him on the sofa, and receives a manuscript from his hand.*] It's going to be awfully embarrassing to cast the parts. People will think that Miriam and Speedy should play the leading parts because they go together so much. But when I wrote the part of Belle I really had myself in mind, and of course Reggy ought to play the male lead.

JOSEPH. Maybe his foot will not be well enough.

CONSTANCE. He can get around all right. My only question is —will he stay here long enough? Oh, I do hope so. Just think,—acting with a real actor, and maybe having him—

JOSEPH. Having him what?

CONSTANCE. Well, of course, if he and I took the leads, there would be that scene, you know, at the last, where they embrace.

JOSEPH [*shocked*]. Constance!

CONSTANCE. Well, of course, it wouldn't be real, because it's just acting, but—

JOSEPH. Constance! I certainly don't think that's very modest. Why that sounds like you plotted it to be that way.

CONSTANCE. Well, I certainly don't want Miriam Upjohn to play the part.

JOSEPH. I think it would be much better for her to do it.

CONSTANCE. But how about Speedy?

JOSEPH. They aren't engaged.

CONSTANCE. They might as well be.

JOSEPH. Well, you could say the same about us.

CONSTANCE. Well, that's beside the point.

JOSEPH. It certainly is not. I think I had better play the man's part.

CONSTANCE. Well, we'll see about it.

JOSEPH. The only time I ever saw Reggy Riggs in the talkies, he ran away with somebody else's wife.

CONSTANCE. Of course he was just playing a part.

JOSEPH. I know. But it might have put ideas into his head. He must be an awfully reckless person to break his ankle on Friar Hill.

CONSTANCE. He had to do a fall for the picture. That's one of his specialties.

JOSEPH. What? Doing falls?

CONSTANCE. Yes. [*Rising.*] Sometimes from cliffs. Sometimes from horse-back.

JOSEPH. That ought to be easy.

CONSTANCE [*she sits and turns to her papers*].—I suppose they'll want me to read the whole scenario. [*She hands it back to him.*] If I get tired, I may call on you to read part of it.

JOSEPH. I'm afraid I'd be horribly embarrassed.

[EMMA JANE *and* SOCK *enter up stage center.*]

EMMA JANE. Oh, hello, you two.

CONSTANCE. Oh, Emma Jane, do you know how long Mr. Riggs is going to stay?

EMMA JANE. Quite some time, I believe.

CONSTANCE. Oh, is he really?

EMMA JANE. Yes. He likes it here.

SOCK [*down to* JOSEPH]. Hello there, Josephine, how's tricks?

JOSEPH. How's what?

SOCK. Tricks. You know—every little thing. [*Crosses up stage right.*]

JOSEPH. I never heard such expressions!

[MRS. UPJOHN *comes on from right, followed by* MIRIAM, *who goes directly off up stage center to left.* MRS. UPJOHN *crosses to left.*]

MRS. UPJOHN. Good afternoon, Constance.

CONSTANCE. Oh, good afternoon, Mrs. Upjohn, I was just saying to Miriam.—

MRS. UPJOHN. Hello, Joseph.

JOSEPH [*rising*]. Good afternoon, Mrs. Upjohn.

CONSTANCE. I was just saying to Miriam—

MRS. UPJOHN [*holding her hand over her eyes*]. Joseph!

JOSEPH. What's the trouble?

MRS. UPJOHN [*to the others*]. Behold Joseph, with his coat of many colors.

JOSEPH. It behooves me to perpetuate the costume of my biblical prototype. [*Crosses down stage left.*]

SOCK [*jesting*]. Why, sure!

MRS. UPJOHN [*sitting with* CONSTANCE]. Pardon me, Constance. I interrupted you.

[*As* CONSTANCE *starts to speak,* JOSEPH *hands her manuscript.*]

CONSTANCE. I was just going to say that I was just saying to Miriam—

MRS. UPJOHN. Hello, what's this? Manuscript?

CONSTANCE. Oh, yes,—my new scenario.

MRS. UPJOHN. Fine, fine,—and we're going to hear it?

CONSTANCE. Perhaps. It's rather long. I don't really know whether I ought to— You see, I was just saying to Miriam—

JOSEPH. Excuse me. [*Handing her more manuscript.*] This is reel three, reel four, reel five, reel six. [*The pile of papers is now high.*]

SOCK. Is that all?

MRS. UPJOHN. What is your part in this, Joseph,—collaborator?

JOSEPH. Oh, no, I'm nothing but a poor amanuensis.

SOCK. Think of that! [*Sits on arm of chair right center.*]

CONSTANCE. As I was saying, I was just saying to Miriam that it's awfully nice of you—

[SOCK *and* EMMA JANE, *who have detected the approach of* MIRIAM *and* RIGGS,—*up stage center—now move down stage, arm-in-arm, humming the wedding march.* MRS. UPJOHN *hastily quiets them, and silence reigns as* MIRIAM *and* RIGGS *appear at the door center from left together; he leans upon his cane at one side and upon her at the other. Sensing the dramatic qualities of the entrance, he stops in the doorway, looks intently into the face of his escort. He only misses the clicking of the camera.*]

MRS. UPJOHN [*rising*]. Oh, Mr. Riggs, I've been wanting to introduce you to one of our young people who is interested in dramatic things,—Miss Constance Bliss.

CONSTANCE [*who has recognized the description and advanced even before the name was out.*] Oh, Mr. Riggs! [*Shaking hands.*] I've been looking forward to this moment for more than just the few weeks you have been in our midst,—I have been looking forward to meeting you ever since I first saw your image on the silver screen nearly two years ago, when you appeared with "The Passionate Princess." I am an ardent and loyal devotee of the—of the—

JOSEPH [*to the rescue*]. The cinema.

CONSTANCE. Yes,—of course, the cinema, because of my work as a—as a—well, perhaps I should not say it myself, but—

JOSEPH. She is a scenario writer of no mean ability.

MRS. UPJOHN. And this, Mr. Riggs, is our friend, Joseph Brady.

JOSEPH [*shaking hands*]. I am very glad to make your acquaintance. [RIGGS *inclines his head.* JOSEPH, *having said the proper thing, backs away to back of sofa.*]

MRS. UPJOHN. And you know the rest of us, so now let's all be seated and enjoy a little surprise which Constance has in store for us. [*Crosses and sits chair down right.*]

CONSTANCE [*as she and* RIGGS *sit on sofa*]. Oh, not just yet, Mrs. Upjohn. I know we all have have questions we would like to ask Mr. Riggs about his art,—if he doesn't mind.

RIGGS. Seems funny to be called Mr. Riggs.

CONSTANCE. What do they call you in the studio?

RIGGS. Reggy, that's my name,—Reggy Riggs.

CONSTANCE. Oh, but we shouldn't call you that,—just yet. We would be guilty of—of—

JOSEPH. Lèse-majesté.

CONSTANCE. Yes, that's it.

RIGGS. I see.

   [MIRIAM *pulls chair left over to the left of the sofa and sits.*]

CONSTANCE. I would like to ask *Mr.* Riggs if the moving picture actors think the talkies will reach the rank of a fine art.

RIGGS. It is still, as you know, a very new development.

CONSTANCE. Oh, yes. It's still so young.

RIGGS. Yes.

CONSTANCE. So—so—so—

JOSEPH. Immature.

CONSTANCE. Yes, immature.

MRS. UPJOHN. Miss Bliss is quite a student of the talking pictures, Mr. Riggs.

RIGGS. So I see.

CONSTANCE. It must be thrilling to go to the theater after a picture has been made and see and hear yourself in it. Isn't it, Mr. Riggs?

RIGGS. Yes, rather.

[*The next two lines are spoken simultaneously.*]

CONSTANCE.	EMMA JANE.
Would you mind telling us—	Do very many actors—

EMMA JANE. Pardon me, Constance.

CONSTANCE. Oh, excuse me, Emma Jane. I'm afraid I'm monopolizing Mr. Riggs.

EMMA JANE [*crossing to sit at his feet*]. I was just going to ask Mr. Riggs if many movie actors marry.

RIGGS. Well, some, yes.

JOSEPH. Are Doug and Mary happy?

RIGGS. Well, I couldn't say as to that.

SOCK. How do you like the climate in California? [*Sliding from arm down into chair up stage center.*]

RIGGS. Well, you see we do most of our work at Astoria.

CONSTANCE. Astoria. Oh, isn't that interesting!

EMMA JANE. What were you going to ask, Constance?

CONSTANCE. I was going to ask a rather intimate question. You don't mind, do you, Mr. Riggs?

RIGGS. Quite all right.

[*As* CONSTANCE *continues, the figure of* SPEEDY PACE *appears in the doorway center. He hesitates to enter, for he is still without collar and coat. Presently, with firm determination, but cautious step, he advances toward the sofa, still unseen.*]

CONSTANCE. Well, I want to know something about remuneration. Is it true that actors get as high as five hundred dollars a week?

RIGGS. Well, some do, yes.

CONSTANCE. Do you know what they pay for a real good scenario?

[SPEEDY *has reached the couch, and is advancing an arm toward the pillow when* JOSEPH *sees him.*]

JOSEPH. Oh, my! You scared me! Goodness!

MRS. UPJOHN. We've been waiting for you, Speedy.

SOCK. Why the sneaky stuff, Speedy? You going to be a movie actor, too?

EMMA JANE. Is this a new style of dress for tea, Speedy?

MRS. UPJOHN. Can I get something for you?

SPEEDY [*who has been trying to explain from the first*]. You'll have to excuse my appearance—

SOCK. Oh, that's all right, Speedy.

SPEEDY [*center*]. No, no. I'm not coming to the tea.

MRS. UPJOHN. Why, Speedy!

SPEEDY. That is, not yet. I mean—well, you see, the fact is, I left the rest of my clothes behind this pillow. [*He reaches behind the pillow and brings forth* MIRIAM'S *apron, which he holds up in consternation.*]

SOCK. You're not absent-minded, are you, Speedy?

SPEEDY. Well, I left it there.

MIRIAM. Is that any place to leave a coat?

SPEEDY. Is it any place to leave an apron? [MIRIAM *does not answer, but turns her attention to* RIGGS, *whom she addresses.*]

MIRIAM. Mr. Riggs—

SPEEDY. Well, where did you put it?

MIRIAM [*absently*]. Oh, out there. [*To* RIGGS.] Mr. Riggs, I want to ask—

SPEEDY. Out where?

MIRIAM [*to get rid of him*]. Oh, in the hall! [*Speaks to* RIGGS.] I want to ask if they make real love in the movies, or is it just make-believe.

RIGGS. Well, that sometimes depends on the leading lady.

[*Exit* SPEEDY *center to left.*]

MRS. UPJOHN. What other pictures have you played in, Mr. Riggs?

Riggs. I was in "Sebastian's Seven Sins."

Constance. He played "Sebastian."

Riggs. And "The Devil's Desire."

Constance. He played "The Devil."

Joseph. My goodness!

Miriam. I've always wanted to know if they really destroy property in the movies. When we see fires and sinking ships and such things, are they real, or just a trick?

Riggs. Real, mostly. We filmed the Spanish Armada last year and all the Spanish galleons were sunk in the sea.

Constance. "Sunk in the sea." Isn't that interesting!

Miriam. You must be a wonderful swimmer, Mr. Riggs.

Riggs. Yes, I swim fairly well.

Constance. Did you have any trouble getting to shore?

Riggs. Well, you see, I was on one of the English ships.

Constance. Oh, I see.

Mrs. Upjohn. Where was this done, Mr. Riggs?

Riggs. Just off Coney Island.

Constance. "Just off Coney Island." Isn't that interesting!—

[Enter SPEEDY—who sits, chair up center by door.]

Mrs. Upjohn. And now I think we should give our attention to Constance Bliss, who has a little surprise in store for us.

Constance. I suppose I ought not to *promise* a surprise, because my surprise depends entirely upon someone else, and that person is Mr. Riggs.

Riggs. Me?

Constance. But as I have found him to be a very courteous and obliging person, I am sure I shall not be disappointed— Well, to make a long story short,—or rather, to begin at the beginning: Mrs. Lewis of the Footlights Club was looking around for a good one-act play for their next bill. So it occurred to me that I could fix up one scene of my latest scenario as a regular one-act play, and then read the rest of the scenario to the audience so that they would know how it comes out. Well, just about that time we heard about the accident on Friar Hill, which has, unfortunately for him, but fortunately for us, kept Mr. Riggs in our midst; and then I had a brilliant idea.

RIGGS [*as in pain, his hand to his head*]. Oh. [*All turn to him.*]

MRS. UPJOHN. What is it, Mr. Riggs? Your ankle?

RIGGS [*hand from face to ankle*]. Yes—my ankle.

CONSTANCE. Oh, that's too bad!

RIGGS. Quite all right. Pardon me. You were saying?

CONSTANCE. I was saying,—I had a brilliant idea. It occurred to me that if Mr. Riggs would only consent to taking part in "The Clutches"—

RIGGS. In what?

CONSTANCE. In "The Clutches." That's the name of my play.

SOCK. Who are the other actors going to be?

CONSTANCE. Why, *we* are. Let's see— [*Counting.*] One, two, three, four—there are eight of us here, and only seven in my big scene. So that makes one to spare.

MRS. UPJOHN. I'll be the one to spare.

CONSTANCE. No, indeed. I want you for the part of Mrs. Underwood.

JOSEPH. Aren't you counting your chickens, Constance? Mr. Riggs hasn't said anything yet.

CONSTANCE. Oh, I'm just hoping—!

RIGGS [*hesitating*]. Well—ah—well—

CONSTANCE. Maybe you'd like to hear the play before you decide. I brought it along.

RIGGS. Well, I was just going to say, how long would it take—

CONSTANCE. Only about an hour and a half.

RIGGS. No, no. I mean how long would it take to rehearse the play? As much as ten days?

CONSTANCE. Well, for a one-act play we usually take a month. But in this case I think, with your help, and if we all work hard—you weren't thinking of leaving?

RIGGS. Well, that depends. Perhaps if you would tell us something about the play.

CONSTANCE. Yes, of course. I'll read it, shall I? Joseph can help me when I get tired.

RIGGS. Oh, no, don't tire yourself. Just tell us the story in your own words.

CONSTANCE [*about to launch forth*]. Well—

RIGGS. Not too long. Just a brief—ah—

JOSEPH. Résumé.

RIGGS Yes. That's the idea.

CONSTANCE. Yes. Well— First of all, the cast of characters. The heroine's name is symbolic.

RIGGS. That's a queer name.

CONSTANCE. No, no. That's not her name. Her name is Belle Underwood. But I say that is symbolic because Belle is the French word for beautiful, and she is beautiful, and because it is the second syllable in the word "rebellion," and she is in rebellion against her tyrannical father who wants her to marry a rich man many years older than she is. And the rich man's name is Mr. Goldman. But she is really in love with another man whose name is Alfred Armstrong,— and that's symbolic, too, as you will see in a minute. Then there is a young clergyman who comes to officiate at the wedding, and his name is Rev. Matthew Mark. And Belle's father and mother, and Mary the maid, and that's all. Now the scene that I have made into a one-act play is the wedding scene in which Belle is supposed to marry Mr. Goldman, much against her will. Mr. Underwood is notified at the last minute that the clergyman who was to preside is unable to come—

SOCK. I'll play that part.

CONSTANCE. Now listen— And so they send a younger clergyman who is a stranger to the family. That's Mr. Matthew Mark. He arrives and is waiting in the parlor when Alfred Armstrong, the disappointed lover, comes in stealthily, sneaks up behind Mr. Matthew Mark, and gives him a blow with his fist under the chin. Then he and Mary, the maid, carry the preacher out. And that is the last we see of Mr. Matthew Mark. Well, pretty soon Belle comes in for the wedding, and her father and mother and Mr. Goldman. But what has happened to the preacher? Well, just then Alfred

Armstrong enters, dressed in the preacher's clothes. Belle gives a faint gasp which she quickly conceals, but the others don't recognize him because they have never seen him before.

MRS. UPJOHN. Does she marry the old man?

SOCK. I hope not!

CONSTANCE. No, she doesn't. But how does she escape him? Can anyone guess? Can you, Mr. Riggs?

RIGGS. The young lover ought to pick her up in his arms and run off with her.

CONSTANCE. "Run off with her." Oh, isn't that interesting.

EMMA JANE. Is that right?

CONSTANCE. I hadn't thought of that. But I think that's a brilliant idea. I believe I'll revise the ending.

SOCK. Is there any kissing in the play, Constance?

CONSTANCE. Oh, yes, at the very start, before the preacher comes, Alfred and Belle are together and he tells her not to worry, that he will surely find a way. And then he kisses her.

EMMA JANE. Are you going to have real kissing!

CONSTANCE. Oh, I think it should be real. This is the age of realism on the stage.

SOCK. Who's going to play Alfred Armstrong?

CONSTANCE. Well, of course, I had Mr. Riggs in mind for that part.

EMMA JANE. And who's going to play Belle?

CONSTANCE. I would be willing to play Belle, if you want me to— But of course we haven't heard yet whether Mr. Riggs can take part.

RIGGS. I really can't say just yet— Did you say that you would play Belle?

CONSTANCE. Yes, if you think best?

RIGGS. I was just going to say I think some other arrangement would be better. You see, in the professional world, the author never takes part in his own play.

CONSTANCE. No, of course not, but—

RIGGS. And then I think we need you to coach the play.

CONSTANCE. Yes.

EMMA JANE. Then it's between me and Miriam. And I don't want to play it.

SOCK. I think Mim should play it.

RIGGS. Will you play opposite me, Miriam?

CONSTANCE. Then you are going to stay and work with us, Mr. Riggs?

RIGGS [*to* MIRIAM]. Did you nod your head?

MIRIAM. Yes, I'd like to play Belle.

RIGGS. All right. I'll play Armstrong.

CONSTANCE. Fine! Now we are sure of success.

EMMA JANE. Speedy should play the old rich man.

CONSTANCE. Yes. I had Speedy in mind for that.

SPEEDY. All right. I can pretend I'm rich. [*Turns up to join* SOCK *in chair up center.*]

CONSTANCE. And Joseph can be the preacher.

JOSEPH. All right.

SOCK. Ha ha! You get hit under the chin.

JOSEPH. Oh, dear me, that's so. [JOSEPH *joins* SOCK *and* SPEEDY *up right center. These three look over their shoulders in disgust at the demonstration which the girls are making over* RIGGS *as they group about him.*]

EMMA JANE. And mother will be Mrs. Underwood.

CONSTANCE. Yes.

SOCK. And I'll be the father, since there's nothing else left.

EMMA JANE. And I'll be the maid, for the same reason.

CONSTANCE. That's just fine. That's going to work out splendidly. And I'll coach it— Fancy me giving directions to Reggy Riggs! But of course [*to* REGGY] I'll ask your opinion about things.

JOSEPH. Yes, of course.

CONSTANCE. Now when shall we have the first rehearsal? Tomorrow?

[*General affirmation is heard. "Yes"—"The sooner the better"—"Let's not waste any time," etc.*]

MRS. UPJOHN [*rising*]. I'm going to interrupt this for a few minutes until we serve the tea.

CONSTANCE. Oh, Mrs. Upjohn, you shouldn't have gone to so much trouble.

MRS. UPJOHN. This is the Upjohn Cafeteria. Everybody has to go out to the pantry and get a tray and a napkin, and then stand in line for their tea.

CONSTANCE. Isn't that interesting!

MRS. UPJOHN. Emma Jane, you lead the way.

[EMMA JANE *is lost in* RIGGS.]

MRS. UPJOHN. Emma Jane!

[SOCK *goes down to her and pulls her away by the arm and off right.* RIGGS *and* MIRIAM *follow.* CONSTANCE *trips after them, watching* RIGGS' *feet and exclaiming:*]

CONSTANCE. Oh, Mr. Riggs, be careful of your ankle. Mr. Riggs! Mr. Riggs! [*and she follows them off, followed by* JOSEPH.]

[*During this exodus* SPEEDY *has slipped into the hall, secured his hat, and now, as* MRS. UPJOHN, *left alone on the stage, looks about for him, is to be seen passing along the hall at back as if departing.*]

MRS. UPJOHN. Speedy, where are you going?

SPEEDY. Well, I just thought I—

MRS. UPJOHN. You can't go now! Listen to me. [*He comes down center.*] I'm going to give you a piece of advice. You'll think it strange for me to say this, and you mustn't ask any questions— If you ever intend to propose to Miriam, you must do it now.

SPEEDY. Now?—But—

MRS. UPJOHN. Before you leave the house.

SPEEDY. But—

MRS. UPJOHN. But nothing, put away your hat. I'll send her in for something—that tray [*at left*] and leave the rest to you. [*She exits right.* SPEEDY *stands helpless for a moment then turns up stage, and goes out center to left.* MIRIAM *enters from right and crosses to left for tray. As she is returning right,* RIGGS *enters, right.*]

RIGGS. Miriam. [*He looks about the room.*] Are you glad I'm staying for the play?

MIRIAM. Why, yes. I think you will make it a success.

RIGGS. No other reason?

MIRIAM. Why, what do you mean?

RIGGS. *I'm* glad I'm staying.

MIRIAM. Why are *you* glad?

RIGGS. Don't you know?

MIRIAM. Why—

RIGGS. I'll show you. [*He suddenly takes her in his arms and kisses her.*]

    [SPEEDY *now reappears in the doorway center, then comes forward, boldly, belligerently. Hearing him, they separate,* MIRIAM *crying out in a mortified "oh!"* RIGGS, *however, retains his composure and* MIRIAM'S *hand. He draws her to him again as he says to* SPEEDY.]

RIGGS. You'll pardon us, won't you? We were just rehearsing the kissing scene. [*He kisses her again, and* SPEEDY, *baffled, chagrined, turns back and out the center door to right.*]

CURTAIN

ACT II

SCENE I

The stage of the Woman's Club House. It is set for "The Clutches." There are doors up stage right and up stage left, and for the other two doors which the play requires, they use, innocently enough, the space between the tormentors and the proscenium on either side.

The scene represents a room in the home of the Underwoods, where the wedding is to take place. There is a large lounge chair down right and at least four other chairs elsewhere in the room. There is a stand or table down left, and at least one other table in the room.

The curtain rises on a dark and empty stage. The sound of voices is heard off stage. The voice of CONSTANCE *may be heard above the others.*

CONSTANCE. Oh, my, aren't you all thrilled? I wish I were going to take part.

RIGGS [*also off stage*]. Yours is the biggest part of all.

JOSEPH [*at the door*]. Oh, my, it's all dark.

MIRIAM. I know where the switch box is.

JOSEPH. Does anybody have a match?

RIGGS. Yes, here's a box.

[*A match is struck in the darkness.*]

JOSEPH. I'll light your way, Miriam.

MIRIAM. All right. Over here. [*She moves off to the left;* JOSEPH *follows, shielding a lighted match. The stage is left in darkness. There is a moment's pause, during which we hear the sound of steps moving across the stage.*]

RIGGS [*suddenly*]. Oh, excuse me!

[*The lights go up, and we find* REGGY *and* CONSTANCE *in very close proximity.*]

RIGGS [*walking away*]. Excuse me. I was just feeling my way around and I—

CONSTANCE. Oh, that's all right, Reggy.

MIRIAM [*off stage*]. There, is that better?

RIGGS. Yes, much better.

[CONSTANCE *and* JOSEPH *enter from left.*]

JOSEPH. Just think! In one hour—

CONSTANCE. Only an hour!

JOSEPH. Yes, I wonder where the others are.

MIRIAM. They're coming.

JOSEPH. Where do we dress?

CONSTANCE. In the dressing room, of course.

JOSEPH. Heavens! Is there only one?

CONSTANCE. No, silly. One for the men and one for the women.

RIGGS. Is this the set?

CONSTANCE. Yes. Do you think it will do? Of course it's not as elaborate—

RIGGS. Perfect. Perfect.

JOSEPH. Well, I guess we'd better get busy.

[SOCK *and* EMMA JANE *enter from the right.* SOCK *carries a wrapped package and a telephone, with the cord wound around the base.*]

EMMA JANE. Hello, everybody. [*Brief greetings, ad lib.*]

SOCK. How are all the little clutches this evening?

MIRIAM. Where is mother?

EMMA JANE. She's dressing at home. Speedy's waiting for her.

SOCK. They'll be along.

CONSTANCE. Now everybody get dressed first.

[*They start off, the women at the right, and the men at the left.*]

CONSTANCE. People! People! [*They stop.*] The women use this dressing room [*indicating left*], and the men this one [*indicating right. They start off again.*] People! People! [*They stop.*] As soon as you are dressed come back here to be made up. Reggy is going to show us how to do it *professionally.* Oh, did you bring the mirrors, Sock?

SOCK. You bet. [*He takes a package to the table left where he also deposits the telephone.*]

[EMMA JANE *goes off left;* JOSEPH *and* RIGGS *go off right.*]

MIRIAM. I'd like to make up now, Constance.

CONSTANCE. All right. Belle should be a bit pale. No rouge. [MIRIAM *sits in chair down stage right.* CONSTANCE *goes out left.*]

SOCK [*who has been unwrapping mirrors, at table left, takes one to* MIRIAM]. Here you are. Ten cents per— Guess I better get my duds on. [*He goes off left. We hear his voice off stage saying . . .*] Excuse me! [*and he reappears saying . . .*] Wrong pew. [*and crosses to right and goes out.*]

MIRIAM *is left alone. She examines the articles in the make-up box on the table left. She takes up a rabbit's foot and looks at it. She picks at it. She caresses it with her finger, pensively. She sighs.*

RIGGS *steps on to the scene from the right.* MIRIAM, *without turning, busies herself suddenly with the make-up box.* RIGGS *looks about and comes down to her, quietly. He stands behind her.*

MIRIAM. I see you. [*She points to his image in her mirror.*]

RIGGS. [*coming to her side*]. You won't be saying that to-morrow.

MIRIAM. Tomorrow? You're not leaving tomorrow?

RIGGS. Tonight.

MIRIAM. Tonight! Why Reggy!

RIGGS. Got to.

MIRIAM. You have an engagement? [RIGGS *nods his head.*] You never said . . .

RIGGS. I know. I didn't want to think about it.

MIRIAM. Oh, Reggy! [*There is a pause.* MIRIAM *looks away.* RIGGS *walks away. He takes a photograph from his pocket, turns back to her, and hands it to her.*] Oh, Reggy! For me? [*He nods; she looks at the picture a moment, then up at him.*] How did you know I wanted this, Reggy?

RIGGS. It's nothing. Put it away in the bottom of your trunk.

MIRIAM. I won't any such thing!

RIGGS. And then some rainy evening, when your husband is away on a business trip, take it out and look at it, and think of a poor vagabond actor who once knew you, and—cared for you.

MIRIAM. You seem to think I'm going to marry a business man.

RIGGS. Well? He's hanging around just waiting for me to clear out.

MIRIAM. Speedy?

RIGGS. He won't have to wait much longer.

MIRIAM. I'm not going to marry anyone.

RIGGS. Don't say that. It isn't true. You'll forget about me soon enough.

MIRIAM. I won't.

RIGGS [*closer*]. You *will* think of me sometimes, won't you, Miriam, and maybe send me a—a Christmas card?

[CONSTANCE *enters at the left. She stops on seeing these two together.* RIGGS, *aware of her presence, immediately changes tack.*]

I think you need a little more rouge on your cheeks.

CONSTANCE. Oh, do you think so, Reggy? Remember, she is sad.

RIGGS. Perhaps you're right.

MIRIAM. But she might put rouge on to conceal her sadness.

RIGGS. Yes, sure.

CONSTANCE. Well, whatever you say. I'll send Joseph to you whenever you are ready. [*She crosses right, then turns again.*] Oh, has Speedy come?

MIRIAM. Not yet, Constance, but he'll be here.

RIGGS [*more to* MIRIAM *than to* CONSTANCE.] Yes. You can always count on him.

CONSTANCE. Tell him I have his wig. [*She goes out right.*]

RIGGS [*as he continues to apply the cosmetics to* MIRIAM]. Confound that woman! Look up. [*He lines her lower lid.*] [*Pause.*] Are you going to answer my question?

MIRIAM. About the Christmas card?

RIGGS. Must I wait till Christmas?

MIRIAM. No.

RIGGS. How long?

MIRIAM. Do you want me to write to you, Reggy?

RIGGS. If you have time.

MIRIAM. I'll have *time* enough— Oh, Reggy. I wish you weren't going.

RIGGS. But I must.

MIRIAM. Do they need you right away?

RIGGS. It's not just that. But I can't stay here any longer.

MIRIAM. Why can't you?

RIGGS. Don't you see?

MIRIAM. If you think you're imposing on mother—

RIGGS. Not that.

MIRIAM. What then?

RIGGS [*very dramatically*]. Suppose you were a man whose life was a wandering life, swayed by the chances of fate, now living in luxury, now in want, and you had resolved never to ask a girl to share such a life with you. And suppose that you met a girl, a charming girl, and that you came to care for her more than you had ever cared for anyone in all your life. And you broke your resolution and asked her to marry you. And she did what any girl with common sense would do—she turned you down. Now would you want to go on living in the same house with her, and seeing another man taking her out of your very arms?

MIRIAM. Reggy, you mustn't talk like that! You—I—can't you see—

RIGGS. It's all right, dear. Don't try to explain. [*With liner poised.*] Now close your eyes. [*She does so. Instead of applying the liner to her eyes, he bends over and kisses her lips.*]

[*At this moment* SOCK, *mirror in hand, steps on from the right. He takes in the situation at a glance, grins, and disappears.*]

RIGGS [*rising*]. I'm sorry. I'd no business doing that.

MIRIAM [*emotionally*]. Reggy!

RIGGS. Forgive me, dear, I'll have to go away. I just can't stay near you.

MIRIAM [*in spite of herself*]. But I don't want you to go away.

RIGGS. I could never stay and just be a "*good friend.*"

MIRIAM. Oh, Reggy, why do you talk like that? Don't you see?

RIGGS [*to her*]. See what, dear?

MIRIAM. That I don't want you to be a "good friend."

RIGGS [*emotionally*]. Do you mean that, dearest? [*She nods. He leaves her side for a moment of intense thought, then returns.*] Miriam, if we are to be married, there is only one way it can be done. It can't be done here. We've got to go away, don't you see? Go away quietly somewhere and be married. Perhaps tonight. After the show. Here there would be all kinds of complications and delay, but in New York— Don't answer now. Think it over. And maybe tomorrow you'll be Mrs. Reginal— [*Voices are heard off stage.* RIGGS *immediately alters his manner.*] Now with a little powder, you'll be all right.

[JOSEPH, *in passing across the stage behind the window,*

has caught sight of the pair, paused, and listened to this last speech of RIGGS. *He now dodges out of sight, as* MRS. UPJOHN *enters right, wearing a cloak over an evening dress.* SPEEDY *follows carrying a sofa pillow.*]

MRS. UPJOHN. Tickets are all sold out. What do you think of that?

RIGGS. Splendid.

MRS. UPJOHN. Met Jack Davis down stairs with a fist full of money. "Full house," he said.

RIGGS. I hope we shan't disappoint him.

MRS. UPJOHN. Of course not— Where do I go, Miriam?

MIRIAM. In here. [*She precedes her mother out left.* RIGGS *and* SPEEDY *are left alone. After a pause,* RIGGS, *who is lining his eyebrow, looks up.*]

RIGGS [*lightly*]. Oh, hello, there.

SPEEDY. Hello.

RIGGS. Going to have a pillow fight? [*He laughs.* SPEEDY *says nothing.* CONSTANCE *enters from right. Goes to* SPEEDY *right. During this scene,* RIGGS *wanders off stage.*]

CONSTANCE. Oh, here you are at last. I've got your wig. Here, bend over. [*He is obedient, she puts a wig on his head. The hair is awry.*] There, that'll do nicely. Now go brush it, and fix your pillow and get made up. Reggy will help you. [*Exit left.*]

[EMMA JANE *comes in left to get a mirror at stage right. In crossing from left to right, she says—*]

EMMA JANE. Hello, best man! [*and in crossing back again—*] Remember the fourth of July. [*Exit left.*]

SPEEDY [*to himself*]. Best man! Hm. Next-best man!

[*Enter* SOCK *at right, looks around.*]

SOCK [*to* SPEEDY]. Now's your chance. Here's a love letter. [*Hands him purple envelope.*] I'll call Miriam. [*At door left.*] Mim! Mim! [*Crosses hurriedly to right and exit right.*]

MIRIAM [*entering from left*]. Did you want me? [SPEEDY, *feigning preoccupation, is silent.*] Did you want me, Speedy? [*Still no answer.*] Thank you for bringing mother over tonight.

SPEEDY [*absently*]. Huh?

MIRIAM. I say, thank you for bringing mother over.

SPEEDY. Don't mention it. [MIRIAM, *astonished, watches him as he reads further, folds the letter, smells it, sighs, and restores the letter to the envelope and his pocket.* MIRIAM, *aghast, turns and hurries off left.* SPEEDY *watches her, out of the corner of his eye, and smiles to himself when she is gone.*]

[CONSTANCE *and* REGGY *enter simultaneously from opposite doors.* REGGY *starts to go off right again, when* CONSTANCE *calls him.*]

CONSTANCE. Oh, just a minute, Reggy; I want to see you. [*She turns to* SPEEDY.] What are you doing, Speedy? Why, you haven't even started. Why don't you do what I told you? Now hurry. [SPEEDY *goes off right.*] [*To* REGGY.] Is anything the matter, Reggy?

RIGGS. No, why?

CONSTANCE. You seem so quiet—I suppose you want to relax before the performance.

RIGGS. Yes, that's it.

CONSTANCE. You've been doing admirable acting, Reggy. Now don't deny it. It's been really gorgeous.

RIGGS. Well, thank you.

CONSTANCE. So realistic. Especially in the love scene.

RIGGS. Glad you think so.

CONSTANCE. Oh, yes! I only wish you had better support.

RIGGS. Support?

CONSTANCE. Yes, Miriam. She's such a stick.

RIGGS. What you mean "stick"?

CONSTANCE. She doesn't *respond* passionately enough in the love making.

RIGGS. Yes. That's quite true.

CONSTANCE. My! I wish I—

RIGGS. What!

CONSTANCE. Oh, nothing. It's no use now.—Tell me, do you think the play will be a success?

RIGGS. Oh, yes, I think so.

CONSTANCE. Oh, I'm so glad. Because I'm pinning hopes on this production.

RIGGS. Yes. We all are.

CONSTANCE. You see, I'm thinking of having my play produced professionally.

RIGGS. Oh, you are?

CONSTANCE. What do you think about it?

RIGGS. Well, who would do it?

CONSTANCE. Oh, I don't know. I thought perhaps you—if you became attached to the part—you might induce some manager—don't you see?

RIGGS. Oh!

CONSTANCE. I think I'm being rather bold to think of such a thing—but—

RIGGS. Not at all.

CONSTANCE. Oh, then you do think the play has possibilities?

RIGGS. Why—yes, of course.

CONSTANCE. Oh, I'm so glad. I wanted you to be pleased. And if you *do* place it with a manager, I shall of course give you a share in the royalties. And then I'll write another, and you can have that produced. And thus we'll form a kind of partnership, don't you see?

EMMA JANE [*speaking as she enters left*]. Sure, an' I wish it was myself that was gittin' married tonight. With all these pretty posies— Oh, does anybody have the flowers?

CONSTANCE. Oh, I was going to ask Joseph. Will you excuse me Reggy? [*Exit right.*]

EMMA JANE. Now, Reggy, what are you going to do to me?

RIGGS. Huh?

EMMA JANE. Aren't you going to make me look pretty?

RIGGS. Oh, that's easy.—Sit down. [EMMA JANE *sits left.*]

EMMA JANE. I'm Irish, you know.

[*Enter* JOSEPH *right followed by* CONSTANCE, *who is trying to fasten his clerical collar at the back.*]

CONSTANCE. Won't you please hold still! [JOSEPH *gulps as she chokes him.* SOCK *enters right.*] Listen, did you see about the flowers?

JOSEPH. Yes.

CONSTANCE. Where are they?

JOSEPH. Mrs. Martin said she would send them over by George.

SOCK [*at table left, busy making up*]. Mrs. Martin said she would send them over,—by George!

JOSEPH. Sock is trying to hide his nervousness by being funny.

SOCK. I *would* be nervous, if I had your part.

JOSEPH. Why?

SOCK. Getting hit under the chin.

JOSEPH. Oh, shut up!

RIGGS [*to* EMMA JANE]. Now use powder and you'll be finished. [*Exit* RIGGS *right*.]

CONSTANCE [*to* JOSEPH]. There. Now, get your make-up on. [*She goes off right after* RIGGS.]

JOSEPH [*down to* EMMA JANE]. What should I put on, rouge?

SOCK [*inspired*]. Here, rub this on your face.

[JOSEPH *stands for a moment with his back to the audience. Then, as* SOCK *and* EMMA JANE *burst into laughter he turns, and reveals black smears on his puzzled face. Disgusted, he turns and goes off right, saying,*]

JOSEPH. My! I wish this was over!

SOCK [*at table left*]. You should have seen what I saw a while ago.

EMMA JANE. What?

SOCK. Oh, you missed it.

EMMA JANE. What was it?

SOCK. Want me to show you?

EMMA JANE. Yes.

SOCK. You be Miriam. I'm Riggs. I'm putting make-up on your face, see? Now I'm going to do your eye-lids, so you gotta close your eyes. [*She does so. He kisses her. They laugh.*]

EMMA JANE. Did he honest?

SOCK. Sure.

EMMA JANE. I guess I must be responsible for that.

SOCK. How do you figure?

EMMA JANE. I told him he was too slow for this town. What did he say to her?

SOCK. I don't know. I got an eye-full and then ducked out.

EMMA JANE. Gee, Speedy is certainly falling behind in this race.

SOCK. The deuce he is! He's making a big hit.

EMMA JANE. Speedy?

SOCK. Sure, you should have seen him reading his love letters in front of Miriam.

EMMA JANE. Is that your idea?

SOCK [*proudly*]. Sure.

EMMA JANE. I'm not so sure about that method.

SOCK. What's the matter with it?

EMMA JANE. Might have the wrong effect.

SOCK. Not a chance. The trouble with you is you don't know anything about psychology. Now listen. Let's suppose Speedy is a house.

EMMA JANE. A house?

SOCK. Yes. A house. And Miss Miriam Upjohn is looking for a house, and she likes the Speedy house pretty well, but she can't make up her mind to take it because nobody else seems to show any interest in it. Along comes another woman, and offers ten thousand dollars for the Speedy house. What happens then? Miss Miriam Upjohn puts on her hat and rushes around and says, "I'll give twelve thousand." The other woman says, "I'll give fifteen." "I'll give seventeen." "I'll give twenty." "Twenty-five." "Thirty." "Fifty." "A Hundred."—See? That's psychology.

[MIRIAM *enters at left wearing a wedding dress.*]

MIRIAM. What's this? An auction?

EMMA JANE. Yes. You just bought a house.

SOCK. You mean, she just got married.

MIRIAM. How do you like my dress?

SOCK. Swell.

EMMA JANE [*humming*]. Here comes the bride.

SOCK. Where'd you get it, Mim?

MIRIAM. It's mother's made over.

SOCK. Just for the play?

MIRIAM. Yes, why?

SOCK. Not thinking of using it for any other occasion, are you?

MIRIAM. Don't you wish I would!

EMMA JANE. Mim! Have you got anything to tell us?

MIRIAM [*walking off proudly*]. I am so glad you like my new dress. [*When she is gone,* SOCK *and* EMMA JANE *look at each other in amazement.*]

SOCK. Well, what do you know about that?

EMMA JANE. Sock! [*Goes to sofa right.*]

SOCK. What? [*Goes to end of sofa right.*]

EMMA JANE. What are you thinking?

SOCK. Same thing you are.

EMMA JANE. Do you suppose she is.

SOCK. Sure looks like it.

EMMA JANE. Who could it be?

SOCK. Give you two guesses.

EMMA JANE. Must be Reggy.

SOCK. That's my guess.

EMMA JANE. Say, do you realize what that means?

SOCK [*mildly*]. Yes.

EMMA JANE. I mean to us—you and me.

SOCK. I know.

EMMA JANE. Well, you seem very enthusiastic.

SOCK. I was thinking about Mim.

EMMA JANE. What?

SOCK. Say, no kidding, what do you think of Riggs as a husband and father?

EMMA JANE [*after a pause*]. Not so hot—what do you think?
[SOCK *gestures "thumbs down."* EMMA JANE *solemnly seconds him by inverting both her thumbs.*]

SOCK. If things didn't come out just right, I'd hate to think that we—

EMMA JANE. Mm. Me too.
[MRS. UPJOHN *enters left and goes to make-up table left.*]

MRS. UPJOHN. Hello, where's the funeral?

EMMA JANE [*to* SOCK]. Shall we tell her?

SOCK. Yes.

EMMA JANE. Listen, lady, do you realize that your oldest
daughter has just been proposed to?

MRS. UPJOHN. What, again?

EMMA JANE. "Again"!

MRS. UPJOHN. Go on, who is it this time?

SOCK. Riggs.

MRS. UPJOHN. Who told you?

SOCK. I caught 'em kissing a little while ago, and she was just
in here and practically admitted—

EMMA JANE. Oh, there's no doubt about it.

MRS. UPJOHN [*sitting at table left*]. Oh, dear.

EMMA JANE. That's the way we feel about it.

MRS. UPJOHN. You do?

SOCK. Yes. The more I see of Reggy Riggs—

EMMA JANE. —the more I think of Speedy Pace.

MRS. UPJOHN. Speedy doesn't know?

SOCK. Don't suppose so.

MRS. UPJOHN. If Speedy only knew—

SOCK. What would he do?

MRS. UPJOHN. He might—

SOCK. Aw, he'd just feel hurt. [*There is a pause.*]

MRS. UPJOHN. I have it!—Let's tell Speedy that Miriam and
Reggy are going to do something rash—elope, or something.
That would bring him to his feet.

SOCK. Say, how 'bout that!

EMMA JANE. Not bad at all!

MRS. UPJOHN. That would be a challenge to his fighting spirit.

EMMA JANE. All right, mother, you're elected.

MRS. UPJOHN. I'll tell him, I can fib for a good cause.

[SPEEDY *enters from left, dressed for his part.*]

EMMA JANE [*aside to* MRS. UPJOHN]. There he is, mother,
Now's your chance!

[MRS. UPJOHN *turns to* SPEEDY.]

MRS. UPJOHN. Speedy there's something I want to know.

[CONSTANCE *enters left.*]

CONSTANCE. The bell, the bell, what can we do for the bell?

SPEEDY. I've got something to show you. [*He goes off stage right again.*]

EMMA JANE. Curses!

MRS. UPJOHN. Never mind, I'll see him. [SPEEDY *returns.*]

MRS. UPJOHN [*trying again*]. Speedy, there's something I want you to know. [*But* CONSTANCE *interrupts, going to* SPEEDY.]

CONSTANCE [*ringing it*]. Oh, isn't that fine! You're awfully clever, Speedy.

EMMA JANE. Let's see. [*She takes the bell, and rings it repeatedly.*]

[*Enter* JOSEPH *and* RIGGS *from different directions.*]

CONSTANCE. Now don't forget your make-up.

[MRS. UPJOHN *corners* SPEEDY *again, and they sit together at table, left, as* SPEEDY *starts to make up.*]

MRS. UPJOHN. Speedy, there's something I want you to know. [*They continue the talk in pantomime.*]

CONSTANCE [*referring to list*]. Bible, Bible, [*To* JOSEPH.] Oh, here you are. Do you have your Bible?

JOSEPH. Yes, and I've got— [*To* EMMA JANE.] Oh, please keep that thing quiet. I'm trying to talk.

EMMA JANE. 'Scuse me, Josephine. [*She puts it down in her chair.*]

JOSEPH. I've got it all fixed for Reggy. [*He opens the book to where an extra sheet is clipped to a page.*] See? All his cues written in.

CONSTANCE. Why did you do that?

JOSEPH. Well, he's always forgetting to come on. Standing around talking to Miriam all the time.

CONSTANCE. He does that scene with you perfectly.

JOSEPH. Well, all he has to do is to hit me under the chin.

CONSTANCE. But you always act as if you were expecting to be hit under the chin.

SPEEDY [*rising belligerently and moving toward* RIGGS, *who stands down stage right.*] Well, of all the nerve—!

SOCK [*interrupting him, and pushing him back into a chair—*

right.] Hey, let's go over our lines there at the beginning. Good afternoon, Goldman.

SPEEDY. Underwood.

SOCK. Nice day for the wedding.

SPEEDY. Yes.

SOCK. Belle is a bit nervous, but she'll be all right. [*Then to* MIRIAM.] You've got an easy part, Mim; you're *supposed* to be nervous. [*To* SPEEDY.] You're not nervous, are you, Goldman?

[SPEEDY *has risen again and again moves toward* RIGGS.]

SOCK. Hey, you're not supposed to get up there. [*He pushes* SPEEDY *back into his chair. They continue mumbling their "Clutches" speeches—and pace up and down.*]

JOSEPH [*who is occupied with pencil and paper on the bench at right.*] Does anybody know another word for lizard?

CONSTANCE. Snake.

JOSEPH. No. It has ten letters. It has to begin with SA and end with R. Doesn't anybody know? Emma Jane, what do you say?

EMMA JANE [*on sofa right*]. Alligator.

JOSEPH. No! Didn't you hear what I just said? It has to—

CONSTANCE. I have an idea. I want to get the signatures of my cast on the back of a program for a souvenir. Will you sign, first, Mrs. Upjohn? [CONSTANCE *goes to* MRS. UPJOHN *who is seated on bench at right.* MRS. UPJOHN, *instead of answering her question, says suddenly*]

MRS. UPJOHN. Salamander.

EMMA JANE.
CONSTANCE.   }—What?
JOSEPH.

MRS. UPJOHN. Salamander. That's it, Joseph. Another word for lizard, with ten letters.

EMMA JANE. Goodness, mother.

JOSEPH. Yes, that is it. That's it exactly.

[RIGGS *leaves the stage right.*]

EMMA JANE. What are you making up for, Constance?

CONSTANCE. Just a bit of rouge. I thought—

EMMA JANE. But you're not going to be on the stage.

CONSTANCE. Well, I thought in case—

EMMA JANE. Oh, I see. Curtain call. Sure.

SOCK [*clapping his hands*]. Authoress! Authoress!

MRS. UPJOHN. Yes, you and Mr. Riggs should take the curtain call.

JOSEPH. Yes, hand in hand.

CONSTANCE. Oh, where is Reggy?

[REGGY *appears from the right, bearing a long box.*]

RIGGS [*gallantly*]. For the authoress.

CONSTANCE [*thrilled*]. Oh! Am I to understand that these are from—her leading man?

RIGGS. Huh?—Oh, no. A little boy just handed them to me out in the hall.

CONSTANCE. Oh.

JOSEPH. Those are for the stage. Mrs. Martin sent them over.

SOCK. "By George."

CONSTANCE. Miriam, will you take charge of them?

MIRIAM. Beg pardon?

CONSTANCE. The flowers.

MIRIAM. Oh, yes.

[RIGGS *leaves the stage.*]

MRS. UPJOHN [*coming down to* MIRIAM]. Can I help you, dear?

MIRIAM. Let's go over our scene together.

MRS. UPJOHN. You mean *my* scene. All you do is cry.

MIRIAM. Well, I have to cry in the right places.

MRS. UPJOHN [*delivers the speech which begins,*] "Belle, why are you crying? This is no way to behave on your wedding day," etc.

MIRIAM [*punctuates the speech with sobs.*]

[*Meanwhile* SOCK *has approached* SPEEDY *to say*]

SOCK. Won't do you any harm to go over our lines again.

SPEEDY. All right. [SPEEDY *rises and takes seat by* JOSEPH, *on bench, right.*]

SOCK. I say "Good evening Goldman." [*Shakes hands.*]

SPEEDY. No. It's afternoon.

SOCK [*snapping his fingers*]. Gosh, that's right. [*He makes his entrance again.*] "Good afternoon, Goldman." [*Shakes hands.*]

SPEEDY. "Underwood." [*And this dialogue is continued following the lines of "The Clutches.*]

[*Meanwhile* EMMA JANE *moves about the stage hanging curtains.* CONSTANCE *is to be seen up stage walking about in deep thought, and occasionally executing a sweeping curtsey.*]

JOSEPH. Say, what's the name of the highest mountain in Siam?

SOCK. Oh, run along and play, Josephine. [*Exit* JOSEPH *right, and* SOCK *continues his dialogue with* SPEEDY. CONSTANCE *next turns her attention to the property list. She goes to* EMMA JANE.]

CONSTANCE. Do you have your card for the flowers?

EMMA JANE. Yes, some place. [*She exits right.*]

[MRS. UPJOHN *and* MIRIAM *exit right after their weeping dialogue.*]

CONSTANCE [*down to* SPEEDY *left*]. Do you have your cigar?

SPEEDY [*producing it*]. Yes.

SOCK. Better start smoking it before the show begins.

CONSTANCE. And your gloves?

SPEEDY [*to* SOCK]. Did you bring those gloves for me?

SOCK. Gee, I think so. [*He exits right.* CONSTANCE, *mumbling properties, exits left.*]

[JOSEPH *enters cautiously at right, and, finding* SPEEDY *alone, comes down to him and speaks in excited undertones.*]

JOSEPH. Speedy! I overheard Reggy and Miriam before you came and they were talking about running away.

SPEEDY. Did they say when?

JOSEPH. He said—"Perhaps tonight—after the show."

SPEEDY. Hm.

JOSEPH. Well, you don't seem very excited.

SPEEDY. I knew about it already.

JOSEPH. You did? Who told you?

SPEEDY. Mrs. Upjohn.

JOSEPH. Mrs. Up— How did she know? It happened before she came.

SPEEDY. I don't know— Listen, have you told anyone?

JOSEPH. No, just you.

SPEEDY. Don't say a word about it. Now get out. I'll take care of it. [JOSEPH *crosses right.* SPEEDY *ponders a moment, then starts boldly toward the door right. He meets* SOCK *coming in.*]

SOCK. Here you are. [*Gloves.*] Gosh, you look funny!

SPEEDY. Listen! Is Riggs in there?

SOCK. Yeah.

SPEEDY. Ask him to come here a minute, will you? [RIGGS *comes down to* SPEEDY.] Look here, Riggs, you're an actor, and you're attractive and charming and all that, and Miriam likes you. That's all right. I'm willing to play second fiddle as long as the game is out in the open, but I'm not going to stand for any underhanded stuff, and I want you to know it.

RIGGS. What are you talking about, man?

SPEEDY. I guess you know.

RIGGS. I haven't an idea.

SPEEDY. All right. I'll make it plainer. If you try to run away with Miriam Upjohn I'll beat you up so bad, you'll never want to have your picture taken again.

RIGGS. What *is* the matter with you? Who said anything about running away?

SPEEDY. It's true, isn't it?

RIGGS. Who's been feeding you full of bunk? I haven't any time for these small-town girls.

SPEEDY. I wouldn't be so small as to say a thing like that.

RIGGS. Look here, young fellow. You're talking pretty big. You're liable to get yourself into trouble.

SPEEDY. I'm not worrying about that. The point is this— Miriam Upjohn goes home with me tonight, not you.

RIGGS. Oh, is that so?

SPEEDY. And you can find your way to the railroad station alone—the sooner the better.

CONSTANCE [*entering*]. Are you two making up?

MRS. UPJOHN [*entering from right*]. I think Constance and Mr. Riggs should practice their curtain appearance.

CONSTANCE. Oh, shall we, Reggy?

RIGGS. Suits me. [*These two come down stage.* REGGY *takes her hand and bows to the audience and to her, stepping aside to leave her on alone. She bows repeatedly, on every hand, and then begins to speak. In the meantime,* SPEEDY *finds his pillow, and tries to stuff it under his belt with even distribution.* EMMA JANE *secures* JOSEPH *and brings him down center.*]

[RIGGS *turns to the table at left, takes paper and pencil and writes, as* CONSTANCE *begins her "curtain speech."*]

EMMA JANE. Reggy! [*No answer; he is writing.*] Reggy, I want you.

CONSTANCE [*interrupted*]. What's the matter, Emma Jane?

EMMA JANE. I want to practice carrying Joseph out.

[CONSTANCE *looks at* RIGGS, *who is just now handing his note covertly to* MIRIAM. *That done, he crosses to* EMMA JANE *and* JOSEPH. CONSTANCE *resumes her speech.*]

JOSEPH. Let's begin just after the blow under the chin.— Ready?

RIGGS. Yes. [JOSEPH *falls stiffly backward into* RIGGS' *arms;* RIGGS *lets him sink to the floor; then* EMMA JANE *takes hold of the ankles, while* REGGY *holds him under the arms.*]

[CONSTANCE, *meantime, has been delivering her curtain speech—*]

CONSTANCE. My friends: every person in the world has aspirations. I have aspired to write plays, to write good, clean plays, which would be produced by good, clean actors, in good clean theaters. You can understand my great joy and supreme pleasure then— [*At about this point, she interrupts herself. She cries out.*] Oh, heavens!

[*All abruptly stop business.*]

CONSTANCE. I see somebody—oh, it's the audience. The audience is beginning to arrive. We should have dropped the curtain.

SOCK [*going off left*]. I'll do it.

[CONSTANCE, *follows off, in haste. The curtain falls part way, and sticks.* REGGY, *who, with* EMMA JANE *was about to carry* JOSEPH *off, now drops his end of the burden, and reaches up to pull down the curtain.* SPEEDY, *on his side, stops stuffing himself with a pillow, to reach up for the curtain on his side. In the middle,* JOSEPH, *head and shoulders on the floor, and feet still clutched by the preoccupied* EMMA JANE, *waves his hands frantically and cries out, as the combined efforts of the rest of the cast succeed, and*]

THE CURTAIN FALLS

ACT II

SCENE 2

The curtain rises again in a very few minutes, disclosing the same scene, a half hour later. The stage is no longer in confusion. Things have been put in order, and the actors have retreated to the wings to await their entrance. The play is on. EMMA JANE *is the only occupant of the stage. She is fixing flowers in a vase, and evidently, since there is no one to hear her, engaging in soliloquy in the part of* MARY *the maid. She speaks with a hastily-acquired Irish brogue.*

EMMA JANE. Sure, an' I wish it was myself that was gettin' married today! With all these pretty posies, an' a gold ring for my finger. [*She takes card from box of flowers and reads it.*] "Mr. Godfrey Goldman." [*She passes her finger over the card.*] Sure, an' it's engraved it is. But I'm not so sure that I'd want to be married to that! Poor little Belle, an' I don't believe she wants to much herself, an' him twenty years older than her, an' fat an' bald, in the bargain.

[*Here she stops as if waiting for something. There is a pause. She looks off left frowning. She adjusts the flowers. Again she looks off left, and says in a whisper behind her hand*—] Ring the bell! [*A hand is seen projecting from the wings, pointing to the chair down right.* EMMA JANE *looks there. Then she goes to the chair, picks up something covertly, and holds her hand behind the chair. A bell rings, palpably not off stage.*]

EMMA JANE [*going*]. Well, who could be ringing that door bell now?

[*She returns immediately, followed by* SPEEDY. *In the character of* GOLDMAN. *He is puffing his cigar vigorously and looks very stern. He wears gray suède gloves and carries hat and stick. These he hands to* EMMA JANE *before going to his seat. The gloves, too, should be left with her. He tries to get them off gracefully. They are new and they adhere. There is an embarrassing wait while he struggles with them. Then* EMMA JANE, *almost giggling, grasps the finger tips and pulls. When a glove comes off suddenly, she loses her balance for a moment. When he is safely seated,* EMMA JANE *picks up her lines.*]

EMMA JANE [*aside*]. Sure an' I wouldn't marry a man that smoked a cigar five minutes before the ceremony! [*To him.*] Just have a seat, Mr. Goldman. [*He is already seated on sofa right.*] Who would you want to see?

SPEEDY [*very gruffly*]. I don't want to see anybody. I came to get married.

EMMA JANE. Oh, I beg pardon, Sir. [*She backs out center, registering fear.*]

[*The telephone bell rings. He glances toward the phone, but does not rise. It rings again. He does not stir.* MARY (EMMA JANE) *enters and goes to it.*]

EMMA JANE. Hello— Yes— Yes, he's right here— It's for you, Mr. Goldman.

SPEEDY. All right. Bring it here.

[*And* EMMA JANE *carries the telephone across to* SPEEDY.

But the cord, alas, has not been fastened, and the greater part of it is still wound around the base of the instrument, while the short one hangs down unattached.]

SPEEDY. Yes— Yes— Yes— Yes— Yes— Yes— [*He hangs up.*]

EMMA JANE [*replacing the telephone*]. Is that all, sir?

SPEEDY. Yes.

[*She goes out right and in a brief moment appears again with* SOCK *in the character of* MR. UNDERWOOD, *his youthful face painted with lines, but it remains a youthful face. He goes to* SPEEDY *and extends his right hand.*]

SOCK. "Good afternoon, Goldman."

[*Now the glove which* SPEEDY *had succeeded in removing was the glove from the left hand. The right hand is still gloved. He starts to shake with that, stops, tugs at the glove and then to the surprise of* SOCK, *improvises a line.*]

SPEEDY. Excuse my left. [*He shakes with his left hand.*]

[SOCK, *not getting his cue, "*UNDERWOOD*" is a bit confused. He forgets the next line. There is a pause. Then, trying to cover the break he strides over to stage left and inclines his ear toward the wings, where* CONSTANCE *gives him the lines. He continues, but with a telltale "Oh yes" to* CONSTANCE.]

SOCK [*center*]. Oh yes— Nice day for the wedding.

SPEEDY. Yes.

SOCK. Belle is a little nervous, but she'll be all right. You're not nervous, are you, Goldman?

SPEEDY. No— [*A pause.*]

SOCK [*prompting in a whisper*]. They just called up from the rectory.

SPEEDY. They just called up from the rectory.

SOCK. So? Is anything wrong?

SPEEDY. No. Dr. Deuteronomy is suddenly taken ill.

SOCK. Oh, heavens! He was to marry you. What shall we do?

SPEEDY. They are sending a young assistant.

SOCK. Oh.

SPEEDY. Mr. Matthew Mark. Do you know him?

Sock. No.

Speedy. Neither do I. But one's as good as another.

Sock. Yes, of course. I'm so glad this is coming off all right. I've always wanted Belle to marry into a respectable family and be comfortably well-to-do. We've had a little trouble with a young man who's always hanging around trying to take her out. We've denied him the house. We've never seen him, but Belle tells us that he's a young newspaper reporter. He hasn't a cent.

Speedy. I own five newspapers.

Sock. Exactly. There's the difference. [sock *does this well, with a broad sweep of his arm. He has been speaking in his deepest, oldest voice, and strutting about a good deal. Now he goes to* speedy *and speaks in a confidential undertone.*] Shall we step into my private den for a minute?

Speedy. Just as soon sit right here.

Sock. I have a bottle of Four Roses in there. [*Gesture of drinking.*]

Speedy. Oh, to be sure. Why didn't you say that in the first place?

[sock *starts off right.* speedy *turns to go left.*]

Sock [*in whisper*]. Psst! This way. [speedy *turns and follows him off right. In a moment* miriam *as "Belle" enters right alone and walks listlessly around the room. She crushes the paper flowers in her arms; she goes to a chair right and sits.*]

Miriam [*also soliloquized*]. His roses never smell as sweet as Alfred's. Oh, my dear Alfred! [*She buries her face in her hands and weeps.*]

[mrs. upjohn, *in the character of* mrs. underwood, *enters right.*]

Mrs. Upjohn [*going to her*]. Belle, why are you crying? [*No answer beyond a sob.*] This is no way to behave on your wedding day. You should be happy that you are marrying a rich man. [*Another sob.*] Are you disappointed because you are not having an elaborate ceremony? [*Sobs.*] We thought it best to have a quiet home wedding under

the circumstances. Are you packed and ready to travel?
[*More sobs.*] Oh, you are impossible!—You can do nothing
but cry.

[MRS. UPJOHN *starts out left. The voice of* CONSTANCE *is
heard off stage.*]

CONSTANCE. The other way.

[MRS. UPJOHN *wheels and stalks off right.* MIRIAM *is
drying her eyes, when* "ALFRED ARMSTRONG" *enters cautiously at the back. Here we should like to have the audience burst into applause at the appearance of* REGGY RIGGS
(*Himself*). *He goes through the business of exploring the
corners of the room to insure his safety, and then, reassured,
approaches* MIRIAM *and touches her on the shoulder.*]

MIRIAM [*as if startled*]. Oh!—Oh, it is you, my dear Alfred.
What are you doing here? You must not stay. If they find
you, they will kill you.

RIGGS [*in tragic tones*]. I am not afraid of death. I do not
want to live without you.

MIRIAM. Alas! I fear it is too late. These flowers are his, this
my wedding dress, and soon his ring will be upon my
finger.

RIGGS. I know, I heard all. I have been in hiding.

MIRIAM. Sh! I hear someone coming. You must go. Good-by,
my only love!

RIGGS. One word more; trust me. I will find a way. While
there is life there is hope. [*He takes her in his arms in
passionate embrace and kisses her, holding it dangerously
long. A voice off stage whispers, "That's enough." Then he
exits center. The doorbell rings.* EMMA JANE *enters from
right and crosses to left. She sees* MIRIAM.]

EMMA JANE. Oh, Miss Belle— An' you've been cryin'!

MIRIAM. Yes. I must go before anyone comes. [*She hurries
off right, drying her eyes.*]

EMMA JANE [*alone*]. Poor girl! An' her a bride today.

[*She bursts into sympathetic sobbing and exits right, to
enter again, almost immediately, dry-eyed, from the left,
followed by* JOSEPH *in the character of* MATTHEW MARK.

His first vocal effort is frustrated by nervousness. He clears his throat and tries again.]

JOSEPH. You needn't call anyone. Just tell them I am here.

EMMA JANE. Who are you, Sir?

JOSEPH. Mr. Matthew Mark, in place of Dr. Deuteronomy.

EMMA JANE. Yes, Sir.

[*He struts up and down with his hands behind his back. Then he takes out and reads a pocket testament as he walks. —Presently, just as he makes a turn toward stage right, RIGGS enters stealthily from stage left and follows him across the stage at his heels. When JOSEPH turns, RIGGS keeps in back of him, and follows him up for a turn or two, awaiting his chance. During this business, JOSEPH displays nervous antipication of the blow which he knows is coming. RIGGS springs upon him, claps his hand over his mouth, and knocks him none too gently under the chin with the other fist. As JOSEPH falls to the floor, EMMA JANE enters from the right. She stops back aghast, and opens her mouth to scream, then:*]

RIGGS. Sh! Don't scream. Keep quiet and I'll give you five dollars. [EMMA JANE *closes her mouth.*] Come here. [*She advances timidly.*] You don't want to see Belle marry that old Goldman, do you?

EMMA JANE. Oh, no sir, but—

RIGGS. Then you do what I say. Here, take hold of his feet.

EMMA JANE. But this ain't Mr. Goldman. This is the—

RIGGS. I know it. But you do what I tell you and I'll take care of Mr. Goldman. Grab hold of his feet.

[*She obeys.* RIGGS *lifts* JOSEPH *under the arms, and together they carry him out at the left. But the illusion is destroyed when* JOSEPH, *thinking he is out of the view of the audience, gets to his feet before he is completely off.* SOCK *and* SPEEDY, *as* UNDERWOOD *and* GOLDMAN, *enter at right.*]

SOCK. 'Bout time this preacher was here. You're ready to go ahead, aren't you, Goldman?

SPEEDY. Yes—I might call up Niagara for hotel reservations. [*He goes to the telephone left.*]

SOCK. I'll see if the wife knows anything about this preacher. [*Exit right.*]

SPEEDY. Hello— Give me long distance— Long distance? I want to talk to the Honeymoon House at Niagara Falls— Hello, the Honeymoon House? [*In plays, long-distance connections are made very promptly.*] I want to reserve a bridal suite for tomorrow night. E. H. Goldman— Yes. Good-by.

[*Enter* SOCK *and* MRS. UPJOHN, *as* MR. *and* MRS. UNDERWOOD. *She goes to* SPEEDY *left.*]

MRS. UPJOHN [*extending her hand*]. I hope all is well, Mr. Goldman.

SPEEDY. Where's this preacher?

MRS. UPJOHN. He has arrived. Mary told me. I'll have him come in if you are ready.

SPEEDY. I've been ready for the last fifteen minutes.

[*At this moment,* EMMA JANE *enters from the left, patting her hair.*]

EMMA JANE. The preacher is right in there, M'am. He said to go right ahead and he'll be in.

MRS. UPJOHN. Oh, very well. I'll call Belle. [*She does so.*] Belle! Belle! [BELLE *enters from the opposite door.*] Now, Mary, will you arrange the chairs, please, as I directed you.

[EMMA JANE *places two chairs up stage center, a third down stage right, and a fourth down stage left. Meanwhile,* SPEEDY *takes a bill from his purse and hands it to* SOCK.]

SPEEDY. Give that to the preacher after we have gone, will you?

SOCK [*center*]. Oh, you are very generous. [*He lets his hand drop.*]

MRS. UPJOHN. Now, Belle, if you will take this chair— [*Indicating the one down right;* MIRIAM *obeys.*] and Mr. Goldman, that one— [*Pointing down left; he goes to it.*]—Now, Mary, you may tell Mr. John Luke that we are ready.

EMMA JANE. Beggin' your pardon, Ma'am, but it's Mr. Matthew Mark.

MRS. UPJOHN. Oh, very well. [EMMA JANE *exits left.*] Now George, we will sit here. [*She takes* SOCK'S *arm, and they go up stage to sit. All are now seated with backs to the audience.* EMMA JANE *returns by down stage left door and remains standing there. In a moment,* RIGGS *enters by the up stage left. He has robbed* JOSEPH *of enough of his attire to dress himself like a clergyman, and he holds the black book in his hand. At sight of him,* MIRIAM *gives a little cry of surprise. Her mother looks around and gestures silence.*]

RIGGS. First of all, let us bow our heads in prayer. [*All obey excepting* SOCK. RIGGS *goes to* MIRIAM *via* SOCK, *whose head he pushes down, and then* "ARMSTRONG" RIGGS *testifies to the symbolic quality of his name by crossing quickly to* MIRIAM, *picking her up in his arms, and hustling her away. For a moment there is silence. Then* EMMA JANE *manages to say something.*]

EMMA JANE. It's a nice day for the weddin', ain't it?

SOCK. Indeed it is, Mary. [*Pause.*]

EMMA JANE. You know, this is the latest style in weddin's.

SOCK. Yes, they all do it this way. [*Now the voice of* JOSEPH *is heard in a desperate whisper from off right.*]

JOSEPH. Speedy! Speedy! [SPEEDY *looks up, then bows his head again.*]

JOSEPH. Speedy! [SPEEDY *looks again, and rises from his seat. But the voice of* CONSTANCE *is heard from off left.*]

CONSTANCE. Sit down! Sit down! [SPEEDY *sits.*]

JOSEPH. Speedy, come here quick! [SPEEDY *rises and crosses right.*]

CONSTANCE. Speedy, come back to your seat! [*He starts to return.* JOSEPH, *clad lightly, without the clerical coat and vest, rushes on from right, whispers something to* SPEEDY, *and rushes off again.* SPEEDY *stands a moment aghast. Then he cries out.*]

SPEEDY. By golly! [*His hand goes to his head. He becomes conscious of the wig. He tears it from his head, throws it fiercely to the floor, and dashes right off. This sudden outburst brings every actor out of his part.* EMMA JANE *crosses to the door at right. She looks out, then turns back and calls:*]

EMMA JANE. Mother!

[MRS. UPJOHN *and* SOCK *have turned from their up-stage facing positions and now she crosses to* EMMA JANE, *in answer to the call.* EMMA JANE *speaks in her ear.*]

MRS. UPJOHN [*aghast*]. They have! [*She runs off right.* EMMA JANE *starts after her, but is arrested by* SOCK, *who learns from her in hurried whisper what has happened. She runs off.*]

SOCK. Good Lord!

[*He starts to follow, but* CONSTANCE, *all thought of stage decorum thrown to the winds, is at his side, demanding knowledge of the disaster. He whispers in her ear and runs off.* CONSTANCE *utters a scandalized "Oh," and follows, leaving the stage empty. In a moment* JOSEPH *enters, timidly, glancing first to the audience and then to the wings. He steps forward to the footlights.*]

JOSEPH. I have been asked to announce—that we shall not be able to continue with the performance, for the reason that two of our actors have—disappeared. In fact, they have all gone, now. I suppose I should add that if there is anyone in the theater who does not feel that he—or she—has gotten his—or her—money's worth this evening, he—or she—may redeem his—or her—ticket at the door. I thank you. [*He rushes from the stage.*]

[*Immediately* SPEEDY *is seen carrying* MIRIAM *up the main aisle of the theater. He puts her on the stage and jumps up himself. At that moment* RIGGS *runs up the main aisle.*]

SPEEDY. There. Now we can go on. [*He looks about the stage and audience.*] Why! Where is everybody?

[RIGGS *lands on the stage.*]

RIGGS [*to* SPEEDY]. You mind your own business and butt out.

SPEEDY. This is my business.

RIGGS. See if it is. Come on, Miriam. [*He starts to go.*]

MIRIAM. I'm not going.

RIGGS. Come on. [*He takes her by the arm.*]

MIRIAM. Let go. I wont.

RIGGS. You'll think differently tomorrow. [*He draws her nearer the footlights.*]

MIRIAM. Let go. I wont.

[SPEEDY *slaps* RIGGS *in the face.* RIGGS *steps back;* SPEEDY *follows up. He strikes* RIGGS *on the chin. Infuriated,* RIGGS *lunges at* SPEEDY, *with a solar plexis blow, but his fist lands in a sofa cushion.* SPEEDY *takes the advantage and hits* RIGGS *in the side of the head. There follows a moment of wild striking, with no telling effects, until, quite by accident,* SPEEDY *places a blow firmly on* RIGGS' *nose.* RIGGS *staggers back, and* SPEEDY *pauses, placing his hands on his hips.* RIGGS, *with head bent, staggers toward* SPEEDY *and suddenly unbends, striking* SPEEDY, *unawares, in the stomach.* SPEEDY *groans, breathless, and strikes back. But* RIGGS *leaves no opening. He follows up his advantage and clinches.* SPEEDY, *still breathless, stumbles backward almost to the point of falling. The two men pitch this way and that about the scene, doggedly holding the clinch, and wrestling in an attempt to throw one another.* SPEEDY *has had the best of the fight at first, then* RIGGS—*then* SPEEDY—*now* RIGGS *has him completely at his mercy. It is here that* MIRIAM *springs into action. She pounds* REGGY'S *back with her fists, beating like a trip-hammer. Then, changing attack, she lifts her skirts to a practicable position and kicks* RIGGS *in the legs. Now, growing more desperate, she grasps his wrist with her two hands and sinks her teeth into his flesh.* RIGGS *cries out in pain, and relaxes his hold upon* SPEEDY. *Instantly* SPEEDY *takes advantage of his liberty and strikes* RIGGS *in the stomach, a firm, well-placed blow.* RIGGS *groans and sinks to the ground. For a moment all is quiet.* RIGGS *lies in a heap in the center of the scene.* SPEEDY *stands puffing one side of the victim, and* MIRIAM, *wild-eyed, on the other. They regard each other, speechless for a moment.*]

SPEEDY. What happened?

MIRIAM. You hit him.

SPEEDY. I know, but he let go.

MIRIAM. Did he?

SPEEDY. Yes. He was clinching and I couldn't get free, and then suddenly—he let go.

MIRIAM. I see.

SPEEDY. Did you do anything to him?

MIRIAM [*growing formal*]. No, of course not.

SPEEDY. I hope I haven't ruined his pretty face. What's the matter with his wrist?

MIRIAM. It's bleeding a little.

SPEEDY. His *wrist?*

MIRIAM. Yes.

SPEEDY. I don't see how I could have hurt him in the wrist. [*He turns aside and sucks his knuckles secretly.*]

MIRIAM. Reggy! Reggy! [RIGGS *stirs; he groans.*] Are you all right?

RIGGS. No.

SPEEDY. He's all right.

RIGGS. Who's that?

MIRIAM. Speedy.

RIGGS. Hasn't he gone yet?

SPEEDY. No, and I'm not going, but you still have time to catch the last train.

RIGGS. Say, if I were you, I wouldn't talk so big. You'd have been in a fine mess if it hadn't been for your woman.

SPEEDY. What's that?

RIGGS. Nice little wild cat you've got! [*Exit.*]

[MIRIAM *is looking at a picture in her hand. She tears it up and scatters the pieces on the floor. She crosses.* SPEEDY *picks up the pieces and looks at them.*]

SPEEDY. This has been an unlucky spot for Reggy Riggs.

MIRIAM [*turning*]. Speedy!

SPEEDY. First you bite up his wrist and then tear up his photograph.

MIRIAM. You know?

SPEEDY. You're sure you didn't think it was my wrist you were biting?

MIRIAM. Oh, no, I meant to bite him. That is—oh, I guess I'd better find mother and the rest.

SPEEDY. Miriam. Don't go. I want you to sit down here a minute, with the next-best man.

MIRIAM. Well— [*He leads her to the center chairs. They sit.*]

SPEEDY. Miriam, I've got a question to ask you. [*Moves toward her a bit.*] I started to ask you this question before, but I was interrupted. [*Moves further toward her. Finds pillow an obstruction, and saying, "Excuse me," removes the pillow and throws it aside.*] Miriam, I wanted to ask you—

MRS. UPJOHN [*in back of auditorium*]. Miriam!

MIRIAM. Yes, mother. [*She rises,* SPEEDY *rises.*]

MRS. UPJOHN [*ditto*]. Is that you, Miriam?

MIRIAM. Yes, mother.

MRS. UPJOHN [*ditto*]. Are you all right?

MIRIAM [*turns to* SPEEDY; *he stands with open arms; she goes to him; they embrace*]. Yes, mother.

[MRS. UPJOHN *and the rest run down the main aisle, calling out as they go, "Where'd you go?" "We thought we'd never find you." "Are you hurt?" "Is everything all right?" "Where's* REGGIE?" *Then they reach the stage and look back at the audience.*]

CONSTANCE. Why! They're all gone.

SPEEDY. Well, why not? It's all over with. [*Embraces* MIRIAM *again.*]

CURTAIN

MOON MAGIC

A Masque for Midsummer's Eve

BY

ELEANOR ELLIS PERKINS

A ROYALTY PLAY

INVOCATION

Ye fairies that from blossoms peep;
Ye elves that 'neath the mushrooms sleep;
Ye nymphs that close in hiding keep;
Ye spirits that in shadows creep;
Straightway appear!

Ye lovers that in gardens croon
Your world old vows in tender tune;
Ye pensioners of the magic moon
Come share with us this night in June;
Dance for us here!

E. E. P.

FOREWORD

It was in the court of the warrior king Cuchulain that Fergus Fingal told the story of Donal of the Hump. All the women of the household, and Queen Emer too, were sitting sorrowing for their absent lords who were fighting in the north and many of them had already been killed, so that no kind of diversion could take the minds of the women away from their grief, until the Queen thought to send two of her women for Fergus Fingal, the greatest of all story-tellers, so that he would come and give them songs and stories, which he did and they were all cheered by it.

He told them about Donal the cobbler of Cathbad, and how he was a vain silly old man who thought all the ladies would fall in love with him if they once looked on his ugly little face, so he would always be showing it at every kind of celebration in the whole country. On his way home from one of these celebrations late at night the moonlight laid some sort of a spell upon him so that he had the misfortune to blunder right into a fairy rath where the fairies were all dancing and singing. But it so happened that the Good People did not kill him as it was their custom to do with mortals, but gave him three wishes and much came of them.

Fergus Fingal told the women this story from the beginning to the end of it, until word came that the King and all his men were returning victorious from battle, and the ladies ran away to greet them while they were yet in their chariots.

THE CAST

QUEEN EMER
FERGUS FINGAL
BRIDE
BRIDEGROOM
DONAL
LADY MOON
FAIRY QUEEN
KING BYRAN CONNORS
LEPROCAUNS
GOOSE
COW
COURT LADIES
ATTENDANTS
WEDDING GROUP
MOONBEAMS
FAIRIES
GOOD PEOPLE
DANCERS AT THE KING'S COURT

THE SET

The requirements for a simple production of "Moon Magic" are:—1. A proscenium draw curtain. 2. An adequate stage for dancing. 3. A second draw curtain of good color and material to be used as a background. 4. Potted palms or shrubs to be used in back of second curtain as a setting for the fairy ring.

There are many ways to arrange the stage and the lights in order to get a series of beautiful stage pictures. The original production of "Moon Magic" was given on a great flight of stairs with a gauze curtain hung half way between the top and bottom. When lighted from the sides and front the gauze curtain was opaque, when lighted from behind it was transparent. The fairy scenes were played behind the curtain against a background of cut shrubs, and by using flash lights the effect was like a firefly dance. The story-telling group was posed around Fergus Fingal on the steps at left, just in front of the gauze curtain, well out of the picture except when the spot lights were on it.

On a flat stage it would be better to place the story-telling group on some sort of a raised dais, in order to separate it from the action and dancing.

For an outdoor stage, a convenient arrangement of shrubs might make the second curtain unnecessary. In order to illuminate the fairy scene colored torches such as are used on the Fourth of July could be stuck in the ground and lighted. The smoke as well as the color is effective.

The pageant is written however for an interior stage with ordinary facilities for curtains and lights. The necessities for a simple and effective production have already been enumerated, but the setting can be expanded to gain effects. The gauze curtain could be used with regular cut drops of trees behind it, lighted from above by concealed strip lights in alternating colors.

The script is prepared with careful light, action and music scenarios, and is accurately cued so that it can be used as a prompt book.

An orchestra of ten or fifteen pieces would be ideal for production in a large auditorium. Otherwise a piano and harp and violin are sufficient.

THE MUSIC

Irish dances
1. Shamrock—music and notes for dance by Louis Chalif, 7 West 42nd street, N. Y. C.
2. Irish Lilt—same as above
3. Square Dance—Kitty O'Neil. Music in book of "Ten Favorite Jigs" by James O'Malley, to be obtained from Lyon and Healy's, Chicago, Ill.

Dance of the Moonbeams
Notes to dance of Chiffonette by Louis Chalif
Music, "La Polkerina" by Charles Fradel

Fairy Dances
1. Gavotte Menzli by Emma R. Steiner
2. Solo dance—Gavotte by F. J. Gossec

Dance before the Queen
Gypsy Dance by T. Sarsate

For dancing after Fairy Cow
"Feu Feuillett" by Berlioz

THE COSTUMES

COURT LADIES *wear dresses of silk and mantles of velvet of rich dark colors. The dresses are low at the neck, the sleeves are long, flowing and cut in points or scallops at the edge, and the skirts reach the floor. The dresses are fastened by jeweled girdles around the hips or around the chest, some have jeweled breast plates and some have sleeveless loose bodices, laced together. The mantles are fastened about the neck or to the shoulders by metal clasps. They have deep fringes of gold or silver or else richly designed borders. The hair is worn in thick braids to the waist or knees or else caught in a large net at the back. Bright-colored silk strands are woven in the braids and silk fillets about the head. The queen wears a jeweled crown.*

THE ATTENDANTS *wear tunics rolling back loosely at the neck reaching just to the knees, with long flowing sleeves. Over this is worn a sleeveless coat, falling straight below hips and laced up the front. Long stockings, pointed shoes, hair cut short at shoulders, with plain band around. Colors saffron, green, purple, red, etc., in the dark tones.*

FERGUS FINGAL *a white-bearded old druid with oak leaves around his head. Flowing robe and mantle of white. Sandals. Irish harp.*

IRISH GIRLS *wear full skirts to ankles, and buckled shoes. Their bodices are tight-fitting, coming below the waist, fastened up the front, short puff sleeves. The bride's dress is white with a low round neck. Flowers in her hair. Other girls wear colors, have loosely draped kerchiefs about their necks. The three old women the same, but with three-cornered shawls, aprons, and poke-bonnet caps.*

IRISH MEN *wear suits of knee breeches and short-tailed coats of colors. Some wear waistcoats and some plain shirts. All wear tight stock collars, buckles on shoes and high black hats. The groom wears a suit of saffron.* DONAL *wears a suit of green and there is a large hump to his back. He smokes a cob-pipe.*

TWO LITTLE STARS *wear long tights and close-fitting long-sleeved tunics of midnight blue, covered with silver stars; in their hair, worn short and curled, are little green and blue lights attached to a small battery worn in a pocket on the back.*

LADY OF THE MOON *wears a long draped robe of shiny blue, from which hang sparkling jewels. From her neck and bare arms shine long chains of jewels. Blond hair, braided with strands of silver hanging over each shoulder. A moon halo, four feet in diameter and covered with thin china silk, with two handles which rest on her outstretched hands.*

THE MOON SPRITES *wear floating knee-length tunics of white, bear arms, unbound hair, white chiffon scarves, two yards long.*

THE LEPRACAUNS *who are little bent old men with white*

beards reaching to their knees, long tights and close-fitting tunics of dark brown. Shoes much too long for them, and soft peaked caps; each has a hammer and a wooden shoe.

THE GOOD PEOPLE *wear short green breeches and tunics tied in with long scarlet sashes. Short three-cornered loose mantles fastened to shoulders. Close-fitting red caps with owl's feathers in them, and pointed red shoes.*

KING BRYAN CONNORS *wears a fine gold crown and carries a gold sceptre.*

THE FAIRIES *wear knee-length dresses, full and hanging from shoulders, of silvery filmy stuff. Underneath this is a belt around the chest which fastens stiff, little silvery wings to the shoulders. These wings may be cut of cardboard, painted silver, and designed in blue and green and gold like peacock's feathers. Should be shaped like short dragon flies' wings. Loose bracelets around the wrists and ankles, with little bells on them. Hair curled tight all over head, with little bells tied to ends of locks to look like dandelion tops.*

THE FAIRY QUEEN *wears a crown of upstanding peacock's feathers on a gold band, and a long wand with a feather on it. A wide jeweled girdle to which are attached wings, and from which a silvery dress falls to ankles. A long train fastened to girdle in back with a blue and green border painted on it.*

THE FAIRY COW *made with a painted head and movable ears, two boys under a brown blanket with black spots. Brown tights on, with paper cuffs around ankles to look like hoofs. A movable wound wire tail.*

THE FAIRY GOOSE *long yellow tights, a goose head, with yellow bill, a goose body and a tail to be waggled by one hand, made of white paper cambric.*

SCENE ONE

Music. Overture by full orchestra. Selection, Mendelssohn's "Midsummer Night's Dream" continuing for two minutes after curtain is drawn.

Curtain. Drawn to position.

Scene. Banquet hall at the Court of Cuchulain.

Lights. Bunches purple. Floods white. 3 spots red, thrown on Banquet table.

Properties. Long narrow banquet table set center stage. 23 places set along up stage side. A place set at each end. High-backed carved chair for Queen at one end, carved chair without back for court lady at other end.

Table cloth reaching to floor of crimson satin. Garlands looped from table edge. A golden goblet at each place. Gold and silver platters heaped with vari-colored fruits on table. Two very large brass candle-sticks with lighted candles.

Ready outside—the following: Irish Harp Small, 3 tall vessels from which wine is poured. 2 platters with boars on them, garnished with red apples.

Cast. 25 ladies of Court on stage. Attendants and Fergus Fingal ready outside.

Action and Dialogue. Music continues for two minutes after curtain is drawn. At rise of curtain, the COURT LADIES *are standing with raised glasses about to drink a toast. They seat themselves sadly without drinking. 3 attendants enter with vessels of wine and refill the goblets. Music stops.*

QUEEN EMER *speaks—*

It is we who are the sad women of Ireland this night, and it is our husbands who are away to do battle in the north, in great peril of their lives at this instant, and some are dead maybe. Now we are sitting, just women alone in the feasting place of the King of Ireland, in the place where we used to be joyful, eating and drinking with our husbands; and wonder is on our faces if we shall ever see them again. We do not have any enjoyment from the cakes and honey or from the fruits and nuts or from the meat and good wine that used to be giving us delight. Nothing matters until we hear that the foes of our husbands are lying dead. But words of mine keep coming and coming like a river to a sea. I should be telling you of the champion's portion they have been preparing for our feast. Two fine young boars are being brought to us on platters;

they have been fed on milk and nuts for the two years past
since they were born, and I think their tender flesh will
be cheering to us. See them now, bringing them in.

Music. March music—Elgar's "Pomp and Circumstance."

*Action. An attendant enters stage Left, bearing a platter aloft
with the boar on it, followed by six attendants in twos.
Eighth attendant carries the second platter similarly, followed by six more attendants in twos. The followers take
positions Left and Right, on Tier 1. The servers offer
the meat to each lady in turn, and each one refuses it. The
platters are laid on the table and the servers take positions
with the others. Music stops.*

QUEEN EMER *speaks—*

Even the boar's meat which used to be giving us joy
and diversion, the way we would be running with our
skirts to our knees to get a portion of it, is not tempting
us from our sorrow now. I know! It is dancing perhaps
that would hearten us a bit. Let us have music for victory
in battle and let the dancers come to us.

[*A stir of delight among the* LADIES. *Two* DANCING GIRLS
run in and bow before the QUEEN. *Music begins and they
dance with barbaric vigor. At the end the* QUEEN *dismisses
them graciously. They go out. The* QUEEN EMER *speaks.
Applause from* LADIES.]

It is dancing that is not what we are needing to cheer
us, but a story, told to us by the story-teller of the Court
of Cuchulain. Go now Fedelm, and go with her Lendabair
until you are bowing before the chair of Fergus Fingal
the Story-teller, and say to him that Emer, who has the
six virtues of women, and who is the wife of Cuchulain,
is asking him to tell a story to herself and her women in
the place where they are sitting, sorrowing for their Lords
in battle. Tell him he excels the world in knowledge and
nicety of speech and good-heartedness, until he promises
to come to us. Run, Fedelm and Lendabair, while the attendants clear the feast and make the place ready for a
story-telling.

Action. The COURT LADIES *on one side of her rise and disappear stage Right. Music begins, same march as before. Ten more attendants enter to clear the feast. The meat bearers take up their platters again and head the procession which follows down the center stair and hurries out Left. Candle bearers come next. Follow attendants carrying the rest of the platters, bowls and goblets that were on the table. Follow the sections of the table, still draped and garlanded, each carried by two attendants.* COURT LADIES *rise and move to stage Left. Attendants return and bring the carved chair which is placed Left for* FERGUS FINGAL. *Another chair nearby for* EMER. *The cushions are brought by attendants in procession for* COURT LADIES. FEDELM *and* LENDABAIR *return, seat themselves with others, all looking expectantly Stage Right. All attendants withdraw.* FERGUS *enters stage Right, singing and crossing Left. Strikes several chords on harp. Clapping of hands by* LADIES.

Music. March music as before. Cue to begin—Emer, "ready for a story-telling." Song of Fergus—Voice arrangement of "Pomp and Circumstance." Cue to stop—Fergus approaches story-teller's chair.

Lights. Cue—movement of Court Ladies stage Left. Follow group with 2 amber spots. Cue—return of Fedelm and Lendabair. Blue spot on curtain Stage Right following Fergus Fingal.

QUEEN EMER *speaks*—

Fergus Fingal, we are the ones who are mindful of the good-heartedness of you, singing a song for the entertainment of women alone. This is how we have sadness and melancholy on us this night; our husbands are away at battle in the north, and maybe dead at this minute. Do you be stooping yourself now to sorry ladies that you might comfort us by some of the fine stories learned during the sixty years since the day you were born.

FERGUS FINGAL *speaks*—

Would Emer, who has the six virtues of women, and who is the wife of Cuchulain, and would the women of

her household, be caring to hear a story of Irish people,
and they living in the future, hundred of years after we
should be dead, and the grass growing over us in the sod?

QUEEN EMER *speaks*—

A story the like of that would be delightful to us, Fergus
Fingal, but let it happen that fairies and a great many of
the Good People and Lepracauns be in the tale, together
with the plain people of Ireland. There is the place of
eminence and it is there you should be sitting and telling
your tale.

Action. QUEEN EMER *motions to the carved chair which had
been hers, placed Right of group,* FERGUS FINGAL *bows,
moves Left, seats himself there.* COURT LADIES *clap their
hands. He strikes three chords on harp and begins story.
During* FERGUS FINGAL'S *story-telling throughout the play
the* QUEEN *and her ladies exclaim "of course," "how audacious," etc., and interrupt with admiring comments.*

Light. Follow Fergus Fingal with blue spot.

FERGUS FINGAL *speaks*—

Now it happened after a time of five hundred years
from the day when we shall all be dead, that there was
living in the village of Cathbad, a cobbler who had the
name on him of Donal of the Hump, and he a vain, foolish
little man, having no wife and no children to do for, and
not wanting any. And this is how Donal of the Hump
was; he was bad-tempered and homely so that no woman
would marry him; he was boasting and vain so that no
man would be friendly with him; and he was great for
driving hard bargains and being a miser so that the fairies
and good people would help him in no way. But it was a
curious thing how there was a great desire on him to be
having all the women falling in love with him, and all
the men falling into jealousy about him, and to do this
he would give his company to every wake and wedding in
the county, even to the distance of fifteen villages away.
If he should go to these occasions where everyone was
being easy and pleasant together, it is how they would re-

ceive him, by jeering and jibing and making jokes on him, until no one but a man of his foolishness would have gone to another. On one night when it came to the marriage of a man and a woman dwelling in the seventh village away from his, he put on his brogans which were new, and his best caubeen which was tall, and set out to go to it.

Lights. Cue—Fergus "and set out to go to it." All lights out. Stage dark for one minute. Then floods on white, spots amber, focused separately on stage 1.

Scene Two

Music. Cue—lights up. Begin Irish reel.

Scene. An Irish Country wedding set on stage 1.

Lights. Continued the same.

Properties. None.

Cast. 15 Irish girls and 15 men on stage. Donal *ready outside.*

Action and dialogue. Irish men and girls run on stage Right in group, laughing and frolicing. In formation for square dance. All men rush to get bride as partner. Groom puts them jealously aside and takes her himself. Dance goes on. DONAL *comes in Left and stands watching, the only one not included. The girls shake their skirts at him and make faces as they go by. Dance stops.*

DONAL. Come on· now boys and girls, let's be dancing that again, and I'll dance with the bride myself.

BRIDE. You'll not be getting me as a partner, you poor deluded man.

GROOM. Donal of the Hump, you are welcome entirely to have my wife as a partner, if you are able to get her, and that I am doubting.

   [*Much laughter by all save* DONAL.]

DONAL. I'll accept your offer, you decent man, and thank you surely. Let's have music boys, a jig, for my limbs are well-suited to jigging. Come, you pretty red rose, soon you'll be having the pleasure of a jig with Donal the cobbler.

BRIDE. I will not so.

DONAL. She's shy, the little red lark. Come, darling. It's Donal that will treat you as good as himself.

Action. He grabs her by the wrist, she protesting, and kisses her loudly. She screams and slaps his face. DONAL *folds his arms and looks defiantly at* GROOM. *The* GROOM *bends double with laughter. All the rest much amused. Music begins.* BRIDE *takes some one else as partner and* DONAL *is again left out. He tries to steal partners but they all escape him. Dance ends.*

GROOM. I don't suppose you need to be staying if you've not got a partner for the dance. It wouldn't be our wish to detain you, Donal of the Hump.

DONAL. Oh, I'm enjoying myself, thank you kindly, and this partner is the one I'll be having for the next dance.

Action. Music begins. He takes the oldest lady there and draws her into the dance. She slaps his face and joins some-one else. He retires holding his jaw. Mutters and shakes his fist at the company. Finally makes up his mind to leave. Goes out Left slowly.

Light. Cue—Donal goes out. All lights out. Wait 30 seconds. Green spots on Fergus Fingal and group.

Music. 1. Cue—Groom steps forward with bride. Begin first dance and play to end.

2. Cue—laughter by the groom. Begin second dance and play to the end.

3. Cue—Donal—"have for the next dance." Begin third dance, and play until lights go out.

Curtain. Drawn during dance. Hold five minutes till Scene III.

SCENE THREE

Scene. At the story-telling.

Lights. Continue the same on whole group.

Action. LADIES OF THE COURT *sit in rapt attention listening to* FERGUS.

Fergus Fingal *speaks*—

And that is how it happened that Donal decided perhaps he might not have at the wedding such a good time as he had been thinking to have, and so went on his way home where he might find himself admired to a prodigious degree. [*Laughter.*] It was the journey home that was not pleasant and agreeable, without the wedding guests for company or a stomach full of poteen for cheer. So dark the road was and lonely that Donal could not sing to himself, and much less whistle, he being a knowledgeable man about the fairies and all the doings of them during the nights and until cock crow of the morning. Donal was making trials at songs and whistles to keep company with himself and that was poor company too, when he noticed a fairy rath and he passing right by it. The poor man's heart jumped in his throat and his two knees would be knocking together the while he was hurrying by, and before he was well past it he heard a voice singing a song more beautiful than any mortal woman could sing if she kept trying for the length of seven lives. All the time Donal knew if he turned around to look he was a lost man, and all the time he was turning around with all the quickness in him to see who it was could be singing such a beautiful song.

Lights. Cue—Fergus "such·a beautiful song." Spots out. Wait one minute. One purple spot on Donal entering Right and following him across stage.

Scene Four

Scene. A lonely road by a fairy rath, at midnight.
Properties. Ready in hands of actors.
  1. Moon halo for lady of the moon.
  2. For illuminating moon halo, a flash light, largest make.
Cast. Donal on stage. Ready off-stage, behind curtain, 2 stars, the Lady of the Moon and 36 moon sprites.
Action. DONAL *enters stage Right, walks along slowly as*

*though he had been walking a long time. Tries to whistle,
wets his lips and tries to whistle again but fails. Begins
to sing "When first I saw sweet Peggy." Gets center stage.
White spot light flashed on curtain center opening, revealing the two stars standing side by side.* DONAL *jumps. His
song stops abruptly. He staggers with fright and tries to
move stealthily by without being noticed. Stars hold curtain
back on each side letting the spot shine in one narrow beam
on the* LADY OF THE MOON, *shown at extreme rear stage
rising, as though appearing over the horizon. She sings as
she comes through the curtain. The stars sit on floor, knees
bent, still holding curtain apart, and receive moon halo
from her holding it perpendicular to floor while she comes
down singing to stage 1.*

Song of Moon Lady—(Words written for solo from Samson and Delilah).

SOLO

Come unwary mortal and listen to my singing.
Moonshine in the darkness its silver light is flinging
Fairies through the shadows swift their ways are winging,
Closer come and hearken to the magic of my singing.
Donal—Donal—Come near to me.

*Action—*MOON LADY *stops center stage. Song stops. She beckons to* DONAL. *He starts, shakes head and stops. Beckons
again, same business. Repeated till he is within five feet of
her. She begins song again. Fascinated he steps into the
circle of her white light, his own purple light vanishes. He
succumbs to spell of her singing. She retreats. He tries to
follow. She gestures him to stand still. He falls weakly
and seems to go into a deep sleep. She takes up her halo
again. Stage suddenly dark. Moon halo illuminated from
behind by large flash lights held by the two stars, showing*
LADY OF THE MOON *in silhouette. Moon sprites emanate
from behind in six radiating lines. Only the tops of their
heads, their upraised arms, and the chiffon scarves string*

*along from hand to hand are cross-lighted from each side
of stage. Music begins. They dance back and forth waving
the scarves in the light to give the effect of clouds in the
moonlight. At end of dance, their formation is again in six
radiating lines, and they retreat behind the moon as they
came. Stage again dark but for lighted moon. The stars
bring the curtains together. The light of the moon goes
out. Everyone disappears in darkness. End of scene.*

Music. 1. Cue—Spot light on Lady of the Moon, begin "My
heart at thy sweet voice" from Samson and Delilah, by
harp pianissino. Continue to end.

2. Cue—Donal within five feet of Lady of Moon at center stage. Repeat selection to end, by harps forte.

3. Cue—appearance of first moon sprites from behind moon.
Begin dance and play through to end.

Lights. 1. Cue—Donal passes center stage, white spot on
curtain, center opening. Focus to shine on Moon Lady when
curtains are parted.

2. Follow Donal Left, and back to center with purple spot,
then change to white. Follow Moon Lady with white spot.

3. Cue—Moon Lady takes position at moon halo again.
Spots out.

4. Cue—Moon halo illuminated. All bunches white, thrown
across stage to light heads of dancers only.

5. Cue—Withdrawal of dancers, bunches out. Stage dark.
Wait one minute. Throw 3 orange spots on Fergus Fingal
and court group.

Scene Five

Scene. At the story-telling, Stage 2.

Lights. Continue the same.

Action. Listening and whispered approval of COURT LADIES *to
each other.*

FERGUS FINGAL *speaks—*

The Lady of the Moon in one way and another is responsible for a tremendous amount of magic, and Donal

was the man well to be knowing the same, but if the dew on the roses is beautiful, the Moon Lady was more beautiful than that, and if the singing of larks is beautiful, her singing was more beautiful than that, and if the motion of waves in the sea is beautiful, her walking was more beautiful than that.

It was a strange thing, he to be left lying there like one dead, and no one to be telling him how long it was he was there. He was not sure in any way where he had been with himself, not knowing if he had been asleep for a year and a day, or for the time of a day only, when he wakened to the tune of a little hammer, and it pounding near to his left ear. Then Donal sat up with all the quickness there was on him, and after he was rubbing his eyes a while he saw a queer little man at the left side of him, pounding busily on the sole of a fairy shoe. Lo and behold you, it was a Lepracaun, and as you well know, a Lepracaun is the first one of the good little people that should be seen by mortal, which happens rarely even so, and Donal was the man to be very much surprised.

Lights. Cue—Fergus Fingal "the man to be very much surprised." Spots off—stage dark. Wait 1 minute. Amber spot on Donal. Change from dim to full on.

Scene Six

Scene. Just outside of Fairyland.

Properties. Ready in hands of fairies. 24 small pocket flash lights to gain firefly effect. 24 fern fronds, 4 feet in length and very bending. For Lepracauns, 2 hammers and 2 wooden shoes for making a noise when pounded.

Cast. On stage 1, Donal and 2 Lepracuans. *Ready off stage,* 15 good people, and King Bryan Connors. 24 good fairies and Fairy Queen, Fairy Cow and Fairy Goose.

Action and dialogue. Spot light on DONAL *shows him stirring uneasily, waking with difficulty. Tapping hammer heard.* DONAL *listens. Settles back to sleep. Tapping heard again.*

Sits up and looks around. Light shifted Right to show LEPRACAUN *sitting on floor, cobbling busily.* DONAL *discovers him, great surprise,* LEPRACAUN *pays no attention.* DONAL *edges closer to start conversation but gets no notice at all to his remarks.*

DONAL. As I am a living and a breathing man, it's a Lepracaun!

The top of the evening to you, sir, and save you kindly. Good evening to you. I said good evening. Is it that the ugly little fellow is deaf, I wonder?

[*The* LEPRACAUN *raises his hammer as if to throw it at him.*

Excuse me, sir, I was meaning no disrespect to your looks indeed, no more than I was alluding to your character. I would not be putting nails in that shoe if I was you, in places where it does need to be sewed. I'm a cobbler myself—I said I was a cobbler myself.

[*The* LEPRACAUN *feels in his pocket for a snuff-box and and offers it to* DONAL *for a pinch.*]

Snuff! Oh, you decent soul, I'll take a pinch with ease and pleasure, thanking you kindly for that same. Snuff now is the thing to be putting a man in good humor entirely. Perhaps you'll try some yourself, so it is you won't be so tight with your tongue.

Action. DONAL *takes a big pinch and sneezes loudly three times, throwing back his head and shutting his eyes. While he is thus occupied the* LEPRACAUN *scampers through the curtain and disappears unnoticed. The light circle slips Left showing another* LEPRACAUN *on* DONAL'S *other side. He sees him and edges cautiously near.*

DONAL. Well, well, where did he go at all? To think of him getting away and me not knowing it. Aha, another Lepracaun.

Good evening to you, sir, I hope you'll not bother yourself to be hurrying away after the other ugly little fellow and he with no tongue to him. His company was undiverting, saving your presence, and it was no matter to me

surely, he to be leaving me unbeknownst the way he did. I
was after telling him to sew the shoes, not nail them, and
this is how it was I came to tell him that thing. You know
surely that I am Donal the cobbler? Do you know that I
am Donal the Cobbler, or do you not? I said, do you know
that—

[*The* LEPRACAUN *feels around for his snuff-box and offers snuff to* DONAL, *who takes a generous pinch.*]
More snuff. Ah, good fortune follow you and my blessing
rest on you wherever you go, for a good little man with
the politeness on you of an angel!

Action. DONAL *throws back his head, shuts his eyes and sneezes
loudly three times.* LEPRACAUN *scampers through the curtain and out of sight.* DONAL *recovers and looks around for
him. Stage grows lighter. The* GOOD PEOPLE *come stream-
ing in from right and left, going past* DONAL *but not noticing him, following the direction of the* LEPRACAUNS *through
the curtains. The most resplendent of the* GOOD PEOPLE
*comes last wearing a gold crown and carrying a sceptre.
Walks grandly past* DONAL.

DONAL. I know you King Bryan Connors of the Good People, but where is it at all that you are going? I am Donal
the Cobbler of Cathbad you know, and I am wanting
to be told where it is that everyone is going. Is it deaf that
everyone in the place is perhaps? Oh King Bryan Connors!

Action. All the GOOD PEOPLE *disappear behind the curtain.*
KING BRYAN CONNORS, *last, turns to look at* DONAL, *puts his
fingers on his lips and tiptoes through.* DONAL, *overcome
with curiosity, follows. Tries to get up courage to go behind
curtain. Makes several starts, finally dashes through.
Whereupon the whole stage is plunged in darkness, during
which the second curtain is drawn back. Lights on upstage
only, showing fairy ring. All fairies are in a circle, hand
in hand, moving their feet up and down in one spot as if
running very fast to stay right where they are. There is
no sound except the little jingle of the bells in their hair.*

DONAL *watches them unnoticed, in great surprise. His ugly little figure is silhouetted against the bright dancing ones. Rubs his head in bewilderment. Tries to imitate actions of fairies. Sees no sense to it. Shakes his head. Tries again. More annoyed. Finally—*

DONAL. The devil take that for a dance. It's no dance at all.

GOOD PEOPLE. Oh— Oh— Oh—

Action. They all turn around at once and point menacing fingers at DONAL, *repeating the accusing "Oh— Oh—" All stage lights on. Then they rush at him pell mell shaking him and jerking him downstage. He is paralyzed with fright. The* FAIRY QUEEN *walks out of Fairyland and appears before him with her pets, a cow and a goose. The fairies push him before her and he falls trembling on his knees.*

GOOD PEOPLE. Kill him! Kill him!

FAIRY QUEEN. Wait! Wait! Don't you be killing him till I ask him a question. Answer me this you audacious man, and then your head will be cut off, or else you will be drowned in a well, or else you will be buried alive. I don't know which. Now this is the question. Mind well what I say. If the dancing of the Good People is disagreeable to you is there anyone in this world so knowledgeable as to improve on it?

DONAL. I could improve on it.

FAIRY QUEEN. And how would you do so?

DONAL. It would please me entirely to show your Queenship how that thing could be done. But there is a prodigious number of the Little People holding me by one leg, and at least six of them are standing on the tails of me coat, and—

GOOD PEOPLE. Kill him. Kill him. Kill him.

FAIRY QUEEN. Now be patient a little, do! And leave go his coat tails. Get up you undecent, outrageous spalpeen and improve on the Fairy's dancing this minute.

DONAL. Thank you your Queenship, thank you kindly. I'm Donal the cobbler of Cathbad you know and my regular business is cobbling, but I dance very well too. Well now, if I was one of the Good People and had to spend my time dancing, I would do it better than they do. See. Watch now.

Action. DONAL *gets to his feet laboriously. He moves his feet up and down like the fairies, then skips gaily off round and round the* QUEEN. *He stops before her and assumes a triumphant attitude.*

FAIRY QUEEN. Hummmmmmmmm. You dance well for an uncultivated man. Do it again if you please.

Action. DONAL *swells with pride. Starts skipping again. The* GOOD PEOPLE *clap their hands in time to the skipping, and one by one join in after* DONAL *single file. The* QUEEN *at last, unable to resist, skips at the end of the line, her cow and her goose skipping beside her. When the* QUEEN *stops they all stop.*

FAIRY QUEEN. That's good indeed. Now I don't know. Shall I kill him for saying our dancing could be improved or shall I reward him for improving it?

GOOD PEOPLE. Reward him. Reward him.

FAIRY QUEEN. You say reward him. Then I will do so. Donal the cobbler you are an audacious and outrageous man to be blundering into Fairyland the way you are, and it's you ought to be killed this instant, but sure the Good People like it that you should improve on their dancing and are wishful for you to be rewarded. I am willing entirely to grant you three wishes. It would be well you to think carefully before wishing them.

GOOD PEOPLE. Think carefully. Think carefully.

DONAL. It was no trouble at all to improve on such dancing, but I'm obliged indeed for the three wishes. I'll not delay telling you what they are. My first wish is that at one time or another all the ladies should fall in love with me; my second wish is that at one time or another all the gentlemen should be jealous of me; and my third wish is to have on myself the handsomest suit of clothes in the whole county.

FAIRY QUEEN. Your three wishes are granted, you foolish man.

GOOD PEOPLE. You foolish man. You foolish man.

FAIRY QUEEN [*waving her wand*]. Ho, you silver-winged fairies. You have business with this cobbler. Let you be at it.

Action. Music begins. The GOOD PEOPLE *standing upstage sing while the fairies circle round and round* DONAL *in center, shaking their fern fronds over him until he is quite dazed. The stage grows dark. Firefly lights flash.*

Charm Song of the GOOD PEOPLE. (*To aria from Samson and Delilah.*)

Fairies mavo on tiptoe, magic circles weaving.

Fairy feet are dancing, fairy bells are ringing.

Fairy spells are working, mortal eyes deceiving.

Mortals are unwary who harken unto fairies when they're singing.

Donal—Donal— Beware! Beware!

Action. At the end of the spell weaving the fairies drive DONAL *before them upstage and the second curtains are closed shutting them into Fairyland. The* GOOD PEOPLE *follow the fairies and* DONAL *out through the curtains which are held politely aside by the cow and the goose.* KING BRYAN CONNORS *at the end of the procession gives his hand to the* FAIRY QUEEN *and they go out together. One little fairy on the stage continues dancing. The goose comes down and chases her back into fairy land. Lights out. Peals of laughter from the fairies. End of scene.*

Lights. Cue—Donal wakes up. Follow him with one white spot until cue for all lights out. *Cue*—Tapping of hammer stage Right. 1 blue spot on Lepracaun. *Cue*—Lepracaun gets up to go, blue spot off. *Cue*—Tapping of hammer stage Left. 1 green spot on second Lepracaun. *Cue*—Second Lepracaun gets up to go, green spot off. *Cue*—Green spot off, put bunches, on in green and blue. Foots and floods on. *Cue*—Donal steps inside curtain. All lights off at once.

Wait thirty seconds. Light upstage bunches only, in white.
Cue—Donal shoved back downstage. Downstage bunches on
in green and blue. Floods and foots on. *Cue*—Appearance
of Fairy Queen. 1 blue spot on her. Follow. Amber spot
on Donal. Follow. *Cue*—Cow and Goose go out through
curtain. Lights out in following order. 1. Floods and foots
out. 2. Spots out. 3. Bunches out. End of scene. Wait one
minute. 3 spots red on Fergus Fingal and story-telling
group.
Music. Cue—Fairy Queen "Let you be at it." Begin aria from
Samson and Delilah. Play through to end. *Cue*—Littlest
Fairy alone on stage. Play "Gavotte" by F. J. Gossec.
Curtain. Drawn for five minutes till scene VII.

Scene Seven

Scene. At the story telling.
Setting, cast, action, etc. The same.
Fergus Fingal *speaks*—

I would not be saying how long it was that the fairies
kept Donal by them that night. It might have been the
wink of an eye, and it might have been less, but however
that was, by the time of cock-crow in the morning Donal
discovered himself walking alone in the forest, and he
dressed more gorgeously than any man he had ever laid
the two eyes of him on before. It was the best part of a
mile he walked, regretting at each step how it was that
no mirror was to be found in which he could be admiring
the back of him as well as the front, when lo, and behold
you, he came within sound of the jollity and fiddles of
the wedding. He having left it the evening before in dis-
pleasure and disgust. "This is lucky indeed," said Donal,
pulling down the front of his beautifully decorated waist-
coat, the better to fit it to himself. "Donal will be the man
to have that wedding for the scene of his triumph," said he.
Lights. Cue—Fergus Fingal "the scene of his triumph" said

he. Spots out, wait 1 minute. Amber spot on 2nd curtain, center for Donal.

Scene Eight

Scene. At the wedding, stage 1.

Setting and properties. Same as before.

Cast. Ready behind curtain, Donal.

Ready on stage 1, the wedding group.

Action. Spot on curtain. DONAL *stumbles through, as though he had been walking a long time. Stops to admire his clothes. Preens himself and struts. Seems to hear something. Music begins and sound of dancing feet. He identifies sound and reaches a conclusion about it. Stage lighted, and the wedding group is seen dancing on stage 1. Everything as before.* DONAL *swaggers downstairs and joins the dance.* BRIDE *leaves* GROOM *to dance with him.* GROOM *retires in jealous rage, stage Right. At end of dance, all the women cluster around* DONAL *admiring him and his beautiful clothes. Men join groom, shake their fists and wag their heads ominously at* DONAL. *Spot light on curtain reveals the* FAIRY COW *and the* FAIRY GOOSE *watching proceedings.* FAIRY COW *walks downstage through group to footlights. Women scream and fly to* DONAL *for protection. They point and push him toward the cow, to urge him to drive it away. He shakes his head, refusing vehemently. The frightened women rush across to stage Right to urge the other men to drive the creature away. Coax and plead flatteringly.* DONAL *in despair at their desertion tries to coax them back. No use. Finally clamps hat on head firmly and comes to center front to stand beside cow, to talk in its ear.*

DONAL. I know you, you are the Queen's pet cow that I met in Fairyland, and I know you are here for no good purpose. What's the matter at all?

[COW *winks one eye.*]

Is it in love with my manly beauty that you are, you to follow me like this?

[COW *shakes head with vigor.*]

Is this how it is, are you jealous of my conquests as are the young fellows over beyond you?

[COW *shakes head with vigor.*]

Perhaps some one of the Good People does be needing back the elegant suit of clothes that was presented to me fair and square for services rendered in improving their dancing as you well know.

[COW *shakes head more vigorously.*]

Then what do you want, you outrageous, bandy-legged, cross-eyed, black-hearted old villain, with the unpoliteness on you of an uncultivated beast?

[COW *winks other eye.*]

Nothing at all, just as I thought. Then get out of here you disrespectful creature, get out, I tell you!

Action. DONAL *grabs the cow by the tail and raises a foot to kick it along. The* COW *begins to move Right with gradually accelerating steps.* DONAL *finds he cannot let go and is forced to follow faster and faster.*

DONAL. Leave me go, you beast, leave me go! Let me off, you murdering spalpeen. Oh, help! Oh, help! I can't let go, come pull me off, I can't let go.

Action. Music begins, played with accelerating tempo, all the girls rush to pull DONAL *away, but they also stick fast, one behind the other. The men hurry to pull the girls off, and they stick one by one similarly. The cow gets to running and all run after it in a long line shouting and crying, "Leave go, you beast, leave go." Cow runs round and round the stage then back to center and through curtain which goose holds aside. Firefly lights seen again, and peals of laughter heard. All disappear, the goose last. All lights out. Music stops.*

Lights. Cue—Donal starts through curtain. Foots on. Bunches on red. Spots off. *Cue*—Entrance of Fairy Cow and Goose, 1 blue spot on them, to continue on goose alone. *Cue*— Fairy cow runs through curtain bunches and spots out. Wait 2 minutes. White spots on Fergus Fingal and group.

Music. Cue—Donal appears through curtain. Wait 1 minute.

Repeat 3rd dance of wedding group and play to end. *Cue*—
Donal "Oh, help! Oh, help! Begin "Feu feuillet," by Berlioz and play until lights are out.

Scene Nine

Scene. At the story-telling.

Cast. Same as before, with addition of 2 court attendants
ready off-stage Left.

Action, etc. Same as before. Attendants enter and approach
FERGUS FINGAL *as he is talking.*

FERGUS FINGAL *speaks*—

And that is how the lot of them were pulled away into
Fairyland, no one to be seeing hide nor hair of them since.
Everyone was gone entirely, so there was no one left to
be laying the blame of it to that vain man of the Hump,
and to his three foolish wishes. Maybe it will serve as a
warning to you however, not to be keeping company with
people you don't know the tricks of, and to beware of fairy
animals in the likeness of a goose or a cow. For once you've
laid a hand on them, you can't be taking it off again till
the Good People release you. Many is the child who has
been stolen away into Fairyland by such tricks.

[*To* ATTENDANTS *at his side.*]
Do you be waiting for a chance to give me a word? What
is it now?

[*The* ATTENDANTS *say something in his ear.*]
It is good news for Queen Emer and the women of her
court, and this is what it is. Your husbands are coming
back with victory from the battle, wanting you to be running to meet them that you should ride the last piece with
them, standing on the blood-spattered cushions of their
chariots and holding the reins of the horses before the
hands of the chariot drivers.

[*The women jump to their feet, clapping their hands,*
expressing great excitement.]

QUEEN EMER *speaks*—

We are the grateful women to you this day Fergus Fingal
for a fine tale than which no better has been told in Ireland.
Even were we forgetting the danger and peril of our husbands in battle, and before this we used to be mourning and
wailing the day and night long. Now we will be running
with the swiftness of a hunted fox, and jumping over the
chariot wheels of our lords to ride home with them the
way they'll be wanting us to do. Farewell, Fergus Fingal.

*Action. During speech the court ladies have been moving cen-
ter.* QUEEN EMER *joins them, goes first off Left, followed
hurriedly by the others.* FERGUS FINGAL *alone strikes a
few chords on harp. Comes center front stage, playing harp
while curtain is drawn together behind him. At end of
speech he disappears through curtain.*

FERGUS FINGAL *speaks*—

Never for me will the women be letting shouts out of
them, with joy for my home-coming; no more for me have
the women ever watched the hills that are far off for the
sight of my war chariot whirling home with the heads of
my enemies tied to the tongue of it. Never will horses of
mine be descried in the distance with the likeness of a flock
of black ravens about their heads; these same being the
sods kicked up by their heels; or the likeness of snow falling
about them; that same being the foam flying from their
mouths. And the great bronze vats have not been full with
warm water for the bathing of my wounds, nor has the
champion's portion at the feast of heroes been mine. But
there is no one in the world that I am second to, only the
King himself, and the heroes are fighting and performing
feats of strength so that their deeds can be heard about
when the story-teller speaks at the feast. The one who makes
them heroes in the knowledge of men is myself, and I am
the one to be putting blood in their eye for the killing, or
to open their hands in friendship one to another. There
is power in the tongue of a story teller to stir men's hearts

to action, as there is power in the fingers of him to stir harp strings to music. [*Exit through curtain.*]

Lights. Cue—Entrance of two attendants, floods and foots on. *Cue*—Queen Emer and Ladies go out. Foots, floods, and 2 spots out. Diminish 3rd spot gradually. *Cue*—Fergus Fingal "harp strings to music," 3rd spot out. Stage dark. *Cue* —Fergus's exit. House lights up.

Curtain. Drawn quickly. Cue—Fergus reaches center front stage.

THE END